THE HISTORY OF CHINA & INDIA

THE HISTORY OF CHINA & INDIA

JULIA CORNER

GYAN

Published by

GYAN

Gyan Publishing House
5, Ansari Road
Daryaganj, New Delhi-110002
Phone: 011-47034999, 9811692060
E-mail: books@gyanbooks.com

Distribution Network
gyanbooks.com
India, USA, Canada, UK, Australia

ISBN: 978-93-7133-365-8 (PB)

First Published, 1843

2nd Impression 2026

Printed at: Gyan Press, Delhi.

THE HISTORY OF CHINA & INDIA
Author: JULIA CORNER

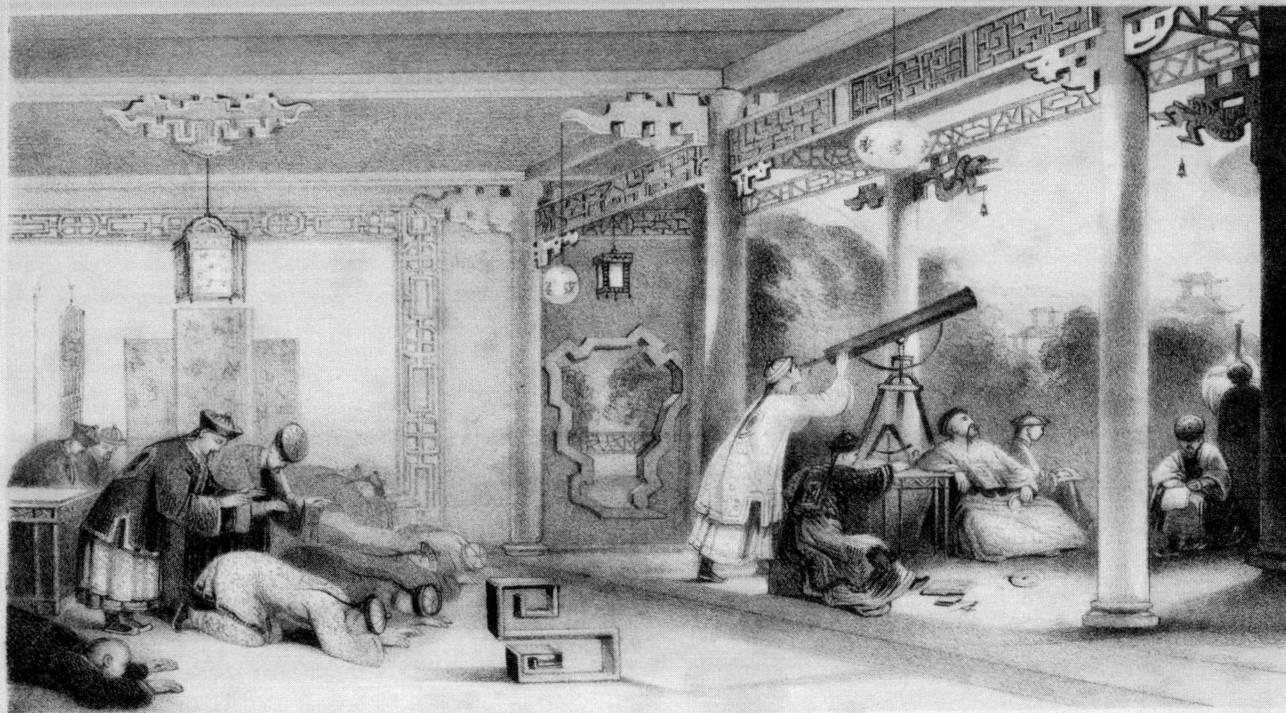

Drawn by G. F. Sargent from a Painting by Ts'hang — On Stone by J. W. Giles

THE CEREMONIES OBSERVED IN EVERY PROVINCE & CITY OF CHINA, ON THE OCCASION OF AN ECLIPSE.

London, Dean & Co. Threadneedle Street.

THE

HISTORY

OF

CHINA & INDIA,

PICTORIAL & DESCRIPTIVE;

BY

MISS CORNER,

AUTHOR OF

"THE HISTORICAL LIBRARY,"

"QUESTIONS ON THE HISTORY OF EUROPE,"

&c. &c.

LONDON:

DEAN & Co. THREADNEEDLE STRt.

THE HISTORY OF CHINA.

INTRODUCTION.

THE Chinese are believed to have been, from very remote times, fond of reading and literary pursuits; yet, as far as our present information extends, they do not appear to possess any regular authentic history of the early state of their ancient empire. From the earliest times, it seems to have been the policy of this singular people to keep themselves distinct from the rest of mankind, to subsist on their own abundant resources, and to bar their country against the ingress of other nations.

To this system, which, there is every reason to suppose, has been invariably pursued from the remote ages of the world, is, in all probability, to be attributed the extraordinary duration of the Chinese Empire, the unchanged habits of the people, and the constant uniformity that has been maintained in the mode of government, which is still, as it was at the commencement, an absolute monarchy, conducted upon patriarchal principles. The Emperor is regarded as the father of the people, who are taught to believe that he derives his right to rule over them directly from the Supreme Being, of whom he is believed to be the vice-gerent and representative upon earth.

The laws that govern the Chinese empire, said to have been framed upwards of two thousand years ago, remain unaltered to this very day; and as they regulate the manners, customs, and education, as well as the moral conduct and political relations of the people, one generation succeeds another, with the same habits, the same occupations, and the same external appearance. Even the conquests of the Tartars, which have twice placed the country under the dominion of foreign rulers, had no effect on the domestic state of the inhabitants; for the Tartar princes, in both cases, adopted the institutions of the land, and governed the people according to their own ancient laws.

There seems no reason to doubt, that the Chinese was one of the first monarchies established after the Deluge. It was cotemporary with those great empires of antiquity which had vanished from the earth, even before the days of the Romans. Time has witnessed the rise and fall of many a mighty kingdom, the names of which may now be sought for, in vain, on the map of the world: yet, China, as a nation, has experienced neither disorganization nor decay, and still remains, with respect to its laws, institutions, language, manners, and learning, almost the same as in those remote ages that long preceded the Christian era.

Considering the extent, the wealth, and the civilization of the Chinese empire, it is remarkable that it should have remained so little known to the rest of the world, both in ancient and modern times. During the middle ages of European history, the Chinese must evidently have been a far more enlightened people than the Europeans; for, while scarcely a nobleman on this side of the globe could sign his own name, reading and writing were common, even among the lower classes, in China, and learning was diffused throughout the country by means of printing, which art was practised, although in a primitive manner, by the Chinese, several centuries before it was known to the Europeans. But, in Europe, when the spell of ignorance and superstition had been broken, knowledge at once made a rapid progress; while, in China, it was not advancing a single step. Debarred by their peculiar laws from all free intercourse with other countries, and kept in total ignorance concerning the rest of the world, the Chinese have had no opportunities of learning more than was known to their forefathers; and, indeed, the nature of their government precludes all possibility of mental improvement beyond a certain extent. Hence, the great body of the people believe that China is the only civilized portion of the earth, and its monarch the supreme lord of all nations. From the most remote times, the essential point of their religious and political creed has been, that all good emanates from the Emperor, as the representative of the Divine power upon earth; and from this belief arises that blind and degrading submission to his will, which is the main support of his despotism.

THE HISTORY OF INDIA.

INTRODUCTION.

FEW countries in the world have experienced more revolutions than India, or been made the subject of so many able and interesting works. Each period of its history furnishes abundant materials for whole volumes, and, at different times, has been more or less connected with that of almost every known civilized nation. From the earliest times, its wealth, and the valuable productions of its soil, have tempted other nations to invade its territories, or visit it for the sake of commercial advantages, in consequence of which, it has always been a scene of constant warfare, as well as of commercial enterprise, and the well-known adage, that

"Might overcomes right,"

has never been more fully or more frequently exemplified, than on the extensive plains of Hindostan.

The history of India embraces four principal eras;—the early dominion of the Bramins; the Greek and Moslem invasions; the powerful and splendid empire of the Moguls; and the rise of the British sovereignty in Hindostan, which has long superseded that of the Mogul emperors as the dominant power, and has extended itself over parts of the country that never owned subjection to those mighty monarchs.

It would be impossible, in a narrative so brief and general as this, to speak individually of any but the most prominent of the numerous kingdoms and principalities into which the country has been divided at every period of its history. The existence of some of these has been but transient, while others have flourished for a considerable period, under a succession of powerful and wealthy princes; but, from the days of Alexander the Great, till now, each succeeding century has witnessed so many revolutions among the native states of India, that very few traces remain of what they have been. The native Indians consist of two distinct people, the Hindus and the Mohammedans, the former being the descendants of the ancient occupants of the country; the latter, of their conquerors, both Turks and Tartars. The Hindus, were, no doubt, in very distant times, a great people; but they have been, for ages, the prey of foreign invasion, and although their princes have always possessed dominions in various parts of the country, and many of them have, even in modern times, been at the head of great monarchies, yet few were able to maintain their independence after the establishment of the Mogul empire; when some of the native kingdoms were totally annihilated, and others became tributary to the conquerors. Still the Hindus have remained a distinct people. They have preserved their religion and peculiar customs unchanged, and have, from time to time, founded new states that have risen to great eminence, but which, like those also of Mohammedan origin, have gradually yielded to British ascendancy.

TABLE OF CONTENTS:—CHINA.

EARLY HISTORY.

CONFUCIUS.

BUILDING OF THE GREAT WALL.

THE HAN DYNASTY.

MIDDLE AGES.

FIRST TARTAR CONQUEST.

THE MING DYNASTY.

THE MANTCHOW DYNASTY.

KANG-HY.

YONG-T-CHING.

KIEN-LONG.

KEA-KING.

MANNERS, CUSTOMS, &c.

ARTS, MANUFACTURES, &c.

TAOU-KWANG.

LIST OF THE PLATES

IN THE HISTORY OF CHINA.

LIST OF THE WOOD ENGRAVINGS.

INSTRUCTIONS TO THE BINDER,

FOR PLACING THE PLATES.

TABLE OF CONTENTS:—INDIA.

MOGUL EMPIRE.

CUSTOMS AND MANNERS.

THE EMPEROR AKBER.

JEHANGHIR.

SHAH JEHAN.

AURENGZEBE.

BAHADUR SHAH.

FAROKHSIR.

MOHAMMED SHAH.

AHMED SHAH.

FALL OF THE EMPIRE.

ESTABLISHMENT OF THE BRITISH EMPIRE IN INDIA.

HYDER ALI.

TIPPOO SAIB.

BRITISH GOVERNMENT.

KINGDOM OF CABUL.

MARQUIS OF HASTINGS.

LORD AMHERST.

LORD WILLIAM BENTINCK.

LORD AUCKLAND.

KINGDOM OF CABUL.

ARTS AND CUSTOMS.

RECENT EVENTS.

LIST OF THE PLATES

IN THE HISTORY OF INDIA.

LIST OF THE WOOD ENGRAVINGS.

INSTRUCTIONS TO THE BINDER,

FOR PLACING THE PLATES.

INSERT

FOLD-OUT

OR MAP

HERE!

CHINA.
English Miles
THIBET
ASSAM
BIRMAH
ANAM
YUNNAN
KWEI-CHOW
FOH KIEN
FORMOSA
HAINAN
TONGQUIN
CHINA SEA
YELLOW SEA
SEA OF JAPAN
COREA
PEKIN
CANTON
NANKING
Formosa Strait
Long.e East from Greenwich

CHINA

EARLY HISTORY.

THE origin of the Chinese monarchy is unknown, but its high antiquity is too well attested to admit of the slightest doubt, and there is every reason to believe that it was founded about two hundred years after the deluge. Two centuries may reasonably be supposed to have elapsed from the time of that memorable event ere any of the posterity of Noah found their way into the distant regions of eastern Asia, which until then must have remained uninhabited by man, and had become covered in most parts with extensive forests, the spontaneous productions of an uncultivated land, which have long since been removed by the hand of industry.

The Chinese have a history which refers to ages still more remote, but it is considered as entirely fabulous by the more learned among them, who do not pretend to fix the foundation of the empire at a more distant date than the period above mentioned, which places it among the first kingdoms established after the flood. It is supposed that the first migratory tribe that passed beyond the deserts of central Asia settled in the province of Shensee, which borders on Tartary, where they laid the foundation of the present monarchy, and became the progenitors of the people known to Europeans as the Chinese, who gradually spread themselves over that vast tract of country which they at present occupy. According to the native historians, the first emperor was Fohi, a chief chosen by his countrymen to rule over them, on account of his manifold virtues, and styled by his subjects "the son of heaven," a title borne by the sovereigns of China to this day. It is quite uncertain how long a space of time elapsed from the reign of Fohi, if such a person ever existed, to that of Yu the Great, who is probably the first real character in Chinese history, the date of whose accession is fixed at somewhat more than two thousand years before the Christian era. Supposing that the monarchy was established before the time of the patriarch Abraham, we may reasonably conclude, that whilst the mighty Pharaohs were ruling over Egypt the Chinese were in existence as a great nation. Whether they held any intercourse with the ancient Egyptians is uncertain, but there is sufficient evidence to prove that they had attained to as high a degree of civilization as that people, and greatly resembled them in many of their laws and customs, which have descended from generation to generation, with so few changes, that there is but little difference between the habits and customs of the Chinese of the present day, and those of their forefathers who dwelt on the land two thousand years ago. The ancient records mention nine sovereigns of the first dynasty, founded by Fohi, whom they suppose to have been gifted with superhuman virtues and knowledge, by which they were enabled to rescue the people from their original barbarism, and to instruct them in the arts of civilized life, which were, undoubtedly, acquired at a very early period, and promoted by the rulers of the country.

The earliest and most useful of these arts were husbandry and silk weaving, both of which must have been taught by necessity as soon as the nation was established, as the people depended for subsistence on the cultivation of the land, and for clothing, on the chief natural produce of the country, adapted for that purpose, which was found in the vast forests of China, where silkworms were abundant on many species of the forest trees. The merit of teaching the people to weave silk into garments, and dye it of various colours, is ascribed to an empress, whose name holds a place in the fabulous history of the empire; and that of instructing them in husbandry is given to Shinnong, the immediate successor of Fohi, whose name is held in veneration accordingly, and even to this day the Chinese offer up annual sacrifices, and hold a festival in honour of the princess who first wove silken garments, and the no less praiseworthy monarch who taught his people to plough the earth, and who is commemorated under the title of "the divine husbandman."

Agricultural pursuits have always been, and still are held in high estimation by the Chinese, who commence the year with a grand festival in honour of the spring; on which occasion the emperor, in imitation of his ancient predecessor, performs the operations of ploughing and sowing seed in a field set apart for that purpose, a custom that has seldom been neglected by the sovereigns of China, who have thus, by their own example, stimulated their subjects to the performance of these useful labours, and maintained the honourable character of the husbandman, who even now holds a rank in society above that of the soldier or the merchant, however wealthy the latter may be. Among the ancients, particularly the Egyptians, Persians, and Greeks, it was a common practice to hold games and festivals, mingled with religious ceremonies, at that season when the earth is ready to receive the seed, thus showing the cheerfulness with which the farmers returned to their rustic toils, and the reliance they placed on a superior Being to reward them with an abundant harvest. The old festival of Plough Monday in England, was probably derived from these customs of the ancients, and was formerly celebrated in all the rural districts with great merry-makings on the Monday following twelfth-day; some of the rites observed being not unlike those among the Chinese, as an instance of which the plough-light was set up before the image of some patron saint in the village church; a custom somewhat similar to that observed among the Chinese, who place lighted candles opposite certain images in their temples. But as a particular description of the spring festival is reserved for a future page, we will return to the subject of the ancient Chinese emperors. One is said to have been the inventor of writing, another of musical instruments, a third the discoverer of the art of working in metals, while a fourth has the credit of having taught his subjects to build bridges. But how these royal instructors acquired their knowledge of the arts and sciences they taught, history does not inform us; and it is rather amusing to read that the Emperor Hoang-ti *ordered* his empress to teach the people to weave silk, although no mention is made that the lady was herself previously acquainted with the art of weaving.

Among the wonderful inventions which there is every reason to believe originated in China, at a very early period, is that of the compass, which, according to an old tradition, was invented by the same Hoang-ti, to guide him through the forests when hunting. This story may be, and most probably is, an utter fiction; but it forms a reasonable ground for supposing that the powers of the magnet were originally discovered by the Chinese, and that an instrument, doubtless of rude and imperfect construction, but similar in its nature and uses to the mariner's compass, was made by them many ages before the Christian era.

The last two emperors of the line of Fohi are celebrated under the names of Yaou and Shun, as the wisest and best of princes, and have always been held up as bright examples to all Chinese sovereigns. They are reckoned among the sages of China, and to them are attributed most of the political institutions by which the country is even now governed. About this time it is first mentioned that the lands were flooded; but the annalists do not say from what cause, so that it remains a question whether they mean to connect this flood in any way with the great deluge, of which there is no particular account in the history of China, or merely refer to some inundation of the rivers. It was then that Yu the Great, one of the ministers of Shun, distinguished himself by draining the lands, which by his means were again rendered fit for cultivation; and for this eminent service, added to his wisdom and numerous good qualities, he was appointed by the emperor to succeed him to the throne, according to the laws of China, by which the reigning sovereign always chooses his successor, and is at liberty to select whom he pleases. By this time the empire was extended over all the northern provinces, as far as the Yangtsekeang river, not by conquest, but by the establishment of new colonies as the population increased. The monarchs, from time to time, bestowed the government of these new settlements on their relatives, so that there arose, by degrees, a number of petty kingdoms, each having its own sovereign, who was dependent on the emperor. Of the southern part of the country very little was then known, but it is supposed it had but few inhabitants, and that those were in a state of barbarism.

Time rolled on without producing any material change, so that after a lapse of many ages the only difference appears to have been, that the country had become more populous, and the people more civilized than in earlier times. The emperors, who succeeded each other without interruption, employed sages to record the principal events that occurred during their several reigns; but in these early annals so much fable is blended with the truth, that they cannot be relied on; and it is supposed that the earliest authentic history relating to the Chinese empire is contained in the works of Confucius, an eminent author and moral philosopher, born in China about five hundred and fifty years before the Christian era, and who was one of the most illustrious characters that ever appeared in that country. The monarchy had probably then existed about sixteen or seventeen centuries, during which great progress had been made in civilization. The people lived under a regular form of government, were skilled in agriculture, and were acquainted with many useful and elegant arts. The government was despotic, and the northern part of the country was still divided into the several small principalities which had been granted by the emperors at different times to their sons and brothers, who constituted the only hereditary nobility of the state, and were all tributary to the chief sovereign. Each of these petty states contained a city, where the prince resided, and all around it were numerous villages and detached dwellings, inhabited by the peasantry, who held small farms which they cultivated for their own advantage, growing rice and vegetables in abundance, so that every poor man could support his family by his own industry. They were not held in bondage by the great, like the peasantry of Europe during the feudal ages; and amongst other privileges which they enjoyed were these:—a ninth part of the land was in common amongst them for pasturage and farming, and all the poor were at liberty to fish in the ponds and lakes, a right that was denied to the lower orders in feudal countries, where the mass of the people were vassals and slaves. The peasants of China, therefore, appear to have been at that period in a better condition than those of any other part of the world, working for themselves, and paying taxes to their respective princes, who by that means raised the tribute which the emperor claimed of them.

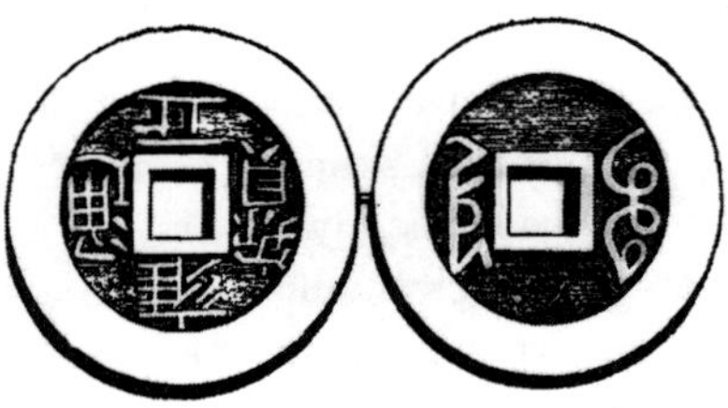

Copper Coin.

At the time of Confucius all taxes and tribute were paid as they are at present, chiefly in kind; but it is supposed there was always some sort of coined money current among the Chinese; and that, at a very early period of the monarchy, they had coins of gold and silver, as well as of lead, iron, and copper; but many ages have elapsed since any other than copper money has been in use among them. A very usual medium of exchange was silver beaten out into thin sheets; the buyer cutting off so much as was required to pay for his purchase, which was weighed by the merchant, who was always provided with a small pair of scales for that purpose. Their reckonings were made by means of a machine, which is still in use for buying and selling, and answers all the purposes of numerical figures. It consists of a number of little balls of various colours strung upon wires fixed in a box, and divided into compartments; the balls in one division being units, in another fives; and with these they add up and multiply with as much facility as we do by the aid of figures.

This is the Chinese system of arithmetic, and has been so long practised that its invention is attributed to the emperor who succeeded the divine

husbandman, and the same who is said to have found his way through the forests by means of the compass.

There were public markets in the towns, to which the people generally resorted about noon; and there were shops also, where the artizans pursued their various callings, and sold, or exchanged with the farmers, the produce of their labours for rice and other commodities of which they stood in need. Beyond the cultivated lands were pastures for sheep; and the rest of the country generally consisted of extensive forests, inhabited by tigers and other beasts of prey, which were so destructive, especially among the flocks, that great hunting parties were made every spring for the purpose of destroying them; and this dangerous sport seems to have been the favourite amusement of the sovereigns and great men of the land.

The principal weapons used both in war and hunting were bows and arrows; consequently the practice of archery was a constant and favourite sport of the great, and there were particular rules by which it was conducted; as for example, the imperial target was the skin of a bear, while that of a stag was set up as a mark for a prince to aim at, and of a tiger for the grandees of the court. Yet the Chinese were never distinguished as a martial nation, holding literature, as they did husbandry, in far higher estimation than military achievements: regarding the man who distinguished himself by his literary attainments beyond him who gained renown by his warlike exploits; and the husbandman who laboured in the field as a better member of society than the soldier who fought in it. Yet the petty princes were frequently at war with each other, so that the empire was seldom quite at peace.

The education of youth was considered of so much importance, that every district was obliged by law to maintain a public school, where boys were sent at eight years of age to be instructed in reading, writing, arithmetic, and their several duties to parents, teachers, elders, and magistrates, as well as to their equals and inferiors. They were also taught to commit to memory a great number of wise maxims and moral sentences contained in the writings of the ancient sages; and many of their lessons were in verse, that they might be the more readily learned and remembered. A new school was always opened with much ceremony, in the presence of the chief magistrate, who delivered a discourse to the boys, exhorting them to be diligent and submissive to the master, and setting forth the advantages of learning, which has been, in every age, the only road to wealth and honours in China. At fifteen, those who had most distinguished themselves were sent to higher schools, where public lectures were given by learned professors on the laws and government of the empire, and such subjects as were best calculated to fit them for offices of state, to which those who attended these schools usually aspired, but which were never bestowed on any but such as had studied profoundly, and given proofs of their knowledge.

Among the arts that are held in high estimation among the Chinese is that of writing, which was known at so distant a period of their history that it must have been one of their earliest steps in civilization. This art, as practised in China, may perhaps be rather difficult of attainment, on account of the number and not very simple formation of the characters; yet it was rare to meet even with a poor peasant who could not read and write; for rich and poor were all educated alike, in the manner just described, which is mentioned as "*the ancient system*" in books that were written more than two thousand years ago.

The general occupation of the females of China, from the empress to the wife of the meanest peasant, was the spinning and weaving of silk, which material, from the earliest times known, was used for clothing by the poor as well as by the rich, for the same reason that wool was used by the ancient Britons; because it was the material of which they had the greatest abundance. It is therefore no proof of superior wealth or grandeur that the peasantry of China wore silk garments, but merely a simple evidence of the fact that silk was the staple commodity of their country, as wool was of ours.

The empresses of those days were as zealous in promoting the branches of industry adapted for females by their own example, as were the emperors in encouraging agriculture by similar means. A plantation of mulberry trees was formed within the gardens of the palace, and a house built purposely for rearing the worms, which were tended by the ladies of the court, and often fed by the fair hands of royalty. Every autumn, a festival was held to commemorate the invention of silk weaving, when the empress, attended by the princesses and ladies of her train, made sacrifices in the temple of the earth, and then proceeded to her mulberry grove, where she gathered leaves and wound the cocoons of silk, which was afterwards spun and woven by her own hands into small webs. These were carefully preserved for the grand spring festival, when they were burned in sacrifice.

Great attention was bestowed on the management of silkworms throughout the whole of the empire; and as it had been discovered that those which were fed on mulberry leaves produced a finer kind of silk than the wild worms of the forests, a law was made by one of the early emperors that every man possessing an estate of not less than five acres, should plant the boundary with mulberry trees.

The difference between the garments of the higher and lower orders consisted in the quality and colours of the silks of which they were composed, and the fashion in which they were made. The robes of the grandees were often richly embroidered with gold and silver, and ornamented with various devices, according to their rank and occupation. As instances of these distinctive marks, the dress of a literary man was ornamented by a bird worked on a square of black silk on the back; while that of a military chief was adorned with the figure of a tiger, or

Drawn by Clayton from a Painting by Lo Shang. On Stone by M. Giles

THE EMPRESS AND HER ATTENDANTS PROCEEDING TO THE TEMPLE FROM THE MULBERRY GROVE.

London. Dean & Co. Threadneedle St.

some other savage animal; and these are among the many customs that have been continued from that time to the present.

The wars among the princes, and the efforts of some of them to render themselves independent of the Emperor, led to a vast deal of disorderly conduct in the several states, each petty sovereign being more intent upon his own aggrandizement than on keeping good order among his people, who, finding that the affairs of government were neglected, and the laws seldom enforced, paid very little attention to them. Such was the state of the Chinese empire when the celebrated philosopher, Confucius, was born in the kingdom of Loo, one of the small sovereignties in the north of China. This event occurred when the ancient Greek republics were in all their glory, and Rome was just beginning to rise into power and greatness. The Greeks and Romans, however, it is believed, knew little or nothing of China, nor did the Chinese imagine there was any great empire in the world besides their own: an opinion they have maintained even until now.

CONFUCIUS,

Who lived between five and six hundred years before our Saviour appeared upon earth, and was contemporary with Solon, the lawgiver of Athens, was the son of the chief minister at the court of the King of Loo, and was himself of royal descent. Being of a studious disposition, he had no taste for the sports of youth, but devoted even the hours of recreation to reading the ancient books, and storing his mind with the wise maxims contained therein, so that at an early age he had made great progress in the learning of the times. He married when only nineteen, and had one son; but soon finding that a matrimonial life opposed many obstacles to the pursuit of his studies, he divorced his wife, and turned his whole mind towards framing a perfect system of government, founded on the works of the ancient sages. It is mentioned by Chinese historians that he had only one wife; we may, therefore, infer that, in his time, the laws of China permitted the practice of polygamy. The talents and virtues of this great man caused him to be appointed one of the chief magistrates of his native country, the kingdom of Loo, in which capacity he had sufficient opportunities for observing that the people in general were in the habit of breaking the laws with impunity, of acting dishonestly towards each other, and were altogether guilty of so many vices, in consequence of the negligence of their rulers, that a complete reformation was necessary throughout the country.

This important change he was desirous of promoting, both by instruction and example, with which view he made a progress through the different states, giving public lectures on the benefit of virtue and social order, which produced such good effects, that in a short time he was at the head of about three thousand disciples, who were converts to his doctrines, and practised the rules he laid down for their conduct. His fame increased with his years, and at length the King of Loo appointed him chief minister, and for a long time he was engaged in affairs of government. It is said that while he continued in power, justice was so well administered, that if gold or jewels were dropped on the highway, they would remain untouched until the rightful owner appeared to claim them. But a similar story is told of Alfred the Great, Robert Duke of Normandy, and others, and it may be considered as only a figurative mode of depicting the extreme good order that was preserved in the state. At length the philosopher, finding that all his efforts to produce a reformation at the court were unsuccessful, voluntarily resigned his dignity, and devoted himself, with a few chosen friends, entirely to the study of philosophy, and the composition of those works which have rendered his name immortal, and the precepts of which, like those of the Koran of Mohammed, even to this day, regulate both the government and the religion of the state. The latter may be more properly termed a system of morality than a religion, as it is intended to inculcate the duties of men towards each other, rather than those which they owe to a superior being. The Confucians believe in one supreme Deity, and adore the earth as the mother of all things; but they have no particular form of worship, nor any regular priesthood; their religious rites consisting solely of sacrifices made in the temples on stated occasions, when the Emperor officiates as high priest, and the chief mandarins of the court as his subordinates. The books of Confucius, which are studied by the Chinese as sacred volumes, teach them that the true principles of virtue and social order are, obedience to parents, elders, and rulers; and the acting towards others as they would wish that others should act towards them. In the works of this great moralist, the duties of the sovereign are as strictly laid down as those of his subjects; and while they are enjoined to obey him as a father, he is exhorted to take care of them as though they were his children. There was nothing new in this patriarchal system of government, which had existed from the very beginning of the monarchy; but it was brought into a more perfect form, and the mutual obligations of princes and people were more clearly defined, than they had ever been before. But it was not only on the government of the empire collectively that this celebrated teacher bestowed his attention; he also made laws for private families, founded on the same principle of obedience from the younger to the elder, and submission from the inferior to the superior. Indeed, all classes of persons, including even young children, were instructed in the duties of their several stations by this highly gifted individual, who employed all the energies of his mighty mind for the benefit of mankind.

The writings of Confucius are chiefly on the subject of moral philosophy; but there are among them two books which may be considered historical, the one relating to his own, and the other to more ancient times. From the former is gathered all that is known of the state of the country at that period; but the latter is regarded more as traditionary than as historical, as it is supposed to be merely a collection and arrangement of the records kept at the courts of the early monarchs by their historians. This work is entitled the Shoo King, and there is another called the Shi King, containing all the ancient poems and songs of the country, which, it is recorded, used to be sung or recited before the Emperors. It may, therefore, be imagined that there were bards among the Chinese in those olden times, who celebrated in verse the great and good actions of their heroes and sages. These traditional poems were collected and revised by Confucius, who formed them into a volume, which is still one of the standard works of the Chinese, and must be studied by all who aspire to preferment, as it forms the subject of a part of their examination, ere they can be admitted as candidates for any high office. The same great man formed into a code of laws all the ancient observances, both in public and private life, being of opinion that the preservation of order in a state depended much upon the outward forms of society in general. This code, which is called the "Book of Rites," entirely regulates and governs the manners and customs of the whole community, from the Emperor to the most obscure of his subjects; and as it has maintained its influence from that time to the present, we may readily account for the little change which has taken place in the habits of the people. The study of this book constitutes an important branch of the education of every Chinese, and is, in fact, a part of his religion. Confucius died at the age of seventy-three, having spent the whole of his long life in the practice and teaching of virtue. Two thousand and nearly four hundred years have elapsed since his death, yet his name continues to be held in as much veneration as ever throughout the Chinese empire; and, although he did not pretend to divine inspiration like Mohammed, or profess to be endowed with more than human attributes, he is worshipped as a superior being, and many temples are dedicated to him in all the provinces of China. His descendants, who are very numerous, are the only persons who enjoy the dignity of mandarins by inheritance, and they are also exempt from taxes, and have many other privileges on account of their great ancestor. In the time of Confucius, another sect was founded in China, by a sage named Laou Keun, whose disciples assumed the title of Taou-tse, or "Doctors of Reason;" but their claim to this distinctive appellation appears doubtful, their principal studies being alchemy and the art of magic. From them emanated the absurd notion, which in former times was very prevalent in Europe, that a liquid might be prepared, the use of which would prolong human existence beyond its natural term; and also that an art might be discovered of turning inferior metals into gold: the former termed the elixir of life, the latter the philosopher's stone. The Taou-tse mingled religious rites with their pretended skill in magic, and were in fact the priests of their sect. They long possessed great influence in China, and were patronized by many of the emperors, but they have now fallen into disrepute, and the few who remain are treated as impostors.

THE BUILDING OF THE GREAT WALL.

For three hundred years after the death of Confucius, the internal peace of China was incessantly disturbed by the wars and quarrels of the petty kings, whom the emperors were unable to keep in subjection, and who constantly refused to pay their tribute; until, at length, there came to the throne a prince named Chi-hoang-ti, a great warrior, who resolved to put an end to these troubles by uniting all the small kingdoms into one monarchy, of which he intended to be the sole and absolute sovereign. There was no difficulty in finding pretexts for invading the several states of the tributary kings, as scarcely a year passed but one or other of them rebelled against his authority. By degrees, however, he conquered them all, and, after some years of civil warfare, became master of the whole empire, about two hundred years before the Christian era; and was the first monarch of the dynasty, called Tsin, or Chin, from which it is supposed the country took the name of China. When Chi-hoang-ti had subdued all the petty princes, he next turned his arms against the Tartars, who had become very

troublesome neighbours, making frequent hostile incursions into the Chinese territories. They were the same people who, in European history, are called Huns, and belonged to that extensive race known in ancient times under the general denomination of Scythians. They consisted of numerous tribes who wandered about the barren plains of central Asia, living partly by hunting, and partly by plunder; and as they were a much more warlike people than the Chinese, they were enemies very greatly to be dreaded. The Emperor, therefore, devised a plan to keep off their invasions, by erecting a wall along the whole extent of the northern frontier, of such a height, thickness, and solidity, as to be proof against any attempts which might be made, either to scale, or to effect a breach in it. The means by which this grand design was carried into execution were cruel and arbitrary in the extreme, yet not more so than those frequently adopted by monarchs of much later ages, and of countries esteemed infinitely more civilized than China; for what could be more tyrannical, more arbitrary, than the laws of conscription, or custom of impressment, by which the armies and navies of Europe were supplied with men during the late extensive wars.

In order to obtain a sufficient number of workmen for so vast an undertaking as the building of the Great Wall, the Emperor ordered that every third labouring man throughout the empire should be compelled to enter his service; and they were forced to labour like slaves, without receiving any compensation beyond a bare supply of food. It was by a similar exercise of power over his subjects that Peter the Great of Russia raised his splendid city of St. Petersburg in the midst of a morass. But the acts of one tyrant do not excuse those of another; and the conduct of Chi-hoang-ti in sacrificing the lives of many thousands of his people to the vanity of completing a wonderful work in a short time, certainly reflects

no credit on his memory. The wall extended fifteen hundred miles from the sea to the most western province of Shensee. It was carried over the

Drawn by Clapton, from a Painting by Fo-Shang. — on Stone by J.W. Giles.

BURNING OF THE CHINESE BOOKS, BY ORDER OF THE EMPEROR WHO BUILT THE GREAT WALL.

London. Dean & Co. Threadneedle St.

highest mountains, through the deepest valleys, and, by means of arches, across the rivers. Its breadth was sufficient to allow of six horsemen riding abreast on its summit, and it was fortified by strong towers, built at equal distances of about one hundred yards, in which guards were stationed. The exterior was formed of stone and brickwork of the most solid construction, which was filled in with earth, so as to render it impenetrable; and the whole was finished in the short space of five years.

Such is the account generally given of the Great Wall of China, which has been regarded as one of the wonders of the world; and, except the Pyramids of Egypt, may be considered as the most ancient monument of human labour now existing.

Chi-hoang-ti, a title which literally signifies the First Emperor, seems to have been a prince who, in all things, was extremely ambitious of fame; for although he had rendered his name immortal by the stupendous work just described, he aspired to still higher renown, and even entertained the vainglorious desire that his name should be handed down to posterity as the founder of the Chinese monarchy. But there was one great obstacle to the attainment of this end, which none but the veriest tyrant would have thought of removing; and that was the existence of a vast number of books, wherein might be read the histories of those who had reigned before him. The Emperor, however, was one of those who would sacrifice every thing which stands between them and the object on which they have set their hearts; therefore, he issued a peremptory order that all books and writings of every description should be collected and burned by the magistrates of each district throughout the whole empire; and the decree was so strictly enforced, that many literary men were put to death for being detected in an attempt to save some valuable records.

There can be little doubt that in the general conflagration many important documents must have been lost for ever; but the tyrant, whose mischievous ambition had tempted him to commit such an act of madness, missed the end he had in view; for, in spite of all his precautions, several copies of the works of Confucius, and some other eminent authors, were hidden behind the walls, and under the floors, of different houses, where they remained until the death of the Emperor rendered it safe to bring them again to light.

It is somewhere related of this same prince that, when dying, he commanded that his favourite wife, and a number of slaves, should be buried with him. This dreadful custom had existed in the barbarous ages, and was common among the Tartars and Hindoos, not only at the death of princes, but also at those of all classes of the people, from a superstitious belief that the wives and domestics thus interred would pass with the deceased into the next world, and be ready to attend upon him there. With the same idea, the Chinese used in later times to bury clothes, furniture, and even food, for the use of the departed, with a number of effigies in the likeness of slaves; and this harmless custom has been continued down to the present time, with this difference, that every article now sacrificed is made of paper; millions of bundles being consumed annually in these pious, but superstitious rites. The revolting practice of immolating human beings had, however, been so long out of date, that it is mentioned in reference to this period as a relic of the barbarism of distant ages.

Chi-hoang-ti appointed his eldest son to succeed him, a case of rare occurrence, for the imperial throne was not hereditary, neither was it, strictly speaking, elective, it being customary for the Emperor to make choice of a successor during his lifetime, and the choice, in most cases, very naturally fell upon one of his sons; but it has seldom happened that the eldest has been the favoured individual. Some of the early emperors, indeed, set aside family claims altogether, and among these patriotic princes was the famous Yaou, who is highly commended in the ancient writings for having chosen a stranger to succeed him, because that stranger was wiser and better than any of his own children.

The custom of bestowing territories on the princes of the royal family was abolished by Chi-hoang-ti, who saw that these petty sovereignties were sure to occasion civil warfare. He therefore provided for his family by giving to each of his immediate male relatives a palace in one of the great cities, with a suitable maintenance, and the privilege of wearing yellow, which was then, as it is now, the imperial colour, and, as a distinctive mark of rank, is highly valued. A yellow girdle has the same degree of importance in China as a blue ribbon in England, and is always a sign that the wearer is nearly related to the Emperor. The prince chosen by Chi-hoang-ti as his successor happening to be absent at the time of his father's death, a younger son took advantage of the circumstance to seize on the sovereignty, and contrived to have his brother secretly strangled. But the usurper did not long enjoy the fruits of his crime, for he made himself so unpopular by neglecting the affairs of the state, and attending to nothing but his own pleasures, that a formidable insurrection broke out in the country, headed by the chief of a band of freebooters, named Liu-pang, a man distinguished by many noble qualities, although he was no better than a robber. It is related of this adventurer, that just after the breaking out of the rebellion, he happened to meet a fortune-teller on the road, who, falling at his feet, said, he offered him this mark of homage, because he saw by the lines in his face that he was destined shortly to become emperor. In making this prediction, the soothsayer, no doubt, foresaw the probability of its accomplishment, for it was not an unlikely termination of the rebellion, that the leader, if successful, should be placed on the throne; with this belief, therefore, the stranger followed up his prophecy by offering his only daughter in marriage to the chief. Liu-pang accepted the proposal, and married the lady, who was thus, by her father's artifice, raised to the dignity of empress; for, after many scenes of violence and bloodshed, in which the Emperor lost his life, the insurgents were victorious, and their leader was raised to the imperial throne.

THE HAN DYNASTY.

The new sovereign, who assumed the name of Kaut-sou, was a native of the kingdom of Han, one of those small states into which the empire had formerly been divided, therefore he is called the founder of the Han dynasty, and the princes of his race occupied the throne for more than four centuries. During this period, the Chinese made considerable advances in civilization. The arts and sciences were improved; literature was encouraged, agriculture was in a progressive state, and several useful inventions date their origin from the same era. Among the latter, one of the most important is the manufacture of paper, which is supposed to have been commenced towards the end of the first century. The Egyptians had long possessed the art of making paper from the rush called papyrus, which was also used at Rome for the same purpose in the first century; but whether the Chinese obtained their knowledge from either Rome or Egypt, or whether the discovery was their own, is uncertain. Before they were acquainted with this useful art, they were accustomed to write on thin slips of bamboo, not with ink, but with pointed tools, similar to those used by engravers, with which they cut or engraved the characters. The bamboo is a gigantic species of reed or cane, that grows as high as a large tree, and is used in China for various purposes, as for the building of houses and boats, and the manufacture of furniture, mats, ropes, boxes, and toys of various kinds; and, although it is extremely light, it is very strong and durable. Books were formed of bamboo by taking off the outside bark, and cutting it into thin sheets, all of the same shape and size, which, after the writing was finished, were strung together in such a manner as to form a compact, though rather clumsy volume. At length, about the year 95, it was ascertained, by what means does not appear, that bamboo might be made into a better material for writing upon, than it furnished in its natural state, by pounding it in a mortar with water until it became a thin paste, which being spread out on a flat surface, was dried into what we call paper. The earliest specimens of this new art in China were probably of a very rough description; but the manufacture was gradually improved by the mixture of silk and other materials, until the Chinese were able to produce a paper of the most beautiful texture, adapted for printing, which we now call India paper, and another kind for painting, known by the name of rice paper. The invention of paper naturally leads to that of ink, which, in China, is always made in those cakes, known by us under the name of Indian ink; and is used with the camel's hair pencils for writing by the Chinese, who do not require such pens as ours in the formation of their hieroglyphical characters. The art of manufacturing paper was first brought into modern Europe by the Arabians, after the conquest of Spain, in the early part of the eighth century, and might possibly have been derived by them from the Chinese, by means of an indirect intercourse through some of the Oriental nations. It has already been noticed that the empire of China is supposed to have been unknown to the ancient Greeks. Even Alexander the Great, who, long after the death of Confucius, penetrated very far into India, did not suspect there was so rich a country beyond it. It happened, however, somewhat later, that the Greeks, in the course of their commercial transactions in the East, now and then obtained small quantities of manufactured silk, which they thought so extremely beautiful, that they were desirous of knowing something of the country from which it came; but the approach was found so difficult, either across the Indian mountains, or along a dangerous coast with which they were unacquainted, that they never gained any accurate information respecting those distant regions. At a subsequent period, when the Romans had grown so wealthy by their numerous conquests, that they were able to indulge in every kind of luxury and extravagance, silk became a fashionable material for the dress of all the fine gentlemen of Rome, on account of its rarity and high value. Such silks as were commonly worn by the peasantry of China, were sold at Rome for their weight in gold; consequently, the merchants of Alexandria, by whom the trade was chiefly carried on, were tempted to brave all dangers in order to obtain large supplies of so profitable a commodity; but as even the most enlightened people of those days knew nothing of the geography of distant countries, it has never been ascertained, with any degree of certainty, how far they actually ventured, or by what route. Their journeys were long and perilous, and they describe a country to which they give the name of Serica, or, the land of silk, but whether it was or was not China is a point that may ever remain undecided; and, like many other doubtful questions, each side has its advocates, whose arguments are often more ingenious than convincing. It appears that the natives of this unknown country, whom the Egyptians called Seres, met those traders at certain frontier stations to transact their business, and would take nothing but gold or silver in exchange for their goods. They are described as a sedate and peaceful race of people, who never suffered strangers to enter their territories; and, as such has been the law of China ever since that country has become familiar to Europeans, many persons consider it as a proof that the Seres were no other than the Chinese: but it is no where remarked that they wore any article of silk clothing, a point that certainly would not have been overlooked by those who set so high a value on that commodity, and paid such large prices for it on account of its supposed scarcity. The Seres, therefore, if not actually the Chinese, might have belonged to some of those numerous tribes of Tartars that peopled the vast regions of central Asia, and who bought silks of the Chinese to sell again to foreign merchants.

To return, however, to the interior of the empire, which, under the dominion of the Han sovereigns, was in a very happy and prosperous

condition. Most of those princes were munificent patrons of learning; they bestowed the highest dignities on men of literary fame, and thus learning, as in earlier times, continued to be the only sure road to wealth and honours. Nobility was not hereditary, except in the imperial family, but depended entirely on personal merit; and as it was always bestowed by the emperor, so it could be taken away at his pleasure. Thus the nobles, or highest class of mandarins in China, are not necessarily persons of high birth, but are men of learning, who must have passed a public examination with credit, before they can aspire to rank and office in the state. This peculiar constitution of the government of China, which has continued down to the present time, is one means of keeping up its despotism, as it prevents the rise of a powerful aristocracy, which has never yet failed to prove a dangerous rival to an absolute monarchy.

Under the Han dynasty lands were, for the first time, frequently bestowed on men of rank, with people to cultivate them, who were bound to the soil, and who were, to a certain extent, slaves: but it is not very clear how far the authority of their masters extended; how large a proportion of the peasantry was thus held in vassalage; or how long the system continued; therefore we may suppose that the duties exacted were light and not of long duration, although considered as a grievous imposition at the time by a people whose liberty had never before been infringed upon.

About this time, the religion of Budha was introduced into China from India, where it was then the prevailing faith. The sect of the Budhists is supposed to have been founded about 450 years before the birth of Confucius, by an Indian sage of royal birth, who is said to have devoted his whole life to the instruction and moral improvement of the people and the reformation of their religion, which was that of the Brahmins. The name of the illustrious sage was Budha; and one of the leading features of his spiritual doctrines was the Metempsychosis, or transmigration of souls; according to which doctrine, the Budhists believe that the soul only quits one corporeal frame to animate another, not necessarily of the human species; and for that reason a Budhist is forbidden, by the laws of his creed, to destroy animal life in any shape. When Budha died, his followers believed that he was transformed into the god Fo, by which name he is also worshipped; and is said to have three different forms, which the priests represent in their temples by three great gilded idols, which they term the three precious Budhas.

Budhism was first brought into China in the reign of Ming-ti, the fifteenth emperor of the Han dynasty. This prince, in studying the works of Confucius, met with certain words which appeared to him to mean that the true religion was to be sought for in the west, a passage which some suppose to have prophesied the coming of Christ. The emperor sent messengers abroad to inquire concerning the faith of the western nations; but they only went as far as India, where Budhism prevailed, but where there were no teachers of Christianity, therefore they concluded that Budhism must be the religion they were in search of, and returned to China, taking with them some bonzes or priests of that persuasion, which has ever since been tolerated by the Chinese government, but has never superseded the Confucian system, which has always been upheld as the chief religion of the State. This happened in the early days of Christianity, about the time when the Jewish empire was overthrown, and the city of Jerusalem destroyed by the Roman emperor Titus. The Budhist priesthood dwell together in communities in the manner of monks, subsisting chiefly upon alms, like the mendicant friars of the Catholic church. The temples are their monasteries; and the pagodas, of which so many are seen in different parts of China, were first erected in that country by the priests of Budha, to whose worship they belong. The head of this religion, who holds the same rank among the votaries of Budhism as the Pope does among those of the Catholic church, is called the Grand Lama. He resides with much state in Thibet, and is supposed to be immortal; for when he dies, it is given out that his soul has passed into the body of some infant, whom the priests pretend to identify by certain signs, and who is brought up in the belief that the same spirit which animated the form of his predecessor, exists within himself. Thus the office of Grand Lama always commences with infancy, and lasts till the close of life. There are a great many female devotees belonging to this faith, who live like nuns secluded from the world, and never marry; but they are not so numerous in China, as in Thibet, Japan, and Tartary. The Budhists have five prohibitory commandments, which they strictly observe. These are, "Not to destroy animal life; not to steal; not to speak falsely; not to drink wine; and to the priests, or bonzes, not to marry." Their belief as to their final state is, that after having passed through a certain term of probation upon this earth under various forms, they shall at length be received into the paradise of Budha, and partake of his divine nature. Some of the Chinese sovereigns adopted this faith, while others encouraged the sect of Taou, and among the latter was Han-ou-ti, one of the early emperors of the Han dynasty, a prince who was famed for many virtues, but was strongly addicted to a belief in magic, and maintained a number of the Taou-tse at his court, who were constantly engaged in studies which he was credulous enough to believe would lead at last to the discovery of the elixir of life, a draught of which he was extremely anxious to taste. In this hope, he was continually supplying the sages with large sums of money, to enable them to procure the rare ingredients for making the wonderful liquid; some of which they pretended were hidden in remote corners of the earth, and only to be obtained with great difficulty, and by the aid of magic.

In vain did the ministers remonstrate with him on the folly of squandering the public money in such idle pursuits. He turned a deaf ear to their exhortations, and gave his whole attention to the Taou-tse and their experiments. At length, it was announced that the coveted draught was really prepared, and the chief of the sages was deputed to convey it in a golden cup to his royal patron; when, in crossing the great hall of the palace, one of the ministers feigning a desire to look closely at so miraculous a compound, suddenly snatched the cup from the hands of the astonished priest, and drank off its contents. The enraged and disappointed Emperor ordered that the offender should instantly lose his head, a consequence that had been foreseen by the daring courtier, who had provided himself with a very clever defence. "O most mighty prince!" said he, "how is it possible for thy commands to deprive me of life, if the potion I have just swallowed has really the power ascribed to it? Then make the trial; I willingly submit to the test; but remember, that if I die, thy system must be a false one, and in that case my poor life will have been well bestowed in convincing my prince of his error." The monarch pondered on these words for a few moments, and then pardoned the offender; not so much, perhaps, from motives of clemency, as from reluctance to be undeceived, or to let the world into the secret of his credulity; so that it is evident he began to waver in the faith he had professed. The Taou-tse were engaged in other researches no less chimerical than that of finding means of prolonging human life beyond its natural term; and many of them spent the greater part of their lives in the search after the philosopher's stone. Yet we need not wonder at the folly and credulity of the Chinese princes in bestowing attention on such fruitless speculations so early as the first century, when we find the most profound scholars of Europe, fifteen hundred years later, engaged in the same visionary pursuits; and may read of one of the German emperors, at the beginning of the seventeenth century, neglecting the affairs of the state to shut himself up with the alchymists whom he maintained at his court, assisting them in their experiments, and expecting that they would at length discover the two great secrets which would bestow on him the gifts of endless life and inexhaustible riches.

The princes of the line of Han were much harassed by the incursions of the Huns, against whom the great wall had proved a very insufficient barrier, and who were a terrible scourge to the peaceful farmers of the frontier provinces. As the object of those fierce invaders was plunder rather than conquest, they laid waste the lands, set fire to the dwellings, and carried away every thing of value, not even sparing the people, for they were in the habit of making slaves of their prisoners. Some of the emperors made peace with these barbarians by giving their daughters in marriage to the chiefs, a cruel mode of purchasing their forbearance, as the Chinese princesses were accustomed to all the luxuries of a palace, and but little able to endure the hardships of a wandering life, and the privations to which they must have been subjected in the rude tents of the warlike Huns. Towards the close of the second century, the power of the Han dynasty began to decline. Some of the princes were weak, others wicked; and, at length, a formidable insurrection broke out, called "The revolt of the yellow caps;" a cap of that colour being the badge of the disaffected party, whose object was to depose the reigning family, and place some warlike chieftain on the throne.

In the mean time, the unsettled state of the empire had afforded opportunities for the establishment of two independent kingdoms or principalities; that of Shensee in the north, and that of Ou in the east, the capital of the latter being Nanking, which had long been a large, wealthy, and populous city. Each of these states was governed by its own sovereign, who assumed the title of king; and they both disclaimed dependence on a superior, who had no power to reduce them to subjection. The troubles occasioned by the yellow caps led to several usurpations of the imperial dignity, and opened a new field of ambition to the kings of Ou and Shensee, who boldly asserted their claims to the throne, the possessor of which was a prince of a distant branch of the Han family, and against him these two sovereigns declared war. A fierce contest ensued, which lasted forty-three years, and is celebrated in Chinese history under the title of "The war of the three kingdoms." It would be vain to seek for any rational account of the events that marked this unhappy period of civil warfare. It was the Chinese age of chivalry, and each chief was exalted into a wonderful hero by the writers of the time, who blended so much romance with history, that nothing certain can be gathered from their works beyond the fact that the country was divided into three separate states, the sovereigns of which were at war with each other for nearly half a century. At length, there appeared among the competitors for the imperial throne a prince who was descended from a branch of the family of the famous Chi-hoang-ti, the builder of the great wall, and for him was reserved the glory of putting an end to the war, and reuniting the three kingdoms under one sceptre. He assumed the title of emperor, and in a few years succeeded in conquering both the states of Ou and Shensee, and thus became master of the whole empire about the year 264.

It is rather a curious coincidence, that two princes of the same race, at the distance of five hundred years, should have established their empire under much the same circumstances, by subduing and uniting the petty states into which the country had, in consequence of the weakness of the government, become divided. The dynasty founded by the conqueror just alluded to, like that of which Chi-hoang-ti was the founder, took the name of Tsin, and ruled over China somewhat more than a century and a half, during which period fifteen sovereigns succeeded each other on the throne.

The war of the three kingdoms furnished the Chinese authors with abundant materials for poems, novels, and dramatic compositions; for this was the golden age of literature in China, where talent had been honoured and rewarded during the whole period of the Han dynasty, and the literati, as before observed, formed the highest class of the community.

Next to them, in point of consideration, were held the agriculturists; husbandry being, in fact, of much more importance than commerce to a people whose remote position on the globe, ere navigation had brought them into contact with distant nations, rendered them wholly dependent on their own resources for subsistence; therefore the wise sovereigns of China endeavoured to promote agriculture by rendering it the most honourable of all pursuits, except that of learning. Ou-ti, the fifth emperor of the Han, restored the annual spring festival, which seems to have been neglected during the War of the Three Kingdoms, but was revived by this prince to keep up a remembrance of the high estimation in which field labour was anciently held; and it has ever since been regularly celebrated, except when war has occasioned a temporary interruption of all customary rites. There were at this period large tracts of pasture land, and fine flocks of sheep, the wool of which was manufactured into cloth; but not in sufficient quantities to supply the place of silk, which was far more plentiful, and, in consequence, much cheaper.

Cotton was then only known as the produce of a rare and curious plant in the gardens of the great; nor was it cultivated to any extent till many centuries later; but it is now produced in great abundance, and has long superseded silk as clothing for the generality of the people. The population of the country had so considerably increased, that it had been found necessary to clear and cultivate much of the forest land, that a sufficiency of food might be raised for the people, who lived chiefly on rice, which is a kind of provision as much used by the Chinese as bread corn is by us. The peasantry were exceedingly industrious; the women and children working in the fields as well as the men; and as the farms on which they laboured were in most cases their own, they had the greater motives for exertion.

Many people, at this period, were employed in rearing horses for war: and most of the farmers grazed cattle on the commons; but this kind of farming was gradually discontinued, as the necessity of bringing the public land under culture increased, till at length there were very few commons or pastures left; cattle became scarce, and sheep were only to be found in the mountainous districts. The country people lived together in clans, all the members of a family joining their property to form a common stock, which enabled them to live much better than if they had been divided. It was therefore customary for a son to bring his wife home to his father's house, where she was expected to submit entirely to the authority of her mother-in-law, whose province it was, as elder matron, to rule over the female part of the household; and if this part of the domination was not always exercised in the most gentle manner possible, it was no less the duty of the daughters-in-law to yield implicit obedience. Hence, perhaps, arose the singular and affecting custom prevalent among Chinese maidens, when any one of their young friends is about to marry, of going to sit and weep with her before she leaves her parental home to take up her abode with strangers. The birth of a son was always celebrated with great rejoicings, but that of a daughter was considered as rather a misfortune than otherwise, especially if the parents were poor; for a girl could in no way advance the fortunes of her family, whereas a boy always had the chance, at least, by applying himself to

learning, of attaining high honours; and, in that case, his parents were sure to be exalted also, as a reward for the attention they had bestowed on his education, which was regarded as a benefit to the state; and if even he were not gifted with extraordinary talents, he was looked up to for future support, as every young man was obliged by law to maintain his aged parents, and taught by his religion that it was one of his most sacred obligations so to do. This point of filial duty was held in so much importance by the government, that a law was made which enacted that the life of a criminal, who would otherwise be condemned to death, should be spared, provided his parents were old, and had no other son or grandson above the age of sixteen to work for them.

A boy had several names given to him at different periods of his life. The first was bestowed soon after his birth by his father, who, having assembled all his relatives, took the infant in his arms, and pronounced its name with numerous prayers and ceremonies; the next name was conferred on the boy's first entrance into school by the master, and was called "the book-name;" the third appellation was assumed at his marriage, when, if he were the eldest son, the father also added another syllable to his own name, all which alterations, one would suppose, must at times have created some confusion, and must do so still; for these customs are even to this day continued, as well as a law that was instituted about this time, prohibiting any person from marrying one of the same surname, even though the parties were not related to each other. It has been asserted by many writers that female infants were often suffered to perish from neglect, and that such an unnatural practice still exists in China to a very great extent; but those who know most about the Chinese give very little credit to this statement, although they do not absolutely deny that parents are sometimes driven by extreme poverty to destroy their female offspring—a crime that might possibly be more frequent among the poor of other countries, if it were disregarded by the law, as it is in China.

In ancient times, the law of primogeniture existed among the Chinese, and remained in force until the reign of the Emperor Outi, who thought it so unjust that the whole of a man's estate should come into the possession of the eldest, while the rest of his sons were unprovided for, that he abolished this law of inheritance, and instituted a new one, by which, on the death of a father, his lands were divided among all his male children, the only difference being that the eldest had two portions. The right to this double portion still exists, and is established by a singular ceremony of very ancient date, called "buying water," which is performed immediately after the decease of a father by his eldest son or next heir, who places some copper coins in a bowl, and being supported by his brothers or near relatives, proceeds to the nearest well, where he throws in the money, and takes some water, which he carries home, and with which he washes the face of the deceased. A daughter had no inheritance, neither did she receive any marriage portion from her parents. On the contrary, she was in a manner bought of them by her future husband or his friends, who sent presents according to their means, as was the custom as far back as in that primitive age when Abraham sent his steward to seek a wife for his son Isaac, who took with him jewels of silver and jewels of gold, and raiment, which he presented to Rebekah and her friends on his asking the damsel as a bride for his young master. As daughters and wives, the women of China were not held in much consideration; but as mothers, they were treated with the utmost respect, especially by their sons, who, even when themselves advanced in years, paid great deference to the commands and counsels of an aged mother.

Among the most sacred rites observed by the Chinese was that of visiting the tombs of their departed relatives twice a year, to make sacrifices, sweep the tombstones, and clear away any weeds that had grown near them. The burial-places are always at some distance from the towns, and very generally on the side of a hill, which is cut into terraces one above another, covered with monuments of the dead. The coffins are not put into the ground, but laid upon it, and covered with a tomb, which is more or less handsome, according to the circumstances of the relatives, some being only mounds of earth, while others are of stone, having in front a slab of black marble, bearing an inscription in letters of gold; and they present altogether a picturesque appearance amid the trees and shrubs which are planted about them. When the time arrives for the performance of the commemorative rites, all the male population of the town or village, both men and children, repair to the place of interment, carrying with them wine and meats, sticks of incense, and paper offerings, to burn at the tombs, which they sweep very carefully before they make their sacrifices; and at the conclusion of the ceremonies, each individual sets up a long streamer of white or crimson paper, which is fastened to a stick fixed in the ground, as a token that he has performed his duties to his deceased kindred; for these usages, which are of great antiquity, are considered so important, that any one who should neglect them would be looked upon as unworthy of the favour of the Gods. The veneration of the Chinese for these observances is one great reason why they are reluctant to remove from the place of their birth, at least to any distance that would prevent them from paying their periodical visits to the tombs of their relatives; and however unnecessary the custom may appear to us, yet it springs from a feeling so admirable, that it cannot fail to be respected. The rites to the dead are always concluded with feasting and merry-making, for it is considered rather a joyful than a mournful occasion, as the visitors believe that they are holding communion with their departed friends, and ministering to their wants by offerings of food and raiment.

Every rich family in China has a temple, or large building, called the Hall of Ancestors, in which are placed tablets of stone or wood, bearing the names and ages of all deceased relatives, with the dates of the days on which they died, and the occupation each had followed in this world. Here, at certain times of the year, all the male members of the family assemble to shew their respect for the memory of the deceased by prostrating themselves, and placing wine, meat, and incense, before the tablets.

Those who cannot afford to have a distinct building for this purpose, hang up the memorials in some room of their house, which they call their Hall of Ancestors, and where they perform the customary ceremonies. There is, in fact, no country in the world where so much respect is paid to the memory of the dead, or where they are held so long in remembrance. A son would sometimes keep the body of a parent in his house for years, enclosed in a varnished coffin, usually very richly ornamented, which was placed in the best apartment, and on all particular occasions candles were lighted, and incense was burnt before it; the room being hung with white, which is the colour appropriated by the Chinese for mourning, and is worn as such by all classes of people. Some wore dull grey, or ash colour; but the deepest mourning was an outer garment of sackcloth, with a cap of the same, every other part of the dress being white. At this period, the male part of the community did not disfigure themselves by shaving their heads, as they do now; but suffered the hair to grow very long and thick, and fastened it in a knot at the top of the head. The male attire was long and flowing, with loose sleeves; and in the winter, men of rank wore costly furs; but the winter dresses of the poor were made of sheepskin. As to the ladies, it does not appear that they have once altered the fashion of their dress from that time to this. Their costume is not altogether unbecoming. It consists in a full robe gathered into a narrow band round the throat, from which it hangs in graceful folds, unconfined at the waist, while the large falling sleeves almost touch the ground. The most striking difference in the appearance of the gentlemen of ancient and modern times relates to the head; that of the ladies to the feet, which were then suffered to grow to the natural size, and were not distorted and squeezed into shoes only four inches long, as they are at present; an absurd custom, that will be noticed in its proper place.

It is doubtful whether tea was in use among the Chinese so early as the Han dynasty; and in fact not much is known respecting their domestic habits at that period, as the country was inaccessible to strangers, and very few of the books then written have been translated into any European language. But in the ordinary affairs of life they were much governed by superstition, putting implicit faith in omens, dreams, and spells innumerable. A belief in astrology was universal, and charms and talismans were frequently resorted to even by the most learned men of the age, by the power of which they hoped to avert an impending evil. One of these popular superstitions was exemplified in a singular manner during the War of the Three Kingdoms, by a chief named Kung Ming, who was a great astrologer, and very often consulted the stars on the subject of future events. One night, being thus engaged, he fancied he saw signs in the heavens predicting that his own death would take place in a few hours; but as he was not willing to die so soon, he lost no time in endeavouring to avert the fatal doom by means of a spell. He lighted a number of lamps in his tent, which he placed in a particular order, corresponding with the position of the heavenly bodies at the time, and then composed a sort of prayer, which he continued to repeat incessantly as he sat on the ground before the lamps. But all was unavailing; for ere the sun arose he had breathed his last sigh, most probably in consequence of the excited state of mind produced by his own superstitious dread. The inefficacy of the charm was thus clearly proved, yet the superstition still remains, and many of the Chinese occasionally light lamps, and arrange them in correspondence with the position of the stars, in the full persuasion that a threatened misfortune may be thus averted.

It was during the period that followed the War of the Three Kingdoms that the Chinese began to erect those elegant villas, in which their taste is so eminently displayed; and as one of the chief beauties of such buildings is that they are invariably placed in some picturesque situation, either on the top of an eminence, at the foot of a rock, or perhaps on a wooded island in the midst of a lake, all these features of the landscape had in most cases to be assisted by art, and thus arose the singular style of ornamental gardening in China.

THE MIDDLE AGES IN CHINA.

THE ancient capital of the Chinese empire was Hang-chow-fou, a large, wealthy city, situated at no very great distance from Nanking, and containing an immense population, chiefly engaged in the manufacture of silk. The Imperial palace, standing in the midst of extensive gardens, was adorned with eastern splendour, and near it were several magnificent temples, and many fine residences belonging to the grandees of the court. Like all the great cities of China, it was surrounded by a high wall, and covered an immense extent of ground; for as none of the buildings exceeded one story in height, they occupied the greater space: so that a Chinese town of six miles in circumference did not contain, perhaps, more houses than one not half the size in Europe, where the style of architecture was different, and the dwellings were high rather than of wide extent. The first sovereign of the new dynasty of Tsin removed the seat of government to Kai-fong-fou, another large city, standing in the centre of the empire, in the province of Honan, one of the most fertile and beautiful parts of all China, and this was the royal residence until the reign of Ouenti, the fifth emperor of the line of Tsin, who built a very magnificent palace at Nanking, where the court was held with more splendour than had been exhibited by any of the former sovereigns.

After the War of the Three Kingdoms had ended, there was an interval of repose which lasted some years, when a new invasion of the Huns again spread terror and desolation throughout the western provinces. They were led by a barbarian prince, who laid claim to the empire on the ground of being descended from one of those princesses of the race of Han, who had married a chieftain of the Huns; and the fierce invader, having made a captive of the emperor, obliged the unfortunate monarch to wait upon him at table, for several days, in his tent, and then had him cruelly put to death; soon after which, some of his generals captured the son of the murdered sovereign, who was treated with every insult, and in the habit of a slave was compelled to attend the barbarian chief on his hunting excursions, and perform the degrading office of carrying his parasol; for parasols to screen them from the sun were luxuries known to the Chinese and Tartars as early as the fourth century, and probably long before, but they were ensigns of dignity, and only used by persons of rank.

This unhappy prince was not destined long to endure these mortifications, for he was beheaded by command of the tyrant, in consequence of an attempt made to effect his liberation. Another prince of his family was immediately proclaimed Emperor, and the Huns were soon driven out of the Chinese territories, but not before they had done a vast deal of mischief in the provinces that bordered on their own country. The monarchs of the Tsin dynasty were not so illustrious as those of the race of Han. The country does not appear to have been so well governed; and the people were very much dissatisfied with the heavy taxes levied to support the extravagance of the court, which had never been held with so much magnificence as at this period. Grand feasts and expensive entertainments were constantly given at the palace, where the royal banquets were usually enlivened by dances performed by female slaves, who were splendidly attired in dresses sparkling with gold and jewels. Their movements were accompanied by very noisy music, for the Chinese have always been fond of cymbals, drums, trumpets, and those deafening instruments called gongs. They had, however, many softer instruments, such as the lute and guitar, which were often touched by other female fingers, and accompanied by other female voices besides those of the young slaves; but dancing was treated merely as an exhibition, and not resorted to for amusement, as in

European countries. The excessive luxury of the court, which could be maintained only by burthening the people with taxes, excited much popular discontent, which manifested itself as usual by a number of petty insurrections, which broke out from time to time in different parts of the empire, and at length ended in the overthrow of the Tsin dynasty; a revolution that was effected in a very remarkable manner, and of which the following are the incidents. A poor boy named Lieouyu, born in the city of Nanking, had been left a destitute orphan at a very early age, and must have perished from want, had not an old woman, who took compassion on him, brought him up as her own. As soon as he was old enough he learned to make shoes,

and sold them in the streets of the city; but he was so idle and careless, that those who knew him predicted that he would come to no good; little thinking that they were speaking thus irreverently of the future Emperor of China. For a long time Lieouyu carried on his shoe-trade, by which he earned a scanty livelihood, without concerning himself much about his condition, until he happened to attract the notice of a military officer, who had probably stopped him to make a purchase, and who, being pleased with his replies to some questions he had put, proposed to him that he should become a soldier. As fighting was an occupation better suited to his taste than shoemaking, Lieouyu at once accepted the offer, and having been introduced into this new scene of action, he displayed so much courage and ability, that he was promoted in his profession by degrees, till he became chief commander of the Imperial forces, and in that capacity rendered such important services to the Emperor, during a serious rebellion, that he was elevated to the rank of chief minister of state. By this time he had become very ambitious, and, like all ambitious people, was not content to stop at any point while there was a still higher one to attain; therefore he took advantage of the prevailing disaffection towards the reigning family, and having made himself exceedingly popular, seized a favourable opportunity of aspiring openly to the throne, and, by the aid of a powerful party, compelled the Emperor to abdicate in his favour. Such was the remarkable career of

F

Lieouyu, who was proclaimed Emperor in the year 420, by the name of Outi, and was the first sovereign of a dynasty called "Song."

The first care of the new Emperor was to reward those who had been kind to him in his adversity, especially the good old dame who had taken care of him in his infancy. He then caused all the schools and colleges, which had been neglected during the late troubles, to be re-opened, and the ancient studies to be resumed; for, although he was not an educated man himself, he was well aware that if learning were not promoted, the constitution of the empire could not be preserved. Towards the close of the dynasty of Tsin, China had become divided into two kingdoms, each having its own sovereign, which could scarcely fail to occasion many troubles, particularly as one was considered subordinate to the other, and was expected to pay him tribute—a mark of inferiority that was almost invariably refused. The superior prince, who alone bore the title of Emperor, resided at Nanking, while the king of the northern part of the country kept his court at Honan; and they were frequently at war with each other. It was fortunate for the people that the Huns, about this time, turned their attention towards Europe, and, under their renowned king Attila, invaded the Roman empire, which had long been declining in power, and was overrun by the Goths, and other barbarous nations. The Chinese were thus relieved from their most formidable enemies; yet there is no period of their history more confused or more disturbed, than the two hundred years that followed the downfall of the Tsin dynasty. During that unhappy period, no less than five different families reigned in succession, each having obtained the throne by usurpation, attended, in some cases, by crimes of a more serious nature.

In consequence of these violent proceedings, the literary men lost their influence in the state, and the highest honours were bestowed on the military; for, as the Emperors had no chance of maintaining their dignity except by force, they had more need of soldiers than of scholars, and raised to all the chief offices such men as were best qualified to aid them against the rebellions that were constantly occurring, and which were headed by the many petty chiefs who aspired to rule the empire. There is every reason to believe that the Chinese, during this time, were carrying on an extensive trade with the Arabians and Persians, whose caravans made regular journeys to the frontiers, from whence they returned laden with silks, of which a portion was sent to Constantinople, for the use of the luxurious inhabitants of that city. We must here remember, that after Rome had been taken by the Goths, Constantinople, where the Roman Emperors had held their court ever since the time of Constantine the Great, remained, with a large portion of what was termed the Empire of the East, in possession of the Romans. It was then the most wealthy city in the world, and its inhabitants indulged in every rare and costly luxury. Silks were in great demand, and were supplied at immense prices by the merchants of Arabia and Persia, who, however, could afford no information respecting the Chinese, because they were never permitted to pass beyond the boundaries of the empire; neither did they know that silk was produced by insects; therefore we may reasonably infer that the Chinese were studious to keep that fact from the knowledge of foreigners. It was about the middle of the sixth century, and during the time that China was in the state of anarchy above described, that the secret was discovered, and brought into Europe by two Persian monks, who went as Christian missionaries into distant lands; but whether it was in India or in China that they made the valuable discovery alluded to, has never been ascertained. However, it is certain that they carried the intelligence to the Emperor Justinian, and undertook, for a large reward, to procure for him a quantity of silk worms' eggs; an exploit that would have subjected them to the punishment of death, had their meditated theft been discovered by the natives. But the monks were fortunate enough to escape with the stolen eggs, which they carried to Constantinople inside a cane; and as they had made themselves acquainted with the art of rearing the worms, the little creatures multiplied very fast in the warm climate of Greece, and were the progenitors of all the silkworms propagated in Europe.

Towards the end of the sixth century, the northern and southern kingdoms of China were again united into one, of which the city of Honan was declared the capital; and not long afterwards the country was restored to order by the accession of a new and illustrious race of sovereigns, called "Tang," who re-established the old system of government which had been so happily pursued by the Han princes. The founder of the Tang dynasty was a chief or general named Ly-yuen, who deposed the last prince of the five families that had so long kept the country in confusion, and ascended the throne in 622. The greater part of his reign was spent in subduing rebellions raised by the princes of the late dynasty, and making such regulations as were likely to lead to future prosperity; but as soon as he saw that peace was restored, and that the stream of government was again flowing in its proper channel, he chose to abdicate in favour of his son, the great Tait-song, after having occupied the throne about nine years. Tait-song is celebrated by the Chinese as one of their most illustrious sovereigns; and he appears to have merited the praises bestowed on him for his clemency, wisdom, justice, and general attention to the welfare of the people, over whom he exercised that paternal authority which distinguishes the government of China from that of all other great empires. Under the auspices of this enlightened prince, learning and the arts flourished as in the ancient times, and all the high offices were again filled by men of letters; while, in order to promote the revival of literature, which had so long been neglected for war, an academy was instituted within the precincts of the palace, where not less than eight thousand students received instructions from the most able professors. Tait-song also founded a similar school for archery, where he often attended himself, for the purpose of practising that warlike art, in which it was important for the Chinese to excel, as bows and arrows were their principal weapons. The ministers sometimes remonstrated with the Emperor on the imprudence of trusting himself among the archers, but the good prince only replied, "Am I not the father of my people? What, then, should I fear from my children?" The attention of Tait-song was constantly directed towards improving the condition of the lower orders, which he effected in a material degree, by lessening the taxes, and sending commissioners into all the provinces to inquire into the conduct of the magistrates, and to see that the poor were not oppressed by them; for he often expressed the benevolent wish that every poor man should have enough of the common necessaries of life, to make him comfortable in his station; which may remind us of the well-known speech of Henry the Fourth of France, that he should not be satisfied till every peasant in the kingdom could afford to have a fowl in his pot on the Sunday. His strict sentiments with regard to the administration of justice induced him to pass a law for the prevention of bribery, by making it an offence punishable with death for any magistrate to receive a present as a propitiation in the exercise of his power; and in order to ascertain whether this law had its proper effect, he employed a person to offer a bribe to a certain magistrate, of whose

integrity he had some suspicion. The bribe was accepted, and the guilty magistrate condemned to death; but his life was saved by the interference of one of the ministers, who were always at liberty to speak freely to the Emperors on the subject of their conduct. "Great prince," said the monitor, "the magistrate is guilty, and therefore deserves to die, according to the law; but are not you, who tempted him to commit the crime, a sharer in his guilt?" The Emperor at once admitted that he was so, and pardoned the offender.

It is recorded, and apparently with truth, that during the reign of Tait-song, some Christian missionaries first arrived in China, where they were well received by the Emperor, who permitted them to build a church, and preach Christianity among the people; but it does not appear that their efforts were very successful, nor have any subsequent endeavours been effective in establishing the Christian religion permanently in the Chinese empire.

It was about this time that the Chinese first discovered the art of making that fine porcelain, which has ever since been one of their principal manufactures. A common kind of earthenware had been in use from time immemorial, and there were potteries in various parts of the country where it was made; but it was not till about the middle of the seventh century that the Chinese began to make the beautiful semi-transparent ware so much valued and admired in Europe, and to which the European manufacture of porcelain owes its origin. The discovery of the materials and the composition of them, in the manufacture of this fine ware, was probably owing to some accidental circumstance which occurred in the potteries, and which gave an idea to the workmen, that it was possible to manufacture a kind of ware much superior to that which they had been in the habit of making. The first furnace on record was established at Changnan, a great city, on the banks of a river, in the province of Keangsy, situated about half-way between Canton and Nanking, in the neighbourhood of which the earth and stones were found that are employed in the manufacture of the fine kind of porcelain; a certain portion of which, made there, was sent annually to the Emperor as tribute, under the name of imitation gem ware.

The Emperor Tait-song died, after a reign of twenty-three years, universally regretted by his subjects, who looked up to him as a pattern of wisdom and virtue, and preserved many of his excellent maxims, which are frequently repeated with great veneration to this very day. It is a singular feature in the character of the Chinese nation, that the surest way of gaining immortal fame has ever been by leaving good examples and good advice to posterity. The successors of Tait-song maintained the peace and prosperity that had been established by that great prince; and under their dominion the country was much improved, and the people enjoyed a considerable share of comfort and tranquillity.

Among the great national works of the seventh century were several extensive canals for the convenience of inland commerce, with locks of a very peculiar construction, placed in embankments, over which their flat-bottomed vessels, without being unloaded, were hauled by ropes attached

to large capstans. By means of this inland communication, the trade with Persia and Arabia was so much increased that a great number of vessels came every year to the port of Canfu, supposed to be the same now called Canton; and in the year 700 a regular market was opened there for foreign merchandise, and an Imperial commissioner appointed to receive the customs on all goods imported from other countries, which produced a large revenue to the government. The manner in which the duties were collected was this:—When a vessel arrived, the commissioner took possession of the cargo, which was laid up in warehouses until an account of it had been taken by the proper officers, and a portion of each commodity had been deducted by way of duty, which was at that time paid in kind, and amounted, towards the end of the government of the Tang dynasty, to the enormous proportion of thirty per cent., or nearly one-third of the whole cargo. The remainder was then restored to the merchants, and the portion taken away was sent to the Royal storehouses.

The Arabians were, at this period, more enlightened and civilized than any European nation. Their merchants were rich, and lived in a style of princely magnificence in their own country, and they were the first foreigners who formed a settlement at Canton, where so many of them went to reside that they were permitted to have a cadi, or magistrate of the Mohammedan religion, to preside over them; and in evidence of their freedom to exercise their own form of worship, there is an ancient mosque at Canton, which has all the appearance of having been built so long ago as the time here referred to. The Mohammedan faith is now professed by a great number of the Chinese people in different parts of the empire, but is perhaps chiefly confined to those of Tartar origin, as there must have been many Moslems, or "true believers," as they call themselves, among the followers of the great Tartar chief Zinghis Khan, an account of whose conquests in China will commence an important era in the history of the country.

The sixth Emperor of the Tang dynasty founded the Hanlin College, the great literary institution of the Chinese empire, consisting of forty members, from amongst whom the ministers of state are generally chosen, and from whom all successful candidates for honours receive their degrees. The members of the Hanlin are mentioned in old histories as the learned doctors of the empire, and in fact possessed quite as much knowledge in those days as they do now; for the members of the present day are all educated according to the ancient system; nor have any new branches of learning, as it is believed, been introduced into the schools of China; yet, when the Hanlin College was founded, the Chinese were far in advance of the Europeans both in knowledge and refinement, for the modern nations of Europe were then only just emerging from the barbarism into which they had been plunged by the conquests of the Gothic tribes. England was divided among the Saxon princes of the Heptarchy, and France was in that rude state which preceded the reign of Charlemagne, who was then in his early boyhood. Thus, while the princes and nobles on this side of the globe were ignorant even of the arts of reading and writing, there was scarcely a peasant in China who did not possess these acquirements; and while Europe was desolated by fire and sword, the happier land of the Chinese was covered with the fruits of the earth, raised by the careful hand of the industrious husbandman. In Europe the great mass of the people were despised, oppressed, and in slavery; whilst in China they were not only free, but enjoyed equal rights with their superiors, and might even aspire to the attainment of equal rank. The possibility of arriving at wealth and honours by means of learning was a great inducement to parents to send their children to the schools, although they might be but ill able to afford it; for as there was but one system of education for rich and poor, the son of a peasant was likely to distinguish himself as much as the son of a grandee; and the public examinations, though strict, were conducted with the utmost impartiality. It may be imagined that only a very small proportion of the boys in any school were gifted with such great talents as would entitle them to attain preferment; therefore, of the many who presented themselves as candidates for honours at the hall of their province, where an examination was held once a year, very few perhaps were chosen; and those had to pass other halls, before doctors of a higher degree, before they were eligible to be appointed to offices of state. Still each aspirant had a chance, and as the object was so important, great pains were taken to instil into the minds of youth a due sense of the value of learning, and many little stories, written with that intent, were read to children as soon as they were of an age to comprehend them. These juvenile tales are mostly very simple, but are not uninteresting as illustrations of the character and manners of the people. The following are specimens of their general style:—"There was a boy, whose father was so poor that he could not afford to send him to school, but was obliged to make him work all day in the fields to help to maintain his family. The lad was so anxious to learn that he proposed giving up a part of the night to study; but as his mother had not the means of supplying him with a lamp for that purpose, he brought home every evening a glowworm, which, being wrapped in a thin piece of gauze and applied to the lines of a book, gave sufficient light to enable him to read; and thus he acquired so much knowledge that in course of time he became a minister of state, and supported his aged parents with ease and comfort in their old age." Another youth, who was rather dull of intellect, found it a very laborious task to apply himself to learning, and made such slow progress that he was often rather disheartened; yet he was not idle, and for several years continued to study with unceasing diligence. At length the time arrived for his examination, and he repaired, with many others, to the hall of the province, where he had the mortification, after all his exertions, of being dismissed as unqualified to pass. In returning homeward, very much depressed in spirits, and thinking it would be better to give up literary pursuits altogether and turn his attention to some other employment, he happened to see an old woman busily employed in rubbing an iron pestle on a whetstone. "What are you doing there, good mother?" said he. "I am grinding down this pestle," replied the old dame, "till it becomes sharp enough to use for working embroidery;" and she continued her employment. Lipe, such was the name of the student, struck with the patience and perseverance of the woman, applied her answer to his own case. "She will no doubt succeed at last," said he, "then why should I despair?" So he returned to his studies, and in a few years, on appearing again before the board, he acquitted himself so well that he passed with honour, and rose in time to one of the highest offices in the state. These short and simple tales, of which the Chinese have whole volumes, serve to shew the bias they endeavoured to give to the minds of their children, and account for the studious habits of so large a portion of the community. From the beginning of the ninth century the power of the Tang dynasty gradually declined, till at length the dominion of that race of sovereigns, who had ruled over the empire for nearly three hundred years, was terminated by the usurpation of a daring chief, who obtained possession of the throne in 897, by the murder of the Emperor. It was about this period that the strange custom was first adopted in China of binding the feet of female children to prevent their growth. The origin of this absurd and unnatural practice is unknown, nor is it easy to imagine what could have induced women in the first instance thus to deform themselves; for although vanity may be a powerful incitement for the continuance of a custom that distinguishes the higher from the lower classes, it hardly accounts for the first introduction of this practice, as any other distinctive mark, less painful and less inconvenient, might have answered the same purpose. The daughters of all people of rank are obliged to submit at an early age, to have their feet cramped up and tightly confined with bandages, which are not removed for about three years, when the bones are so far compressed that the feet never assume their natural shape and size. The health of the children generally suffers much from the want of proper exercise during this cruel process, and the enjoyment of after-life must be greatly diminished by the difficulty which females find in walking, or even standing without support. Yet they are proud of their very helplessness, and would think it excessively vulgar to be able to walk with a firm and dignified step. The lower classes cannot follow a fashion that would disable them from pursuing their daily labours, yet many parents in a very humble station of life are not free from the vanity of desiring to have one daughter with small feet, the prettiest child

Ancient Foot

Modern Foot.

being usually selected for that distinction; and such is the force of fashion, that the little damsel who is thus tortured and crippled, is looked upon as an object of envy rather than of pity.

For the space of fifty years after the extinction of the Tang dynasty, the government was in much the same state as it had been three centuries before, when the Tsin dynasty was set aside by the usurper Lieouyu; and although the present period of anarchy was of so much shorter duration, it witnessed the accession of five different families, numbering in all thirteen emperors, whose reigns were very brief, most of them dying by some kind of violence. Yet it was in these turbulent times that printing began to be practised in China; an event which occurred about five hundred years before that art was known in Europe,—and as there is no invention which has contributed so largely towards the improvement of mankind, it may reasonably be said that until the Europeans were possessed of the means of multiplying books by printing, they were not so far advanced in civilization as the Chinese. The method first adopted in China was to engrave the characters on stone, consequently when the impressions were taken off, the ground of the paper was black and the letters were white; but this mode was shortly superseded by the invention of wooden blocks, cut in such a manner that the letters were raised instead of being indented, and thus were impressed in black on a white ground. This mode of printing from wood is still practised in China, and is better adapted to the written language of the Chinese than the use of moveable types, as the words are not formed of separate letters like those of European languages, but a single character expresses a whole word, and sometimes more than one; and as there are many thousands of characters, it would cost the printer much unnecessary time and trouble to compose a page according to our plan. Before the invention of printing there must have been a vast number of the Chinese constantly employed in writing, as they were always a reading people, and even the poorest peasants were able to obtain books in manuscript, while in Europe a book was a thing unknown among the lower classes, and seldom to be met with except in monasteries or the palaces of princes.

The troubles that followed the fall of the Tang dynasty encouraged the Tartars to make new irruptions into the empire, and one of their chieftains having aided a fresh usurper to mount the Imperial throne, received from him in return the grant of a large territory in the province of Peche-lee, with an annual tribute of silks; and thus the Tartars gained a footing in the north of China, which laid the foundation of those long and terrible wars that ended in the first Tartar conquest. But ere these wars commenced, there was a long interval of repose, in consequence of the downfall of the last usurping family of the five petty dynasties, and the elevation of an illustrious race called Soong, of which there were eighteen emperors, who ruled over the Chinese empire 319 years. The founder of the Soong dynasty was a popular minister, who had also had the command of the armies, and had distinguished himself by his courage no less than by his ability in affairs of state; therefore, as the Emperor was dead and his son was but a child, it was decided by all the military leaders and other great men, that it would be better to place on the throne a man who was able to defend the country against its enemies. They accordingly fixed on the chief minister, and sent a deputation to his palace to invest him with the yellow robe, and he was proclaimed by the title of Tait-sou, in the year 950. The names assumed by the Emperor usually had some appropriate meaning; thus Tait-sou signifies "Great Sire," and the name of the present Emperor, Taou Kwang, means "The Light of Reason." The conduct of the new monarch justified the high opinion that had been formed of his virtues and abilities, and he holds a place in the history of China as one of the greatest of its sovereigns. His mother, too, is reckoned among the illustrious females of the empire, for the Chinese annals have preserved the names of many women distinguished by their superior understanding, whose wise sayings, and exemplary conduct, are recorded as examples for others. The following is among the numerous instances preserved in Chinese history of the heroism of the sex, in having preferred death to a dereliction from the established rites of the country.

An Emperor of one of the petty dynasties, who occupied the throne before the race of Tang, going on a party of pleasure, took with him one of his wives, whom he left at a summer-house on a beautiful little island, desiring her to amuse herself until his return. He had not proceeded far on his excursion, when he heard that the waters had suddenly risen to a great height, on which he despatched some of his attendants in all haste to save the princess from the danger in which he had so unintentionally placed her. By the time they arrived the tide had already covered a part of the island, and as it was still rising, they lost no time in endeavouring to rescue the princess. It happened, however, that the Emperor, in his alarm, had forgotten to send his seal, as was customary when he wished to see any one of his wives; and it was quite irregular for them to enter his presence without this token. The princess, therefore, when told that her Imperial lord desired that she would accompany his messengers without a moment's delay, asked for the seal; and as it could not be produced, she refused to follow them; and, in spite of their earnest entreaties, persisted in remaining whilst they rode back for the signet; but although they made what speed they could, they were too late; as, in the interim, the island had been overflowed, and the princess and her attendants had all been drowned. This and many others of a similar nature are related as examples of heroic virtue; as it is considered a meritorious act to sacrifice life rather than infringe the ancient customs. Many female names are also immortalized by the historians of the empire, as mothers, who by their excellent advice have guided their sons in the paths of rectitude; and among these was the mother of Tait-sou. We are told, that when the nobles presented themselves before this illustrious lady, to offer their congratulations on her son's advancement to the throne, she made this sensible reply—"I have been told that the art of ruling is a very difficult one. If my son governs with wisdom and justice, I shall receive your compliments with pleasure; but if he should fail in these qualities, I shall have no reason to rejoice in my present exalted position, but would rather return to my former obscurity." Tait-sou reigned seventeen years; and it is said that the empire had never been better governed than it was during that period; part of the merit being due to the Empress mother, who had a share in the government, and aided her son by her good counsels, to which he paid the utmost deference, according to the laws and customs of China; for, as we may observe, although the wife of an Emperor was of little importance in the state, his mother possessed a considerable share of influence; and, in case of a minority, usually acted as guardian of her son, and regent of the Empire.

As the Tartars still occupied some of the cities of Peche-lee, the Emperor paid great attention to the improvement of his army; and made a law, that no soldier should be promoted to command, until he had written a treatise on the art of war, and given proofs of his skill in horsemanship and archery. Several of his successors, although they were sometimes obliged to make expeditions against the formidable foes by whom the northern districts were held in perpetual terror, preferred keeping at peace; and were even content to purchase temporary cessations from war by the payment of tribute; a plan that was pursued by the Saxon king of England at that very time, in order to keep off the invasion of the Danes; and in both cases it proved equally ineffectual. In the meanwhile the great mass of the people were quietly engaged in their ordinary pursuits; for there were no signs of warfare in any other part of the country; and they felt no inconvenience elsewhere

Drawn by E. Clayton from a Painting by Fochang

On Stone by J. W. Giles.

THE EMPEROR WEI-T-SOONG AND HIS COURT, TAKEN PRISONERS BY THE TARTARS

London, Dean & C°. Threadneedle Street.

from what was passing in the north. Literature was promoted by the aid of printing; and the commercial intercourse with Arabia and Persia had continued to increase; so that, on the whole, the empire was in a very prosperous condition. In the reign of the third Emperor of the Soong dynasty were established the famous porcelain furnaces at King-te-chin, a large village in the province of Keang-sy, where all the best china is still made. These manufactories were erected in the year 1000, and still afford employment to many thousands of people. At that time porcelain was one of the principal articles of export; to which were added silks and spices; for although the Chinese had no spice in their own country except coarse pepper, still they were able to obtain abundance of the finer sorts of spices in their trade with the neighbouring islands; and about this time they took possession of the Moluccas, or Spice Islands, which they retained above sixty years, when they were dispossessed by the Malays, who were soon obliged to give them up to the Arabs and Persians. Tea had not yet become an article of foreign trade, although it was in very general use among the natives of China.

We are now approaching the commencement of those terrible wars which occasioned many sad scenes of desolation and misery among the peaceful Chinese, until the native sovereigns were expelled, and a prince of the Mogul race was seated on the throne of the empire.

In the reign of Weit-soong, the eighth emperor of his line, the horde of Tartars who had settled in the north, forming a tribe belonging to a great nation called the Khitans, grew so formidable, that, contrary to the advice of his wisest ministers, Weit-soong was imprudent enough to solicit the assistance of the Kin, or Eastern Tartars, another powerful tribe, who were at war with the Khitans, and very readily entered into an alliance with the Chinese Emperor against their common enemy. The result was such as had been foreseen by those who had endeavoured to dissuade their Imperial master from seeking such aid; for no sooner had these dangerous allies accomplished the object for which they had been called in, and had driven the Khitans out of the country, than they took possession of the vacated provinces; and, having found that they were a stronger and more warlike people than the Chinese, they soon began to meditate the conquest of the whole country. Weit-soong perceived his error when it was too late to remedy the evil; but still hoping he might be able to make terms with the barbarians, he repaired to their camp, accompanied by several princes of his family, when he and his whole party were made prisoners, and conveyed into Tartary; while the Tartar chief, having caused himself to be proclaimed Emperor, commenced his march towards Honan, the Imperial city. The Chinese, on receiving intelligence of the capture of their sovereign, had placed his eldest son, Kint-soong, on the throne; but this prince neglected to take measures for stopping the approach of the enemy, who crossed the Hoang-ho, or Yellow River, without opposition, and proceeded direct to Honan, which they took and plundered, while the Emperor, with his wife and some of the chief lords of the court, were carried away into captivity. There were many, it is said, who avoided this melancholy fate by putting an end to their own existence, which is not even now an uncommon practice among the Chinese, under any misfortune from which there is no other hope of escape. The Tartar prince, who was called King, or Khan of the Kin, fixed his residence at Honan, so that there were two distinct kingdoms in China; the Tartars keeping possession of the northern and the Chinese of the southern provinces, where the court was sometimes held at Nanking and sometimes at Hang-chow-fou, the ancient capital. The two sovereigns were equal in power and dominion; and as the Chinese princes were desirous of recovering the provinces they had lost, and the invaders were no less anxious to conquer the rest of the empire, the wars between them were carried on with scarcely any intermission during several long reigns, by which the country was reduced to very great distress, when at length a fresh foe appeared, to whom both parties were obliged to yield, and thus commenced a new and eventful era in the history of China.

THE FIRST TARTAR CONQUEST.

ZINGHIS KHAN, whose original name was Temudgin, and who was one of the greatest conquerors that has ever appeared on the face of the earth, either in ancient or modern times, was the chief of one of the numerous hordes of Moguls that inhabited the countries to the north of the Great Wall, extending from Eastern Tartary to Bukharia. They were a wandering people, who had no settled place of abode, but formed their cities of tents, which they could set up where they pleased, and carry away with them whenever they chose to change their locality. Every tribe had its own chief, but there was one superior to the rest, who was called the Great Khan, and to him the lesser chiefs paid homage and tribute. Some of them were also tributary to the two great Tartar empires of the Khitan and the Kin,—the former extending over Western Tartary to the shores of the Caspian Sea, and containing several great cities, of which Cashgar was the capital; the latter comprising the whole of Eastern Tartary, with the North of China, and to this empire the particular horde of Moguls, of which Temudgin was the chief, had long been accustomed to pay tribute. This celebrated warrior was gifted by nature with a mind of vast capacity, which served to render him more terrible to the rest of mankind, since it made him ambitious, and led him to plan and execute the widely extended schemes of conquest that have rendered his name distinguished in history as one of those wholesale destroyers of the human race, whose fame rivals that of Alexander of Macedon, generally called "the Great,"—a term that has too often been most strangely misapplied to those who have done the most mischief in the world, and proved themselves the worst enemies of their species. Temudgin had been accustomed to war from his earliest youth, for his father had died while he was yet but a boy; and several of the subject hordes, not choosing to acknowledge the authority of so inexperienced a leader, deserted the young chieftain to join others, so that he had but a very small band of warriors when he first set out on his career of conquest. Being successful, however, in several expeditions, the number of his subjects was increased, and he married the daughter of the Great Khan, whose real name was Vang, but who is better known by the fabulous title of Prester John, or Priest John, which he seems to have obtained among Europeans in consequence of the visits of some Christian missionaries to that part of the world, by whom it is supposed he was converted to Christianity. The Khan and his son-in-law did not remain on friendly terms, but were frequently at war with each other, till the death of the former. Temudgin then invaded the territories of his deceased father-in-law, and conquered one by one many of the Mogul tribes, whose princes did him homage as their Great Khan, or supreme chief. His ambition being thus flattered by success, Temudgin, on finding himself head sovereign of the Moguls, began to indulge the vain fancy that he was destined to rule over the whole world, and being fully impressed with this romantic and mischievous notion, he assembled together all the princes of the different tribes which were subject to him, and the generals of his armies, to hold a diet on the subject of the vast enterprise he meditated.

The place of rendezvous was on the banks of the river Onon, where all the chiefs arrived at the appointed time, and the whole army was ranged in order, each band displaying its particular standard. The Khan was seated in the midst of the assembly, when a certain pretended prophet, who enjoyed a great reputation for sanctity, suddenly appeared, and in a loud voice declared that it was the decree of Heaven that Temudgin should rule over all the earth; that all nations should bow down before him; and that he should thenceforth bear the title of Zinghis Khan, signifying Most Great Emperor. Such was the rise of this renowned chief, who began his reign as Emperor of the Moguls by giving a new code of laws to his subjects, which he did with a view to keep peace among them, and make them formidable to other nations. The men belonging to the Mogul tribes were prohibited from pursuing any occupations but those of war and the chase, all servile employments being left to slaves and strangers; the regulations

Painted by Tschang

Drawn on Stone by Dean & Co.

THE CHINESE PEOPLE SOLD FOR SLAVES BY THE TARTARS, AFTER THEIR CONQUEST BY ZINGUIS-KHAN.

London Dean & Co. Threadneedle Street

for hunting, on which the subsistence of these rude nations chiefly depended, were strictly defined; and death was made the punishment for murder, as well as for the theft of a horse or an ox, the two most valued articles of Tartar property. With regard to religion, the barbarian prince granted universal toleration; nor did he suffer his people to interfere with each other on that point, but all were permitted to worship in their own way, to enjoy equal rights, and to receive equal protection from the laws, whether they were Heathens, Jews, Mohammedans, or Christians, for Zinghis numbered among his subjects people of almost every different persuasion. The rapid conquests of Zinghis Khan speedily established his authority over the greater part both of Western and Eastern Tartary, from the banks of the Volga to the wall of China, which proved no barrier to his victorious arms. The contest was still continued between the northern and southern potentates of China. The territory of the former was called Cathay by the Moguls, and by that name the Chinese empire generally is mentioned in the European histories of those times. It has already been stated that the Moguls were tributary to the Kin race, then reigning in Cathay; but as the tribute had not been regularly paid for some time, the Emperor Yongtsi, who had just succeeded to the throne, sent an ambassador to demand it from Zinghis Khan, who treated the message with the utmost contempt, and made it a pretext for the invasion of China. The descriptions that are given of the dreadful cruelties of the invader are probably very much exaggerated; but the sufferings of the people must have been extremely great, as the Tartar mode of warfare was barbarous in the highest degree, and it was one of the maxims of Zinghis, never to make peace till after conquest.

It is said that in the first expedition he burnt down as many as ninety cities in the north of China, put to the sword many thousands of the inhabitants, and carried away vast numbers of both sexes into slavery. The Emperor of Cathay then offered terms of peace, which were accepted by the conqueror, who received, as the price of his forbearance from all further hostilities, immense presents in gold, silks, horses, and slaves. He then withdrew his army; but it was not long before he commenced a new invasion, which put an end to the empire of the Kin, and established that of the Moguls in the north of China. On this occasion, the invaders laid siege to the ancient city of Yea-King, which stood nearly on the site of the modern Pekin, and had become the capital of the kingdom of Cathay, as the Tartar kings had, during their wars with the Chinese sovereigns, found it expedient to remove their court from Honan. Yea-King was stormed and taken, after a long and desperate resistance, during which the inhabitants were reduced by famine to the last extremity; and when the conquerors entered, they immediately set fire to the Imperial palace, from which, however, the king had fled before the commencement of the siege. It is needless to dwell on the horrors of these barbarous wars; suffice it to say, that Zinghis was in the end completely victorious, and took absolute possession of the northern part of the country, while the king of the Kin was obliged to retreat farther towards the south.

The conqueror now turned his eyes towards other regions, and having appointed governors to preside over the provinces he had won, he left a part of his armies to defend them, and departed, with a numerous host, to spread war and desolation throughout the countries of Western Asia, the greater portion of which was divided into small sovereignties, under the dominion of the Turkish sultans of the race of Seljook, who had established a powerful empire on the ruins of that of the Arabian caliphs, but were now much weakened in consequence of their wars with the European crusaders. It is not therefore surprising that they should be unable to resist so powerful an enemy as Zinghis Khan, who first subdued all the states around the Caspian sea, and then proceeded southward with equal success, through Persia and Arabia, to the shores of the Indus. All the rich and populous provinces of Chorassan, Carizme, and Transoxiana, the last of which afterwards took the name of Zagatai from one of the sons of the conqueror, fell under the power of the Moguls, who plundered them, and sold great numbers of their Turkish prisoners for slaves to the Syrians and Egyptians.

During the progress of this fearful war, the eldest son of Zinghis Khan, Toushi, who was also a great warrior, headed an expedition into the Russian empire, which led the way to the conquest of that country a few years afterwards. Zinghis, on his way back to China, brought under subjection several of the kingdoms of Tartary that had either revolted from his authority or had not yet been subdued; but he did not live to complete the conquest of the Chinese empire, as death put an end to his destructive career very soon after his arrival in Cathay, in the year 1227. He left four sons, of whom the third, Octai, with the unanimous consent of his brothers, succeeded as Great Khan of the Moguls and Tartars, and was styled Emperor of China, while the others were content to hold states dependent on him. Octai, in pursuance of the dying commands of his father, carried on the war against the Kin, whose last monarch, after a long and desperate resistance, killed himself in despair, and the remnant of that once powerful nation fled to their native deserts, where they founded the tribe of the

Mantchoos, by whom the Chinese empire was conquered at a later period, and whose princes still occupy the throne of China.

While Octai was thus employed in extending his empire in China, he sent out a powerful army to Russia, headed by his nephew, Batou, by whose successes the dominion of the Moguls was established over that portion of Europe, and was maintained for upwards of two centuries. In the mean time the Chinese kept possession of the southern half of the country, and several Emperors of the Soong dynasty had succeeded each other, none of whom were particularly distinguished; nor had they yet been involved in wars with the Moguls, when Houpilai, better known by the name of Kublai, one of the grandsons of Zinghis, became Emperor, or Great Khan, about the middle of the thirteenth century, and for him was reserved the glory of completing the conquest begun by his great predecessor. Kublai was born in China, and in him the ferocity of the Tartar race appeared to be blended with the mildness of the Chinese character. He was a terrible foe, but a most beneficent ruler, and possessed all the great qualities of his grandfather, with a more enlightened mind; but he was not much less ambitious, and not being satisfied to reign over half an empire, he projected the conquest of the southern kingdom, which was at that period styled Manjee, and accordingly went to war with the Chinese Emperor, who happened to be a weak and indolent prince, who was wholly addicted to pleasure, and concerned himself but little about the conquests of the Tartars, so long as he was not personally inconvenienced by them. Under these circumstances, many of the Chinese cities opened their gates to the great Tartar general, Peyen, who was entrusted by Kublai with the chief conduct of the war; and those which offered any resistance were speedily forced to surrender, by the usual violent means.

Such had been the miserable state of the country for several years, when the Chinese monarch died, leaving three infant sons, who all in succession received the title of Emperor, for it cannot be said they reigned, as the eldest was but eight years of age when his father died. The Empress mother, who was appointed Regent, sent an embassy to the Great Khan with proposals of peace; but received for answer, that as the Soong princes had obtained the throne originally in consequence of the minority of a reigning prince, so it was but just that another family should dispossess them, under the same circumstances. The young Emperor was taken prisoner and conveyed to the Desert of Shamo, in Tartary, where he soon died, and the second brother lived only two years; when the now empty title was bestowed on the last prince of the Soong dynasty, who was about six years of age.

In the mean time the Tartars (as the Moguls were generally called, in common with all the nations of central Asia) were rapidly approaching the Imperial city, from which the whole Court fled in the utmost consternation, and went on board some barks that were lying near the mouth of the Canton river. Some Tartar vessels were sent in pursuit of the wretched fugitives, whose terror at the sight of the hostile fleet seems to have amounted to madness; for one of the grandees, seizing the infant Emperor in his arms, jumped with him into the sea, and was instantly followed by the Empress and the chief ministers—who thus all perished.

The Tartar sovereign was left in undisputed possession of the whole empire, but the conquest had not been achieved without much bloodshed, and numerous acts of revolting barbarity; but when the great object was accomplished, and the Mogul Emperor acknowledged by the Chinese as their sovereign, he endeavoured to win their affections by conferring benefits upon them; and sought to establish his power on the firm basis of popular esteem, rather than suffer it to rest on the uncertain foundation of that terror which his name had hitherto inspired.

Never did a more illustrious prince ascend an eastern throne, and never was there one more beloved and respected than Kublai Khan; and although a conqueror, and of a foreign race, he was deservedly called the father of his people, who had no cause to regret, beyond their previous sufferings, the revolution that had placed him at the head of the empire.

He wisely abstained from making any alterations in the political institutions of the Chinese, nor did he interfere with any of their ancient customs; the high functionaries who had submitted to his authority were suffered to retain their employments, and in the distribution of offices of State no unjust partiality was shewn towards the Tartars, and thus peace was preserved between the conquerors and the conquered.

The tribute or rent imposed on the natives of the country was a tenth part of all the silk, rice, wool, hemp, and other produce of their land, except sugar and spice, on which only a very small duty was levied; but these duties were not levied on the mechanics, who, for their tribute, were obliged to work for the Government one day in the week, which amounted to a seventh part of their labour; and on these days they were employed in keeping the public edifices in repair, and making clothes and warlike implements for the army. The Chinese pay no observance to a Sabbath.

The new Emperor fixed the seat of government at Kambalu, called also Peking, which signifies the Court of the North; but it was at that time generally termed Kambalu, and must have been the same as the ancient city of Yea-King, which was probably enlarged, and received the addition of a new palace built by the Mogul prince, as the old Imperial residence was destroyed, and the town also partly ruined, when it was stormed by the Tartars under Zinghis Khan.

The more modern and handsomest part of Peking was not built till the beginning of the fifteenth century, after the restoration of the native

princes. Kambalu, in the time of Kublai Khan, was a wealthy and populous city, containing plenty of shops, well stocked with the rich merchandize of Persia and Arabia; for, as soon as peace was restored, a considerable trade was carried on overland with those countries, from which the caravans arrived regularly every year, and the merchants were lodged in hotels or caravanserais, of which there were many in the suburbs, built expressly for the accommodation of foreign traders, each nation having its own particular hotels and storehouses.

The commerce of the empire had now increased to such an extent that it was found necessary to adopt a more convenient kind of money than the small copper coinage that was in general use; therefore Kublai Khan invented a species of paper money, similar to our bank-notes, made of the inner bark of the mulberry-tree, and stamped with his own mark, to counterfeit which was a crime punishable with death. This great prince seems to have paid more attention to the interests of commerce than any of the emperors who had preceded him, and to him the Chinese are indebted for one of the grandest of their national works, which is the Great Canal, that forms a direct communication, by water, between Canton and Peking, the two extreme points of the empire.

The want of good roads has always been a check to the internal trade of China, and this disadvantage was at once perceived by the Emperor, who projected and carried into execution a design for facilitating the intercourse between the chief cities. This was effected by turning the waters of some of the lakes into artificial channels, which were made to communicate with the rivers; many branches also extending to towns that were not in their course. 170,000 men were employed for years in the construction of this mighty work, which was completed under the immediate successors of Kublai, and which, for real utility, far surpasses the Great Wall of Chi-hoang-ti, being at this moment of the utmost benefit to the Chinese, whose inland trade would be very limited without it, as the means of land-carriage are few, and both tedious and expensive. Another great advantage of this canal was, that it answered the purpose of draining large tracts of marshy, but fertile land, which had till then been quite useless, but were thus rendered fit for cultivation.

It was in the early part of the reign of Kublai, before he had become master of the whole empire, that China was for the first time visited by European travellers, who were fortunate enough to be admitted to the court of the Great Khan, and honoured by his confidence and friendship.

Matteo and Nicolo Polo were two merchants of Venice, who, having occasion to make a journey into Persia, which formed part of the dominions of Kublai (being one of the countries conquered by his grandfather, Zinghis), heard so much there respecting the splendour of the Imperial court, that they felt a great desire to become acquainted with the distant city of Kambalu, which they found means to visit, by accompanying a Persian ambassador, who was charged with despatches for the Emperor. They were received with the greatest courtesy by Kublai, who was well pleased at meeting with such an opportunity of gaining some correct information respecting the people of Europe, and made many inquiries on the subject of the manners, religion, and form of government, of different European countries; from which it may be inferred, that he was more enlightened as to the state of the Western world, than the present monarch of the Chinese empire, who seems to be possessed with the infatuated belief that the Europeans are all in a most pitiable state of barbarism. In consequence of the conversations he held with the Venetians, Kublai, who was himself a votary of the Buddhist faith, was nevertheless so highly impressed with their representation of the excellence of the Christian religion, that he despatched by them a letter to the Pope, containing a request that his Holiness would send proper persons to instruct the Chinese in the doctrines of Christianity; and the Venetian travellers departed on this extraordinary mission.

Several years had passed away, during which the Khan had been so much engaged in prosecuting the war against Manjee, the southern kingdom of China, that he had almost forgotten the Venetians, whose first visit had taken place long before the conquest; nor was the war yet quite ended when they returned, accompanied by Marco Polo, the son of one of them, and the most celebrated of the three, since it was he who wrote, on his return to Italy, an account of the Chinese empire, or kingdom of Cathay, where he had resided no less than seventeen years, during which he had enjoyed, without interruption, the favour of the Emperor.

At this period, so little was known of China in the Western world, that the history of Marco Polo gained but little credit, and failed to enlighten the people of the age with regard to that fine country. In fact there were very few who knew any thing about the traveller, or the book he had written, for the art of printing being then unknown in Europe, knowledge was but slowly and partially diffused, and those who read the work thought it so improbable, that they treated the whole narrative as a fiction. The extent and wealth of Cathay, the splendour of its court, the number of its cities, the beauty of its manufactures, the order of its government, all faithfully described by the author, were read with a smile of incredulity, nor was it till a much later period, when the country was visited by other Europeans, that justice was done to his veracity.

But to resume the subject of our history. When the Polos set out on their return to China, they had with them two preaching friars, deputed as missionaries by Pope Gregory the Tenth, who also sent letters to the Khan; but some of the states of Syria, through which the travellers had to pass, were in a state of warfare, and the friars were, from some untoward circumstance, prevented from proceeding, while the Polos, after encountering many difficulties and dangers, safely reached their destination. This was about the time when the Crusades were drawing to a close, and the year that the three Italians arrived at the court of Kublai Khan, was the same as that in which Edward the First returned to England from the Holy Land.

The Emperor testified much delight at the return of his former visitors, and was so much pleased with young Marco, that he conferred on him a high post at the court, and employed him on missions to various parts of the empire. Marco had therefore sufficient opportunities of observing the state of the country, as well as the manners of the court.

The cities were, at this period, thronged with industrious manufacturers, who all worked at their own homes, and sold the produce of their labour to the wealthy merchants, who traded principally to India, from which country the manufactures and produce of China were conveyed to Alexandria, and from that port were transported to Venice, where they were all received under the general name of Indian goods, and thus the Chinese were for a long time considered the same people as the Indians, and their country was supposed to be the most remote part of India. It is believed by many persons that an acquaintance with the narrative of Marco Polo was a powerful inducement to Christopher Columbus to undertake his first voyage of discovery, by which he expected to arrive at the wealthy land described by the Venetian under the name of Cathay.

Among the many improvements made by Kublai Khan, during his beneficent reign, was the establishment of inns or post-houses, commencing from the capital and continued at intervals of about thirty-six miles to all the principal places in the empire, and at these stations relays of horses were always kept in readiness for the Emperor's messengers, who were there also furnished with the requisite food, and lodging. There were also ferry-boats at convenient stations to carry them across the rivers and lakes without delay, so that in case of need, a messenger could travel two hundred miles in the twenty-four hours; and by these means, fine fruits and other luxuries, for the court and rich citizens, were often conveyed from the most distant provinces to Pekin; an advantage which that city would not so readily have enjoyed otherwise, since it stands in a cold and barren plain, and depends for its supplies on the more fertile districts of the south.

These supplies are still obtained by the generality of the inhabitants by means of the Great Canal, which is constantly covered with barges, laden chiefly with grain. A great number of these barges were employed between the different provinces and the capital, in conveying the tribute, out of which, when the harvest was abundant, the Emperor laid up in his granaries stores of rice and corn, which in years of scarcity he sold to the poor, at a cheap rate; although, therefore, the taxes were heavy, the people derived benefit from them when they stood most in need of assistance, and they were always remitted, or at least much lightened, in a season of public calamity. Every thing, indeed, appears to have been done by this beneficent prince that could tend to increase the prosperity and happiness of his subjects, who seem to have enjoyed, under his paternal government, the blessings of peace in their fullest extent.

In all the cities, good order was preserved by the establishment of a strict police, and no one was allowed to be abroad after dark, except on urgent business, when he was required to carry a lantern—a regulation that prevented robberies or disturbances in the streets at night. In the centre of the capital there was an enormous bell, suspended in a lofty building, so placed, that it could be heard all over the city; and this was tolled every evening at a certain hour, as a signal for all persons to retire to their homes; as the curfew, in olden times, was rung at eve, to warn the people of England that it was time to extinguish the cheerful blaze, and betake themselves to repose.

As soon as Kublai had completed the conquest of China, he sent an ambassador to the sovereign of the Japan Islands, who was an independent prince, ruling over a numerous and not uncivilised people. The object of this embassy was to demand submission and tribute of the Japanese monarch as a vassal of the Chinese empire; and when the indignant chief refused to comply with so unjust a requisition, the Emperor declared war against him, and sent out a large fleet, in the hope of making another important conquest.

It would be difficult to conjecture upon what ground the Emperor of China founded his claim to the supremacy of Japan, which had for ages been a distinct sovereignty; nor does it appear, as far as their early history is known, that the Japanese had ever been dependent on the Chinese empire. A tradition certainly existed, that at some remote period these islands had been conquered by a Chinese warrior, who became the founder of the Japanese monarchy, and whose descendants still occupied the throne. Powerful princes are not always very particular about making a good title to the territories they covet, wherefore the Emperor might have thought it a sufficient reason for his assumption of superiority, that the first Prince of Japan was a subject of China. The Japanese, however, made a successful resistance; and by the help of a storm, which destroyed the greater part of the Tartar fleet, they were fortunate enough to preserve that independence which they have maintained to this very day.

The Tartar conquest produced no alteration in the manners and customs of the native Chinese, which indeed, as before observed, appear not to have been affected by any of the revolutions that have taken place in the country; all the national festivals being observed as in former times, and the same laws remaining in force that have so direct and powerful an influence on the character and social habits of the people of China.

The garments worn by the mass of the population were at this time still made of silk, for although cotton was then cultivated for the purpose of being manufactured, it was not so plentiful as silk, consequently it was much more expensive, and only used by persons of high rank; but the case is now entirely reversed, since at the present day the rich alone wear silks, while the poor are universally clothed in cotton.

One of the great festivals observed in China in the reign of Kublai Khan was the birth-day of that great prince, which was a universal holiday, and celebrated throughout the empire with all kinds of public rejoicings. Sacrifices were made in the temples, the cities were illuminated, and people of all classes spent the day in feasting and amusements. Among the latter were dramatic pieces performed by companies of strolling players, either in temporary theatres set up in the streets for the delight of the com-

Painted in Bokhara. Drawn on Stone by Dean & Co.

THE ANNUAL FESTIVAL CELEBRATING THE EMPEROR'S BIRTH DAY, REVIVED BY KUBLAI-KHAN.

London Dean & Co. Threadneedle Street

monalty, or in the houses of the great mandarins, who usually hired actors on grand occasions, as they do still, for the entertainment of their guests.

The Emperor appeared on this festive day arrayed in a robe of cloth of gold, his whole dress glittering with jewels, and was attended by all the chief officers of his court, in their magnificent state dresses, who stood around the throne, while he received the homage of the tributary princes, who came to offer their congratulations. The banquet given at the palace on this occasion was extremely sumptuous, and graced with the presence of the Empress and ladies of the court, for the Tartar ladies were less secluded in their habits than the Chinese; and when they first arrived in the country, were frequently seen on public occasions; but they have since adopted, in a great measure, the more reserved manners of the ladies of China.

The banquet took place in a large hall, where the guests were seated according to their rank. The Emperor's table stood on a daïs at the upper end, and the ladies were ranged according to their rank, at tables by themselves. The meats were served on silver, and the drinking cups were of gold. A band of music was in attendance the whole time; and at the lower end of the hall a temporary stage was erected, for the performances of the players, and the feats of jugglers and tumblers. But it must be observed that the mirth of the guests was never indulged to an extent that might have been deemed disrespectful to the Emperor. There was no noisy laughter; and whenever the Imperial host raised the cup to his lips, a signal was given, and all present knelt down and bowed their heads until he had finished his draught. Such is the homage paid to Majesty in the East.

On the occasion of the birth-day, presents of great value were sent to the Emperor from all the provinces; but as they were too numerous, and some of them too bulky to be laid at his feet, they were merely passed in review before him, borne by a train of camels. This was a very general custom in the East, and the presents made to Eastern princes by their subjects must have very materially contributed towards keeping up the extraordinary splendour for which their courts were so remarkable.

Since the Tartars had occupied the throne, hunting had been the grand amusement of the court, the sports of the chase being regarded by that people as emblematical of warfare, and the fearless hunter being respected as a brave warrior. The annual hunting expedition into Tartary was conducted with all the solemnity of a campaign, the Emperor taking the head of a numerous train, which had all the appearance of a vast army marching to the field of battle. The three winter months were entirely occupied with this pursuit, which, during the season, was deemed the chief business of the state; so that the holding of these hunts is among the principal duties of a Tartar sovereign, and he who neglects them occasions discontent and rebellion.

Falconry was a less important pastime, but not a less favourite one of the Emperor, who kept a great number of falconers in his train, and very frequently went out with them in pursuit of cranes and pheasants, on which occasions he was always carried in a richly-ornamented pavilion on the back of an elephant.

When the sporting season was over, it was customary for the whole court to repair to a city of Tartary, where the Emperor had a palace, with an extensive park and pleasure grounds; and to this summer residence he was accompanied by the Empress, and all his other wives, for he had many, although only one of them enjoyed the dignity and title of Empress. This favoured lady was surrounded with as much state as her lordly husband, having no less than three hundred female slaves to attend upon and amuse her, for which purpose many of them had been taught music and dancing, according to the custom of the East; and

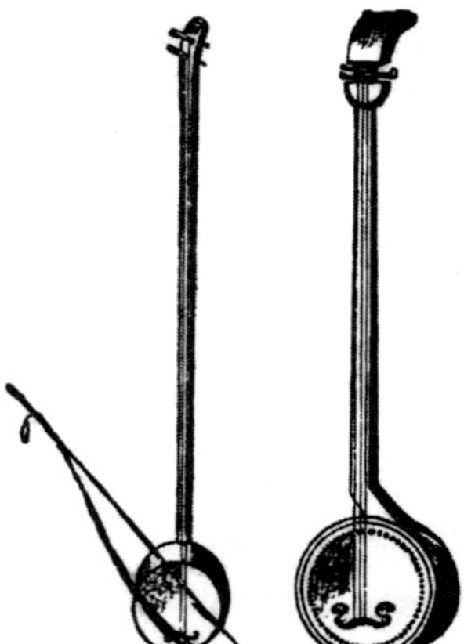

Violin. *Guitar.*

besides these damsels, there were elderly females, whose occupation it was to relate entertaining stories to the Empress and ladies of the court, amongst whom reading was then an art unknown.

Kublai Khan lived to the advanced age of eighty-three, and had ruled over the whole of China about eighteen years, when he died, in 1294, and was succeeded by his grandson, Timur.

The empire of the Moguls had now attained its utmost magnitude. It extended from the Chinese sea and the Indies, to the northern extremity of Siberia, and from the eastern shores of Asia to the frontiers of Poland in Europe; and all this vast portion of the globe was governed by princes of the family of Zinghis, who were all vassals of the Great Khan, or Emperor of China. The chief of these were the Khans of Persia, Zagatai, and Kipzac, who were tributary to Kublai, but after his death they became independent sovereigns.

The Chinese empire continued under the dominion of the Moguls about seventy-three years from the death of Kublai, and in that time eight princes of his family reigned in succession; not one of whom equalled their great predecessor in ability, although most of them were mild and beneficent rulers. Kublai had, with the wisdom of a superior mind, accommodated himself to the habits and prejudices of the conquered nation; but his successors, less politic, made innovations on the ancient form of government, and lost, by degrees, the confidence and affection of the Chinese, who are extremely jealous of the slightest interference with their established customs, and whose dissatisfaction at length began to exhibit itself by frequent insurrections.

During the whole of the Yuen dynasty, Buddhism was the religion of the state; and so many of the Bonzes, or priests of that sect, came into China, that the people found them very burthensome, as they were a mendicant race, who went from house to house asking alms. Many Buddhist temples were built in the reign of Kublai Khan, who was himself a professor of Buddhism; a faith which never possessed so much influence in China as during the sway of the Mogul emperors.

Shunty, the ninth and last sovereign of this race, ascended the throne in 1331; and reigned thirty-five years, or rather suffered his ministers to reign, for he himself was too indolent and fond of pleasure to take much share in state affairs. When the Tartars first arrived from their own wild deserts, they were a bold energetic race of barbarians; but the ease and luxury in which they were enabled to indulge, in the genial climate of China, had softened their manners, and had thus destroyed the warlike character by which their ancestors had gained possession of the country, and by which alone they could hope to retain it.

The revolution that placed the empire once more under the dominion of native princes, took place under the following circumstances. There was a poor labourer in the province of Nanking, who had a son named Choo, a lad whose constitution was so delicate that he was quite unfit for hard work, his father therefore placed him in one of the monasteries, to be brought up by the Bonzes, with a view to his becoming a member of that order. The boy, however, had no taste for so inactive a life, and growing stronger as his years increased, he enlisted as a common soldier in the Imperial army, in which capacity he distinguished himself so highly on two or three different occasions, that he was promoted, step by step, till he had attained to a high rank; when he married a widow of fortune and influence, whose family was among those who were disaffected towards the Tartar government. Choo soon imbibed similar principles, and took the lead in a formidable insurrection that broke out in the province of Nanking, or as it was then called, Keang-nan. The many changes of name that have occurred in the provinces and cities of China, have caused great confusion in the geographical history of the country, and made it very difficult, in some cases, to identify even places of importance. However, as soon as it was known that the famous General Choo was at the head of the insurgents, the whole province was speedily in arms, the capital having already declared for the rebel chief, who met and defeated the Imperial forces. The numbers of the rebel army increased daily; the most considerable cities opened their gates to them, and at length Peking itself was taken, and Shunty, with his family, fled into Tartary, leaving his capital in the undisputed possession of the victor, who was proclaimed Emperor by the title of Tait-sou, in the year 1366; and this was the commencement of the Ming dynasty, which was displaced about three hundred years afterwards by the present reigning family.

Shield.

THE MING DYNASTY.

AS soon as Tait-sou was firmly seated on the throne, ambassadors were sent by the kings of Corea and other tributary princes, to congratulate him on his elevation, and express their satisfaction that the country was once more under the dominion of a native ruler. The success of Tait-sou and his excellent government are attributed in great measure to the prudent counsels of his wife, by which he wisely suffered himself to be guided, and was thus, perhaps, restrained from falling into those excesses which often stain the victories of a conqueror. It does not appear that the Tartar ladies ever possessed that influence in the state which was constantly exercised by the ladies of China, which is a clear proof that the Chinese had a higher opinion of female intellect than the more barbarous nations, although much has been said to the contrary. The new Emperor chose Nanking for his capital, and erected Peking into a principality, which he bestowed on one of his sons, Yong-lo, who when he became Emperor, again removed the court from Nanking to Peking, the latter city being better situated for keeping the Tartars in check, who were constantly at war with the Chinese after the fall of the Mogul dynasty. Tait-sou began his reign by restoring those institutions which had been disregarded since the time of Kublai Khan, whose successors had broken in upon one of the most important usages of the Chinese government, by placing military men in all the chief offices of state, which, under Kublai, had been filled, as usual, by the learned. This was one of the innovations that had led to the revolution, and was among the first grievances redressed by the new Emperor, who restored the literary Mandarins to their former rank and influence, and granted great privileges to the Han-lin College. He made several new regulations intended to promote the happiness of the people, and among others, that women should not devote themselves as priestesses to the religion of Buddha, and that no man should enter a monastery till he was forty years of age; for Tait-sou knew by experience that young people sometimes were induced to adopt a life of seclusion before they were old enough to judge whether it was exactly suited to their dispositions, and were thereby doomed to many years of misery and regret.

Tait-sou reigned thirty-one years, and having lost his favourite son, appointed his grandson, a boy of thirteen, to succeed him, which gave great offence to one of his sons, Yong-lo, who raised an army at Peking, and placing himself at its head, marched towards Nanking to demand from his nephew the surrender of the throne. He was opposed by the Imperial troops, and a battle ensued, in which many were killed on both sides; but the cause was still undecided, when the gates of the city were opened by some traitor, who had probably received a bribe for so doing. The assailants instantly rushed into the town, put many of the inhabitants to the sword, and set the palace on fire. The youthful Emperor perished in the flames, and Yong-lo took possession of the vacant throne. Some of the ministers were condemned to death, others killed themselves, while many of the Mandarins, who expected to be punished for their adherence to the cause of the late unfortunate prince, shaved their heads and assumed the sackcloth habit of the Bonzes, and thus disguised were not recognized, for it was not the custom at that time for the Chinese to shave off their hair.

Although the new Emperor had obtained the throne by cruelty and violence, he was not a bad sovereign, but on the contrary exhibited great moderation and justice in many acts of his government. It was he who removed the court to Peking, which has been the Imperial residence ever since; but he established separate tribunals at Nanking, which city was occupied and governed by his eldest son.

It was in this reign that the great Mogul chief, Timour, or Tamerlane, as he is more generally called, whose conquests almost equalled those of Zinghis Khan, being ambitious of adding China to the vast dominions he had already acquired by a long and successful course of warfare, set out with the intention of invading that empire; but happily for the Chinese he died on the way, and the expedition was abandoned. From time to time, however, the Tartars renewed their invasions in the hope of recovering the empire, and were a terrible scourge to those provinces which bordered on Tartary. When there happened to be a powerful prince at the head of the state they were kept in check, but whenever the government was weak they did not fail to turn that advantage to account; so that the Chinese were never entirely at peace during the whole period of the Ming dynasty, which lasted three centuries.

It was in the reign of the twelfth Emperor of this race, that the rapid progress of navigation, which followed the discovery of America, first brought the ships of Europe to the shores of China. The Portuguese, who were the great navigators of the age, having made several voyages to India by the newly-discovered passage round the Cape of Good Hope, ventured still farther eastward in the year 1516, and were the first Europeans who reached the port of Canton. Some alarm was experienced at Canton on the appearance of strange vessels, of a form altogether new to the Chinese, who very naturally supposed an invasion was intended; consequently the fleet, which consisted of eight vessels, was immediately surrounded by Chinese war junks, and it was with great difficulty that the commander, Perez de Andrada, obtained permission to proceed up the river to Canton with two of his ships. The Viceroy of the city granted an audience to the Captain, who explained, by means of an interpreter brought from Malacca, that they were merchants, who had no hostile intentions, but desired to trade with the people of the country; to which he received a favourable answer; and an express was sent to the Emperor, to inform him of the arrival of the strangers, and their object. The Emperor graciously signified his pleasure that they should have leave to establish a factory on the coast, and send trading vessels to Canton once a year; and thus a regular treaty of commerce was concluded between Portugal and China.

The Portuguese were the first who called the great men of the Chinese empire Mandarins. The first place where they established a settlement was at Ningpo, from which port they long carried on a profitable trade with other parts of China and the Japan Islands; but unfortunately, many of the Portuguese who went thither were daring adventurers, who were ready to undertake any desperate exploit for the sake of gain, and conducted themselves so improperly, that they were at length expelled from Ningpo by the provincial government. They had, however, been allowed to build some warehouses at Macao, a port on a small island at the entrance of the

Canton river, for which privilege they paid an annual tribute, and Macao, in the course of time, became their chief settlement. They erected there, by degrees, a number of good houses, and the merchants who went to reside there, took with them their wives and families, which was contrary to the laws of the empire, but connived at by the Mandarins, who probably derived some advantage from granting this indulgence. Macao was honoured by being the place of banishment of the well known poet, Camoens, whose beautiful poem of the Lusiad was here written in a grotto which still bears his name, and which is represented beneath.

The new Portuguese town of Macao, being situated at the extremity of a small peninsula, joined by a narrow isthmus to the island of Meang-shan, the Chinese government caused a wall to be built across the slip of land as a barrier; for although the Chinese were not insensible to the advantages of foreign commerce, they adhered to their system of exclusion, and while they strictly prohibited the strangers from entering their cities, or even passing the bounds of their own settlement, they jealously watched all their proceedings. A Mandarin was appointed at Macao, who governed the town in the name of the Emperor, and whose duty it was to give information to his superiors of the conduct of the inhabitants.

Not long after the Portuguese had opened a trade with China, the Spaniards began to send out ships to the Indian Ocean, and in the reign of Philip the Second, established a colony at Manilla, in the Philippine Islands, where they entered into commercial dealings with a company of Chinese merchants, who carried silks and porcelain thither for sale. There had been some warfare between the Spaniards and the natives of the Philippines, before the former had gained their object of settling a colony upon one of those islands; but at length, having subdued the Prince of Luzon, and forced him to acknowledge the King of Spain as his sovereign, they established themselves at Manilla, where they built many good houses, and three monasteries, which were speedily filled with Spanish monks, who took great pains in endeavouring to convert the natives. But their grand object was to introduce the Christian religion into China, and with that view, they earnestly solicited the Chinese merchants to admit them into the country. This request was long refused, as it would have been a violation of the laws that would have subjected any persons concerned to very severe penalties; but at length a circumstance occurred, that afforded the desired opportunity.

The coasts of China and the neighbouring shores had from time to time been infested with pirates, who were the terror of all the maritime towns and villages, and who sheltered themselves in some of the small islands that abounded in the adjacent seas. One of these lawless chiefs, whose name was Limahon, having committed frightful ravages in different parts of the empire, made an attack on the town of Manilla, and treated such of the inhabitants as were unfortunate enough to fall into his hands with the utmost barbarity. A Chinese fleet, under the command of Admiral Omon-con, was sent out in search of the formidable corsair; but the latter had already been defeated and driven from the Chinese seas by the Spaniards, in return for which good service the Admiral consented to introduce some of their priests into China; and two Augustine friars were permitted to embark on board one of his vessels, accompanied by two of the Spanish officers who had assisted in the defeat of Limahon. The strangers were received with much courtesy by the governors of several cities which they were allowed to visit, and were magnificently entertained at the houses of some of the chief Mandarins: but whenever they applied for leave to preach to the people, the request was studiously evaded.

The appearance of foreigners in a Chinese city was so rare a sight, that the house in which they lodged was constantly surrounded by the populace, who mounted the walls and the house tops to obtain a glimpse of the men from an unknown land. When they went out, sedan chairs were provided for their accommodation; but they could scarcely make their way along the streets, in consequence of the crowds that were assembled to see them. They found the country through which they travelled extremely fertile and well cultivated, and the people, who were then generally employed in harrowing and seed sowing, appeared to be in comfortable circumstances; but the strangers were so closely watched, that they had little opportunity of gaining much information respecting the real condition of the natives, or of visiting the interior of their abodes.

Chinese Harrow, and Mode of Harrowing.

At this period, which was late in the sixteenth century, no mention is made of silk garments among the poor, whose clothing was mostly of the strong cotton stuff, called by us Nanking, or nankeen, which was manufactured in large quantities, and usually dyed blue. The cultivation of cotton had been improving from the commencement of the Ming dynasty, and had become a material of importance both in the agriculture and manufactures of the country.

At length the Spaniards were informed that their visit had been sufficiently prolonged, and without having received a direct reply with regard to the object of their mission, they were politely escorted to Canton, where a bark was in readiness to convey them back to Manilla, and thus ended their hopes of propagating Christianity among the Chinese. Other attempts were made, with as little success, until the Jesuits undertook missions to China, and as they were in general more enlightened men than monks of other orders, and in the habit of mixing more with the world, they succeeded better than those who had gone before them. They commenced the great work they had in view, in a very cautious manner, giving out that they were holy men from the West, who, having heard of the wonders of the Celestial empire, had come to finish their days in that celebrated land; and one of them gained the reputation of being a great astrologer, by constructing a sun-dial, and an armillary sphere, which excited much admiration.

Having conciliated the good will of the natives, they were permitted to remain, and when they had gained sufficient influence to make the attempt, they obtained leave to build a Christian church, and succeeded in making many converts. It was just at this time that the great invasion of the Mant-chow Tartars threw the whole empire into confusion, and in bringing war into all the provinces, put a stop to the labours of the Jesuit Missionaries.

In the mean time the Dutch had begun to send out ships to the Indian seas, and being at war with the Spaniards and Portuguese, had dispossessed them of some of their best settlements, particularly some colonies which they had established in the Island of Formosa; and they also obtained a settlement in the Island of Java, where they built the town of Batavia, which still belongs to the King of Holland, together with the greater part of the island. The British merchants, likewise, in the latter part of the reign of Queen Elizabeth, and towards the close of the Ming dynasty, began to make commercial voyages to the East, and established factories at Bantam, in Java, whence they opened a trade with the Chinese, who sent every year four junks to Bantam, laden with raw silk, porcelain, sugar-candy, and japanned ware; but no mention is made of tea, till after the Tartar conquest, which happened in the time of the English Commonwealth.

The Mantchow Tartars were descended from the Kin, who were conquered and driven out of China by the Moguls, but had re-established themselves in Tartary, and had again become a powerful nation. It is a striking instance of the caprice of fortune, that when the Moguls were expelled by the founder of the Ming race, they sought refuge among the Kin, and marriages were made between the Royal families of the two races, whose posterity, the Mantchow sovereigns, who have now reigned in China about two hundred years, may thus claim a descent both from the Kin and the Mogul princes.

At the time when the Portuguese first arrived in China, the Mantchows were, and had long been, on friendly terms with the Chinese, to whose markets they brought for sale, horses, furs, and ginseng, a medicinal root much used in China. As long as they were but an inconsiderable tribe this kind of intercourse was continued; but as they grew more numerous and powerful, they also became more haughty, and disputes arose between them and the Chinese, which led first to petty hostilities, and by degrees to serious warfare. Sometimes a peace was made, the conditions of which were sure to be violated ere long by one or other of the parties, and then the war was renewed with increased violence.

Such was the state of affairs when Wanlie, the thirteenth Emperor of the Ming dynasty, ascended the throne of his ancestors, in the year 1571. Wanlie is highly spoken of in Chinese history as being just, wise, and benevolent, and altogether as a prince of an excellent disposition. It was he who caused to be published every three months, for the convenience of the public, a book containing the name, rank, and native city of every Mandarin in the empire—a custom that has been continued ever since. It is called the Red-book, we suppose from the colour: red having some important bearing in connexion with that distinguished class; for instance, there are before the portals of every mandarin's mansion, two high poles, which are uniformly painted red, to denote the office of the occupier.

There are nine degrees of rank among the Mandarins, and alterations are continually being made among their body, either by the degradation of some to a lower or the elevation of others to a higher grade, as well as by the appointment of new magistrates, and the admission of fresh candidates after every examination. The nobility is therefore, in fact, a constantly fluctuating body, and the Red-book is a sort of Court Calendar, corrected every three months, according to the changes that have occurred.

The long reign of Wanlie was disturbed from its commencement by the irruptions of the Mantchows, whose power was fast increasing, while that of the Ming princes was as rapidly declining; and at length the Mantchow prince, Tien-ming, provoked by the oppressive conduct of some Chinese mandarins on the frontiers, formally declared war against the Empire, and published a manifesto, stating his reasons for so doing.

The injuries which he complained of were seven in number; the following being the heads of what are called the seven grievances:—The Chinese had commenced hostilities without just cause; they had passed a certain boundary line agreed upon between the two nations as the limit of their respective territories; and this they had done to assist an enemy of the Mantchows, in violation of a solemn treaty, by which neither party was to cross the frontier; they had put to death a Tartar envoy sent to complain of the above grievances; they had carried off a Tartar princess, and married her to a Chinese prince; they had expelled the Tartars who dwelt on the frontier; they had spoken insultingly of Tien-ming himself; and, lastly, they had excited several nations which he had conquered and made tributary, to rebel against him. "It is to revenge these seven injuries," continued the manifesto of the Tartar prince, "that I have now resolved to subjugate Ming and his whole empire;" and having thus justified his contemplated invasion, he lost no time in proceeding to action. He entered the province of Pechelee at the head of fifty thousand men, where he assumed the title of Emperor, and gained some victories; but the Chinese raised such a numerous force that he was obliged to retire.

Just at this juncture Wanlie died, and was succeeded by his grandson, Hit-song, who reigned only seven years, during which the war was continued with varied success, and was still undecided when the last of the Chinese sovereigns, Whey-t-song, ascended the throne, in the year 1627.

The late Emperor, Hi-t-song, and the Tartar King, Tien-ming, died within a few months of each other, the latter being succeeded by his son Tien-song, who prosecuted the war against Whey-t-song with a view to the conquest of the Empire. The whole country was now in a most dreadful state of anarchy, for the regular troops being all engaged in the contest with the Tartars, there were none to stop the progress of rebellion, which began to shew itself in all the provinces. Several daring chiefs raised revolts, and collected large armed bands, with which they ravaged the country and plundered the cities with impunity; nor had the magistrates any power to prevent such outrages by enforcing the laws, which they could only do by military aid.

The boldest of the insurgent leaders, whose name was Li Kong, even aspired to the Imperial dignity, and having raised an immense army, he made himself master of the provinces of Honan and Shen-see, where he secured his authority by putting to death the principal mandarins of the cities, and freeing the people from all taxes and contributions. The support of the commonalty being thus gained, he marched towards Peking, the capital, sending several of his party before him disguised as merchants, who went into the city, where they hired shops, and carried on trade till an opportunity offered for executing their project, which was to gain over some of the soldiers of the guard, and by their assistance to open the gates to the rebel army. All happened according to their wishes; and the night on which the treacherous soldiers were to keep guard, was fixed for the entrance of Li Kong and his troops, who on the gates being opened rushed into the town, and commenced a furious attack on the palace. The mandarins fled in dismay; the guards of the palace went over to the enemy; when the unfortunate Emperor, seeing no other means of escaping from the foe, stabbed his daughter with his own hand, and then put an end to his own existence. The young lady was carried off by a faithful slave, and having survived the effects of the blow, was afterwards married to a Chinese grandee; but the Empress, and many ladies of the court, dreading nothing so much as falling into the hands of the rebels, killed themselves in despair.

In the mean time the triumphant chief caused himself to be proclaimed emperor, and taking possession of the palace, proceeded to exercise the sovereign authority, to which the people of Peking and the northern provinces universally submitted; but one of the Chinese Generals, Woosankwei, who still had an army under his command, held out with determined bravery, and fortified himself in a city on the confines of Tartary, which was speedily besieged by the usurper, whose cruelties had already made him hateful to all except his own soldiers. Enraged at the opposition of Woosankwei, the tyrant caused the aged father of that general to be brought, loaded with chains, under the walls of the city, and sent word to the General, that if he did not surrender, the old man would be instantly put to death; on which the unhappy son appeared on the wall, and on his knees, whilst the tears streamed down his face, received the commands of his venerable parent never to acknowledge the base usurper as his sovereign. Scarcely had the father uttered the words, when his head was severed from his body: a sad sight for the eyes of a son, whose filial affection was of that deep character so frequently met with among the Chinese.

Woosankwei had now a double cause for vengeance—the death of his prince, and the murder of his father. He therefore made peace with the Mantchow Tartars, and aided by them soon expelled the usurper from the capital, where the Tartar prince was hailed as a deliverer, and proclaimed Emperor in 1644. Scarcely, however, had he been invested with this high dignity, than he was seized with a fatal disorder, of which he died in a few days, having named as his successor his son Shun-che, a child only six years of age, whose uncle was appointed to govern as Regent during his minority.

Such was the revolution that placed the present Imperial family on the throne of China; but some years elapsed before the whole country was brought under submission to a foreign ruler; for although the provinces of the north, which had been disgusted by the tyranny of the usurping chief, had not hesitated to bestow the title of Emperor on a Tartar, some of the southern cities supported the claims of the native princes, and a long civil war ensued, during which the loyalists kept possession of the south, and two or three princes of the Ming family were successively proclaimed Emperors at Nanking, and held their courts in that city.

The Chinese general, Woosankwei, was raised to a very high rank, and a principality was bestowed on him, with the government of one of the principal cities of Shensee. The fate of the usurper Li Kong was never known: but it was generally supposed he was killed in some engagement with the Tartars.

THE MANTCHOW DYNASTY.

SHUN-CHE, FIRST EMPEROR, FROM 1644 to 1662.

AMA VAN, Regent of the empire and uncle of the youthful Emperor, engaged excellent tutors for his royal nephew, who not only instructed him in the literature of the country, but instilled into his mind such principles as were likely to fit him for the government of the conquered nation. Under the care of these able monitors, he learned to be just and moderate towards the people over whom the fortune of war had placed him; and being naturally well inclined, he attained to manhood with just such principles as were best calculated to reconcile the Chinese to foreign dominion.

While Shun-che was pursuing his studies, the Regent and his generals were engaged in reducing the southern part of the country to subjection; and all the finest provinces were devastated by the long and fearful contest. Many of the great cities were laid in ruins; for wherever the Tartars met with resistance they set fire to the houses, and demolished all the public buildings, except the Budhist Temples, which, being regarded by them as sacred edifices, they thought it would be sinful to destroy.

The traces of this war are still visible in China, where many an empty space is bounded by a dilapidated wall, that once surrounded a populous town, but now encloses only a few market gardens; and some of the chief cities are not much more than half their original size, as may be seen by the extent of their walls, which at present encompass large spaces of ground where no houses are remaining, and which are usually devoted to the culture of vegetables for food. A great part of Nanking, with the Imperial Palace, was destroyed at this time; and there are now within its walls, orchards, fields, garden grounds, and scattered farm-houses; not above one-third of the area being occupied by the present city.

One of the most formidable opponents of the Tartars was a maritime chief, or pirate, known by the name of Koshinga, a noted character in the history of these times, not only for his loyalty to the Chinese royal race, but also for his exploits against the Dutch, who had by this time considerably increased their Indian trade, and had formed a settlement in the Island of Formosa.

Ching-che-loong, the father of Koshinga, one of the richest merchants in China, had, in the early part of the war, fitted out a fleet at his own expense to support the native princes; but after the accession of Shun-che, he accepted the offer of a high post at court, leaving the command of his fleet to his son Koshinga, who, instead of following the example of his father, remained faithful to the cause of the legitimate princes. This chief was the terror of the Indian seas, where no foreign vessels dared to appear during the wars, so that all trade was for a long time suspended. At length the Tartars, having taken Nanking, laid siege to Canton, which, by the aid of Koshinga's fleet, was enabled to hold out for eight months; but was at the end of that time obliged to surrender, and the last prince of the Ming family fled to the court of the king of Pegu, where he was received with the greatest hospitality.

Every place of importance having now submitted to the conquerors, the new government was acknowledged throughout the empire; and shortly afterwards, on the death of the Regent, Shun-che, although only fourteen years of age, took the government into his own hands, A. D. 1652. The young sovereign, who no doubt acted by the advice of prudent and experienced ministers, suffered the Chinese to retain all the rights and immunities they had enjoyed under their native rulers; but as he found it necessary to satisfy his Tartar subjects also, by admitting them to a share of the honours and emoluments of the empire, he doubled the number of officers of state and members of councils, making one half Chinese and the other half Tartars, a regulation which continues to this day.

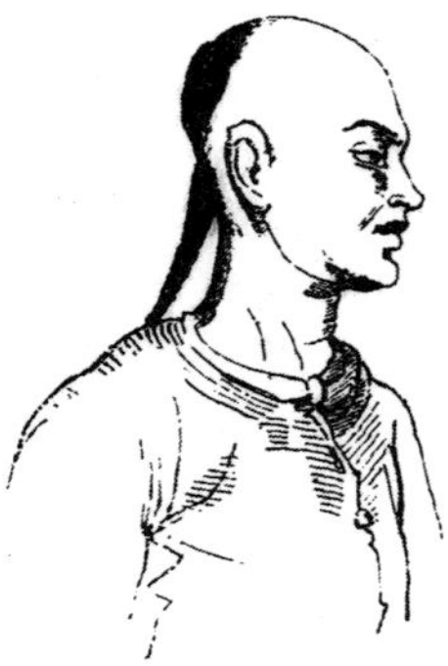

The Chinese, however, were required to submit to one mark of subjection that was far more obnoxious and spread more general discontent among them than any changes that could have been introduced into the form of government. This was, that they should divest themselves of the thick raven locks, which they had been accustomed to cherish with peculiar care, and adopt in their stead the frightful Tartar fashion of wearing a long plaited tail hanging from the crown of a bald head. The hair is an ornament highly prized by most people; and as nature had been especially bountiful to the Chinese in that particular, they were extremely reluctant to part with it; and it is asserted that many chose to submit their heads to the executioner, rather than to the barber, for that was the cruel alternative, as it was found impossible to enforce the decree by any gentler means than treating disobedience as rebellion, and punishing the offender accordingly. The tails were thus fully established, and have been worn ever since, to the great satisfaction, no doubt, of the barbers of China, whose services are in constant requisition among all classes of people, since the poorest mechanic must have his head shaved and his tail plaited as well as the most wealthy mandarin.

There were some few alterations made also in the national costume, but they were not very striking, nor would it be very easy for an English pen to describe them. With regard to the laws, the religion, and the system of government, the conquest produced no change, for the Tartar sovereigns governed like their Chinese predecessors, according to the rules laid down in the ancient books; so that, although the Emperor of China is absolute lord of the lands and the people, he is in some degree restrained by the laws as well as his subjects. He has four chief ministers, two Tartars and two Chinese, who together with certain high officers of state form the Imperial council; but the ordinary business of the government is conducted by a tribunal called the Li-pou, consisting of six boards, each of which has its particular department.

The Li-pou Courts are as ancient as the monarchy itself, having been instituted, according to the Chinese annals, by the famous Emperor Yaou;

a proof at least that they were among the earliest institutions of this singular empire. The business of the first court, or Board of Official Appointments, is to take care that all offices under the government are properly filled, and that those to whom authority is entrusted shall use it with moderation, and discharge their several duties with punctuality. The members of this tribunal are responsible for the conduct of all the viceroys, magistrates, and civil officers of every description, and are obliged at stated periods to send in an account of their proceedings to the Emperor; so that if any of them are guilty of misconduct, it is almost sure to be made known, and they are punished according to their misdemeanours. Each governor of a province or city is obliged to send a report to the Li-pou once in three years as to the conduct of all magistrates under his jurisdiction, and also of any injuries done by himself to his poorer brethren when seated on the magisterial bench to dispense justice; and this statement is compared with that of others, who have perhaps been secretly keeping a watchful eye upon him; so that it is a dangerous experiment for a magistrate to attempt to conceal his own delinquencies, since they are almost certain to come to the knowledge of the Board, and he is then punished, not only for the offence, but also for the concealment. These regulations are intended to protect the people from oppression, and must certainly act as a check to an undue exertion of power on the part of the authorities, although they may frequently be evaded.

The second court, or Board of Finance, has the charge of the government revenues, and its members have to see that all taxes and duties are regularly paid into the Imperial treasury and storehouses; some being collected in money, and others in kind. They make out orders for salaries and pensions, distribute the proper quantities of rice, silks and money, that are allowed to princes and officers of state, and keep exact accounts of all that is received and expended by the government. The third Li-pou court is the Board of Rites, to which belongs the direction of all the customs and ceremonials observed among the Chinese; not only in public, but also in private life. This Board appoints the days for holding festivals and royal hunts; and for the performance of sacrifices, and all other religious rites. It regulates the costume to be worn by the different orders of the people; the etiquette of the Court, as well as of private society; the reception of ambassadors; the entertainments given by the Emperor; and, in short, it has the superintendence of all those outward forms and usages which in China are considered of so much importance. The fourth is the Military Board; and the fifth the Board of Punishments, which superintends the execution of the penal laws. The sixth court is the Board of Public Works, which is charged with the care of the roads, canals, bridges, temples, palaces, and all public buildings, its chief duty being to see that they are kept in repair throughout the empire.

During the Ming dynasty these tribunals were held both at Nanking and Peking; but Shun-che suppressed the courts at Nanking, and united the members with those at Peking, where all the business has since been transacted, each of the six councils having its own separate hall.

As soon as the Tartar prince was firmly seated on the throne, the Russian Emperor Alexius, the father of Peter the Great, sent an embassy to China, with a view to establish a commercial treaty between the two empires; but the attempt failed from a rather curious circumstance, and one that has since been a cause of dispute with the British government. It was a custom of the Tartar sovereigns to exact from all those over whom they claimed supremacy an act of submission, called the Ko-tou, which consists in making nine prostrations, touching the ground each time with the forehead. This ceremony is equivalent to an acknowledgment of vassalage, therefore the Russian ambassador very properly refused to perform it, as it would not have become him thus to compromise the dignity of his master, who was an independent, as well as a powerful prince. The refusal of the envoy gave great offence to Shun-che, who, in consequence, declined receiving the embassy. But this was not the only point of disagreement between the two monarchs; for the Russians had taken possession of some territories in Siberia, which were considered as a part of Mantchow Tartary; and as they would not give them up, but on the contrary erected a fort there for the purpose of defending them, the Tartars commenced a war for their recovery, which was continued for a long time, the Russians still approaching nearer and nearer to China by new conquests, until at length the dominions of the Emperor of Russia actually joined the territories of China.

Not long after the failure of the Russian embassy, the Dutch, who were very anxious to open a trade with Canton, and establish a factory there, sent ambassadors to the Emperor with a petition to that effect. They were very courteously received by the Viceroy of Canton, who accepted the presents they carried to him, according to the custom of the East, where a request to a great man is invariably accompanied by a present; nor would any foreign ambassador be admitted to the presence of the Chinese sovereign unless prepared with some costly gift to lay at his feet.

The Viceroy of Canton was a handsome young Tartar of prepossessing manners, who invited the Dutch envoys to dine with him, and entertained them in a very sumptuous style. They were received in the great hall of the palace by his mother, who had just arrived from Tartary, and, according to the habits of the Tartar ladies, made no scruple of appearing before strangers of the opposite sex. The dinner was served in the Chinese fashion, on a number of small tables, not covered with cloths, but ornamented with painting and gilding, at each of which two guests were seated. The meats were served in silver dishes, and the wine in golden cups; and during the banquet a party of actors, splendidly habited in the ancient costume of the country, performed a play at one end of the hall for the amusement of the company.

The Dutchmen were not a little surprised at the magnificence displayed by the Tartar governor, and departed highly gratified with the reception they had met with, and from which they augured favourably for their mission; but in this they were mistaken, for when they arrived at Peking, they were scarcely treated with common civility by the authorities there, who provided them with a miserable lodging, and very scanty entertainment, until the time was appointed for their audience.

The sovereigns of the East usually hold their levees at break of day, consequently the ambassadors, to their great annoyance, were conducted to the palace overnight, and obliged to sit up in their state dresses that they might be ready at the moment their attendance was required. Seated on the floor in an outer apartment, which was quite destitute of furniture, they had leisure to contemplate by the light of a few lamps, a motley group of beings in the same uncomfortable situation as themselves, all waiting also for the honour of being admitted to the presence of the Emperor. In one corner of the room was a barbarian envoy from a Prince of the Southern Tartars; dressed in a long coat of sheepskin, dyed crimson, with large boots, bare arms, and a horse's tail dangling from his cap. Contrasted with this rough-looking personage, was the ambassador of a Mogul Khan, who wore a blue silk dress, so richly embroidered that it looked like beaten gold; and very different from either of these, was the representative of the Grand Lama, who was attired in a yellow robe, with a broad hat, like that worn by a cardinal, and a string of large beads round his neck. There were many other figures, all equally novel to the eyes of the Europeans, who were no less objects of curiosity to the strangers.

At length the welcome dawn appeared, when on a given signal, all started up, and shaking off the weariness that had oppressed them, followed the official persons, whose business it was to conduct them to the hall of audience. This hall is of white marble, the entrance to which is by five flights of steps; the middle flight being reserved exclusively for the Emperor, and never profaned by the foot of any other person. Here a scene of extraordinary pomp and splendour exhibited itself to the astonished eyes of the plain and homely Dutchmen. The glittering dresses of the attendants; the gorgeous banners displayed by the soldiers ranged on each side of the hall; the superb throne, around which were held on high, figures of the sun made of gold, and silver circles representing the moon; with the crowd of officers and Mandarins in their state robes, produced a most imposing effect.

The Emperor had not yet made his appearance, but all the ambassadors were directed to prostrate themselves three times before the empty throne, and at each time of kneeling to bow down their heads to the ground three times till their foreheads touched the marble flooring. This was the very ceremony the Russian envoy had refused to perform; but as the Hollanders were extremely anxious for the success of their embassy, they did not think it prudent to make any scruple about the matter, and went through the kotou with a good grace. The sound of bells soon announced the approach of Shun-che, all present fell on their knees as he ascended the steps, every eye being bent towards the earth, as if none were worthy to look upon him. He walked up the hall with a stately air, and seated himself on the throne, when the whole assembly arose, and the different envoys were led forward to do him homage by a repetition of the nine prostrations; but not a single a word, nor even the slightest mark of notice, did the haughty Tartar vouchsafe to the disappointed Europeans, who withdrew with no very kindly feelings towards a prince before whom they had humbled themselves to so little purpose. Both the Tartars and Chinese had, in fact, a great contempt for the Dutch people, in consequence of having learned that there was no emperor or king of Holland; for they did not understand the nature of a republic, but thought the Dutch must be a very poor and mean nation that could not afford to maintain a king. However, before the ambassadors quitted Peking, they were officially informed that they might come to China once in eight years, to bring presents, but not to trade.

The presents brought by ambassadors were received as a kind of tribute, and acknowledgment of vassalage; and thus the Chinese have imbibed the absurd notion that all the countries of Europe, from which embassies have been sent to the Emperor of China, are subject to him, and they are only now beginning to discover their mistake. It is scarcely possible to believe that the Emperors themselves could have been under the same impression, although it was their policy to keep up the delusion among their subjects, who were taught to look upon them as absolute monarchs of the whole earth. Shun-che, especially, must have been better informed, since he had placed himself under the tuition of a German Jesuit, named Adam Schaal, for whom he entertained so great a respect that he raised him to the dignity of Chief Minister of State, and consulted him on every affair of importance; so that, however strange it may appear, the Empire of China was for a time governed in reality by a Christian Missionary. The Emperor was so much attached to this excellent man, that he would often spend the whole day with him at his own house, in order to profit by his profound learning; and although he himself never became a convert to Christianity, he did not prohibit others from embracing that faith, and allowed two churches to be built at Peking, where several missionaries came to reside. It may be supposed that under such favourable circumstances many were converted to the Christian faith; and if all the successors of Shun-che had adopted the same liberal policy with regard to religion, China might perhaps by this time have been a Christian country.

In the mean time some thousands of families who still preserved their attachment to the late dynasty, emigrated to the Island of Formosa, where they were received and protected by the Dutch, who had erected two forts there, and were in possession of a great part of the country. But they soon had cause to repent of having admitted the Chinese loyalists into the island, for their numbers rapidly increased to an alarming extent; and it was discovered that they were holding a secret correspondence with the maritime chief Koshinga, who openly persisted in his opposition to the new government of China. This discovery excited some apprehension on the part of the Dutch, whose fears were not without foundation; for Koshinga, who had formed the bold project of conquering the island, and setting himself up as an independent sovereign, landed with a force of twenty thousand men, and being joined by the Chinese emigrants, demanded the surrender of the Dutch forts. A desperate conflict took place, in which the Dutch suffered very severely, and were obliged to retire within the forts, from which they sent a deputation to the camp of the invader to propose terms of accommodation; but Koshinga refused to make any terms, saying, that Formosa had always belonged to the Chinese, although they had allowed strangers to reside there; but as they now required it for their own occupation, the foreigners must immediately depart, as it was no longer convenient to let them remain. A regular warfare was then commenced for possession of the island, which lasted many months, when the Dutch were obliged to give up the contest, and betake themselves to their settlements in Java; on which Koshinga assumed the sovereignty in 1662, and was called by the Europeans, King of Formosa. Great numbers of Chinese loyalists, from time to time, left their country to place themselves under his protection, so that the number of his subjects was constantly increasing; and as he still remained faithful to the exiled royal family of China, he made frequent descents on the maritime provinces guarded by the Tartars, who were much harassed by his attacks. The Dutch had endeavoured to civilize the original inhabitants of the island, but the Chinese made slaves of some of them, while others escaped to the mountains, where their posterity still live, in a state of barbarism.

About the time that Koshinga achieved this conquest, the Emperor Shun-che died, at the early age of twenty-four, and was succeeded by his son Kang-hy, who was then only eight years old.

Kang-hy, from 1662 to 1722.

The new Emperor Kang-hy was one of the greatest monarchs that ever ruled over the Chinese territories. Being so young when his father died, four of the ministers were appointed to conduct the government during his minority; but as they were all rather advanced in years, and strongly prejudiced in favour of the ancient usages of the country, they employed the authority with which they were entrusted to abolish the innovations made by the late Emperor, and restore all things to their former state. Their principal cause of dissatisfaction was the toleration that had been granted to the Christians, which they feared might, in time, if it were continued, be prejudicial to the ancient forms of worship which had endured for so many ages; and as this was in their eyes the greatest evil that could possibly befal the country, they used their best endeavours to prevent it, by putting in prison the good Father Adam Schaal, and another Jesuit called

Father Verbiest, who had also stood high in the favour of Shun-che, and had been employed to assist Schaal in the affairs of the state. The two churches were then destroyed, and all who had professed the Christian faith were persecuted with the utmost severity, by fines, imprisonment, exile, and some even with death. The two Jesuits were, after a time, liberated; but the general persecution of the Christians was continued till the young Emperor was of an age to take the government into his own hands. One of his first acts was to put a stop to the cruelties to which the Christian converts had been subjected; and he made amends to Father Verbiest for the sufferings he had endured, by raising him to the same rank which his father had bestowed on Adam Schaal, who had lately died of old age.

During the Regency, the pirate Koshinga had died; but his son had taken upon himself the government of Formosa, and as he inherited his father's hatred towards the Tartars, and was equally powerful at sea, he constantly ravaged the whole line of the south-eastern coast of China. The naval force of the empire not being sufficiently strong to contend with that of the pirate king, the government issued an order, that all subjects of the Emperor of China dwelling near the sea shore, should withdraw ten miles into the interior, so as to leave only a barren tract of country to the invaders. The inhabitants of the Portuguese settlement of Macao were the only persons exempted from the general order, probably because the government was indifferent about the safety of a foreign colony, particularly as the country beyond was defended by the barrier wall that confined the Portuguese within certain limits. A great number of villages near the coast

were entirely destroyed, and thousands of families who had lived by fishing were reduced to great distress by being obliged to remove from the vicinity of the sea. The fishermen, however, converted their boats into smaller ones, in which, with the assistance of their families, they could continue their occupation in more shallow waters. Each of these boats was furnished with a peculiar and ingenious contrivance. It consisted of a net suspended at the end of a bamboo pole; the latter projecting from the boat somewhat like a bowsprit, was fixed on a pivot by which it was moveable, and was also attached by means of ropes to a balance board. The fisherman, as he wished to raise his net out of, or to sink it into the water, had only to walk either up or down the balance board. This mode of fishing is still practised in many parts of the island of Hong Kong, and other places; but the nets in use are often of a large size, and are raised out of the water by means of ropes attached to wheels fixed on the shores. The expulsion of the inhabitants from the sea coast, produced the desired effect; for the Formosan Chief, whose principal resources had been derived from plundering the maritime towns and villages, found his power decline with his means of acquiring wealth; and although he contrived, with some difficulty, to support his authority till his death, his son, about twenty years after the accession of Kang-hy, gave up his island in consideration of a title and a pension for life.

Formosa was thus united to the Chinese empire, and has proved a valuable acquisition, as it is extremely fertile, producing in abundance fruits, corn, and rice, of which large quantities are sent annually to China. The loyalists who had taken refuge there, having lost their leader, made submission to the Tartar Emperor, and received a full pardon; but were obliged to shave their heads, like the rest of the nation.

The minority of Kang-hy is remarkable, among other events, for the commencement of the trade in tea, a very small quantity of that article being sent to England by the East India Company, who had been in the habit of sending trading vessels to several of the Chinese ports, and had formed a settlement at Amoy before the Tartar conquest. They purchased vast quantities of silks, both raw and manufactured; but tea had not yet attracted much attention, and the little canister sent by one of the resident merchants to a friend was intended merely as a curious present.

Some years afterwards, the Directors of the East India Company, in writing out to Bombay for certain goods to be shipped for England, desired that one hundred dollars should be laid out in tea, to be sent with the rest of the merchandise. This order having been executed, they wrote again, desiring that five or six chests should be sent every year; and then the enormous duty of five shillings a pound was levied by the English government upon this article, which made tea so dear that, even when larger quantities of it were brought to this country, a long time elapsed before any but very rich people could obtain it. Still the trade continued to increase, till at length the quantity of tea sold to the foreigners attracted the notice of the Chinese government, and a very heavy tax was laid on the exportation of that article, which has ever since produced a considerable revenue to the Emperor.

Kang-hy was exactly the sort of prince to make himself exceedingly popular; for he was a great hunter, and thus acquired a high military reputation among the Tartars, who regarded hunting and war as pursuits equally honourable and important; and he gained the good-will of the Chinese by honouring and rewarding literary merit, and by attending in person to the welfare of his subjects. Every year he made a progress through some of the provinces, to see that the magistrates performed their duties, and that the people were not oppressed by them. On these occasions the people of the cities usually made a grand display; as for instance, on his visit to Nanking in 1689, triumphal arches were erected in all the principal streets, at the distance of about twenty paces from each other, gaily adorned with ribbons, silks, and fringes; and when he made his entry on horseback, with a numerous train of guards and gentlemen, he was met by a deputation from the citizens, bearing silken banners, canopies, parasols, and other ornamental ensigns used by the Chinese on great occasions. The streets were crowded with people as he passed along; but, although so many thousands were assembled, such was their habitual awe of Majesty, that not even a whisper disturbed the solemn silence which prevailed.

From Nanking the Emperor proceeded to the wealthy city of Soo-chow, which from the beauty of its situation, the luxury of its inhabitants, and the circumstance of many of the streets being intersected with canals, on which pleasure boats are continually gliding, has been called the Venice of China. Here the people laid down rich silks and carpets along the streets through which the royal train was to pass; a mark of respect that was highly pleasing to the Emperor, who, instead of riding over them, as was expected, dismounted at the gate of the city, and desiring his whole suite to do the same, proceeded on foot to the palace. This little mark of consideration probably did more towards raising the monarch in the public estimation, than any of his greater acts; so easy is it sometimes, by an act of courtesy, for a sovereign to win the affections of his subjects. Another incident is said to have occurred during this progress, which may serve to shew the summary mode in which justice was executed upon those Mandarins who were found to have abused their authority.

Kang-hy, who was a little apart from his attendants, saw an old man sitting on the ground weeping bitterly. Riding up to him, he inquired the cause of his grief. "My lord," said the old man, who was ignorant of the rank of his interrogator, "I have cause enough for sorrow. My only son, who was the joy of my life, and the support of my declining years, has been taken from me to serve the governor of the province; and I have no one to comfort me in my old age, or to mourn over my tomb. The Emperor asked if he had endeavoured to obtain some redress. "Alas!" replied he, "how is it possible for me, a poor weak old man, to force a great Mandarin to do me justice?" "We will presently see that!" said the monarch, "get up behind me, and shew me the way to this governor's house; perhaps it will not be so difficult to obtain justice as you may imagine." The poor man mounted as he was desired, and they forthwith rode to the Mandarin's palace, where the imperial guards, and a large party of grandees who had missed the Emperor, arrived just at the same time in great consternation. Kang-hy entering the palace, charged the governor with his violent conduct. The offender, not being able to deny the accusation, was condemned to lose his head, and the sentence was executed on the spot; when the Emperor, turning to the old man, said, "To make you ample amends for the injury you have sustained, I appoint you governor of this province in the room of him who has proved himself so unworthy of that office. Let his crime and punishment be a warning to you, to use your power more justly."

It was during this reign that the Chinese learned the art of casting cannon, in which they were instructed by Father Verbiest, under whose inspection about 450 pieces of artillery were founded, to the great satisfaction of the Emperor, who made a solemn feast under tents in the fields, on the occasion of their being tried; his Majesty and the court being lodged in an immense splendid tent, or temporary palace, containing a grand hall of audience, and other apartments, all lined with embroidered silks. Gunpowder had been known and made in China from a very early period, but it had only been used in the composition of fireworks, of which the Chinese always made a great display at their festivals; nor was it till the early part of the seventeenth century, that they became acquainted with its application as an agent in warfare; when the Portuguese, during the war with the Mantchows, lent them three cannons for the defence of the city of Nanking, with men to manage them; and great was the surprise created by their deadly effects. The fame of Father Verbiest was considerably raised by the important service he had rendered to the state in furnishing it with artillery, and a title of honour was bestowed on him in consequence; besides which, he gained much credit and influence by reforming the calendar, which had been suffered to fall into such confusion, that it was found necessary to leave out a whole month of one year to bring it into regular order. Yet the composition of the almanacs is considered an affair of so much importance, that it is the chief business of an assembly of learned Mandarins, who compose what is called the Astronomical Board; and when the error in their calculations was discovered, the president was banished to Tartary, for his incompetency to the duties of his office, and Father Verbiest was placed at the head of that department in his stead; for it is one of the singular features of the Chinese government to punish inability in office as a crime, on the ground that no man ought to undertake that which he is not able to perform; and on the same principle a military commander is sometimes disgraced in consequence of the loss of a battle, or the failure of an enterprise, in which he may have done his best to succeed.

The Astronomical tribunal is subordinate to that of the Board of Rites. The grand business of its members is to make the almanacs; and they have also to calculate the eclipses, and to present to the Emperor at the end of every forty-five days an exact statement of the position of the heavenly bodies, together with the observations that have been made during that time. An eclipse is considered a great event in China. Some time before it takes place, notices are sent to the governors of every province and city throughout the empire, that they may prepare for the performance of the accustomed solemnities that are always observed on the occasion. Large printed bills are immediately posted on the public buildings, and orders are sent to the Mandarins to assemble in the large halls appointed for that purpose, whither they repair on the morning of the given day, in their robes of ceremony, and take their seats at tables on which are delineated all the eclipses that have happened for more than 4000 years. It is stated in evidence of the antiquity of the Chinese monarchy, that the ancient records mention a total eclipse of the sun that took place 2155 years before the Christian era, which is also noticed by the Chaldeans and ancient Egyptians, and as the correctness of the statement has been proved by subsequent calculations, it affords an additional reason for supposing that China was inhabited and had its learned men at that early period.

The ceremonies observed on the occasion of an eclipse have somewhat of a religious character, and originated in ignorance of the causes of the phenomenon, which was anciently believed to be the forerunner of some dreadful calamity; and although the Chinese are now aware that the effect is produced by natural causes, they are too much attached to their old customs to discontinue them. The Mandarins being assembled in the Hall of Astronomy, place themselves at the tables before mentioned, waiting for the commencement of the eclipse. The moment the sun or moon, whichever it may be, begins to be darkened, drums and gongs are sounded in the town, and the people all prostrate themselves, bowing their heads till their foreheads touch the earth, and in this position they continue as long as the orb remains shadowed; while some of the members of the Astronomical Board are at the observatory watching the progress of the eclipse, and noting down their observations, which are afterwards examined and compared with the computations made by the chief tribunal, and a report is transmitted to the Emperor.

The distribution of the almanacs at the beginning of every year is also attended with many solemnities. There is no work in the world of which so many copies are printed as the Chinese calendar, the number being estimated at several millions; which is not improbable, considering the amount of population, and the fact that every family uses an almanac as an oracle; since, besides the usual information, it not only predicts the weather, but notes the days that are reckoned lucky or unlucky for commencing any undertaking; for applying remedies in diseases; for marrying or for burying; and, in short, it is consulted by the people in many cases where their own reason would be a better guide; but the government gives countenance to all superstitions that disincline the people from exerting their own reasoning faculties. The calendar is an Imperial monopoly, and no other than that prepared by the Astronomical Board is allowed to be published, the law on this point being so strict that a violation of it would be punished with death. The almanacs are all printed at Peking, and are distributed through the empire in the following manner. On a certain day appointed for the ceremonial in the capital, the Mandarins repair early in the morning to the palace, while the members of the Board, arrayed in their state dresses, proceed to their hall to escort the books, which are carried in procession to the Imperial residence. Those which are intended for the Emperor, the Empress, and the queens, are bound in yellow satin, and enclosed in bags of cloth-of-gold, which are placed on a large gilded machine, borne by forty footmen clothed in yellow. Then follow ten or twelve smaller vehicles, surrounded with red silk curtains, and containing the books to be given to the princes, which are bound in red satin, and enclosed in bags of silver cloth. These are followed by men bearing on their shoulders several tables, on which are piled the calendars intended for the grandees of the court and the generals of the army; the cavalcade is completed by the president and members of the Board in sedans, followed by their usual attendants. On arriving at the palace, the golden bags are laid on two tables covered with yellow damask, when the members of the tribunal, having first prostrated themselves, deliver them to the proper officers, who receive them

kneeling, and carry them with great ceremony to the foot of the throne. The silver bags are sent in a similar manner to all the princes of the royal family; after which the ministers, and other great officers of state, present themselves in turn, and kneel with reverence to receive their almanacs, which are regarded as gifts from the Emperor. The ceremonies of distribution at the Court being concluded, the books intended for the use of the people are sent by the tribunal into every province of the empire, where the forms observed at the Imperial palace are repeated at the court of the head Mandarin, after which the people are allowed to purchase their almanacs; and as this is a privilege of which few omit to avail themselves, the sale must be immense, and must largely add to the revenue.

The Chinese had many astronomical instruments at a very early period of their history; but they were greatly improved, and some new ones introduced, by the Jesuits, who certainly owed the extraordinary influence they once possessed in China to their inculcation of the arts and sciences most esteemed in that country. The first clocks and watches seen in China were presented to Kang-hy by one of the Jesuit fathers; and another member of the fraternity, to gratify the ladies of that Emperor's court, constructed for them a camera-obscura, an instrument with which they were much delighted, as it enabled them to see what was passing outside the palace gates. In consequence of the encouragement received by the Jesuits, Christianity made greater progress in China during the reign of Kang-hy than at any period either before or since. Many members of the royal family, both male and female, openly professed the Christian faith, and a church was built for their accommodation within the precincts of the palace; besides which, several places of worship for Christians were erected in different parts of Peking, as well as in other large cities. Among these new edifices was a church built by a French Jesuit named D'Entrecolles, at the famous village or town of King-te-ching, where the great porcelain manufacture was carried on; and there he made himself acquainted with the whole process of that beautiful art, which was first brought into Europe by him, when, on the death of Kang-hy, the Christian missionaries were obliged to quit the country. Among the Jesuits resident at this time in Peking was Père Gerbillon, a native of France, who was employed by the Emperor on a mission into Tartary, the object of which was to negotiate a peace with the Russians, who had been at war with the Chinese ever since the rejection of their embassy by the late Emperor Shun-che, who refused to acknowledge their right to the territories they had occupied in Mantchow Tartary.

The negotiations were successful; peace was concluded, and a free trade established between Russia and China by a treaty signed by the two Emperors Alexius and Kang-hy in the year 1689. The boundaries of the Russian Empire, which had been the ground of dispute, were precisely defined, and it was agreed that caravans should be sent at stated periods to Peking, and be allowed to remain there till they had disposed of their goods. A caravansery in the suburbs was allotted for the residence of the merchants, and their expenses while they remained were to be defrayed by the Emperor of China. The trade thus conducted was a monopoly of the Russian government; but there were private merchants also who travelled to China, and transacted business on their own account with the Chinese merchants, at an annual fair held on the frontiers; but they were not permitted to proceed to Peking, like the government agents, nor even to enter the Chinese territories.

The principal wars of Kang-hy, after the submission of the pirates of Formosa, were with the Elenths or Kalmuc Tartars, who had been a very numerous and powerful tribe, but were almost annihilated in the course of three years warfare, by the victorious arms of the Chinese Emperor, who by this conquest greatly extended his dominions in Tartary. In the year 1721, Kang-hy, then far advanced in years, celebrated the sixtieth anniversary of his accession to the throne, and as he was the first sovereign of China whose reign had been lengthened to this term, a grand jubilee took place on the occasion throughout the whole empire. Sixty is a number held in especial veneration among the Chinese, and the sixtieth birth-day of any private individual is always celebrated with great festivities by the family; but the event of a monarch having arrived at that epoch of his reign, particularly one who was so much beloved and respected, was an especial cause of rejoicing, which was testified in the usual way by sacrifices to the gods, illuminations, feastings, fireworks, and a variety of amusements.

On all festive occasions in China, the sacrifices constitute an important part of the ceremonials, and as there are no priests of the order of Confucius, the Emperor officiates as high-priest in the capital, whilst in all the other cities the Viceroy or Chief Mandarin acts in that capacity. The greatest annual festival on which the sovereign appears in his sacerdotal character is that of the celebration of the season of spring, which takes place about the middle of February, and is one of those ancient observances that help to preserve the primitive character of the nation. It is then that the Emperor performs the part of the husbandman by ploughing and sowing seed in an enclosure set apart for that purpose near the palace, a ceremony never omitted by Kang-hy, who was very attentive to all observances that are held in reverence among the people. The day for the royal ploughing was fixed by the Board of Rites, and this ceremony was accompanied by many solemnities on the part of the Emperor, and those who were to assist at the sacrifices, such as fasting for three days until the evening of each, and abstaining from all kinds of amusements during that period. Several princes were also deputed on the eve of the festival to visit the Hall of Ancestors, a temple dedicated to the memory of the Imperial relatives who had departed this life, where many rites and ceremonies were performed before the tablets on which their names were engraven.

Early on the morning of the festival the Emperor, attended by the great officers of state, repairs to the Temple of the Earth, where he makes sacrifices, and implores a blessing on the labours of the spring, that they may produce a plentiful harvest; and when these rites are ended he descends from the temple into the field, where all the requisite preparations have been made by forty or fifty husbandmen, who are in attendance. The

Emperor ploughs a few furrows with his own hand, and sows five sorts of grain; after which twelve grandees of the first rank plough and sow in turn, and then the work is completed by the professional husbandmen, each of whom receives a present of a piece of Nanking cloth. The produce of this field is held sacred, and carefully preserved in a granary by itself, to be used for the most solemn sacrifices. The ploughing by the Imperial husbandman takes place only in the capital, but in every large city a ceremony is performed called "meeting the spring;" when the governor assumes the character of high-priest, and goes out in state, carried in a finely ornamented sedan chair, preceded by banners, lighted torches, and music. He is followed by several Mandarins in their sedans, and by a number of litters, in which are placed children, who are fancifully dressed and crowned with flowers, representing various deities connected with the labours of the field. But the most prominent figure among the *dramatis personæ* is a huge earthen buffalo, the representative of the spring, which is borne in procession to meet the high-priest, who delivers a lecture on the benefits of husbandry, which is one of sixteen discourses read annually to the people. At the conclusion of the lecture he strikes the buffalo three times with a staff, when it is immediately broken in pieces by the populace, and a number of little porcelain cows with which it was filled, furnish materials for a scramble. The rest of the day is devoted to amusements, among which the most popular are plays performed by companies of strolling actors, who set up temporary theatres in the streets, the expenses being paid, on this occasion, by the government.

It is thus that the rulers of China, both by precept and example, stimulate their subjects to the pursuits of agriculture, so essential to the support of the empire; and as the Emperor in person, ploughs the land and sows the seed; so the Empress also performs her part to encourage another most important branch of industry by going through in appearance at least all the labours connected with the culture of silk. The Empresses of ancient times were wont in reality to occupy themselves with their maidens like the royal dames of Europe in days of yore, spinning and weaving, and stitching with indefatigable zeal; but at the period to which I am now alluding, they contented themselves with gathering a few mulberry leaves in the Imperial orchard, and winding off some cocoons of silk; having first made sacrifices in the Temple dedicated to the inventor of the silk manufacture. The intention of these ceremonies is obviously to countenance that superiority in point of rank which the farmers and manufacturers have invariably held over those engaged in mercantile pursuits; for the rulers of China, from the earliest period to the present, have always deemed it better policy to make the empire entirely dependent on its own resources for food and clothing, than to obtain those necessaries or add to its wealth by foreign trade, which has hitherto been only tolerated, and never encouraged by the government.

Kang-hy endeavoured, with the assistance of the Jesuits, to make some improvements in the arts and sciences of China, especially in that of medicine, which has always been in a most deficient state; but the prejudices of the Chinese with regard to the dissection of human bodies is so strong that, although several books on the subject of anatomy were published under the patronage of that enlightened Emperor, the study was never prosecuted to any advantage; and so little is yet understood of the medical art, that the greater portion of the Chinese people put more faith in spells and charms, than in any remedies derived from professional science, and place very little reliance on the efficacy of a medicine, unless it be taken on a lucky day. Kang-hy died in the year 1722, having ruled over the Chinese empire sixty-one years, the longest reign recorded in the history of China, since the fabulous times.

The sovereign power had never been greater or more absolute than during this period, nor had it ever been equalled, except while the sceptre was swayed by the powerful hand of Kublai Khan. Besides extending his dominions by his conquests over the Elenths, Kang-hy obliged the Monguls to remove three hundred miles beyond the Great Wall, where he gave them lands and pastures, while he settled his own subjects of the Mantchow race in the provinces they had vacated, thus uniting to China a large extent of territory without the intervention of a foreign nation. The Monguls, however, are still a constant source of uneasiness to the Chinese government, and are watched with the utmost jealousy by the Mantchows, whom it is well known they heartily detest as the usurpers of that empire, once so gloriously ruled by their own princes. They have no cities, but dwell in tents, some of which are as richly furnished as the halls of a palace; the flooring being covered with Turkey or Persian carpets, the sides adorned with silken hangings, and every other article for domestic use being of a costly and luxurious description, and obtained in exchange for valuable furs from the Chinese. The Monguls are great hunters, and thus procure the skins of various animals that are highly prized. They are all trained to arms and are also addicted to horse-racing, wrestling, and other athletic sports. Their ordinary costume is a long dark blue robe, fastened round the waist with a leather belt; under-garments of Nanking cotton, leather boots, and a cap of cloth or fur, according to the season. Their princes attend as vassals at the Imperial court, and very often marry the daughters of the Emperor, who is not unwilling to promote such alliances as a means of securing their fidelity. With the same view he sends rich presents to them every year, except when any signs of rebellion appear, in which case the gifts are withheld, until submission has been made, and the disaffected have returned to their allegiance. Their lands are held in fief, and descend to the eldest son, who cannot take possession until he has received his investiture from the Emperor; another means of keeping them in subjection.

Yong-t-ching, from 1722 to 1735.

Some time before his death, Kang-hy had nominated as his successor his fourth son, who happened to be in Tartary at the time when his father was seized with the sudden illness that terminated his existence; and some say he then named his fourteenth son to succeed him; but others assert, and apparently with more reason, that Yong-t-ching, availing himself of his brother's absence, possessed himself of the document that bequeathed the empire to the fourth son, and by adding the character that expresses ten, converted fourth into fourteenth, and thus by forgery and usurpation mounted the throne, having caused the true heir to be imprisoned in Tartary, where he died. Such is the account given of the accession of Yong-t-ching, who was installed with great pomp on the day following the death of his father. The ceremony of the installation, which is equivalent to a coronation, takes place in the great hall of the palace, which is decorated with the splendour always displayed by the Chinese on state occasions. This ceremony consists in the act of homage performed by the princes and grandees of the empire there assembled, who acknowledge with certain forms the right of the new monarch to ascend the throne, and make the nine prostrations before him. In former times, if the successor were the son of the deceased sovereign, the government was left, during the period of mourning, to the care of the ministers, while the prince remained in the deepest seclusion, even shutting himself up within the tomb, or causing a hut to be erected near it, where he would spend months in the indulgence of his sorrow. But this custom has not been followed by the Tartar rulers, who appear to be fully aware of the impolicy of leaving the management of the state to others, and therefore profess to respect the ancient practice, while at the same time they evade its performance by pretending that their own inclinations have been overruled by a consideration for the welfare of the people. The enthronement of an Empress is not a matter of right, but a mark of favour conferred by her husband, which raises her above the rest of the queens, of whom there are several, but does not place her upon an equality with the Empress-mother, who still holds the first rank among the females of the empire. The name of Yong-t-ching signifies "lasting peace;" but the title was not at first very appropriate to the prince who assumed it, since he began his reign by a violent and unrelenting persecution of the Christians, who, in consequence of the toleration they had so long enjoyed, had grown very numerous. The Jesuits were banished from the court, the churches either destroyed or converted into heathen temples, and all Christian missionaries ordered to leave the country. Even his own relatives, those princes who, in the time of Kang-hy, had embraced Christianity, and been allowed by that liberal-minded monarch to have a church for the exercise of their worship within the very bounds of the palace, were involved in the general fate of the converts, and sent as exiles, with their wives and families, to the dreary deserts of Tartary. The banishment of the Jesuits put a full stop to the progress of improvement in China, where every trace was soon lost of the benefits derived from their unwearied exertions; and as the succeeding Emperors have neither tolerated the Christian religion, nor given any encouragement to the introduction of European science, the Chinese are not more enlightened now than they were before the natives of Europe first visited their shores.

In every respect, except his enmity to the Christian religion, Yong-t-ching is spoken of as a mild and beneficent sovereign, anxious to do good, and extremely charitable in seasons of public calamity, such as failure of the crops, or earthquakes, which latter are not unfrequent in China. The province of Pe-che-lee is particularly liable to these awful visitations, which were severely felt at Peking twice during the reign of Kang-hy, who is much and deservedly praised for his humanity to the sufferers; nor was Yong-t-ching less benevolent on the occasion of a similar calamity which occurred in 1730, when many houses and temples were thrown down in the capital, and a great number of lives lost. Large sums of money were distributed by order of the Emperor to repair the damage; and those families who were reduced by the destruction of their shops and goods, to temporary distress, were relieved and supported at the expense of the government until their houses had been rebuilt and their trade had re-

commenced. In 1725, a terrible famine afflicted the land, when the public granaries in every province were opened for the purpose of supplying the people with corn and rice at a small price, and the Emperor, according to established custom, made solemn sacrifices in the Temple of the Earth; released numbers of prisoners who were confined in the dungeons of the capital, and performed other acts of propitiation, hoping thereby to avert the calamity.

The care that is taken to make a provision for the poor in time of need, by laying up stores of grain in every province, constitutes an admirable features of the Chinese policy; and, according to the ancient laws, is one of the chief duties of the sovereign, who is enjoined by Confucius, the revered instructor both of the prince and his people, to take care that the lands are cultivated so as to produce the necessaries of life for all; to attend to the fisheries and planting of trees; to be moderate in imposing taxes; to see that the means of instruction are furnished for every class; but above all, to assist the people in times of scarcity, as a father would provide for the wants of his children. Yong-t-ching revived an old custom that had fallen into disuse, of inviting to a feast all persons eminent for their virtues. In his reign also the Mandarins who had conducted themselves well in an inferior station were promoted to a higher rank. He encouraged agriculture by bestowing rewards on the most diligent labourers, and he brought under cultivation new lands at the extremity of the province of Yunnan, on the borders of Tartary, where he settled colonies, and conferred honours on those who had exerted themselves to improve the country. He modified the restrictive laws with regard to emigration, allowing the inhabitants of the maritime provinces to repair to Siam, Malacca, and the neighbouring islands; on condition, however, that they should return to their native country—a stipulation that was perfectly in unison with their own feelings, which would lead them, even without such an injunction, to end their days in the place of their birth, that they might be entombed among their ancestors. During this reign some fresh disputes occurred with the Russians, which occasioned an alteration in the mode of trading between the two empires. Instead of being permitted to visit Peking once a-year, as they had been in the habit of doing ever since the peace concluded by the late Emperor, the Russian caravans were only allowed to repair thither once in three years; but a medium of communication between the merchants of both countries was established by a trading station on the banks of a small stream in Tartary, called the Kiackta, which is about 1000 miles from Peking, and more than three times that distance from Moscow. On each side of this stream was erected a small town, or rather village, with a fort garrisoned by a few soldiers, that of the

Russians being called Kiackta, that of the Chinese Maimatschin, which means the fort of commerce. The Chinese residents in Maimatschin were agents employed by the merchants of great manufacturing cities to carry thither such goods as were likely to be marketable; as silks, both raw and manufactured, tea, porcelain, japanned ware, tobacco, rice, pearls, precious stones, spices, and those elegant toys of carved ivory for which the Chinese are so famous. They exchanged these articles with the Russians for rich furs, woollen cloth, linen, Russia leather, glass, and cutlery. The Chinese were not permitted to take their wives with them, nor could the Russians take theirs, on account of the length and difficulties of the journey, so that there were no women in the place, which must have been dull enough for those who were obliged to remain there a whole year, the term specified for the residence of the Chinese traders, who at the end of that time returned to their homes, when others were sent out to replace them, with a fresh assortment of goods.

An embassy from the Russian court to that of Peking, in the latter part of the reign of Kang-hy, was accompanied at setting out by several ladies, who, had they not been thwarted in their wishes, would perhaps have braved all dangers for the sake of seeing the capital of the Chinese empire; but when they had proceeded some way, the ambassador was informed that there was no example of European females ever having been admitted into a city of China, and that they could not be allowed even to enter the Chinese territories without permission from the Emperor. They were therefore sent back to Russia, by which they avoided hardships greater than they had perhaps contemplated; for the travellers, in crossing the sandy desert of Shamo, were forty days without seeing a human habitation, except a few Mongul tents; while, to augment their miseries, the snow fell in abundance, and they could not always obtain a sufficient supply of fuel to make a fire when they halted. This embassy was sent by Peter the Great; and some years afterwards, the Empress Catherine the First despatched an ambassador to the court of China, where he was well received by Yong-t-ching, who consented to a treaty, by which the Russians were to have a church in the capital, with priests of their own faith; and there were to be four young Russians always resident there, to study the languages and act as interpreters between the two nations. These students were to remain for ten years, and then to be replaced by others. The Empress afterwards gave up the monopoly of the regular trade, and the caravans ceased to visit the Chinese capital, but the merchants of both countries still resorted to Kiackta, where a great trade has been carried on to the present time. During the whole of this reign, the British merchants of the East India Company trading to China were so much oppressed by the heavy duties imposed by the government, and the extortions privately practised by the Mandarins, that, although the commerce was never entirely stopped, it was very often interrupted.

The reign of Yong-t-ching was not distinguished by any very remarkable event, neither was it disturbed by foreign wars or domestic rebellion, therefore had it not been for the cruel persecution suffered by the Christians, the name of the Emperor would not have been a misnomer. He died in 1735, having reigned about fourteen years, and was succeeded by his eldest son, the warlike and highly talented Kien-long, the first sovereign of the Chinese Empire whose court was visited by a native of Great Britain.

A public mourning in China, especially for the death of an Emperor, is observed with the deepest solemnities throughout the whole country, for it is not, as in Europe, an optional ceremony to put on the outward symbols of sorrow; but the whole nation is bound, both by law and custom, to exhibit the same tokens of grief for the loss of him who is in a figurative sense the parent of every individual, as each would display on the death of his own father or mother. On the death of the sovereign, despatches announcing the event, written in blue ink, which is emblematical of a royal demise, are immediately forwarded to all the provinces. The Board of Rites then issues directions for the mourning, when the many millions of human beings that constitute the population of China, clothe themselves in coarse sackcloth or white serge, lay aside every kind of ornament, and refrain from all festivities, either in public or private. During the first hundred days, the men are obliged to leave their heads and beards unshaven. Marriages are not celebrated, nor are any sacrifices performed in the temples. Similar ceremonies are observed at the death of an Empress-mother, but do not continue for so long a period; fifty days being the usual term of mourning on such an occasion; but the wives of the Emperor are not thus publicly honoured at their deaths, although in some instances the Mandarins of the court have been ordered to take the balls that designate their rank from the tops of their caps, and not to partake of any amusements for a certain time.

Kang-hy had raised successively three princesses to the dignity of Empress, and on the death of the last, to whom he had been exceedingly attached, he commanded that all the great officers of state should go in turn to weep and prostrate themselves before the coffin, while he shut himself up alone to indulge his grief. Being afterwards informed that four of the gentlemen of the bedchamber had been seen eating and laughing together, when they ought to have been sunk in sadness, he banished them from the court, and deprived their fathers also of their employments. "Is it to be suffered," said he, "that my servants, whom I treat with indulgence and honour, should be so little touched with my affliction as to make merry whilst I am overwhelmed with sorrow?"

The funeral processions of the great are very magnificent. When a

favourite brother of the Emperor Kang-hy was carried to the place of interment, no less than sixteen thousand persons attended, most of whom bore ensigns denoting the rank of the deceased, or offerings to be burnt at his tomb. Trumpeters and mace-bearers, umbrellas and canopies of cloth-of-gold, standards, camels and horses laden with sacrifices, the coffin under a large yellow canopy, borne by eighty men, princes, princesses, mandarins, and bonzes, made up the great and imposing spectacle.

The reigning family have some very magnificent places of sepulture, one of which is in Eastern Tartary, near the city of Shinyang, four or five hundred miles to the north-east of Peking. It is there that the bodies of Shun-che, and his father, the great conqueror of the Chinese, are entombed; and several Mandarins of the Mantchow race reside there to take care that the tombs are kept in order, and to pay the customary honours and make the sepulchral sacrifices at the proper seasons. The tombs are built of white marble, in the Chinese style of architecture, and the large space of ground on which they stand is surrounded by a thick wall with battlements, as though the builders had feared that the sacred spot would have need of defence.

The Chinese, whatever may be their rank, make as much display as they can possibly afford in their funeral rites. The procession is usually extended to a great length, and preceded by solemn music; the melancholy tones of an instrument resembling the Scottish bagpipes, being accompanied at intervals by three strokes of the drum. White standards inscribed with the name and age of the deceased, and a vast number of white lanterns, are carried in the train. The coffin is surmounted by a canopy, and followed by the chief mourner, dressed in a garment of sackcloth, fastened round his waist with a cord, and a cap of the same material with a white bandage. He is supported by his brothers, or two nearest relatives; after whom succeed in a numerous procession, the friends and relations, all habited in coarse white cloth, some on foot, others in sedan chairs covered with white serge, these being mostly the females of the family, who utter loud lamentations the whole way. One of the principal objects in the procession is the tablet, which is sometimes carried in a gilded chair, and is taken back, after the interment, to be placed in the hall of ancestors. At the side of the tomb are erected temporary buildings, of mat or bamboo, where refreshments are laid out on tables by the attendants, while the friends are making the sacrifices and burning incense at the tomb. If the deceased has been a Mandarin of high rank, it is not uncommon for his sons to remain several weeks on the spot, living in bamboo huts, that they may renew their expressions of grief, and make new offerings each day to the manes of the departed, and, in obedience to the injunctions of the ancient sages, "sleep upon straw, with a sod of earth for a pillow."

Kien-long—1735 to 1795.

The great Emperor Kien-long, the grandfather of the present sovereign of China, succeeded his father Yong-t-ching, in the year 1735. On the day of his installation, while performing the customary rites in the hall of imperial ancestors, the young monarch made a vow, that "should he, like his illustrious grandfather Kang-hy, be permitted to complete the sixtieth year of his reign, he would shew his gratitude to heaven by resigning the crown to his heir, as an acknowledgment that he had been favoured to the full extent of his wishes." The vow was made in all sincerity, and the noble prince was spared to fulfil it. The first public act of his reign was to recal from exile all who were still living of those unhappy members of the royal race who had been banished by his predecessor in consequence of their attachment to the Christian religion. The exiles returned in a very destitute condition, for all their property had been confiscated to the state, and as no portion of it had been restored, they had no means of subsistence but small pensions, to which they were entitled as princes of the blood, and which were wholly inadequate to the maintenance of a family.

It is a custom of long standing in China, to provide for all the relatives of the Emperor, by granting them pensions in money, silks, and rice; which allowances are larger or smaller, according to the degree of affinity in which the pensioners stand to the throne; those who are more than five degrees removed, being allowed only a bare subsistence. These princes, who are very numerous, occupy a most unfortunate position in society; for, with the exception of a few of the highest rank, who may happen to be honoured with the Emperor's especial favour, they are of necessity an idle, useless class of beings, treated as mere appendages to the court, and debarred from those opportunities of distinguishing themselves which are freely accorded to all other members of the state. A prince of the blood is excluded from holding public employments, or from the pursuit of any occupation with a view to emolument. He has therefore no inducement to give much of his attention to study; since learning does not procure for him the same advantages that are derived from literary attainments by men of humbler birth. As a body, therefore, the princes of the empire are the most illiterate men in China, and the least respected; for the Chinese pay very little regard to rank, or even to wealth, if unaccompanied by learning. They know that a magistrate must be a person of literary acquirements, otherwise he would not have arrived at that dignity, and he is revered accordingly; but a prince, who owes his title to the accidental circumstance of birth, is not supposed to have the same claim to respect as a Mandarin, whose rank is owing to personal merit; and hence the hereditary princes are inferior in point of consideration to the Mandarins, notwithstanding their relationship to the Emperor.

There are two branches of these idlers: the first being descended in a direct line from the famous Mantchow conqueror, Tien-ming; the second, from the uncles and brothers of that great hero. The former take precedence in rank, and are distinguished by a yellow girdle; while the latter being more distantly allied to the Emperor, are only permitted to wear a red girdle. They are all obliged to live within the precincts of the court, to attend all the levees, to follow in the train of the Emperor whenever he appears abroad; and in fact, they are mere living automatons, who seem to exist for no other purpose than to increase the pomp of the Imperial retinue.

Such is the greater proportion of the hereditary nobility of China; much more debased, and far less to be envied, than the hard-working peasantry of the country; yet more deserving of pity than contempt, as being a class of the community held in an irksome state of bondage, from which there is no escape.

The recal of the exiles gave hopes to those who were interested in the great cause of spreading the doctrines of Christianity over that vast portion of the globe, that the Emperor was inclined to countenance, or at least to tolerate the preaching of the missionaries; which he did for some time, and the churches were again attended, as in the reign of Kang-hy. At length, however, the Mandarins, dreading the extinction of their ancient religion, presented a memorial on the subject to the Emperor, who suffered himself to be persuaded against his better judgment, not to afford any farther protection or encouragement to the teachers of Christianity. He was even induced to sanction the demolition of the churches, and the expulsion of all the Christian priests from the country.

This was about the time when the order of Jesuits was abolished in Europe; since which, all traces of the progress that had been made by the indefatigable exertions of that once influential body, towards establishing the Christian religion in China on a firm footing, have entirely disappeared.

The reign of Kien-long was not very peaceful, for he was addicted to warfare, and his ambition was gratified by some important conquests in Western Tartary, where several Tartar tribes were rendered tributary, and the rich city of Cashgar was brought under his dominion. But a later attempt which he made, to subjugate the Birman empire, was less fortunate, and a fine army sent out with that view was entirely destroyed.

The reasons given by Kien-long for invading the country of the Burmese were as little justifiable as those of the great Tartar sovereign of China, Kublai-khan, when he interfered with the Emperor of Japan. The invading army commenced hostilities by plundering a town and mart, which the Chinese had long been in the habit of frequenting with goods for sale. The Burmese monarch took immediate steps to repel the invasion, by dividing his forces into two separate bodies; one of which marched direct towards the enemy, while the other, by a circuitous route came behind them, and thus cut off their retreat. A terrible conflict took place, which lasted three days, and was most disastrous to the Chinese, who were hemmed in on all sides, and cut down by thousands, while numbers were made prisoners; so that, of all the vast army that entered the Burmese territories not one man returned to tell the miserable tale of their defeat, for those who escaped the sword were conducted in fetters to Ava, the Burmese capital, where they were made government slaves, according to the custom of that country. Those who understood any trade, were obliged to practise it; those who did not, were employed as gardeners and field labourers, and compelled to work very hard, without fee or reward, beyond a scanty supply of the coarsest food, just sufficient to keep them from starving.

But, notwithstanding the unfortunate result of this expedition, the Emperor made some important acquisitions to his dominions; amongst which was the kingdom of Thibet, an extensive country, which is but very little known, and chiefly remarkable as being the seat of the Budhist religion, and the residence of the Grand Lama, or high-priest of that faith. Thibet is an advantageous possession to the Chinese empire on account of its situation between the north-western frontier of China and the countries of various Indian and Tartar tribes, who might possibly be very troublesome neighbours, but that their veneration for the Grand Lama keeps them from disturbing his dominions; so that Thibet forms a sort of neutral ground, which prevents the approach of an enemy on that side of the empire, of which it now constitutes a part. But of all the wars of Kien-long, none has so much interest as the contest with the Meaou-tse, a singular people, who are supposed to have existed in the very heart of China from a most remote period of its history, yet have preserved their original freedom, and remain to this day an independent nation, though less numerous and powerful perhaps than before the armies of Kien-long appeared among their mountains, spreading death and desolation on every side.

Between the provinces of Canton, Kuang-sy, and Kuei-chow, are several ridges of high hills, extending from three to four hundred miles, inhabited by many different tribes of this race, who are quite distinct from the Chinese, whose government they do not acknowledge, and whose civilization they do not share. They are believed by some to be the aborigines of the country, as it is well known that the southern part of China was in a state of barbarism long after the north had been comparatively civilized; but how it happens that they have been permitted to remain unsubdued and independent has not been accounted for. But the mountainous nature of the region which they inhabit, and which gives them advantages over an enemy, may, with other causes, have tended to discourage all persevering attempts to subject them. They are governed by their own laws, and have their own princes; but it is remarkable, that in all the revolutions that have taken place in China, the Meaou-tse are never mentioned as having taken any part, nor does it appear that they were ever called upon to pay tribute. Their perfect independence of the Tartar government has been shewn by the retention of their hair, which is allowed to grow over the whole head; and being of great length is tied up in the ancient Chinese fashion. They preserved their hair, and continued this mode of wearing it, after the Tartar conquest, when the vanquished Chinese were compelled to shave their heads in token of subjection. The Chinese consider them as a people totally different from themselves, insomuch that in their maps they even mark off that part of the country occupied by them, as though it were inhabited by a foreign race.

The intercourse of the Chinese with the Meaou-tse was sometimes of a friendly, sometimes of a hostile nature; for, like most barbarians who dwell in the vicinity of a fertile country, the Meaou-tse were addicted to plunder, and would occasionally make incursions into the plains, and carry off such spoils as fell in their way; while at other times they pursued a peaceful traffic with the Chinese, who purchased their forest timber, which abounds on the mountains, but is scarce in the level country, where all the ancient forests have long since been cleared away, in order to afford space for the cultivation of rice and cotton, to feed and clothe the overflowing population. As the Meaou-tse do not allow the Chinese to enter their country, the latter make an agreement for a certain quantity of timber, which is then thrown into the rivers that intersect the hills, and floats down into the plains; the price being paid usually in oxen, cows, and buffaloes, which are received by persons appointed for that purpose when the wood is committed to the stream.

Although the Meaou-tse are not subjects of the Emperor, yet every hostile incursion which they make against the Chinese is regarded by the latter as an act of rebellion. In the year 1770, one of the tribes made several marauding expeditions into the plains, and committed such extensive depredations that a military force was sent to invade their mountain territory, the Emperor being resolved to subjugate or destroy their whole race. The Imperial army entered the hills, which soon presented frightful scenes of bloodshed, for the people fought desperately in defence of their liberty; and so great was their dread of being brought under the authority of the Chinese government, that even the women were seen fighting in the common cause by the sides of their husbands. At length the Chinese General gained possession of the principal town, when the chief took refuge in a strong fortress at some distance; from whence he sent a deputation to the

General, offering to acknowledge himself a vassal of the Emperor, provided he might be permitted to retain his territories and rule over his people as before. But the mighty monarch, bent upon crushing the liberties of the mountaineers, sent forth his Imperial mandate that the whole population should remove from their native hills to some distant part of the empire, where they might be kept in subjection, which they scarcely could be so long as they maintained the strong position they had hitherto occupied. The chief of the unfortunate tribe, to whom this sentence of expatriation was far worse than death, collected his warriors around him, determined to resist to the last; declaring that he would rather perish on his native soil than rule as a sovereign in a foreign land. But a still more melancholy fate than either awaited the brave barbarian; for being at length made prisoner, he was conveyed, with many other captives, to Peking, where he was condemned to suffer an ignominious death, together with nineteen individuals of his family, who were beheaded at the same time with him; while all his people, men, women, and children, were dragged from their homes, and distributed as slaves through various parts of the empire.

This appears to have been an act of ferocity on the part of Kien-long quite inconsistent with that mildness and benevolence of disposition that manifested itself in his conduct towards his own subjects during the whole of his long reign; but he was a prince who could not brook the slightest opposition to his will, and who never spared those who dared to question his authority. Still the Meaou-tse were not conquered; for although that one particular tribe was exterminated, there were others in different parts of the mountains who soon afterwards appeared in great numbers, and are still frequently engaged in hostilities with the Chinese who dwell in their vicinity.

The latter part of the reign of Kien-long is remarkable for the first intercourse ever held between the courts of Great Britain and China; when an embassy was sent by his Britannic Majesty to the Sovereign of the Chinese Empire, under the following circumstances. Soon after his accession to the throne, Kien-long had established a company of merchants, called the Co-hong, consisting of the principals of ten hongs, or mercantile houses, who were invested with the exclusive privilege of transacting all business with Europeans; consequently, the English, as well as others, were prohibited from dealing with any other Chinese traders, and were obliged to purchase their tea, silks, and other commodities of importance, from these hong merchants, who fixed the prices of all goods, either exported or imported, and regulated the terms on which foreigners were to conduct their trade with China. They were responsible to the government for the customs and duties on all goods brought into or sent out of the country; and they were also answerable to the foreign merchants for the value of their cargoes after they were landed; so that any losses sustained on either side were to be made up by them: yet their profits were so enormous, that they grew in general very rich, and lived in great splendour.

In the year 1771, however, the partnership of the co-hong was dissolved, and then there was no restriction to prevent other Chinese merchants from trading with the Europeans; yet the hong merchants contrived to maintain their monopoly, by making handsome presents frequently to the Mandarins at Canton, who, in return, suffered no one to interfere with their trade. This led to very unfair dealings on the part of the hongs, who, to indemnify themselves for the large presents they were obliged to make for the protection of their monopoly, charged most exorbitant prices for their goods, and practised all kinds of imposition on the European traders. The British merchants, who were the greatest sufferers by their extortions, endeavoured to get a memorial presented to the Emperor; but their petitions were never allowed to reach the court, and they had no alternative but to submit to imposition, or to give up the trade altogether. Some of the hongs had contracted very heavy debts with the English, which they refused to pay; and serious disputes arising on that point, as well as on many others, the British government at length determined to send an embassy to the court of Peking, to lay all these complaints before the Emperor and solicit redress. Lord Macartney, late governor of Madras, was appointed ambassador on this extraordinary occasion, and being furnished with many valuable presents for the great Eastern autocrat, set sail from Portsmouth, in September 1792, and arrived at Canton, in June, the following year. The ambassador and his train were received with the highest marks of distinction, for the Emperor had been apprised of their coming, and had sent orders to the governors of the different cities and provinces, where they would stop in their way to Peking, that every attention should be paid to them, and all things provided for their accommodation; a command that was most scrupulously obeyed, so that they were not only well entertained when they went on shore, but ample stores of provisions, with wine, tea, and baskets of porcelain were sent to their ships by the Mandarins of several places where they cast anchor on the voyage from Canton to the capital; for, as the empire is not open to the admission of strangers, except by favour, those who visit it on state affairs are considered and treated as guests of the sovereign, or persons in his service for the time being, and not as travellers, who are free to go where they please, and to have what they choose to order in return for payment; consequently the accommodation they meet with, depends very much on whether the mission is agreeable or not to his Majesty. This fact was fully exemplified by the following circumstances, which occurred at Chusan.

The British ships having to sail round the coast to the gulf of Pechelee, required experienced pilots to conduct them along the shore, with which the English sailors were totally unacquainted. The governor was solicited to furnish proper persons for the purpose, on which he sent into the town of Tinghae, the capital, to order all who had ever performed that voyage to repair immediately to the hall of audience. A great many men presented themselves, and among others, two tradesmen who had been to Tien-sing, a great trading town on the Peiho river, on their own affairs, and these were the individuals selected to perform the office of pilots to the British embassy. It was in vain they desired to be excused, on the plea that their business would be ruined by their absence, and their families reduced to great distress; the governor only replied that the Emperor's commands were explicit, and must be obeyed; the poor men therefore were obliged to go, inconvenient as it was to them. The Peiho river runs from Peking to the gulf of Pechelee, and has many populous towns and villages on its banks.

The number of barges or junks continually passing up and down this busy stream is a proof of the wealth and populousness of the country, many of them being engaged in commerce, while many are government boats employed chiefly in conveying to the capital grain and other produce of the land, collected from the people of the neighbouring provinces, who pay their taxes, or rather rents, chiefly in kind. The junks are strongly built, and curved upwards at each extremity, one end being much higher than the other. The sails are of matting or cotton, made like a fan to fold up with bamboo sticks. Great labour is required in setting them, as the Chinese have no proper machinery for that purpose, so that all their manœuvres in working a ship are performed by actual strength. Most of the sailors, with their families, live constantly on board the junks, having no home on shore, and there are many companies of actors also, who have no other dwelling place than a covered boat on the river.

The government yachts that conveyed the embassy up the Peiho were extremely handsome and commodious; but as the Mandarins had no idea that an ambassador could come for any other purpose than to bring tribute, and do homage to the Emperor on the part of his master, they had caused flags to be attached to the yachts, displaying these words in large Chinese characters, "Ambassadors bearing tribute from the country of England;" nor would they believe that the presents brought for the Emperor were to be viewed in any other light. The viceroy of the province of Pechelee, a venerable old man about eighty years of age, had travelled nearly one hundred miles in obedience to the commands of his Imperial master, to be in readiness at Tien-sing to receive the English ambassador, who went on shore, accompanied by several gentlemen of his suite, to pay a visit to that high functionary.

Tien-sing is the great emporium for the north of China, as Canton is for the south. It extends for several miles along both sides of the river, on the banks of which are many quays and dock-yards, with large public buildings, the chief of which are the custom-houses, warehouses, and temples. The shops are handsome and well furnished, but the private houses are no ornaments to the streets, being built as in all large Chinese cities, within a court, enclosed by a brick wall.

The Chinese are never at a loss for a hall of reception, as they can construct, at a few hours' notice, a temporary building of bamboo, which, being carpeted, and adorned with silken hangings, and other tasteful ornaments, answers all the purpose of a palace for occasions of ceremony. It was in a hall or pavilion of this kind, raised within sight of the river, that the gentlemen of the embassy were received by the Viceroy of Pechelee, with all the attention due to their rank, and the well-bred politeness that generally characterizes the manners of a Chinese gentleman.

It is remarked by Lord Macartney, that men of rank, in China, appear to treat their domestics with a degree of kindness and condescension seldom met with in Europe; and yet it is most probable that the servants alluded to were slaves, for domestic slavery is very common among the Chinese, and does not seem to be a very hard lot. In the higher walks of life, the customs of society were found not to be devoid of the elegance and refine-

ment of the most polished circles of Europe; as for instance, the Viceroy of Pechelee, whose advanced age made it extremely inconvenient to him to go on board the yachts, returned the ambassador's visit by being carried down to the shore in a chair, and sending an officer to the boat to present his visiting ticket; which is exactly the same thing in China, as leaving a card in London. The Chinese visiting tickets however are large sheets of crimson paper, folded like a screen, the name and titles of the visitor being written down the middle.

From Tien-sing, the embassy proceeded to Tong-soo, a city distant from Peking about twelve miles, where the whole party landed; and as it was necessary to remain there a few days, a Budhist temple was prepared for their accommodation, the Bonzes being obliged to remove for the time to another monastery in the neighbourhood, with the exception of one, who was left to watch over the lamps at the shrine. These temples are always used as hotels on all occasions connected with the government; but the priests are not required to furnish the guests with entertainment as well as lodging, their table being supplied, free of cost, by the governor of the city, wherever they may be. The only thing difficult to be procured was milk, which is never used by the Chinese, neither do they make cheese or butter; but when it was understood that the strangers were in the habit of mixing milk with their tea, and that it was not pleasant to them without this ingredient, much trouble was taken to procure two cows, which formed a part of their train during the remainder of their sojourn in China.

The appearance of foreigners in that part of the country was an event of extraordinary interest to the inhabitants, who ran in crowds to every point where they were likely to obtain a sight of them. The whole way from the landing-place at which the yachts were stationed, to the temple where the ambassador and his suite were lodged, was like a fair; for besides the vast concourse of people assembled merely for the purpose of seeing the European strangers, a great number of petty tradesmen, such as pastry-cooks, dealers in spirituous liquors, and persons who keep eating-houses, set up booths for the sale of various refreshments, among which were tea and rice prepared for eating, which may always be had in the streets of every town in China, where a working man may dine very well at any time for less than a penny.

The English travellers went by land from Tong-soo to Peking, some in palanquins, others on horseback, and the rest in small tilted-carts with two wheels, which is the only kind of carriage known in the country, and, having no springs, is a very uneasy conveyance. The road is very broad, bordered on each side by willow trees of immense size, and paved with large flat stones. The pavement is in the middle of the road, instead of at the sides as with us, which is easily accounted for by the rarity of wheel carriages, which are less common, even for long journeys, than sedans and horses.

The party was escorted by a guard of soldiers, whose chief employment the whole way, was to keep off the crowd with their whips, of which they did not scruple to make very free use; but curiosity was stronger than fear, and no sooner did the whips cease to play, than the mob again pressed forward, while every wall, house-top, and tree, was thronged with spectators.

It was now the middle of August, and the Emperor had not yet returned to the capital from his palace at Zhehol in Tartary, one of his numerous residences, where it was customary for the court to reside during the summer months. Zhehol is a small, mean, and crowded city, about fifty miles to the north of the Great Wall, and standing about five thousand feet above the level of the Yellow Sea; consequently it is much cooler than in China, and on that account is pleasant as a summer retreat. The country beyond the wall is wild and mountainous, and bears in its principal features a great resemblance to Savoy and Switzerland. There is a good road for general traffic, all the way from Peking to Zhehol, parallel to which there is a private road, kept in the highest order by the soldiers, expressly for the use of the Emperor and court. Travelling palaces, or Imperial hotels, are erected at certain distances all the way from the capital, as the Emperor never, on any occasion, condescends to take refreshment or pass the night at the house of a subject, although the palaces of some of the viceroys are little inferior to his own.

The palace and gardens of Zhehol are situated in a romantic valley, on the banks of a fine river, overhung by rugged mountains. The park, which is very extensive, presents the most magnificent specimen of the Chinese style to be found in the whole empire; as the objects that are usually crowded together in too small a space to produce a pleasing effect, are at

Zhehol distributed over a vast area, the Imperial park being not less than eighteen miles in circumference, including the palace and gardens of the ladies, which are enclosed within a separate wall. The western side of the park is occupied by thick woods of oak, pine, and chestnut trees, covering the sides of the steep mountains, where a great number of deer are kept for the chase; but the rest is laid out in ornamental pleasure grounds, adorned with as many as fifty handsome pavilions, magnificently furnished, each containing a state room with a throne in it, and some of them having a large banqueting-hall, where entertainments are given on special occasions to the great mandarins of the court.

Among the ornaments of these beautiful pleasure grounds are small transparent lakes filled with gold and silver fishes; and a broad canal, on which are several islands, adorned with pagodas and summer-houses of various forms, sheltered by groves of trees and fragrant shrubs. All Chinese buildings of this description are highly decorated, and generally bear some resemblance to a tent, which is evidently the model from which the architecture of China was originally designed.

Near the palace of Zhehol, on the side of a steep hill, stands the magnificent temple of Poo-ta-la, the largest and richest in the whole empire, covering above twenty acres of ground, and built at an immense cost by Kien-long, who was a worshipper of Fo, for whose service this splendid pile was erected. It consists of one large temple or monastery, with a number of smaller buildings and pagodas attached to it. The great temple is an immense square, eleven stories in height; these stories being distinguished by galleries running round the four sides of the building, containing the apartments of the Lamas, or priests, of whom there were not less than eight hundred at the time of which I am now speaking, so munificently was the establishment endowed by its founder. In the centre of the great temple is the golden chapel, where the priests perform their devotions. It derives its name from its gilded roof; and in the middle is a small space railed off, in which, elevated by steps, stand three altars richly adorned, each supporting a colossal statue, said to be of solid gold, but of course only gilded. The priests, who wear yellow robes, chant their service in a kind of recitative, striking drums at intervals; but there is no congregation, and although people sometimes go into this and other Budhist temples from curiosity to observe the rites, none ever join in them.

It was at Zhehol that the Emperor chose to receive the English embassy; which, until his pleasure was known, was lodged at Yuen-min-Yuen, about seven miles from Peking, where there is another fine palace, with an extensive park and beautiful gardens. The president of the Board of Rites, and several other great mandarins, who visited the ambassador very frequently, were extremely anxious that he should consent to perform the nine prostrations before the Emperor, which he decidedly refused, knowing that if he submitted to this ceremony, it would be construed into an acknowledgment of the supremacy of the Emperor over the King of Great Britain.

The Kotou is, in China, the act of homage exacted from a vassal by his liege lord; and the same degree of importance is attached to it, as, in the feudal ages, belonged to acts of a similar kind in all European countries. It was, therefore, of material consequence that the ambassador should be firm on that point, which was at length given up by the Chinese; and the English party, escorted by a guard of Tartars and several mandarins of rank, set out on their journey to Zhehol, where, for the first time, an English nobleman was presented at the court of the most ancient monarchy in the world, and, as he himself expresses it, beheld "King Solomon in all his glory."

The court of the Tartar princes having already been described, it is needless to speak again of the glittering display with which majesty in China is surrounded; as all that has been said on that subject with respect to Kublai and Shun-che, applies equally to every other monarch of that race.

It is very well known that the custom of Eastern sovereigns has always been to hold levees soon after day-break; and such was the practice of the Emperor Kien-long, although he had arrived at the advanced age of eighty-three. At the first appearance of dawn, on the day appointed for the reception of the embassy, were assembled all the princes of the Imperial family, the principal officers of state, with a great number of mandarins, and several Mogul chiefs, who had come, as was customary, to be present at the celebration of the Emperor's birthday, which was drawing near, and was always kept with much ceremony. The hall of audience, on this occasion, was a magnificent tent in the park, supported by gilded pillars, at the upper end of which was placed a throne under a canopy, raised several steps from the ground, which last was covered with rich carpets, and furnished with embroidered cushions of exquisite workmanship. From the top of the tent hung several of those elegant painted lanterns, so conspicuous among Chinese decorations, and unequalled for beauty in any part of the world. The Emperor's approach was announced by the sound of gongs and trumpets—the never-failing accompaniments of all state processions in China, whether of the monarch or the mandarins. He was carried in a palanquin by sixteen bearers, a number that is not permitted to any other individual in the empire; and was surrounded by the usual appendages of Chinese dignity—flags, standards, fans, and parasols. He was plainly dressed, as suited his venerable years, in a robe of brown silk, with no ornaments about his person except a large pearl in the front of his black velvet cap.

The British ambassador, who was presented by the president of the Board of Rites, was most graciously received, although he did not pay that homage to which the great autocrat was accustomed, but merely bent one knee in presenting his credentials. Some compliments were exchanged, and several presents also; for the etiquette of the court of China requires that every envoy who approaches the throne shall be provided with a suitable offering, for which he usually receives a gift in return; but it should be observed, that the former is accepted as a humble tribute due from an inferior, while the latter is conferred as a mark of extreme condescension. When the ceremonies were ended, a sumptuous breakfast was served up in the tent in the Chinese fashion; and while all present partook of the repast, a band of music played on the lawn, where tumblers and rope-dancers exhibited various feats of agility, and a play was performed on a raised stage.

It is somewhat singular, that a people so fond of theatricals as the Chinese are and have been for many ages should have no regular theatres, nor any actors of celebrity; but in this, as in all other respects, their taste and genius are stationary. They have no scenery, but very fine dresses; and as no women are allowed to appear on the stage, the female characters are always performed by boys.

At Zhehol, the ladies of the court had a theatre for their own especial amusement, where plays were acted every day, and were sometimes attended by the Emperor and his ministers, but more frequently by the ladies only, who, having but little occupation, naturally fly to any frivolous pursuit that may help to beguile the time. One of their greatest enjoyments was to form parties of pleasure on the canal, for which purpose there were yachts always in readiness, fitted up in the most elegant manner, but so contrived that the fair occupants were entirely screened from observation.

There was no Empress at this period, for the princess who had enjoyed that dignity was dead, and Kien-long had not thought proper to raise another to the throne. The laws of China admit of only one lawful wife; but the Tartar sovereigns do not restrict themselves to this rule, although they generally give to one a rank above the rest, and she alone is called Empress, while the others have the title of queen. There were eight queens at this time, two of the first and six of the second rank; and these had each a certain number of ladies in her train, making altogether upwards of one hundred females belonging to the court. As long as the Emperor lives they probably lead pleasant lives, but their subsequent lot is not very enviable; as they are then removed to a building near the palace which may be termed a nunnery, since they are obliged by the customs of the country, to pass the remainder of their lives within its walls, in utter seclusion.

The English visitors staid a week at Zhehol, and were present at the anniversary of the Emperor's birthday, which is a holiday throughout the empire. The ceremonies of the court consisted principally in the grand Birthday Ode, sung in chorus by voices innumerable, accompanied by deep-toned bells and solemn music. The Emperor was present, but not visible, being seated behind a screen in a large hall, where all the courtiers were assembled in their state-dresses to pay the customary homage, which was done by falling prostrate at the conclusion of every stanza of the Ode, which has been thus translated, "Bow down your heads, all ye dwellers on the earth; bow down your heads before the great Kien-long!" an exhortation that was literally obeyed.

The two or three days that succeed the birthday are entirely devoted to festivities, in which all classes participate; the rich in visiting or receiving their friends with feasting, the poor in such enjoyments as their station enables them to obtain.

As soon as the gaieties were over, it was intimated to the British ambassador, that it would be proper to take his leave of Zhehol, and return without delay to Canton, whither the Emperor's answer on the subject of the embassy would be forwarded. It was not left to themselves to regulate the mode or the route by which they should return, neither were they allowed to travel through the country without an escort of mandarins, who, under pretence of polite attention, directed all their movements, and effectually prevented them from gaining more information than was deemed desirable by the jealous and watchful government.

Instead of returning by sea as they came, the strangers passed by the Imperial canal and rivers, through the provinces of Shan-tong, Keang-nan, Che-keang, Keang-se, and Kwang-tung or Canton, a journey that occupied about ten weeks.

The highly cultivated state of the country, the number, wealth, and greatness of its cities, its abundant resources, and myriads of inhabitants, were subjects of wonder and admiration to our travellers, whose representations on their return home drew the attention of the English more particularly towards this vast empire, on which till then scarcely a thought had been bestowed. The institutions, the manners, and the history of the Chinese became subjects of inquiry; and although but little knowledge, comparatively speaking, has yet been gained on any one of these interesting points, we may now reasonably indulge the hope that a few years will clear away much of the obscurity.

The Emperor wrote a very friendly letter to our king, George the Third, but did not accede to the request that he would allow the subjects of the latter to trade to Ning-po, Amoy, and other maritime cities besides Canton, as they used to do before they were restricted to that one port by an edict of Kien-long in 1755. The mission however was in some degree successful, as the Viceroy of Canton, who had encouraged the frauds practised on British merchants, was removed from his office; while the governor appointed in his room received peremptory orders to put a stop to the grievances complained of, so that for a short time the trade was conducted on a fairer footing, when the abdication and subsequent death of Kien-long afforded an opportunity for the renewal of all the former oppressions.

It was in the next year but one following that of Earl Macartney's embassy, that the aged Emperor of China completed the sixtieth year of his felicitous reign, and in accordance with the vow he had made at its commencement, prepared to resign the throne he had filled with so much ability. He had had twenty-one sons, of whom only four were then living; but he had not yet nominated either of them as his successor, an omission which had for some time been a source of considerable anxiety to many of the chief officers of government, who had some reason to fear that he intended to set aside the claims of his own sons, in favour of a young man on whom he had bestowed one of his daughters in marriage. The individual in question was the son of the chief minister, or Kolau, an officer possessing much the same degree of rank and influence in China, as in former times was held by the grand viziers at the court of the Arabian Caliphs.

The Kolau, a man of great talent, whose name was Cho-chang-tung, had risen from the station of a private soldier to the eminent position he then occupied in the state; and had for many years enjoyed the uninterrupted favour and confidence of his sovereign, who gave a signal proof of his high regard for the minister by admitting him to the claims of relationship. The union of Cho-chang-tung's son with one of the princesses spread the utmost alarm through the court, where it was fully expected that the new son-in-law would be named as the future sovereign of China. The excitement produced by this belief was so great, that a certain mandarin, high in office, taking upon himself the perilous task of mentor, ventured to write to the Emperor on the subject, entreating him to select without delay one of his own sons as successor to the throne he was about to vacate. In all probability, the temerity of the mandarin was founded on the ancient laws; which enjoin the ministers to admonish the prince when they find him acting contrary to the interests of the people: but although the sage counsellors of olden times exercised this privilege with impunity, it seems to be a dangerous experiment in modern ages; for the stern monarch, incensed at the presumption of the imprudent meddler, replied to the letter by giving orders that the writer should be instantly beheaded—a sentence that did not occasion the least surprise, notwithstanding its undue severity. The unfortunate mandarin had needlessly exposed himself to this danger, since it does not appear that the Emperor ever entertained a thought of placing his son-in-law on the throne. Of his own four surviving sons, the youngest was his favourite; and to that prince, who assumed the name of Kea-king, he determined to resign his empire. The sixtieth anniversary of his accession was celebrated by a grand jubilee throughout China, when many acts of munificence were performed by the Emperor; and among others, he desired that all the old men who had passed the age of seventy should be invited to a feast, prepared for them at his expense in every district over the whole country.

The chosen successor, Kea-king, ascended the throne in 1795; and Kien-long died about three years afterwards, at the advanced age of eighty-eight. His character is very differently represented by different Chinese writers; some painting him as another Nero, while others speak in the highest terms of his benevolence and the mildness of his administration. Both statements are perhaps equally foreign to the truth; for although there is no reason to believe that Kien-long was habitually a tyrant, yet it is hardly to be supposed that a sovereign so entirely despotic should have ruled over a numerous people for the space of sixty years without having been guilty of some acts of cruelty and oppression. He was highly distinguished as a patron of literature, to which he was himself a valuable contributor, being a poet of no ordinary talent. He was indefatigable in his attention to business; and his extensive charities in seasons of public distress do honour to his name, and give him a true right to that title which it is the aim of every ruler of China to attain, that of—The Father of his People.

Kea-king.

The late Emperor had chosen his fourth son to succeed him, because he entertained a very high opinion of his disposition and talents for government; but the conduct of the new monarch soon proved that both his virtues and abilities had been very much overrated by the partiality of his fond father; for, as soon as he was his own master, he began to indulge in pleasures that would have been extremely unbecoming in a prince of less pretensions, but were more especially so in the supreme head of the Celestial Empire, who styles himself the Son of Heaven and the August Ruler.

Kea-king seems to have imbibed a great distaste for the restraints and etiquette of the Chinese court, which are no doubt excessively fatiguing, as every word and movement of the Emperor ought to be in accordance with that dignified and even sacred character with which he is invested, and which most of the Imperial rulers of China have made it their study to maintain. The Mantchow Emperors had all been eminently distinguished by the stately air and grave deportment naturally looked for in those who are venerated as beings partaking of a superior nature; but Kea-king was utterly destitute of these lofty attributes, and not only indulged in an immoderate love of wine, but selected his favourite associates from amongst the actors, who, in China, are considered the very lowest class of the community. It is even said that, when heated with wine, he sometimes degraded himself so far as to take a part in the dramatic performances of his chosen companions. The ministers openly remonstrated with him

respecting these disgraceful propensities, but their admonitions were in vain; and one of them, Soong-tajin, a man of very high talent, who was exceedingly useful to the state, was banished for presuming to speak freely on the subject of his faults. The people soon became dissatisfied with a monarch whom they could not respect, and insurrections broke out in many parts of the country; incited in some cases by the elder princes, who felt themselves aggrieved at the preference that had been given by their father to their younger brother.

Kea-king was as unpopular among the Tartars as among the Chinese; for while the latter were shocked at his indifference to ancient customs, the former were discontented at his neglect of the annual hunting excursions, esteemed as the grand business of life by all the Tartar soldiers, as well as by the tributary nations dwelling beyond the Wall, and which had never been omitted by his three predecessors. One of the consequences resulting from this state of affairs was the formation of secret associations, called Triad Societies, which are known still to exist to a great extent—their object being to overthrow the present government, and restore the native princes to the throne. The Triads, who may be called revolutionists, knew each other by secret signs like the Freemasons; and although it may appear extraordinary that a people so entirely under 'espionnage' as the Chinese, should be able to keep up such an institution, it is confidently asserted that the Triads form, at this moment, a considerable party in China, and in that case a revolution is not a very improbable event.

In consequence of the disturbed state of the empire, numerous bands of robbers infested the interior of the country, while the pirates of the Ladrone Islands renewed their depredations on the coast. Among these was a noted Corsair named Ching-yih, who was no less renowned and feared than the famous Koshinga had been in the time of the first Emperor of the Mantchow race. This formidable chief was in the habit of levying contributions on all the merchant vessels that appeared in the Chinese seas; he plundered the villages on the coast, and did not hesitate to engage in battle with the Imperial fleet. It was strongly suspected that he received secret assistance from many Chinese merchants of Amoy and Canton, who were disaffected towards the reigning family; but whether this were true or not, he had a very powerful force at his command, and committed the most horrible barbarities with impunity.

Ching-yih was accidentally drowned, but his death did not put a stop to the lawless practices of his people; for his widow, who might have been esteemed as a great heroine in a worthier cause, took the command of the fleet, headed the rovers in all their piratical expeditions, and actually fought in several engagements with the government forces. These Amazonian qualities were combined with very extraordinary talents as a ruler; for the chieftainess drew up a regular code of laws for the government of her people, by which they were bound to act equitably towards each other; and thus order was preserved among them. For some time, this female corsair maintained the sovereignty of the Chinese seas; insomuch that no merchant ships could navigate them in safety without a pass from her, which she granted on payment of a certain toll, and this pass protected them from any pirate vessels they might encounter on their passage. At length, disputes arose among the pirate captains; and the chieftainess, beginning to find her position a difficult one to maintain, concluded a regular treaty of peace with the governor of Canton, who was rewarded by government with a peacock's feather, the usual mark of distinction bestowed on a military or naval commander for any eminent service rendered to the state. The lady, who had assumed so unfeminine a character, withdrew from the conspicuous situation in which she had placed herself, to live in retirement; while most of the pirates, being thus left without a leader, made submission, and were received into the service of the government.

In the meantime, the whole country was in a very unsettled state. The province of Pechelee was overrun with armed bands, composed partly of those who had become robbers by profession, and partly of revolutionists, who joined with the banditti as a means of strengthening their force. All were equally terrible to the peaceable inhabitants, who were plundered with impunity, the robbers coming in such numbers as to intimidate the magistrates, some of whom were possibly more inclined to encourage than to oppose them.

In the year 1813, the palace at Peking was suddenly attacked by a numerous body of armed men, who forced the gates, and rushed into the great hall, with the intention of seizing the Emperor, and obliging him to abdicate the throne. A similar attempt had been made ten years previously, since which time, Kea-king had taken care to have a strong body guard in constant attendance; and besides this precaution, a double guard was posted at every gate; therefore, it is supposed the conspirators must have had confederates within the palace, who facilitated their entrance; otherwise there must have been a desperate struggle with the soldiers, which does not appear to have been the case. A terrible scene of confusion ensued. The princes and attendant officers surrounding their sovereign made a gallant defence; and the present Emperor, Taou-kwang, had the good fortune to save his father's life, by shooting two of the insurgents who were in the act of rushing upon the Emperor.

Much blood was shed before the palace was cleared of the assailants, who were, however, at length dispersed, and the insurrection was eventually subdued. No more disturbances of any importance happened during the reign of Kea-king, who named as his successor the young prince, whose timely aid had preserved his life.

About three years after this rebellion, another embassy was sent by the British government to the court of Peking, to complain anew of the manner in which the trade with England was conducted at Canton. The good effect produced by the interference of Kien-long had been but temporary, for his successor, being as narrow-minded as he was weak and vicious, hated all Europeans, and suffered the Chinese merchants to impose upon them in the most unscrupulous manner. Lord Amherst, the ambassador on this occasion, proceeded to Peking by the same route that Lord Macartney had previously taken; but his reception at the various places he stopped at on the journey, was very different from that given to the former ambassador; nor did he meet with similar attention with regard to accommodation and entertainment, all which clearly indicated the unfavourable disposition of the sovereign respecting the object of the mission. In short, on the arrival of the embassy at Peking, the old dispute relative to the Ko-tou was revived, and the conduct of the ambassador was so entirely misrepresented to the Emperor, that no audience was granted; and thus the English not only failed in obtaining a redress of grievances, but were disappointed of seeing the Imperial court of the Chinese empire.

One grand object of this unsuccessful Embassy had been, as before, to solicit a restoration of the privilege formerly enjoyed by British merchants,

Drawn by B. Clayton from a Painting by W. Alexander Esq. On Stone by J. W. Giles.

APPROACH OF THE EMPEROR OF CHINA, TO RECEIVE THE BRITISH AMBASSADOR.

London, Dean & Co. Threadneedle Street.

Drawn by [illegible] from a Painting by [illegible]

On Stone by J. W. Giles.

THE PRESENT EMPEROR OF CHINA WHEN A YOUNG MAN SAVING HIS FATHER'S LIFE DURING AN INSURRECTION.

page 122

London Dean & Co. Threadneedle Street

of trading to other ports besides that of Canton, a privilege now obtained by other means, and not likely to be lost again. All European trade, as already stated, had been restricted to the single port of Canton, by an edict of Kien-long in the year 1755, when it was ordered that foreign vessels should only go thither at a certain season of the year, and not remain there longer than a given time, at the expiration of which they were either to depart entirely, or withdraw to Macao; and this arbitrary decree had never been revoked. In consequence of the ports being thus closed against them, the British merchants were obliged to pay for the transport of tea from an immense distance, by which its price was considerably increased, for between Canton and the principal tea districts there were ranges of lofty mountains to be crossed, and shallow rivers to be navigated, which made the carriage of goods a difficult, expensive, and tedious process, the more especially as chests of tea, or any other large or heavy packages, are not conveyed over land in wagons or by horses, but are slung on bamboo poles, and carried by men, however long the distance may be. The boats on the canals and many of the rivers, have to be tracked, or drawn along

by ropes, and this labour also, which in most countries is done by horses, is in China performed by men; so that, either on land or water, the number of labourers employed in the transit of merchandize is immense. The tracking of the government barges is a sort of tax on the people, who are usually pressed into this service by order of the magistrates, on whom the duty devolves of seeing that each district furnishes a certain number of men for that purpose, even the wealthiest farmers not being exempt, except on finding substitutes, whom they must pay.

The principal tea districts are in the provinces of Fokien, Keang-se, and Chekeang; the first and second of which are adjacent to Canton, stretching far to the north-east; and Chekeang is the next maritime province to the north of Fokien. Each of these provinces is of immense extent, that of Chekeang alone being nearly one-fourth of the size of France, and containing a population more than equal to that of Great Britain and Ireland. The journey, from one province to another, is therefore no trifling matter, and it was calculated that the difference in the expense of bringing tea to Canton for exportation, or taking it to the eastern ports nearest to the districts where it is chiefly grown, amounted annually to two hundred thousand pounds sterling, being about twenty-five shillings on every pecul weight, which is one hundred and thirty-three pounds. The effect of the prohibitory laws on the price of tea is therefore obvious, and all lovers of that pleasant beverage may well rejoice at the removal of these difficulties by the event of the late war, which has opened the desired ports to British vessels, so that teas will be henceforward shipped at more convenient stations.

China, properly so called, is divided into eighteen provinces, some of them even larger than those above-mentioned; therefore it may easily be imagined how impossible it is for the Emperor to take cognizance of the whole of his vast dominions. The actual administration is, in fact, completely in the hands of the Viceroys, to whom a great share of power is necessarily given, and who exercise in their respective spheres the same absolute authority that the Emperor does over the whole. Each Viceroy maintains a splendid court, and, when he appears abroad, is attended by a numerous retinue, bearing the symbols of his high office, among which are standards emblazoned with the golden dragon, carried before none but the greatest dignitaries. He is borne in a gilded chair, and always followed

by the public executioners, some carrying chains, others that universal instrument of justice, the bamboo, which is very unceremoniously applied on the spot to any unlucky wight who may chance to be detected in a misdemeanour; consequently, the approach of the high functionary never fails to inspire a degree of awe, which is manifested by the respectful haste with which the people make way for the procession, ranging themselves close to the wall, where they stand perfectly still and motionless till the whole cavalcade has passed. The Viceroys are entrusted with despotic authority; but they must be careful how they use it, as they are always liable to the visits of the Imperial Commissioners, who frequently arrive from the capital without giving notice of their approach, for the purpose of seeing whether all is as it should be; and if they find any thing wrong, it is immediately reported at the court, when the offender is visited with a prompt, and often a severe punishment. A single word from the Emperor is sufficient at any time to deprive the first grandee in the land of his rank, his property, or even his life; nor is it a very uncommon case for a mandarin of the highest order to enter the palace with all the pomp of a petty sovereign, and to come forth, within one short hour, loaded with chains, and stripped of every ensign of his late dignity. The governor of a province or city is particularly liable to such a reverse, from the nature of the laws, which hold him responsible for all those public calamities which are attributed to accident in other countries; as, for instance, the overflowing of rivers, the scarcity of crops in a favourable season, or the destruction of property by fire; all evils supposed to arise from want of vigilance on the part of the chief magistrates, who are required to see that all subordinate officers are attentive to their several duties. Every one holding an official situation is answerable for the conduct of those below him, and if the inferiors are negligent in their respective departments, the superiors are liable to punishment. Thus, if the country is inundated by the sudden rising of a river, the viceroy is considered in fault for not having attended diligently to the repairing of the embankments; if the crops are not so abundant as they ought to be in any particular province, the failure is attributed to the governor, in not having seen that the husbandmen were more intelligent or industrious; and, again, should lives or property fall a sacrifice to fire, it is presumed that they might have been saved by more active measures; consequently, the magistrates are blamed for not keeping a more efficient police, and the viceroys or governors are blamed for appointing such careless magistrates. The most usual punishment for mal-administration is degradation to a lower rank, according to the nature and magnitude of the offence. If the fault be a very serious one, the offender, if of the highest degree, is perhaps degraded to the lowest, that is, from the first to the ninth class of mandarins; but if it be only a trivial error, he is lowered one, two, or three degrees, and in most cases the punishment is only for a certain time, at the expiration of which, he is restored to his rank and office, and resumes his former place in society, as though nothing had happened, for a temporary disgrace of that kind leaves no stigma on the character of the individual.

Crimes that are considered in the light of treason are visited with a heavier penalty. Banishment, or death, is the doom of him who has in aught neglected or disobeyed the commands of the Emperor, and, in either case, the whole family of the culprit share his fate, although they may be wholly innocent of any participation in his crime. The enactment of this unjust law was no doubt originally intended to deter people from ill-advising their relatives, or encouraging them in any act contrary to the interests of the government, and even to make them watchful and anxious for the good conduct of each other.

In the year 1819, the sixtieth birth-day of the Emperor Kea-king was celebrated by a great jubilee throughout the empire, when the ancient customs were observed, of remitting all arrears of land tax, of granting a general pardon to criminals, and of admitting double the ordinary number of candidates for literary honours to the public examinations for that year. As these examinations were first instituted, and are still held, for the purpose of selecting the fittest persons to fill all offices of state, without regard to rank or fortune, they are conducted with the utmost impartiality, no advantage being gained through the influence of wealth or patronage. A strict adherence to this principle is one of the chief causes of the prevalence of learning in China, where a man has no occasion to fear that, because he is without either money or powerful friends to aid him, his talents will avail him nothing. One of the favourite maxims of the Chinese is, "By learning, the sons of the poor become great; without learning, the sons of the great are mingled with the common people." The beneficial influence of this maxim is observable in the village schools, which are generally well attended, since it is natural for every father to hope that one of his children at least may distinguish himself by a superior capacity, and thus make his own fortune, as well as that of his family; for as parents are frequently degraded in consequence of the misconduct of a son, so they are often honoured and rewarded on account of his virtues; so that every inducement is held out to the people by their rulers to pay strict attention to the conduct, as well as to the education of their children.

It is somewhat remarkable that, in a country where the system of instruction is entirely regulated by the laws, and forms so material a part of the constitution, there should be no free schools supported by the government, nor any establishments for education founded by the munificence of those who, in every age, have acquired fame and riches by their literary attainments. The master of a district school is paid at the rate of about ten shillings a-year for each boy; yet even this small sum cannot very easily be spared by a labouring man, whose wages are not more than fourpence a day; so that many families of the poorer classes send only one son to school, selecting, of course, him who shows the most promising genius. The boys are incited to industry and good behaviour by the hope of prizes, which are distributed at stated periods, and consist of pencils, Indian ink, paper, and little pallettes for grinding the ink, which are all much prized by the Chinese, who call them "the four precious materials," and teach the children to keep them in very neat order. In most of the country villages, and in all large cities, there are evening schools for boys who are obliged to work in the day-time; for the children of the poor are inured to labour from a very tender age, so that little fellows of five or six years of age may be seen trudging along the roads, with a stick across their shoulders, carrying loads; and they are set to work in the fields almost as soon as they can walk. It is the usual practice, now, for persons of rank and wealth to engage private tutors for their children; but whether the latter are educated at home or at a public school, they must undergo the regular examinations before they are eligible to office, nor are they taught in any way differently from the boys at the village seminaries.

Many years of laborious application to study are required to fit a youth for becoming a candidate for literary distinction; and to us it would seem a subject of regret that so much time should be devoted to the acquirement of such unprofitable lore as that which constitutes the limited knowledge of a Chinese scholar. Five or six years are entirely spent in committing to memory the works of the ancient sages, particularly the five canonical books, of which Confucius was either the author or the compiler; and thus a mandarin must know by heart all the laws, rules, and maxims by which the empire has been regulated from time immemorial. Six years more are devoted by the unwearied student to the making himself master of the art of composition, to which end, he studies innumerable set phrases, and apt similes; so that all the learned Chinese write in the same figurative style, and use the same metaphors.

The district examinations take place twice in three years, when those young men who are looking for preferment and are qualified for trial, assemble at the public hall, before a council of the literati, who are to judge of their merits, when each candidate is furnished by the president with a theme, on which he has to write an essay, and an ode, to test his fitness for a further trial. The best of these compositions being selected, the authors are sent to the chief literary mandarin of the department in which their district is situated, who subjects them to a much more rigorous examination than the former one, which ends by giving certificates to a certain number, who thus gain what is called "a name in the village," while the rest either give up the pursuit, or wait for the next opportunity of making another trial. The chosen few have then to appear before a still higher tribunal, which is yet stricter than the last. The hall where this trial takes place is provided with a great number of small apartments, so that each candidate may be shut up alone, and the judges thus assured that their performances are entirely their own. They are even searched on entering these little cells, to see that they have neither books nor papers about them, and this being ascertained, all are supplied with writing materials and themes to try his skill in composition, both in prose and verse. To guard against any partiality being shown by the president and members of the board, these papers are laid before them, unsigned, and they select the best, without knowing who are the authors. The fortunate individuals whose pieces are thus approved, then receive the first degree, which is equivalent to that of our Bachelor of Arts; but the numbers are so considerably diminished at each fresh trial, that, on an average, it is reckoned that not more than ten arrive at this degree, out of every thousand who present themselves, in the first instance, at the hall of the district; but as the districts are very numerous, these tens amount to many hundreds in every province.

A graduate of the first degree wears a blue gown with a black border, and has a silver bird on the top of his cap. The second degree is that of Keu jin, which is translated "elevated men," a rank equal to that of Master of Arts at our universities. All those who have attained the first step are qualified to try for the second, but the task is a much harder one, and as the number to be chosen is very small in proportion to that of the can-

didates, being not much more than one out of every hundred and forty, the emulation and excitement are of course very great. This trial takes place only once in three years, in all the provincial capitals, before a board composed of an Imperial Chancellor, and the great mandarins of the province. On this occasion, as before, the competitors write their essays in separate cells, which are guarded by soldiers, to prevent the possibility of communication with any one outside. They have to pass through three ordeals, with an interval of two days between each. On the first day, two or three thousand pieces are, perhaps, sent in for inspection to the judges, who are so strict, that, if one word of the composition be incorrectly written, it is thrown aside, and the mark with which it is signed, for no names appear, is put up at the gate of the hall; which spares all the mortification of a public rejection, as no one knows the signature but the candidate himself, who, on recognising his own mark, returns quietly home; so that on the second day there are not, perhaps, one quarter of the original number; and on the third, there are fewer still. At length, the names of the successful candidates are declared; on which hand-bills notifying the same are printed and posted up in all directions; their parents and nearest relatives are sent for, to share in the honours that are bestowed on them; they are invited to the houses of the great, and overwhelmed with presents and congratulations. The blue dress is exchanged for a brown gown with a blue border, and the silver bird superseded by a golden or gilt one. The happy scholar is now on the high road to wealth and fame; he is qualified for any office, and if his conduct and ability are such as to entitle him to advancement, he is sure to rise.

Such are the means by which nobility is acquired in China; and, before the reign of Yong-tching, they were the only means; but in the reign of that prince, and since his time, rich merchants and others, who have not gone through the ordeal above described, have been allowed to purchase rank, and have thus become mandarins without possessing the necessary qualifications; but this innovation causes much dissatisfaction, and is not carried to any great extent. There are still two degrees above those already mentioned, to which all who have taken the second degree are privileged to aspire. Once in three years, those who are ambitious of rising another step, repair to Peking for the examination by the Doctors of the Han-lin college, who elect three hundred out of about ten thousand, which is the average number of candidates for the honour of a rank somewhat similar to that which among us is called Doctor of Laws. The three hundred elected to this dignity are again examined in the presence of the Emperor, and a few of them chosen to fill up the vacancies that have occurred in the Han-lin college, from which the ministers and other high officers of state are usually appointed. The attainment of this grade is the grand object of every one who enters upon a literary career in China; a grade equally open to all, yet reached only by a few.

When the last election is decided, three of the new members, whose names stood highest on the list, are paraded round the city for three days, with flags flying, drums beating, and all the usual pompous appendages of a Chinese procession.

The number of civil officers in China amounts to about fourteen thousand, all of whom are paid by the government. Every province has its Viceroy, every city its governor, every village its ruling mandarin; and each of these is assisted by a council of inferior magistrates, and has a number of officers in various departments subordinate to him.

The mandarin rulers, whatever may be their rank, are only elected for three years, at the expiration of which they are appointed to the government of some other place. It was formerly a custom, which is probably still observed, that when a good magistrate of a village or district had fulfilled his term of office, the people should testify their respect and gratitude by sending a deputation to invest him with a robe of many colours, which was proudly preserved in his family, as a memorial of his virtues; and on such an occasion, when the time for his departure had arrived, the villagers would set up lighted sticks of incense for some distance along the road by which he was to pass, and kneel down by the way side to receive his farewell greeting.

The Emperor Kea-king died in the year 1820, and was succeeded by his second son, Taou-kwang, the present Emperor, whose reign will in all probability prove the most eventful era that has yet occurred in the history of China; but ere we enter on the subject of those interesting occurrences that have given a new aspect to the affairs of the Celestial Empire, let us turn our attention more particularly towards the general state of Chinese society.

MANNERS AND CUSTOMS, AND GENERAL CONDITION OF THE CHINESE.

THE habits of social life in China, as far as they are yet known to us, are as peculiar to the inhabitants of that country, as their political institutions, their religion, or their literature; and, although not destitute of refinement, present a striking contrast to those of any other existing nation. In the many allusions that have already been made in the preceding pages, to the manners and customs of this singular people, it must have appeared that it is not the difference between civilisation and barbarism that distinguishes the Chinese of the present age from their contemporaries, but it is the more remarkable dissimilarity between ancient and modern civilisation, which marks them as a nation belonging to other times.

To speak of the Chinese as a rude or uninformed race, would be quite as erroneous as to style them a highly-civilised people, a term that can only be applied with propriety to those who are enlightened by modern science, which in China has hitherto made no progress. The refinement of the Chinese consists in the elegance and luxury with which the higher and richer classes are surrounded in their own houses, and that strict attention to the forms of good breeding which prevails generally through all the grades of private life. Politeness is an indispensable accomplishment, and the rules of etiquette are studied in all the schools of China, as regularly as the Latin grammar in those of England. A knowledge of the forms and ceremonies to be observed both at home and abroad, in the drawing room of a friend, as well as at the court of the Emperor, is essential to every one who studies with a view of taking degrees, as he knows not to what rank he may be called, and ought to be prepared to conduct himself with propriety in different grades of life, from the station of the petty mandarin of an obscure village, to that of the chief Kolau or minister of state. It must be understood, that to conduct himself with propriety does not altogether refer to his integrity in office, or his moral character, to both of which, however, his most careful attention is requisite; but he must know how many bows to make to his visitors; what compliments to address to them, according to their rank; whether, at their departure, he should attend them as far as the door, or only so many paces towards it; and other minute observances, too numerous to mention, must be studied and practised. These trivial ceremonies impart a dulness and formality to Chinese society, which are found excessively tedious by most Europeans, whose easy unstudied manners would be thought quite barbarous among the well bred of the celestial empire. It is possible, indeed, that more freedom may exist between intimate friends than we are aware of, since very few Europeans have had opportunities of seeing much of the in-door life beyond the little that can be observed in a mere visit of ceremony, which is always received in the same formal manner; so that we have yet much to learn respecting the private domestic habits of a Chinese family.

The houses of the wealthy are built, like those of the Egyptians, within a court, surrounded by a wall; consequently, they are not visible to the passers by; but those of government officers are always known by two red poles which are set up before the gate. The handsomest dwellings are those which consist of a number of separate buildings, or ranges of apartments, all on the ground floor. The principal entrance is threefold, namely, by a large folding-door in the centre, and a smaller one on each side, at which hang two handsome lanterns, inscribed with the name and titles of the master of the house. This entrance leads to the saloon, where visitors are received, which is usually the first of a suite that may be called the state apartments, since they are chiefly used for the reception and entertainment of distinguished guests. They are elegantly and commodiously furnished, for the Chinese are not deficient in taste, nor do they spare expense in the interior decorations of their houses, which are often fitted up in a very costly style. The walls of the best rooms are generally adorned in different parts with scrolls of white silk or satin hanging from the ceiling to the floor, on which are imprinted, in large characters, maxims and moral sentences extracted from the works of the ancient sages, which are considered far more ornamental than the finest paintings. Many of these sentences bear a close resemblance to the Proverbs of Solomon. Their chairs, which, it may be remarked, are articles of furniture not used by the natives of other parts of Asia, are rather clumsy and heavy in appearance, but they are made of a very beautiful wood, which grows in China, and is not unlike rosewood. They are all made with arms, and sometimes are furnished with silk or satin cushions, and hangings for the back, embroidered by the ladies of the family, who devote a great portion of their time to needlework. Japanned cabinets and tables, with a profusion of porcelain jars and other ornaments, are always seen in a Chinese drawing-room; but none of these are so striking or so characteristic as the lanterns, suspended by silken cords from the ceiling, and ornamented with a variety of elegant designs.

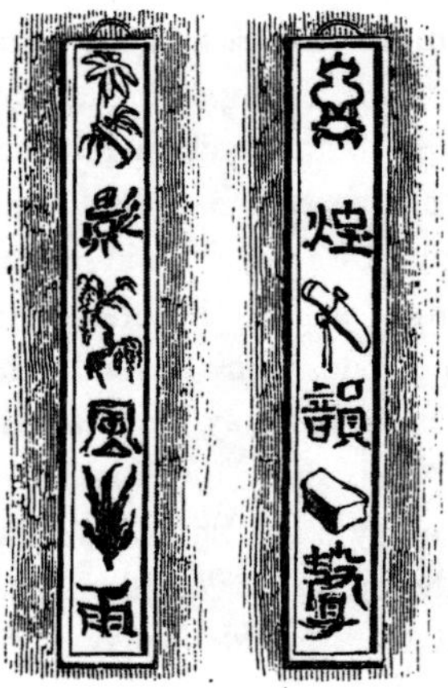

In any civilized part of the world we may find Indian cabinets and porcelain vases; but the lanterns are exclusively Chinese, and are very showy specimens of the national taste and ingenuity. They are made in every form that fancy can invent, and of all sizes, from the small ones carried by pedestrians, at night, to those that illumine the halls of the great, the latter being sometimes eight or ten feet in height, and three feet in diameter. The most costly are composed of transparent silk, adorned with landscapes, birds, flowers, and fanciful devices, in colours of dazzling brightness; the frame work being richly carved and gilt, and the cords and tassels, by which they are suspended, made of silk and gold thread. The possession of fine lanterns is a sort of passion among the Chinese, many of whom spend considerable sums in the gratification of this fancy.

The Feast of Lanterns, which takes place almost immediately after the celebration of the new year, is a festival of ancient date among the Chinese, and is the occasion of a most brilliant and beautiful spectacle. On the fifteenth day of the first moon, every city, village, and hamlet, throughout the country is splendidly illuminated with an infinite variety of these beautiful lanterns, which are hung up at every house, from the palace of the viceroy to the hut of the humble fisherman, the general feeling being a desire on the part of each to outshine his neighbour. The tradition respecting this festival is, that the wife of an Emperor of one of the early dynasties being extravagant and fond of pleasure, chose to have the palace illuminated every night with a thousand lights, which might supply the place of the sun, and keep up a perpetual day within her abode. This legend, which refers to a period antecedent to the era of Confucius, may be received as an evidence that the Feast of Lanterns was celebrated in China in very ancient times; but its real origin, like that of many other Chinese customs, is lost in obscurity, nor is it likely ever to be discovered. The illumination is continued for three nights, and is attended by a grand display of fireworks, in which the Chinese excel all other nations. Many of the lanterns, made purposely for these occasions, exhibit moving figures, such as huntsmen on horseback, galloping round; ships sailing, troops of soldiers marching, or people dancing, all kept in motion by some ingenious contrivance not visible to the beholder. These are seen only at the houses of the rich mandarins, and, of course, attract vast crowds of spectators. The chief part of the many thousands of lanterns manufactured expressly for this festival are of horn, or a very strong transparent paper, made in the Corea, which is used in most parts of China instead of window glass; but even the commonest of them are elegant in shape, and gaily decorated; so that, altogether, the effect of the illumination must be very brilliant. Even the poor fishermen who dwell on the sea shore, and those who live in boats on the rivers, will bestow as much as they can possibly spare of their hard earnings for the purchase of a fine lantern to exhibit on this festive occasion, so that even the waters are illumined; and as the towns and villages are neither few nor far between, the spectator placed upon any eminence beholds, on all sides, an illuminated panorama of the country. During the festival, the gates of the cities are left open at night, that the country people may enjoy the pleasure of seeing the illuminations.

All the cities of China are walled round, and some of them are described as bearing a great resemblance to the old feudal towns of Europe, except that, in general, they are of wider extent. Peking is supposed to be about twenty-five miles in circumference. It is divided into two distinct parts, the northern, or Tartar city; and the southern, or Chinese city. The former, which is inhabited chiefly by Tartars, is surrounded by a wall, with nine gates, always guarded by soldiers, and contains the Imperial palace, which, with its magnificent gardens, stands in the centre, within a space of about five miles in circumference, enclosed by another wall, and called the Forbidden City, as no one may enter it but privileged persons. The Tartar city contains the residences of all the grandees of the court, the halls of the Six Tribunals, the Han-lin college, several superb temples, a Mohammedan mosque, and many other public buildings. The principal streets are very long and wide, and contain numerous shops, as well as private houses, but they are not paved, which is a great inconvenience in wet weather; neither are they lighted at night; but as no one is allowed to be abroad after dark, unless on some very particular occasion, it is not of much importance that they should be so, particularly as any one who is obliged to go out, must carry a lantern with him. Large spaces of ground in this part of Peking are occupied by ornamental gardens belonging to the rich mandarins, and is adorned with a fine lake, a mile and a half in length, and more than a quarter of a mile in breadth, crossed by a bridge of nine arches, constructed entirely of white marble. The banks of this lake are bordered with trees, among which, the drooping willow bends its graceful branches, and in the midst of this expanse of water, is an islet, adorned with a temple and an elegant pagoda, the never-failing ornaments of Chinese scenery. Peking is therefore, by no means devoid of natural beauties; and even the old, or Chinese town, which is the trading part of the capital, contains large gardens and fields, where vegetables are grown for the daily supply of the markets, and also many nursery grounds, where flowers are cultivated expressly for the adornment of the ladies of Peking, who wear them in their hair. This simple and elegant mode of decorating the hair is generally adopted in all parts of China, and when natural flowers are not to be obtained, artificial ones are substituted; but a female head is seldom seen without the one or the other, which, among the higher classes, are mixed with golden bodkins, jewels, and other ornaments.

The temples in this part of the capital are very magnificent, especially those dedicated to Heaven and Earth, the former standing in the centre of a spacious enclosure, elevated by three stages, each ascended by a flight of marble steps, and surrounded by a handsome balustrade. Within the enclosure is an edifice, styled the Palace of Abstinence, to which it is customary for the Emperor to retire for three days, before the grand ceremony of sacrificing in the temple, which is performed annually, at the winter solstice, when the Emperor officiates in his character of High Priest; and on this occasion, the produce of the field he ploughed in the spring, with the silks cultured and woven within the precincts of the palace, are offered up to the supreme ruler of the universe, under the name of Tien, or Lord of Heaven. The procession to the temple on the day of the sacrifice is very magnificent, as the Emperor is accompanied by the whole court, besides a numerous cavalcade of civil and military mandarins, all in full dress. It is remarkable that, in a religious procession, there should be no priests, nor any symbols of its sacred character, unless we may so consider a vast number of lighted flambeaux, and about four hundred gorgeous lanterns, which are carried in the train. On the day of this solemnity, as well as that of the ploughing festival, the Emperor is visible, but is seldom seen in public at any other time, or passes the boundary wall of his own park, except during the annual hunting expedition, or when he removes from one royal residence to another.

The streets of Peking are crowded, noisy, and bustling, for there, as in all other great cities of China, it is a common custom for men of the lower orders to work at their several trades in the streets, where they sit with their tools around them, as if they were in a workshop. Cobblers, tinkers, and blacksmiths, set up their apparatus wherever they may obtain a job; and medicine vendors, who are generally fortune-tellers also, establish themselves, with their compounds ranged in order before them, in any convenient locality. There are also a great number of pedlars, ballad-singers, and mountebanks, who contribute no less to the noise than to the throng. But the most remarkable persons who exercise their callings in the streets are the barbers, who are all licensed, and shave the heads and plait the tails of their customers with the utmost gravity in the open air. All the men of the lower orders, as well as some of a higher class, have this operation performed in the street, a custom that would probably fall into disuse, if the Chinese ladies were in the habit of walking abroad more freely. The shops have open fronts, gaily painted, and before the door of each is a wooden pillar, covered with gilt characters, describing the nature of the goods sold within; and as these sign-posts are usually decorated with gay streamers floating from the top, they have been not unaptly compared in appearance to a line of shipmasts with colours flying. The windows of all the houses in Peking are made of Corea paper, very frequently of a rose colour, and strengthened by a thin framework of bamboo, for there is no glass in the north of China, nor is it yet very common in the south, although more frequently seen now than in the last century. The houses in Peking are seldom more than one story in height, and have flat roofs, which are often covered with flowers and shrubs; for as there are no fire places, so there are no chimneys, the rooms being warmed by pans of lighted charcoal, of which fuel, great quantities are brought from Tartary on dromedaries, and these animals are constantly seen, thus laden, in the streets of the city.

The new town was partly built, and greatly embellished, by the Emperor Yong-lo, when he removed the court from Nanking to Peking, which was then entirely inhabited by Chinese; but when it was taken by the Mantchows, the native people were all driven out, and the houses given to the Tartar conquerors, since which time, it has been called the Tartar city.

Our knowledge of the great metropolis of the Celestial Empire is still imperfect; but in a country where such strict uniformity prevails throughout, and where the manners and dresses of the people are regulated by the laws, it is not unreasonable to conclude that the inhabitants of Peking resemble those of other Chinese cities. In the new town, the streets are wide and handsome, but the old town presents the same general features that distinguish all the great cities of China, the most striking of which are the high walls, narrow streets, open-fronted shops, gaily decorated temples and triumphal arches, with a constant succession of sedans and noisy processions, the bustle being increased by the incessant activity of itinerant artificers and vendors of almost every commodity; amongst whom, not a few are water-sellers, one of which class is here represented.

The streets of Canton are mostly particularised by their separate trades, one being entirely occupied by shoemakers, another by drapers, a third by jewellers, &c. and this distinctive arrangement of the trades is probably adopted in most of the towns. The triumphal arches, which are seen in most of the principal streets, are ornamental gateways that have been erected in honour of eminent persons, by which may be understood those who have distinguished themselves by their wisdom and virtues either in public or private life. The Emperor Kang-hy, for instance, ordained that every widow who attained to her hundredth year without forming a second matrimonial engagement, should be presented with thirty taels of silver for the erection of a triumphal arch, with an inscription in her praise; for although a woman is allowed to take a second husband if she pleases, and many do so, it is accounted far more honourable to remain faithful to the memory of the first. There is a curious custom with regard to marriage, among the lower orders; which is, that of begging in the public road to raise money for a wedding procession. A few years ago, an English gentleman, in walking near a burial-ground at Macao, observed a number of women standing together, making a doleful noise, which he supposed to be a lament for some departed relative; but, on enquiry, he learned that they were soliciting donations from the passers by, to facilitate the marriage of a young couple, who were very anxious to be united, but had not money to pay the expenses of the bridal ceremonies; and such is the superstition of the Chinese, that no happiness would be expected to result from a union unless the bride were carried home in due form.

The great mass of the people in China are the peasantry, or land cultivators, an industrious, frugal, and, as far as can be judged from the little that is at present known of them, a contented race of people, strongly attached to the habits of their forefathers, and decidedly averse to any innovations in their ancient customs. So vast is the population of this immense empire, that its demands upon agriculture for the necessaries of life could not be satisfied without great activity on the part of the peasantry, hence they labour incessantly to render the soil doubly productive, by constantly irrigating, and frequently manuring, the land. By these means, they produce two crops of rice in the year, and sometimes three; or a careful farmer will raise sufficient cotton in the interval between his rice crops to make clothing for his whole family.

The farms are, in general, small, and are sometimes cultivated by the proprietors, sometimes by the tenants, who rent them of rich landowners, for there are many of the mandarins and merchants who possess very large landed estates, which are always let to cultivators, as no individual, however rich, the Emperor alone excepted, presumes to convert into a park or pleasure ground a large extent of land that may be made to contribute towards the subsistence of the community at large. According to the law, all landed property, on the death of its owner, is divided into equal portions among his sons, with the exception of the eldest, who has a double share; but the system of clanship, which is universal among the agriculturists, renders this law of no real weight, as they all live together and fare alike, each individual labouring for the common benefit of the little community to which he belongs. It is not uncommon, in a large family, for the brothers to make an agreement among themselves to dispense with the services of one of their number, that he may devote himself entirely to letters, the rest supporting him during his studies, in the hope that he will ultimately obtain degrees that may enable him to repay them for the benefits they have conferred upon him. In some few cases this is of great advantage to the whole family; but there are many thousands of these poor students who never rise higher than to the first degree, nor obtain any employment more lucrative than that of a schoolmaster, or tutor in a private family.

All aged relatives, whether male or female, are invariably supported by the younger branches of the family; and instead of being considered burthensome, are treated with the greatest deference by their sons and grandsons, who, so far from thinking it a hardship, are proud of having parents to work for. The force of domestic affection and the respect paid to it, were fully exemplified during the late war, when it was no unusual case for a soldier to obtain permission of the general to return home to visit a dying grandmother, or attend upon a sick parent; duties so sacred in the eyes of the rulers of China, as to supersede all others. In China, therefore, none need fear that they shall be despised or neglected in old age, which not only secures the respectful attentions of their children, but the especial patronage of the highest authorities. The Emperor Yong-tching ordered that the sum of ninety taels should be given to a man who had reached the extraordinary age of a hundred and eighteen years; and one who, in the reign of Kien-long had attained to the age of a hundred and thirty, was presented, by that monarch, with a hundred and twenty taels, and some pieces of silk, with a promise that if he lived ten years longer, he should have another present. The same Emperor commanded that whenever a family of five generations should be found residing under the same roof, a report should be made to him of the circumstance, that he might present the father of the race with a handsome donation. That great sovereign composed some interesting odes on the subject of longevity.

In former times, every male at the age of sixteen paid a capitation tax, which ceased when he had attained his sixtieth year, and a pension for life was then settled on him by the government. There is no capitation tax at present, nor are any pensions granted to the aged; but there is an Imperial gift of thirty taels, to which every man and woman is entitled at the age of one hundred.

The cottages of the peasantry are generally described as being neat and comfortable in appearance. They are but scantily provided with furniture made of bamboo, by the peasants themselves; the articles in use consisting chiefly of tables, stools, and beds, or rather boards; for the bed is but a board laid upon two wooden benches with a mat spread upon it, and surrounded by curtains of coarse hemp, to keep off the mosquitoes. The rich have softer beds, and handsome bedsteads placed in a recess, with curtains of silk or gauze, according to the season.

Every house belonging either to rich or poor, has its household gods, to which offerings are frequently made according to the mode of Chinese worship, consisting of cakes, rice, plates of meats, and cups of tea, which

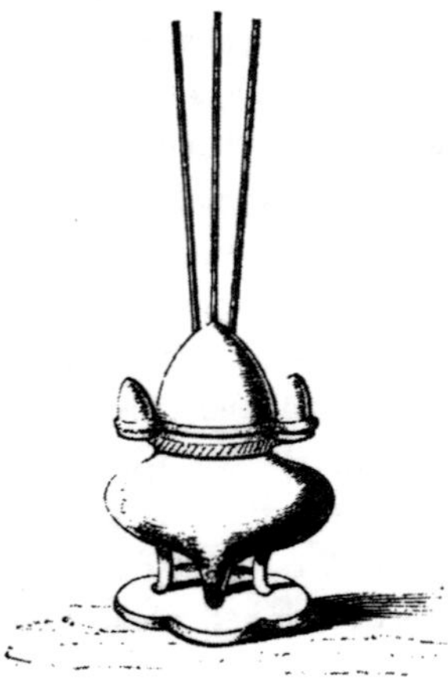

are placed before the images for a certain space of time, and then taken away to be consumed by the family. At the great public festivals, tables covered with offerings, brought by the people, are set in the streets, or in the temples, and are ranged with the nicest care. Each table displays a variety of choice viands, such as ducks, fowls, pigs' heads, large cakes, fruits, and confectionary of all kinds, with wine, and rows of very small cups filled with tea. The tables are illuminated with large wax tapers, and in every offering is fixed a lighted Joss-stick, which burns very slowly, and when exhausted is replaced by another. The word Joss, is supposed to be a corruption of *Deos*, as it does not belong to the Chinese language, nor does it appear to have been in use before the settlement of the Portuguese in China; and this conjecture is the more reasonable, from the fact of there being other words now in common use, even amongst the Chinese themselves, which owe their origin to the Portuguese; as for instance, mandarin, the native term for which is quan. As long as the festival lasts, the tables remain untouched, but as soon as it is ended, the offerings are distributed among the crowd, so that the lower orders may be said literally to share in all public festivities.

The commencement of a new year is the time for feasting and merry-making, in China. The Christmas of the olden time, in England, was not a season of more universal merriment than this is in the flowery land. On this most important of all the Chinese festivals, high and low, the rulers and their people, indulge in a cessation from the cares of life, and give up all their thoughts to pleasure. A regular order is issued by the Board of Rites, that all government business shall be suspended from the twentieth day of the twelfth moon, to the same day of the first moon; thus allowing to all the mandarins in office, a holiday of thirty days, unless any particular business should demand their attention; and they do not fail to avail themselves of this release, by locking up their seals, and preparing to enjoy their long vacation. The rest of the people devote as much time to amusement as they can spare from their ordinary avocations; but those must be miserable indeed who do not join, for two or three days at least, in the general gaieties.

The festival, which begins at the midnight that closes the old year, is ushered in by the ceremonies of offerings, incense burning, and numerous other rites, which last till daylight, the temples being lighted up, the pagodas illuminated, and candles set up before the domestic idols in every house. As soon as the day appears, visits of congratulation are paid and received, and new year's gifts are sent to particular friends, always accompanied by a visiting ticket of red paper, on which is written the name of the donor, and a list of the presents sent, consisting usually of silks, fine tea, sweetmeats, ornaments, toys, and other trifles suited to the occasion. All the actors, musicians, jugglers, and tumblers in the empire, are in requisition at this period of recreation, when grand entertainments are given by the rich, and plays are performed in the streets, at the expense of government, or by a subscription among the inhabitants, for the amusement of the poor. The lower orders are very much addicted to gambling, smoking, and drinking, particularly in the towns where there are plenty of booths for their accommodation, to which they resort as soon as their daily labours are ended. These taverns, which are merely open sheds, are much frequented, at all seasons, but at holiday times they are crowded from morning till night with noisy revellers.

The last day of the year is not quite so joyful a one as the first, for among the many wise regulations of the Chinese government is a law, by which all men are obliged to settle accounts with their creditors on that particular day; and it is considered so disgraceful to leave any debt unpaid, that the unlucky debtor who cannot discharge his pecuniary obligations at the appointed time, is liable to be treated with insult and injury by those to whom the money is owing; and among the vulgar, it is not uncommon for an individual under such circumstances to have his furniture broken, and his family annoyed in every possible way; nor can he apply to the magistrates for redress, however serious the injury he may sustain, because the fact of not having paid his debt would render his complaint of no avail.

The necessity of being punctual in payments, involves also that of economy, one of the moral virtues instilled into the minds of the people by their magistrates, who are obliged, by law, to give instruction in public on the first and fifteenth days of every moon, by reading one of the sixteen discourses that treat on all the principal duties of social life in every station. Thus the mandarins are the pastors of their respective flocks in every town and village throughout China; and the people, in the absence of religious instruction, are taught that system of morality which is the vital principle of the government and social constitution of the nation. The practice is an ancient one, but the lectures now given were written, or probably revised, by the Emperor Yong-tching, all the texts being maxims selected from the ancient sacred books. The first lesson is on filial piety, and the respect which a younger should pay to an elder brother. These duties are so strictly enjoined and enforced, that a few years since a man was put to death for having beaten his mother, and his wife shared the same fate for having assisted him. The act was regarded as a crime so heinous, that the house in which it was perpetrated was deemed unfit for the residence of any human being, and was dug up from the foundation, that not a stone of it might remain. The magistrates were all disgraced; the wife's mother was severely punished; and the scholars of that polluted district were prohibited from attending the public examinations for three years. The second of the sixteen discourses exhorts the people to preserve a respectful remembrance of their ancestors, and enjoins them not to neglect to visit their tombs at the proper periods. The principal subjects of the other lectures are, the benefits of concord in the villages; the respect due to the professions of husbandry and the culture of silk; the advantages of economy and industry; the education of youth; application to business; obedience to the laws; and the punishments incurred by those who are negligent of their duties. The following extracts from one of these lectures will afford a specimen of the plain and simple style in which they are written.

"The Emperor orders you to preserve union in the villages, that quarrels and law-suits may be banished from thence. Listen attentively to the explanation of this ordinance. You live with kinsfolk and acquaintance, with persons advanced in years, and with your schoolfellows; you cannot go abroad without seeing one another, morning and evening, and at all times you will meet. It is this assemblage of families dwelling in the same place that I call a village. In this village there are rich and poor; some of these are your superiors; some your inferiors; some your equals. One of the ancients has wisely remarked, that in a place where there are old men as well as young, the latter ought to respect the former, without considering whether they are rich or poor, learned or ignorant; they ought to think of nothing but their age. If, being in easy circumstances, you despise the poor,—or if, being in indigence, you look with envy on the rich, this will cause perpetual divisions." The lecturer then points out at great length the miseries that arise from quarrels and law-suits, contrasting them with the pleasures that flow from peace and friendship. He then proceeds thus: "The Emperor, whose compassion to his people is unbounded, prohibits law-suits; and having your peace and unanimity at heart, is so good as to give you instructions himself, to prevent the discord that might otherwise arise among you. As for tradesmen and mechanics who are born to a low condition, their happiness consists in living according to their circumstances, in not being uneasy at their own poverty, nor envying others the possession of their wealth. This rule of morality will be to them a source of consolation. You are now acquainted with the intentions of the Emperor, whereto it behoves you to conform; and if you do, as I make no doubt you will, the greatest advantages will accrue from your obedience, for you will content the paternal heart of his Majesty. When you return home, therefore, apply yourselves to the practice of so useful a doctrine."

The delivery of these discourses, which are called the Sacred Instructions, must on no account be neglected; and the government has taken care to ensure the attention of the mandarins to this important branch of their duty, by making them, in a great degree, answerable for the conduct of the people under their control; and, accordingly, the magistrates of the district in which the aged woman was ill-treated by her son were all punished by Kea-king, on the ground that, such a crime could not have been committed, if proper pains had been taken to inculcate the duties of filial piety and obedience, as contained in the first of the sacred instructions.

The care of admonishing the people belongs to the mandarins of small communities; but the viceroys have also to perform their part, as teachers, by assembling all the inferior governors within their province about once a year, to give them instructions as to their respective duties, to which they are bound to listen with respect, as coming from the Emperor himself by the voice of his representative.

The real condition of females in China, and the position they hold in society, are certainly not yet very accurately known. They are seldom seen in the streets, it is true; but that is sufficiently accounted for by their inability to walk with ease; and as they do sometimes appear abroad, and are often observed at the windows without making any attempt to conceal their faces from the gaze of strangers, it is evident they enjoy far more liberty than the Turkish ladies, although it is not the custom for the sexes to mix together in general society. When a mandarin gives a grand entertainment, his wife frequently invites her friends to witness the theatrical performances, and various amusing exhibitions that are going forward during the dinner. These they can see without being seen, from a latticed gallery provided for that purpose; and thus they are not entirely debarred from the enjoyment of the festivities, although they do not mingle with the guests; but whether their exclusion be voluntary or compulsory, seems to be one of those doubtful points that admit of different opinions even among those who have visited the Chinese at their own houses.

As far as European observation has extended, all visiting in China is conducted in a manner which is very formal, according to our notions. The most intimate friend, in making a morning call, does not alight from his chair until he has sent in his visiting ticket, that the master of the house may give him a proper reception, according to his rank, as it is the etiquette to hurry to the door in some cases to receive a guest; while in others, it is only necessary to meet him in the middle of the room; and in the former case, the bowings are lower and more numerous than in the latter. The law has decided that the superior shall take precedence in entering the room, yet it is considered polite to make a pretence of refusing to go in first, and a few unmeaning compliments always pass on the occasion, both parties knowing very well which of them is to take the lead.

It is not the custom in China to uncover the head, unless invited so to do; in warm weather, therefore, a gentleman usually says to his friend, "Pray put off your cap;" and it would be a mark of ill-manners to omit this compliment. Tea is always offered to a morning visitor, and is usually accompanied with sweetmeats and pipes, for the Chinese are as fond of smoking as the Turks, and every gentleman wears an embroidered tobacco

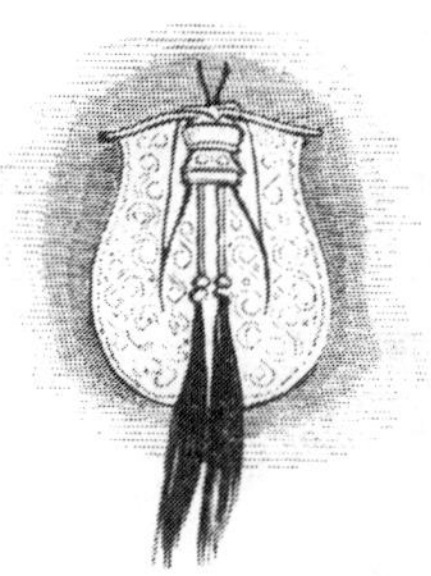

pouch at his girdle. It is not exactly certain when tobacco was first introduced into China, but it is supposed that it found its way there soon after the discovery of America, as the Chinese were in the habit of smoking before the time of the Tartar conquest, although there is no mention of such a custom prior to the sixteenth century.

The forbidden pleasure of opium smoking had also been indulged in to a great extent, until the events transpired that gave rise to the late war; but as the indulgence was illegal, the opium pipe was only used in some inner apartment, where the smoker was secure from observation.

Smoking is not confined to the male sex, nor to the lower class of

females; but every Chinese lady has her richly-ornamented pipe, which would really be an elegant appendage if it did not involve so unfeminine an indulgence. The usual employments among the Chinese ladies are, working embroidery, playing on different musical instruments, and painting on silk and rice paper. It is not supposed that they possess generally any accomplishments more intellectual than these; yet as some ladies are known to write to their husbands when absent, it is clear that there are individual cases where the art of writing has been acquired; and, of course, that of reading; which might lead us to conjecture that, in some of the numerous families where private tutors are now employed, the girls may be allowed to participate to a certain extent in the studies of their brothers; but this is a mere supposition for which there is no authority.

The costume of the Chinese, being regulated by law, is not subject to the caprice of fashion or individual taste, except in such trifling particulars as produce no alteration in the general style. The dress of a Chinese lady is not different from that worn in ancient times: it consists of a short loose robe, confined round the throat with a narrow collar. The robe is worn over a long full skirt; and both are frequently made of richly-embroidered silks. The sleeves are wide, and sufficiently long to fall over the hands, and the hair is gathered up in a knot at the top of the head, and is fastened with golden bodkins, and adorned with flowers. They all wear trousers, like the Turkish women; and their tiny shoes are of satin, silk, or velvet, beautifully worked with gold, silver, and coloured silks, the soles being of rice paper, from one to two inches in thickness, and covered

Domestic scene. Ladies at their usual employments.

outside with white leather, made from pig's skin. The little girls are very becomingly attired in short dresses, reaching to the throat, and worn over the full trousers. The hair, which is combed from the forehead, hangs down in ringlets on each side, and the back hair is plaited into one or two long tails; in which simple style it remains until the young lady is about to become a bride, when the more matronly fashion is adopted, and the braids and curls are formed into a knot, intermixed with flowers and jewels.

A gentleman usually wears, in the house, a loose robe of silk, cloth, or, in summer, of some lighter material, with a cap also suited to the season. If he be a mandarin, a ball is worn on the top of the cap, to designate the class to which he belongs. The summer cap is as light as chip, to which it bears a resemblance. It is made of bamboo, in the shape of a cone; and, if the wearer be a government officer, has attached to the ball a crimson silk ornament, which hangs like a fringe. The winter head-dress is of satin, with a wide brim of black velvet, turned up all round, and the usual adornments of ball and fringe at the top. A mandarin of the first rank is known by a red ball on his cap; a transparent blue one denotes the second class; and the other grades are distinguished by white, opake blue, crystal, gilt, and other balls.

A Chinese is not at liberty to wear his summer or his winter cap when he pleases, but is obliged to wait for the time appointed by the Board of Rites, for making the alteration in his head-gear. The announcement is made in the Gazette, when the viceroy of the province lays aside the cap he has been wearing for the previous six months, to adopt that of the approaching season, and the example is immediately followed by all other mandarins and officers within his government. It is very usual to wear at home a cap of silk or velvet, fitting closely to the head. Furs are very much used in the winter costume, for as the Chinese have no fires in their apartments, they wear a great quantity of warm clothing, putting on one garment over another until they are sufficiently protected from the cold. Dress boots are of velvet or satin, with the universal thick white soles; and a fan, in an embroidered case hanging from the girdle, is as indispensable a part of the costume of a Chinese gentleman as his cap or gown.

One strange fashion, common to both sexes among people of rank, is that of suffering the nails of the left hand to grow to an enormous length; a custom that can only have had its origin in the vanity of showing that the hand thus disfigured is never employed in hard labour.

The lower orders in the towns, men, women, and children, all wear loose frocks of Nanking cloth, usually dyed blue, and gathered round the neck; but the labouring men in the country work in large cotton trousers, with a shirt over them, and a broad bamboo hat, which answers the purpose of an umbrella, to shield them from the sun and rain. But the most extraordinary article of apparel worn by the Chinese labourer is a cloak, made of reeds, which has a very rough, unsightly appearance, but is extremely useful in wet weather, either in the fields or the boats.

The river population in China, as will be noticed more particularly in speaking of Canton, form a very large portion of the community in that province, and were formerly considered as a distinct and inferior race. Until the time of Kien-long they were not permitted to intermarry with the people on shore; but that enlightened sovereign removed the restriction, and those who live on the water now enjoy equal privileges with those who have their dwellings on land, and a boatman may take to wife a village lass without incurring any penalty. It is thought that many of the poor people who emigrate to Singapore, and other settlements, often take their wives with them, notwithstanding the laws that so strictly prohibit women from leaving the country; but there is no doubt that the laws against emigration are altogether very much relaxed; and it is probable that the government may purposely refrain from being very vigilant in seeing them enforced.

It is rather curious that, among the personal decorations of the Chinese, there is not one they prize more highly, or on which they bestow more attention than the plaited tail, which, at first, was detested as a disgraceful badge of dependence, and is still a sign of their subjection to the Tartar rule. The beauty of the tail consists in its length and thickness, and many who have not hair enough to make a handsome braid, supply the deficiency with false hair and silk; but whatever pains and cost a man may bestow upon improving his appearance by the aid of art, he can have no pretensions to personal attraction, unless his figure indicate that he has not been kept upon spare diet; and, indeed, there are no people in the world who are fonder of good living than the Chinese. The tables of the wealthy are supplied with a great variety of rich dishes, among which is a soup that supplies the place of our Turtle. It is made of the nests of some particular birds found chiefly in the island of Formosa, the trade in which is a government monopoly. Beef is not very often eaten, but pork is abundant, and mutton is brought to the tables of the great, although sheep are very scarce in the southern provinces, where the land is little devoted to pasture. Vegetable soups, poultry, and game, dressed in various ways, and many excellent made dishes, are brought to table; and the dinner, which may consist of six or eight courses, is always concluded with a bowl of rice, served to each person.

The Chinese take wine with each other, and when they have done so, turn the cup upside down, to show that they have emptied its contents, this being a point of good breeding. The wine, which is a liquor extracted from rice, is always taken hot, and is poured by a servant into the cups from a silver vessel like a coffee pot. The dinner service consists of porcelain bowls, of various sizes, with plates shaped like saucers, and sometimes a few silver dishes, with a spirit lamp beneath. Instead of knives and forks, they use what are termed chopsticks, which are small round sticks of ivory or ebony, tipped with silver; but they have also spoons of ebony, and silver ladles, for the soups. The dinner is followed by a dessert of fruits and confectionary; after which the company usually adjourn to another room to take tea, and amuse themselves; but the Englishmen, who have dined in a familiar manner with the mandarins, or Hong merchants of Canton, have never been gratified by the company of the ladies.

The shopkeepers of China usually take only two meals in the day; one between eight and ten in the morning, the other between four and six in the afternoon. Their usual fare is rice and vegetables, with a little pork or fish, and their ordinary drink is tea; but they sometimes indulge in Shamsoo, a spiritous liquor distilled from rice, large quantities of which are made at Tinghae, the capital of Chusan.

The bakers in China are chiefly employed in making pastry, and flat unleavened cakes, the latter constituting the only bread which is known in China. Their ovens, or rather baking machines, consist of a flat plate of iron, suspended by chains from a beam over a copper filled with burning charcoal. The cakes are placed on the iron plate, which can be raised or depressed at pleasure, by means of the chains; and as this is the only mode of baking among the Chinese, their bread is necessarily made in the form of cakes, and is eaten only as a dainty. At Canton, the process of cooking is carried on over charcoal fires, and as there are no chimnies to any of the houses, a part of the brick-work above the fire in their kitchens, or cooking places, is left open, to suffer the vapour to escape. There are plenty of eating-houses in that city, both for rich and poor, those for the latter being open sheds, where they can procure a hot breakfast or dinner at any hour of the day, for a very trifling sum. The superior sort are fine handsome hotels, where gentlemen of the higher classes can dine when their families are out of town; but the owners of them are not allowed to entertain foreigners; therefore the English have yet to learn what sort of accommodation is to be met with at a Chinese tavern.

Gambling with cards, dice, and dominoes, which is openly practised among the lower orders, is considered disgraceful among those of higher grade; who, however, play at chess, and have their own peculiar games, which, to judge from the descriptions given by authors, who have had an opportunity of witnessing them, appear to be rather childish pastimes. One of these games consists in playing with a bouquet of flowers, which is passed rapidly from hand to hand, until the beating of a drum in an adjoining apartment suddenly stops, when he who holds the flowers must drink a glass of wine. If some other forfeit were substituted, this certainly is a sport more adapted for children than for those of a graver age.

Among the out-door amusements of the commonalty, that of kite flying is carried to a degree of perfection unseen in any other country. The kites are made in a variety of forms, as of birds, butterflies, or fishes; and the flyers often try their skill in bringing down each other's kites, in imitation of hawking. Foot-ball is a favourite pastime; and a game called jang, which is of very ancient date, and is played with two wooden toys in the form of a pair of shoes, one of which is placed on the ground, and its fellow thrown from a distance, the object being to insert one within the other; and he who succeeds in doing so, is the winner. These games are very much practised at all the festivals.

From this slight sketch of the manners and customs of the Chinese, we are next led to a review of their arts, manufactures, and produce, all which throw additional lights on the state of society, and help to familiarize us both with the country and the people.

ARTS, MANUFACTURES, AND NATURAL PRODUCTIONS OF CHINA.

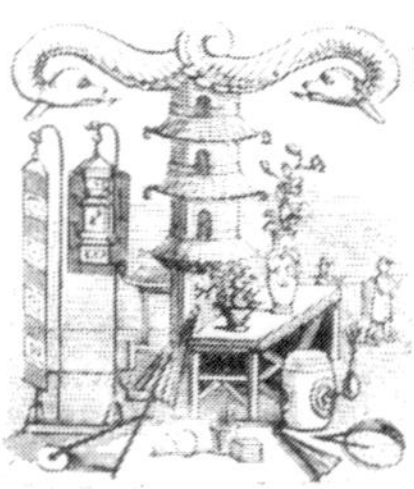

THE Chinese are deservedly celebrated for their industry and ingenuity; yet, in consequence of their reluctance to be taught by foreigners, they possess very little scientific knowledge, and succeed better in ornamental, than in useful works. Those arts which chiefly contribute to the comforts and conveniences of life, are but imperfectly understood; while those that depend on exertion of fancy and neatness of execution, have attained to a high degree of excellence. They have very little machinery, and are strongly prejudiced against the introduction of any improvements that would tend to abridge manual labour; nor can we wonder that such a feeling should prevail in an over-peopled country where emigration is not encouraged, and where many millions depend on the labour of their hands for subsistence. Even their agricultural implements are as few and simple as they were in the early days of the empire, yet by dint of the excessive toil of the vast numbers of people employed, the lands are as well cultivated and as highly productive as they could possibly be by any improved system. The plough, the harrow, and the hoe, all of the rudest construction, are the chief implements used by a Chinese farmer, the spade being only seen occasionally. The plough is usually drawn by buffaloes, but sometimes that labour is performed by men, and even by women, among the lowest class of farmers. Water wheels and chain pumps are used for irrigating the lands. The water wheel is an immense, yet very light, machine, composed entirely of bamboo, its buckets for raising the water being made of the same material; it is fixed adjoining the banks of all such rivers as have the stream running one way, which keeps it going night and day, and supplies water to a large trough which empties its contents into several channels that run through the fields in various directions, and thus keep them constantly watered. The chain pump is used to raise water from the wells and ponds for the same purpose, and being portable, extremely useful to the Chinese labourer, who is never without one; consequently, the making of these machines is a branch of industry that affords employment to a great number of mechanics.

The great object of cultivation is rice, the staple food of all classes, from the prince to the peasant. Most of the plains present an endless succession of rice or paddy fields, which, in the early stage of the crops, exhibit a vast surface of bright green, but turn yellow as the grain ripens. The seed is first sown in small patches, flooded with a particular preparation of liquid manure, which promotes its immediate developement, so that in a few days the shoots are five or six inches in height, when they are transplanted to the fields, some of the labourers being employed in taking them up, others in making holes to receive them, and a third party in dropping them into the holes about six together. All these men stand up to the ankles in water, for it is requisite that rice should be kept constantly wet, or it would be spoiled; but when the rice is ripe, the fields are drained; so that the reapers, whose labours commence about Midsummer, work on dry ground.

The second harvest is ripe in November, after which the ground is usually planted with cabbages, and other vegetables; but in some parts of the country, a crop of cotton is obtained between the two rice crops. A Jesuit writer gives the following account of the cultivation of the cotton, and its extraction from the seed. "On the same day that the husbandmen get in their harvest, they sow the field with cotton seed, first breaking the surface of the ground with the harrow. After the earth has been moistened, there grows, up by degrees, a small shrub, about two feet high, the flowers of which appear towards the middle of August, being generally yellow, but sometimes red; and this flower is succeeded by a pod, about as big as a nut, which opens of itself, displaying, within, three or four little bags of cotton, extremely white, and these contain the seed for the following year. The crop is then ready for gathering, and the cotton is separated from the seed by means of two small rollers, turned by the hand and foot sufficiently close together to exclude the seed while the cotton passes through." The field is then manured for the second crop of rice, the plants of which are transplanted into it in the manner before described.

Keang-nan, and the provinces adjoining, are those where cotton is more extensively cultivated, and in the neighbourhood of Nanking, the cloth known by that name is made in large quantities. The weavers are all women, and work at their own homes; for there are no large manufactories in China, either for silks or cottons; so that there is scarcely a cottage throughout the empire, where there is not some manufacture carried on, either for sale or home consumption, and generally for both.

The introduction of cotton instead of silk for clothing, must have proved a material benefit to the lower classes, being so much more durable, and better suited to their occupations, than silk; yet it was not till after the accession of the Ming dynasty that it was cultivated in sufficient quantities to allow of its coming into general use. The extended cultivation of cotton was one of the causes of the almost entire disappearance of sheep from the southern provinces, for it was found that it would take much more land to supply a certain number of persons with mutton and wool than with rice and cotton; there the pastures were gradually turned into rice and cotton plantations, while sheep were banished to the mountains and less fertile parts of the country. For the same reason cattle, horses, and other domestic animals, are scarce, the few that are kept for the purposes of husbandry, are poor and ill-fed; for there is not a common on which they can graze, so that they are tied up in stalls when not employed in the fields. Dairy farms are unknown in China, where the people use neither milk, butter, nor cheese.

The land tax is said to amount to about one-tenth of the produce; and it is reckoned that about ten thousand boats are constantly engaged in carrying to Peking the tribute goods from different provinces, which serve to

clothe and feed the army, and afford stores of grain for times of scarcity, as well as to furnish the numerous princes and government officers with the silks and rice that are distributed to them annually, as a part of their salaries. The state dresses of the Emperor's guards are of silk, the making of which is a tax on the silk districts. The provinces that produce the finest silk are those of Chekeang, Keang-nan, or Nanking, and the country adjoining; but there is a wild species of worm in many other parts of China that feeds on some of the common forest trees, and from which is obtained a coarse kind of silk, which is very durable, but which will not take any dye, and is far less glossy and beautiful than the silk of the worm that feeds on the mulberry tree.

The Chinese do not sell their best silk fabrics to foreigners, consequently we never see in this country the rich silks which they wear themselves. Their velvets are not equal to those of Europe; but their flowered damasks and crapes are superb. There are women who can earn as much as thirty dollars a month by embroidering the beautiful shawls of China crape that are so much admired in this country.

A large portion of the peasantry in the silk districts are chiefly engaged in taking care of the mulberry plantations, which require constant attention that they may produce fine leaves, and the frequent pruning of the branches for that end, destroys, in great measure, the beauty of the tree. The worms are kept in houses, in the centre of the grove, for it is an essential point in the management of them that they should be always surrounded by perfect stillness, as it is found that noise is extremely injurious, especially to the younger ones. The care of feeding and tending them belongs to the female part of the family, who also manage the silk after it is spun by the worms.

The other principal manufactures of China are porcelain, japanned ware, and paper. The great porcelain factories of King-te-ching are still carried on as they were in former times; but as the Chinese have made no improvements, either in the forms, or the designs with which they ornament their ware, the Europeans now greatly surpass them in both these particulars, although perhaps the China ware may still be superior in quality to that manufactured in Europe.

Another branch of industry, which has never been imitated with success in this part of the world, is that of making the beautiful japanned material that we often see in the shape of folding screens, cabinets, tea-trays, boxes, and ornamental tables, so brilliantly adorned with paintings and gildings in that peculiar style which is at once recognized as Chinese. This is an art, however, in which the people of China yield the palm to those of Japan, from whom it derives its name; and all the most costly screens and cabinets seen in the houses of the Chinese mandarins are the work of the Japanese, who send them to China. The varnish used for japanning them is the gum that oozes from a small tree, or rather a shrub, which grows both in China and Japan. The excellence of the art consists in laying on the varnish perfectly smooth, which is a tedious and difficult process, as many coatings are required, and each must be spread with the same nicety. The varnish will take any colour without losing its brilliancy, so that all the painting is executed upon the japanned surface; and although the Chinese have but little knowledge of the fine arts, we cannot refuse to give them credit for their skill in the execution of the ornamental designs.

Among a people so addicted to reading and writing, the manufacture of paper must necessarily be carried on to a considerable extent, and must be much increased by the annual consumption for the sacrifices, which require an immense supply of paper. The paper used for printing books being thin and transparent, is only impressed on one side, and folded, so that every leaf is double, with the edge uncut. Books are not bound, like ours; but every work is divided into a number of separate parts, each neatly stitched into strong paper covers. The parts, in this shape, are placed all together, loosely, in the outer case; a plan that seems to have been adopted for the purpose of avoiding the inconvenience of holding a thick volume in the hand.

Books are very cheap, for there is no duty on paper, and the wages of printers, as of all other workmen, are very small. There are a great many booksellers in all the principal towns, but as the only books read in China are those of the native authors, none others are to be met with; and thus printing and bookselling go on, year after year, and century after century, without adding to the previous knowledge of the people, or giving them a single new idea.

Printing is still executed, as formerly, by means of wooden blocks, which are prepared thus. The copy is written on very thin paper, and pasted on plain blocks, from which all the blank parts are neatly cut away, and as the letters are left raised on the surface, they are, of course, an exact representation of the manuscript, which must, therefore, be very carefully written. Moveable types are sometimes used, but only for a temporary purpose, as the printing of the Gazette, and the Red Book, the latter of which is altered every three months.

The process of printing, in China, is very different from that used in England, as the Chinese employ no press, nor would it facilitate their operations, while they continue to print on paper of so delicate a texture that any hard pressure would be likely to break through it. The printer works with two brushes fastened on both ends of a stick, which he holds in his right hand, and having inked the characters with one brush, he lays on his paper, and runs the other over it, which makes the impression; and this is done so quickly, that a good workman can take off two thousand copies in a day.

Nothing is allowed to be published in China until it has been examined and approved by the members of the Han-lin College, who take care that not a line shall be printed which might be displeasing to the Emperor, who is, by that means, often kept in ignorance of many public proceedings, which are either prohibited from appearing in the Gazette at all, or are entirely misrepresented in it; a case of daily occurrence during the late war, when every defeat was metamorphosed into a victory.

The useful arts in China are, as before observed, in a very unimproved state. The Chinese do not make good locks, knives, or cutlery of any description, and it has only been of late that they have begun to make clocks and watches, for which the springs, and finest part of the works, are obtained from England. Another step recently taken towards an improvement in the conveniences of life, has been in the manufacture of glass, which had previously been made by melting that which had been broken on its way from Europe; but the Chinese have, for some years, been in the habit of purchasing English flints, and making glass themselves; and although this glass is very inferior to that of Europe, yet the art of making it is gradually improving, and glass mirrors have, in great measure, superseded those of polished metal, which have been in use from very ancient times.

It is almost superfluous to speak of the excellence to which the Chinese have attained in the carving of ivory, since there are few of us who have not had many opportunities of judging for ourselves of the unrivalled beauty of their workmanship in this delicate art; the most perfect specimens of which are perhaps exhibited in the models of ships, and the balls contained one within another, to the number, sometimes, of twenty, or even more. Nothing can afford a greater proof of the patience and perseverance, as well as of the taste, of a Chinese handicraftsman, than one of these elegant baubles, each ball being exquisitely carved, and no two alike in pattern. Each of the balls rolls freely within that which encloses it, and is visible through apertures, so that however many there may be, the beauties of each can be examined, and the number of the whole counted. Much time is spent upon the carving of these toys, for the cleverest artist will employ a whole month in the execution of each separate ball, consequently, the labour of two years is not unfrequently bestowed on the production of a single toy, which is formed out of a solid globe of ivory, and has no junction in any part. The outside of this globe is first carved in some very open pattern, and is then carefully cut with a sharp, fine instrument, through the openings, till a complete coating is detached from the solid part inside, as the peel of an orange might be loosened with a scoop from the fruit, without being taken off. One hollow ball is thus formed, with a solid one inside of it. The surface of the inner ball is then carved through the interstices of the outer one, and when finished, is subjected to the same operation as the first; and thus a second hollow ball is produced, still with a solid one, of smaller dimensions, inside. This process is repeated again and again, the difficulties increasing as the work proceeds, till, at length, only a small ball, of the size of a marble, is left in the centre, which is also ornamented with figures, cut upon it, and then the ingenious but useless bauble is complete. This process is said to be performed under water.

The Chinese display equal skill in carving wood, mother of pearl, and tortoise-shell, out of which they form innumerable articles of great beauty, both for ornament and use, the great market for these trifles being Canton, where they are sold in vast quantities to the Europeans and Americans. There are some streets in the suburbs of the city, outside the walls, full of shops for the sale of such commodities; but the shopkeepers dare not sell tea or cotton, the dealings in which have been hitherto entirely restricted to the Hong merchants.

It is remarkable that in a large country where so much trade is carried on, and where every town is full of retail shops, there should be no coinage, as a medium of exchange, more convenient than that of the little copper coins, one thousand of which are only equal to a tael, or Chinese ounce of silver, worth about six shillings and eight-pence. These copper pieces, called tchen, have a square hole in the centre, and are issued from the mint threaded on strings, each string containing a thousand, divided by knots into hundreds. Large payments are therefore made in ingots of silver, usually called by the Europeans, Sycee; and it is part of the business of a banker in China, to receive from the government officers all the silver collected in taxes, which they melt, refine, and cast into ingots of a certain weight, each being stamped with the date of the year, and the name of the refiner. In making small payments, it is very usual, as in ancient times, to cut off a small piece of silver from a thin sheet of that metal, and weigh it with a fine balance, made expressly for that purpose. There are silver mines in various parts of the country, but more particularly in the province of Yunnan, which borders on the Birman empire.

Of all the natural productions of China, the tea plant is decidedly one of the most important, both as an article of foreign commerce, and of home consumption.

Tea is grown, more or less, in every part of the country, but principally in the provinces of Fokien, Keang-nan, Chekeang, and Keang-sy. It is cultivated on the hills, and in the plains, the former being sometimes clothed to the very summit with the fragrant shrub, which resembles the myrtle, and bears a white flower, not unlike our hedge rose. The difference in the quality of the teas, and the distinctions of green and black, depend partly on the district in which they are grown, and partly on the season when they are gathered, as the young leaves of the spring are of much finer flavour than the full-grown leaves of the summer, or the still coarser ones of the autumn.

The tea growers are generally small proprietors, who, with the help of their families, cultivate their own pieces of land, which are divided from those of their neighbours by a narrow path, or a narrow channel. The farmers, after having gathered their crops, partially dry them in the sun, just sufficiently to prevent their being spoiled, and in that state they are sold to the agents of the Hong merchants, who usually contract with the farmer to take his whole crop at a certain price. The tea is then removed by the contractors, whose business it is to complete its preparation, which is done by drying it in iron pans over a charcoal fire, care being taken to prevent its burning, by stirring it the whole time. Much more labour is expended in preparing the superior kinds of tea, than is bestowed on those of coarser quality; as, for example, the finest sorts of green tea are dried in very small quantities, and after having been carefully sorted, every leaf is rolled, separately, with the hand; while the commonest black teas are dried in baskets, piled one upon another in long rows, in a drying house, where charcoal fires are made upon the brick floor; and when this process is completed, the leaves are rolled by handfuls at a time, without being sorted. All the intermediate sorts are prepared with more or less care, according to their quality. The picking and rolling are performed by women and children; the drying and packing, by men. A difference is observed in the packing of the various kinds of tea, as well as in their preparation, the green being only shaken into the chests, that the leaves may not be broken, while the black is rudely trodden down by Chinese labourers. A popular notion formerly prevailed, that green teas derived their colour from being dried on copper, and were therefore injurious; but this is found to be a mistake, although there is no doubt that the Chinese have, on many occasions, when the demand for green teas has been very great, manufactured them from black, by colouring the leaves with drugs, or juices of some kind.

The annual export of tea from Canton is computed at about fifty-four millions of pounds, of which considerably more than half is brought to England; and when we consider that, in addition to this immense quantity sent abroad, it is the universal beverage of three hundred millions of people at home, we may readily imagine what a vast number of Chinese must be employed in the culture and preparation of this valuable shrub, which may justly be classed among the most important productions of the country.

Sugar is cultivated in some of the interior provinces, where sugar-candy is made in such large quantities as to form an article of export.

Drawn by B. Clayton from a Painting by Tiqua. — On Stone by E. Gilks

CULTURE AND PREPARATION OF TEA.

London, Dean & Co. Threadneedle St.

There are many curious trees in China that are unknown in Europe, among which are those that produce camphor, tallow, and wax. The camphor tree grows to a great height, and is one of the most useful timber trees in the empire, as it does not split, and is never destroyed by insects. It is chiefly used for chests, and household furniture, and sometimes in boat building. The luxuriant foliage of this fine tree is of the brighest green, and from the fresh-gathered branches is obtained the resinous gum, which we call camphor, and with which the wood is highly scented.

The tallow tree has some resemblance to the aspen and birch, the branches being long and flexible, and the leaves of a very dark green, which, in autumn, turn red, with a purple tint. The fruit, or rather seed, is contained in brown pods, that grow in bunches at the extremity of each bough, and on opening, disclose three small white berries, which hang very prettily by their slender strings when the husk has completely fallen off. These have each a small nut in the middle, but the white coating is the tallow, of which candles are made; and thus the Chinese, who, from local circumstances, kill but few animals as compared with the number killed in England, are furnished with a vegetable substance, which supplies the deficiency of the material used here for the manufacture of candles; but as their tallow is softer, and melts more readily than ours, they harden it with a coating of wax, which is also obtained from a tree, or large shrub, of which however it is no part, being formed upon it by little white insects that settle, at certain seasons of the year, in such vast swarms upon the tree, that it is completely covered with them, and becomes encrusted with a white, hard, shining wax, so that it is commonly known by the name of the wax tree. The tallow tree abounds in the Island of Chusan, where the manufacture of candles is extensively carried on; and, in fact, this is a very important branch of Chinese industry, as it is not only for domestic purposes that lights are required, but all the temples have to be supplied with those great candles that are set up at the festivals, before the images.

The Bamboo, and many of the purposes to which it is applied, have already been noticed. There are many varieties of this valuable production of the east, which grows in India as well as in China, some kinds being much larger and stronger than others, and differing also in colour. In the construction of temporary buildings, it is far more useful than timber, on account of its lightness; and from it are made excellent water-pipes, the cabins of the sampans, or family boats, ropes, &c. whilst it enters largely into the manufacture of paper. Its young shoots are a very delicate vegetable for the table, not unlike asparagus; and among the innumerable minor purposes to which it is applied, we may mention its employment at Canton in the manufacture of hats, which are made and sold to foreigners in that city. The making of these hats is a specimen of the ingenuity of the Chinese, who are very clever in imitating any thing they see; and will produce the counterpart of an European hat with the most minute exactness. The body of the hat is made of a composition formed of the inner part of the bamboo, beaten into a pulp, and mixed with glue. It is spread on a block of the proper shape, and, when dried, is covered and lined in the same manner as gentlemen's silk hats in this country.

There is another species of reed that grows in the marshes, very much smaller than the bamboo, seldom measuring more than two inches in diameter, the pith of which is the material commonly called rice paper. The pith is used in its natural state, being only pared in thin slices and rolled out into flat sheets, as we receive it in this country.

The Chinese paint flowers, birds, and butterflies, very beautifully on this paper, of which they also make artificial flowers in large quantities, a trade that has long flourished in Nanking, the reeds being found in great abundance in the neighbourhood of that city.

The Chinese are deficient in certain points of taste: they regard a shadow in a picture as a defect, and brilliancy of colours as the chief beauty; therefore, they succeed admirably in ornamental designs, but fail in landscape or portrait painting, not from want of ability, but from want of that knowledge which is only to be obtained by the instructions of those whose tastes have been better directed. The Chinese style of architecture, though frequently elegant, is deficient in grandeur and solidity. There are scarcely any magnificent stone edifices. The palaces consist of a numerous collection of fantastic buildings, highly ornamented, but, to our taste, without regularity; and many of the temples, although spread over a vast extent of ground, have no pretensions to be called fine structures. The roofs are usually supported by columns or walls of wood, which has always been the chief

Tower of the Thundering Winds.

material used in building; and hence we never hear of the ruins of ancient castles or other buildings of antiquity, which, in many parts of the world, particularly in India and Europe, remain to show what splendid edifices were erected in bygone ages. The great wall is certainly a wonderful monument of ancient times; but it is almost the only one that we read of in China, except a famous temple or tower, partly in ruins, which stands on an eminence in the neighbourhood of Hang-chow-foo. It is called the Tower of the Thundering Winds, and is supposed to have been built about 2500 years ago.

TAOU-KWANG.

The present Emperor of China, Taou-kwang, whose name signifies "the glory of reason," ascended the throne in the year 1820; and if he possess not the wisdom and talents of his grandfather, Kien-long, he has always maintained the dignity of his exalted station, and is consequently more respected than his predecessor, the weak-minded and vicious Kea-king. That sovereign had only survived the celebration of the sixtieth anniversary of his birth-day, one year, when he was gathered to his ancestors; and his second son, who was chosen, as before-stated, in consequence of having saved the life of his father in the insurrection of 1813, was installed on the day after Kea-king's death, with the usual magnificence.

The dominions of Taou-kwang, the first Chinese sovereign whose name is connected with English history, comprise the whole of China proper, Thibet, the greater part of those extensive regions of central Asia comprehended under the general name of Tartary; with the tributary kingdoms of Corea, Cochin China, Loo Choo, and Siam, which are governed by their own princes, who have the title of king, and are vassals of the Chinese emperor, to whom they send tribute. The distant Tartar tribes have always been found very troublesome dependents, and no sooner was Taou-kwang seated on the throne, than a serious insurrection broke out in the western tracts of Little Bucharia, which had been annexed to the empire by Kien-long. Cashgar was one of the chief scenes of the revolt, which, after a struggle of several years, was at length suppressed by the Mongul and Mantchow imperial troops, who are said to have been guilty of dreadful barbarity towards the insurgents.

Peace was scarcely restored in the West, when the internal repose of the country was disturbed by another rebellion of the mountaineers known by the name of Meaoutse, who had again become a numerous and formidable people, notwithstanding the extinction of some of their tribes by the emperor Kien-long. The cause of this fresh outbreak does not appear to be known, but they poured down in great numbers from their native hills, under the command of a chieftain who assumed the title of Wong, or King, and not only displayed the imperial ensign of the Golden Dragon, but wore a yellow robe, which is a direct assumption of the imperial dignity. All the mountain tribes, which are about seven in number, each governed by a separate chief, enlisted under the banner of this daring leader, and descended to the plains, where they defeated the imperial troops, and possessed themselves of four towns, from which they expelled the soldiers and mandarins, but did not injure the rest of the inhabitants, declaring by a public proclamation, that they were not the enemies of the people, but of the government. The viceroy of Canton, Governor Le, received orders from Peking to put an end to the rebellion; and, with that view, he assembled what he supposed would be a sufficient force to defeat them, but they were more formidable than he expected, and his army was repulsed with great loss; in consequence of which misfortune he was degraded and deprived of his government; for the spirit of the law is, that if a general is commanded to conquer, he ought to obey. Another mandarin, the viceroy of Honan, met with better success, and having retaken one of the towns occupied by the mountain bands, was rewarded with a peacock's feather, which is the highest badge of military distinction known among the Tartars. Still, the rebellion was not terminated, and the Meaoutse held out with determined obstinacy, for nearly six years, when in 1838, two imperial commissioners were sent from Peking, to treat with them upon amicable terms, and (by what means is not exactly known, although it is suspected large presents were not spared,) induced them to return quietly to their homes. It was then publicly announced that the rebels had been obliged to make the most humble submissions; but as they are as independent now as they were before, it is quite evident they were rather appeased than subdued; and if they really were bribed to withdraw, will most probably, ere long, repeat the same profitable experiment.

Scarcely had the mountain tribes laid down their arms, and retired once more in peace to their native wilds, than a war broke out of a totally different nature from any that had yet disturbed the Celestial Empire. Hitherto, the people of China had only been called upon to contend with barbarous nations, whose mode of warfare was familiar to them; and moreover, they had been accustomed to look upon the English with a degree of contempt, owing to the fact of never having known them in any other character than that of traders. Unconscious of their own inferiority in knowledge of the art of war, or of the improvement in weapons, and wholly ignorant of the great advantages which discipline always gives over numbers, they treated our countrymen as foes rather to be despised, than dreaded; and entered, without apprehension, into a contest, the result of which has certainly been to them most unexpected. To the Emperor, especially, who, far from the scene of action, and if we may judge from his edicts, fully impressed with the belief that England was some petty state, depending for subsistence on its trade with the Chinese empire, the manner in which the war terminated, must indeed have been a cause of astonishment; but some are of opinion that the Imperial ruler of China, and many of his satellites, know more of the real state of Great Britain, than they think proper, for political reasons, to acknowledge.

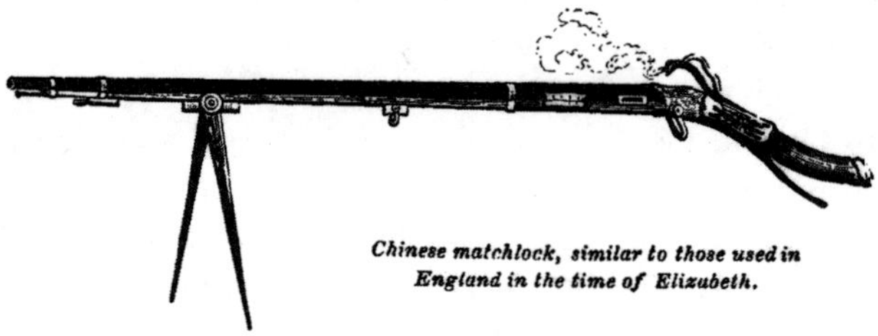

Chinese matchlock, similar to those used in England in the time of Elizabeth.

The commercial intercourse between England and China has been already traced, in the course of this history, from its commencement to the embassy of 1816, at which time the trade was entirely in the hands of the East India Company; and so it continued till the year 1833, when the term of their last charter expired, and all British subjects were equally at liberty to send out ships to China, for tea and other produce of that country, which till then had never been brought by any vessels but those belonging to the privileged Company. This alteration afforded ample opportunities for carrying on a contraband trade in opium, the importation of which was prohibited by the Chinese government; but the drug was eagerly purchased whenever it could by any means be smuggled into the country. In consequence of its injurious effects upon the health of those who indulged in the habit of smoking it, the Emperor Kien-long had issued a very severe edict against its importation; and the opium dealers were obliged to transact their business very secretly, for they continued to take it to China, notwithstanding the prohibition. At that time, however, the drug was so dear, that none but the wealthy could afford to buy it; therefore no notice was taken of the Emperor's command, or little attention was paid to it; for the mandarins and other great men, who ought to have seen that the laws were not violated, were fond of smoking opium themselves; so that the dealers were as much encouraged as before, although not so openly; and the smokers took care to enjoy their pipes in secret, as the Turks and Arabs are said to drink wine. The opium trade continued, therefore, to flourish, in defiance of the imperial mandate; and when the monopoly of the East India Company ceased, and ships belonging to private speculators began to make voyages to Canton, the forbidden drug was imported into China, in much larger quantities; and as it had become much cheaper, in consequence of being more extensively cultivated in India, it came within the reach of the lower classes; and thus opium smoking increased to such a fearful extent, that the attention of the Emperor was at length called to the subject. Anxious to suppress the growing evil ere its contaminating influence should extend itself still further, Taou-kwang consulted his ministers as to the best course to be pursued for that end. Some proposed that the trade should be made lawful, on payment of a heavy duty on the commodity, as was the case before the reign of Kea-king, when opium was used only as a medicine, and brought to China in small quantities. Others contended that nothing less than the strict prohibition of the mischievous drug would have any effect in checking the vice that had become so general, and advised that the penalty of death should be denounced against all who should be found engaged in, or conniving at, the sale of opium. It is thought that one motive for the anxiety of the government to put a stop to this traffic was, to prevent a vast deal of treasure from being carried out of the country, for the opium was never paid for in merchandise, but always in Sycee, that is, pure silver in ingots. At length, the Emperor appointed a mandarin of high rank, Lin-tsihsen, to the office of High Commissioner, with full powers to adopt any measures he might find necessary for the accomplishment of the desired object, and to punish buyers, sellers, and smokers, of opium, with the utmost severity. The new commissioner set out immediately for Canton, where he arrived in March, 1839; and having entered the city with great pomp, proceeded forthwith to the commencement of his duties.

The British trade was at this time, and had been ever since the expiration of the Company's charter, under the control of a superintendent, appointed by the British government, who, in the first instance, was to have resided at Canton; but this arrangement being contrary to the spirit of the Chinese law, the first superintendent, Lord Napier, was obliged to remove to Macao, where he soon died; his death having been accelerated in

Drawn by D. Clayton from a Drawing by Tinqua. On Stone by J. W. Giles

THE ENGLISH FACTORIES AT CANTON.

London, Dean & Co. Threadneedle Street.

consequence of the many vexations he had experienced in his intercourse with the Chinese authorities. Three officers had, successively, filled his place, neither of whom had been allowed to become permanent residents at the British factory, where the merchants are allowed to remain only just long enough to transact their business, the very longest term being four months, commencing from the fourth of December; and if their affairs are not settled by that time, they must leave them in the hands of the Hong merchants.

The Factories belonging to the merchants of Europe and America occupy a small space along the banks of the river, outside the walls of the city, and are built on piles, as their situation renders them liable to inundation. They are railed in, and have a space allotted for garden ground, with a promenade, called the Respondentia walk, which was all that the law allowed to foreigners in the vast empire of China, until the late concessions. The Factories are British, Dutch, American, French, Austrian, Danish, and Swedish, each consisting of several brick or stone edifices, built along the side of an open space of inconsiderable dimensions. Three streets in the suburbs, leading from these factories, contain the shops where foreigners purchase all they require for their own use, for they are not allowed to enter the town, even for the purpose of buying goods. Every one of these shops has a sign, like that of a country inn in England, gaudily painted and gilded. The occupiers are dealers in carved ivory toys, porcelain, and other goods, the trade in which is not restricted to the Hong merchants, whose exclusive privilege is confined to the more important articles of commerce, as tea, silks, and cottons.

When Commissioner Lin arrived at Canton, it happened that there were several British ships in the river, having not less than twenty thousand chests of opium on board. These he demanded should be given up, without delay, to be destroyed, requiring, at the same time, that the merchants to whom they belonged should bind themselves, by a written engagement, never to bring any more opium to China, and they were informed that, in the event of their breaking that engagement, they would be liable to be tried and punished by the laws of China. This unreasonable demand caused the utmost confusion in the British factory, as some of the merchants, chiefly those of Bombay and Calcutta, trusting to the encouragement that had been so long afforded to this particular branch of trade, notwithstanding its illegality, had embarked the greater part of their capital in the cultivation and purchase of the drug, for which there was now no market, so that their ruin would be inevitable, unless they could contrive to dispose of their opium secretly, as they used to do; and as this mode of traffic was always liable to detection, they naturally hesitated to give a bond that would place their lives at the disposal of the Chinese government, provided they should, at any time, be discovered in such illicit dealing.

The governor, finding that his orders were not complied with, issued a command that all native servants should leave the factories, which was instantly obeyed, simply because the poor fellows did not dare to act in a manner contrary to the decree of the ruling power. The factories were then surrounded by a body of Chinese and Tartar troops, who guarded the merchants as prisoners, while the Hong merchants were instructed to ascertain how many chests of opium were on board the foreign vessels, and the names of their owners. In the meantime, Lin published several manifestoes, addressed to the English, in the admonitory style used by the rulers of China towards their own people; thus proving how little he was acquainted with the English character and resources. In fact, the Chinese have always considered that, in permitting the outer barbarians, as they term all who dwell beyond the limits of the Central Empire, to trade to their shores, they are conferring on them inestimable benefits, for which they receive no adequate advantage in return.

The first address of the governor set forth, at great length, the benevolence of the Emperor towards the strangers, and their utter unworthiness of his favours. He reproached them with returning evil for good, in bringing into the country a poisonous drug, to injure both the health and morals of the people, and gave them to understand that, in case of continued disobedience, they would be forbidden to trade to China any longer. "Let our ports once be closed against you," said he, "and where can you look for profits?" In another part of the same remonstrance, he says, "Should you foreigners be deprived of our tea and our rhubarb, you would thereby lose the means of preserving life; yet plentifully they have been granted to you to carry beyond the seas. Can there be favours greater than these! yet are you grateful? Our central Empire, comprising a territory of many thousands of miles, and possessing, in rich abundance, all the products of the earth, has no advantages to derive from the purchase of your foreign commodities, and you may well fear that if your trade should be cut off, the livelihood of your several nations must come to an end."

This extraordinary document, full of that simple eloquence with which the mandarins of China are wont to instruct and admonish the people, was certainly absurd as addressed to Englishmen; but if we take into consideration the light in which the English were then viewed by the Chinese government, we shall only see in it a sincere desire to settle the dispute as amicably as possible, by persuading the barbarians to submit quietly to the Imperial mandate. This was evident from the conclusion of the manifesto, which promised them pardon and future protection, provided they would hasten to make submission, and amend their ways, stating that he, the High Commissioner, was induced to be thus compassionate, by reflecting that they were men from distant lands, and were perhaps ignorant that the pernicious drug they brought was so strictly prohibited. Finding, however, that this exhortation failed to produce the desired effect, the governor continued the blockade of the factories, and even threatened to put the occupants to death; on which the British superintendent, Captain Elliott, deemed it advisable to agree to the surrender of the opium, in order to secure the safety of his countrymen. Several weeks were occupied in the landing of the forfeited drug, during which, the merchants were still detained in the factories; but as soon as it was ascertained that all the chests had been brought on shore, the troops were withdrawn, and the captives left at liberty to depart.

In the meantime, the Commissioner had sent to Peking for instructions how to dispose of the property he had seized, and received the following order, in the name of the Emperor: "Lin-tsihsen, and his colleagues, are to assemble the civil and military officers, and destroy the opium before their eyes; thus manifesting to the natives dwelling on the sea coast, and the foreigners of the outside nations, an awful warning. Respect this. Obey respectfully." In obedience to this command, on the first of June, 1839, the High Commissioner, accompanied by all the officers, proceeded

The Bocca Tigris.

to Chunhow, near the Bocca Tigris, or mouth of the river, where large trenches had been dug, into which the opium was thrown, with a quantity of quick lime, salt, and water, so that it was quickly decomposed, and the mixture ran into the sea.

Some days before this transaction, the British merchants had retired to Macao, where most of their families were residing. This settlement still belongs to the Portuguese, who have their own government, and the privilege of trying any offender by their own laws, even though he be a Chinese. They have forts garrisoned by about four hundred men, some fine churches, a monastery, and a convent for nuns, who are occasionally seen walking in the town. The Portuguese employ a great many black slaves, as servants; but all the mechanics and workmen of every description, as well as the shopkeepers, are Chinese. The houses are built in the European style, the handsomest of them being chiefly let to English families. The most attractive object to strangers is, the cave of the celebrated Camoens, who was both a soldier and a poet, in which latter capacity he drew upon himself the displeasure of the Portuguese government in India, by some satirical compositions directed against the Viceroy, who banished him for five years, to Macao, then a new colony, where he selected, as a favourite retreat, a cool grotto formed by three huge fragments of rock; a spot well suited to the romantic genius of the poet, who there, it is said, composed the famous "Lusiad," a poem of which the Portuguese are justly proud, although the author was suffered to subsist upon charity, during the latter part of his life. The cave stands now in the Casa gardens, but has been disfigured by decorations in very bad taste, its most conspicuous object being, at present, a modern summer-house erected on its summit.

Soon after the British merchants had removed from Canton to Macao, it happened that some English and Chinese sailors quarrelled in the street, when one of the latter was accidentally killed by a random blow. The laws of China make no distinction between murder and homicide; therefore, when the governor of Canton was informed of this unfortunate circumstance, he demanded, as was the duty of his office, that the culprit should be given up to justice; but as the English are not amenable to Chinese law, they, of course, refused to comply. The governor, therefore, gave orders that provisions should no longer be supplied to the English at Macao, on which Captain Elliott removed the whole fleet to Hong-kong, a rocky island, about thirty-five miles to the east of that settlement, inhabited, at that time, chiefly by fishermen, but which has now become an English settlement, with a good town, built by its new occupiers. In the mean time, the British superintendent had written to Lord Auckland, the Governor General of India, requesting that he would send, without delay, as

Drawn by E. Clayton from a Painting by Tiqua. *On Stone by T. Gilks*

THE BAY AND ISLAND OF HONG KONG.

London, Dean & C°. Threadneedle S.t

many vessels and men as could be spared from the Indian station, to assist in protecting the lives and property of Her Majesty's subjects in China; and thus, towards the close of 1839, the clouds of war were gathering rapidly over the Celestial Empire.

The High Commissioner Lin no sooner became aware that the British fleet had removed to Hong-kong, than he issued a decree that all trade between the English and the Chinese should be suspended, until the former had given the bond he had at first required of them, signed with the names of all the owners of vessels engaged in the opium trade, as well as that of the superintendent, whom he termed the 'Barbarian eye,' meaning the chief, or inspector of the foreigners. The arbitrary conduct of the Chinese functionary has been much censured, and was, perhaps, both violent and unjust; but may it not be urged in excuse, that he was sent by his imperial master for the express purpose of putting a stop to an unlawful branch of traffic; and that if he failed in effecting that object, his own ruin might be the consequence. For a time, therefore, the trade was suspended, and the English ships remained in Hong-kong harbour, while the Chinese fleet was preparing to make an attack on them, under the command of Admiral Quan, a gallant veteran, who was greatly respected both by friends and foes. Hong-kong is one of a group of small rocky islands, which are so numerous round the coast of China, that one of the titles given to the Emperor, is

'Lord of ten thousand isles." The inhabitants were mostly poor fishermen, living on the sea-shore, in wooden sheds, and some in huts of a peculiar

character, a description of which, from the work of Mons. Borget, a late traveller, we proceed to give in his own words: Alluding to the narrowness of the space occupied by the habitations, he observes, "The first comers take possession of the ground, and there they place their worn-out boat. * * * Those who come next, place around the boat stakes of wood, thus forming a stage over the heads of their predecessors, either by hoisting up their boat, or when they do not happen to be so rich, by forming a flooring which they surround by mats, and cover in by a roof of the same materials; still poorer individuals follow, who having neither boat nor materials to form a flooring, nestle themselves in the intervals between the other habitations."

Hong-kong is not more than eight miles in length and five in breadth; exhibiting to the eye, on the first approach, a mass of steep rugged rocks, among which, however, are found many fertile spots, where rice is cultivated, and the inhabitants enjoy the luxury of plenty of good water, which in Chusan and many other islands is very scarce. The little town of Chuck-chuen, situated in the most picturesque part of the island, is an assemblage of white houses with blue-tiled roofs, and, when the English first arrived there, was the residence of the mandarin governor of the Island, and his subordinate officers. Hong-kong abounds in granite, which many of the inhabitants are employed in hewing for exportation.

In November, 1839, the British fleet in the harbour was attacked by Admiral Quan, but without success, as the Chinese were soon driven back, with great loss, several of their vessels having been destroyed in the action. This defeat was a serious blow to the authorities at Canton, who had placed great dependence on the admiral; nor did they dare to send a true account of the affair to the Emperor, who was for a time deceived into a belief that the Chinese had been victorious, and under this impression, bestowed a high Tartar title on Admiral Quan. He was afterwards made aware of the truth; but as Quan was a valuable officer, he was unwilling to dismiss him, and therefore affected not to believe the second version of the story. The admiral continued in command of the fleet; but Lin, who had given the false report, was very soon deprived of his seals of office as High Commissioner, although he was allowed to remain viceroy of the provinces of Canton and Quang-se.

This mandarin, whose name is so familiar to English ears, was much esteemed by the people over whom he ruled, being free and courteous in his manners, and extremely good-natured, though subject to be displeased, when his demeanour was haughty and abrupt. He is described as a short man, with a lively intelligent countenance, and by no means deficient in that rotundity without which a Chinese, of the male sex, has no pretensions to grace or beauty in the eyes of his countrymen or countrywomen. While he filled the office of High Commissioner, he kept up the state of a sovereign, and being the representative of the Emperor, exacted all the homage due to him in that capacity; as an instance of which, the Hong merchants were, on several occasions, obliged to remain on their knees, during a very long audience, except Howqua, who in consideration of his advanced age, was allowed to be seated on a low stool. The Commissioner himself was seated in state, behind a yellow satin screen, the emblem of majesty; to which, in fact, the homage was paid.

Just at this time, February 1840, there was a public mourning in China, on account of the death of the Empress, which was observed for one hundred days by all the government officers, who were ordered to take the balls from their caps, and not to shave for that space of time; but all public business proceeded as usual.

In the mean time, edicts were published almost daily, threatening to close the ports for ever against the English, if they continued to act in defiance of the Imperial commands. Lin and his coadjutors were exerting themselves to strengthen the fleet, by building a number of gun-boats of larger size, and superior in construction to the generality of the war junks, which were scarcely different from the trading vessels. Nothing of much importance occurred till the month of June, when an armament arrived from India, under the command of Admiral Elliott, which joined the British ships already assembled in the bay of Hong-kong. The apprehension excited by this reinforcement occasioned a bold attempt on the part of the Chinese, to destroy the whole fleet by sending fire-ships into the midst of it; but most of them exploded before they came near enough to do any mischief, and others did not even ignite; so that the experiment proved a total failure. This was a great disappointment to the chief mandarins, who had been so confident of success, that a proclamation had been issued, warning all foreigners who were not Englishmen, to avoid anchoring their vessels near the British fleet, lest they should be involved in the general destruction.

The scheme of the fire-ships having failed, high rewards were offered to those who should either kill or capture any of the English, or take one of their ships. The rewards were to be proportioned to the rank of the captives, and it was owing to this cause, that many of our countrymen were kidnapped by the Chinese of the lower orders, who were constantly on the

watch for any soldier or sailor who might chance to have strayed away from his companions. In this treacherous manner many were made prisoners and carried to Ningpo, where they were confined for some months, until released, in consequence of a treaty between Captain Elliott and Keshen, the High Commissioner who succeeded Lintsihsen. The persons most active in the service above-mentioned were chiefly fishermen and sailors of the very lowest class; who conveyed their unfortunate captives, some of them British officers, and one a female, to their destination in wicker cages of very confined dimensions; leaving them from time to time thus imprisoned, for hours, in the court yards of the temples, to satisfy the curiosity of the multitude, who came to gaze upon the novel spectacle.

This unwarlike mode of making prisoners was carried to a great extent, at which we cannot wonder, when edicts similar to the one following were constantly published: "Fishermen and other seafaring people are called on to go out and destroy foreign vessels; and whilst thus engaged, are promised that their families will be housed, clothed, and fed in the public offices at the public expense, and they will themselves be entitled to high rewards. The proof required of having destroyed a ship, is the board with her name; that of having killed an Englishman, his head; either of which, on being delivered to any district magistrate, will entitle the bearer to receive the promised reward. Englishmen sailing in small schooners or boats are ordered to be attacked and exterminated. Honours, rewards, and happiness will be the lot of him who kills an Englishman." It was by these unfair proceedings, and not by the chances of war, that British soldiers and seamen became prisoners in China; yet it is very probable that the Chinese, unacquainted as they are with the rules of European warfare, saw nothing dishonourable in taking every means in their power of ridding themselves of an enemy with whom they began to find they should be unable to contend in fair fight, and from whom they anticipated all manner of injury.

The Chinese army is composed of the native troops and the Tartar legions, the latter amounting to about 80,000 men, ranged under eight banners, and always at the disposal of the government. Their colours are

yellow, white, red, and blue; which, variously bordered, form eight different standards. The Tartar soldiers are far more effective than the Chinese, as they are warlike by nature, trained to arms, and regularly organized; whereas, the Chinese merely constitute a militia, as they dwell at their own homes, clothe and arm themselves according to their own fancy, and are very seldom required for actual service. Their chief duty, as military men, is to act as police in the cities; and in case of any local disturbances or rebellions of the mountaineers, they are obliged to take the field; but in general, they spend the greater part of the year with their families, engaged in cultivating the land; and as they receive pay from the government, every countryman is desirous of being enrolled as a soldier, for the sake of increasing his means of subsistence.

The enlistment of soldiers is a very remarkable ceremony, every man being required to give a proof of his strength, by lifting a heavy weight above his head, in the presence of the high officers of the district assembled in some large open space, when those who cannot raise it to the proper height, are at once rejected; and those who can, are sent up to a table to be registered. Five thousand volunteer troops were thus enlisted at Canton, about the time that Chusan was taken by the English, the Hong merchants having been commanded by the viceroy, Lin-tsihsen, to raise that number of recruits, which there was no difficulty in doing, for the stoppage of trade had thrown out of employment so many of those men whose business it was to carry loads of merchandize, that as soon as it was known, they repaired, in large bodies, to the place appointed, where five thousand of them were selected and registered.

The first conquest made by the English was, that of Chusan, which was taken on the fifth of July, 1840. Chusan, where there was formerly a British factory, is a fine island, about fifty miles in circumference, containing an immense population, and situated near the eastern coast of China, about half way between Canton and Peking. It is very mountainous, but between the hills are wide valleys, where rice is abundantly cultivated, and watered by the numerous streams that flow from the heights. Some of the hills are covered with tea plantations, others with sweet potatoes; and those that are not susceptible of cultivation, with tallow and cyprus trees; while in the plains are cultivated the finest fruits, cotton, tobacco, rhubarb, the sugar-cane, and vegetables of all kinds for the table.

Before the Tartar conquest, the rearing of silk-worms was very general in Chusan; but the Tartars cut down all the mulberry-trees in the island, and exterminated the inhabitants, who were among the defenders of the Ming family; since which time silk has ceased to be one of the products of Chusan.

Cotton is extensively grown and manufactured by the people for their own use, so that in every cottage the women are employed in carding, spinning, and weaving the produce of their own fields. The tallow tree is abundant; and the manufacture of candles, one of the branches of industry that affords occupation for the people, numbers of whom are also employed in making bricks and tiles from the blue clay, which is plentiful in this island, and when burnt, retains its original colour. Tinghae, the capital of Chusan, is a large city, standing in a plain, not far from the sea. Its high blue walls are fortified by twenty-two square towers, besides a wide moat, which runs nearly all round the town; but these defences were of little use, without artillery and soldiers, with which Tinghae was but ill supplied; so that the English took possession of it without any difficulty, and almost without opposition. On their first landing, indeed, the Chinese fired upon them from the town, and also from a high hill where a body of troops had been stationed; but these were speedily dislodged by the invaders, who had encamped upon the height which they called the Joss-house hill, from its being the site of a magnificent temple. The mandarins in the capital, on seeing this strong position occupied by the enemy, determined to abandon the city, which they had no means of defending, with any chance of success; and in the course of the night they evacuated it, followed by all the soldiers and the greater part of the inhabitants, who carried away with them such property as could be conveniently removed, so that when the English entered the town, the next day, they found it nearly deserted.

The streets of Tinghae are very narrow, and most of the houses are built of wood, and are painted and highly varnished. The temples are among the finest to be seen in any part of China, particularly that dedicated to Confucius, the walls of which are composed of very beautiful mosaic work; but the British soldiers paid very little respect to the Chinese idols enshrined within any of these buildings, many of which were very roughly handled, and some of them totally destroyed. To all the Budhist temples were attached a number of buildings in which the priests resided, but they were all deserted, on the approach of the enemy, except in one or two instances, where some aged devotee was left to watch over the lights burning before the idols. The joss-sticks which emit these lights, are frequently set in jars filled with earth, and being ignited, burn down very slowly, diffusing an agreeable odour. In one of the temples were observed three gigantic figures, seated in arm chairs, large lanterns being suspended before them, and on

Budhist temple.

a long table, beautifully carved, were placed a great many jars with joss-sticks burning in them, besides several porcelain vases filled with flowers; and what was still more remarkable, at each corner of the table was a jar filled with sticks on which characters were engraved, referring to certain books hung against the wall, which are gravely consulted by the Chusanites in the regulation of their affairs. Thus, if a man is about to undertake a journey, he proceeds to the temple, and having selected one of the sticks, he turns to the page pointed out by it, that he may ascertain whether the expedition will prove fortunate, and which is the lucky day for setting out. Superstitions of this nature are very common among the Chinese, especially of the lower orders; and the priests who receive a small fee from those who consult their books of fate, have an interest in encouraging the practice, for they are in general extremely poor, having little to subsist on but voluntary contributions.

The flight of the inhabitants from Tinghae was followed by the plunder of all the houses and shops in which any property had been left; not by the invaders, but by the Chinese, of whom numbers of the poorer classes are not very remarkable for their honesty. The presence of the English did not deter the pilferers from crowding into the town, and carrying off whatever they could seize; till these depredations were in some measure checked by the British officers, who posted sentinels at the gates, to prevent any thing being taken out, except coffins for interment. These were suffered to pass without question, until their numbers began to excite attention; when they were examined, and as had been suspected, found to contain all kinds of goods that could be put into them.

The peaceful demeanour of the English encouraged many of the citizens to return and re-open their shops, while the country people supplied them plentifully with provisions; but the climate was found very unhealthy for the British troops, many of whom died there, owing, it is supposed to the dampness of the flat lands, which are always so wet that the fields can only be crossed by the narrow paved causeways constructed for that purpose.

The news of the capture of Chusan was received with the utmost displeasure at the court of Peking. The Emperor wrote immediately to Viceroy Lin, with his own hand, or to use the Chinese expression, with the 'Vermillion pencil,' expressing his extreme dissatisfaction that his officers had not put a stop to the rebellious proceedings of the barbarians; and commanding the viceroy to repair immediately to Peking, to answer for his misconduct. The Emperor also wrote to Elepoo, the governor of Ningpo, an aged mandarin and a member of the imperial family, who was very highly respected, desiring that he would cause to be constructed, without delay, several vessels on the model of the English ships of war, to be employed against the British occupants of Chusan. The governor forwarded this extraordinary order to the head of the naval department at Ningpo, who, being utterly ignorant of the construction of English ships, and fearing the consequences of disobedience, killed himself in despair.

Towards the close of the year 1840, Admiral Elliott sailed up the Peiho river, to hold a conference with Keshen, the viceroy of Pechelee, who had just been appointed Imperial High Commissioner, and was on his way to Canton, with instructions to take measures for terminating the war. The great object of this wily politician was the recovery of Chusan, which he knew full well would be more easily accomplished by negotiation than by force; therefore he used all his endeavours to make terms with the admiral, who at length agreed to give up Chusan in exchange for Hong-kong, on condition that the merchants who had suffered by the seizure of the opium, should be indemnified for their losses, and that all the prisoners at Ningpo, formerly alluded to, should be released; and as these terms were not objected to, he consented to go round to Canton with a part of the British forces, in order to meet Keshen, on his arrival in that city, and there to conclude the treaty. The commissioner proceeded on his journey through the provinces, and made his public entry into Canton on the 29th of November, by which time the British fleet had arrived at Toong-koo island, not far distant from the entrance of the Canton river. The ships were plentifully supplied with provisions by the country people of Toong-koo, who brought to them pigs, ducks, eggs, and vegetables, in abundance. As they moved from station to station, these people followed, and at every place where they anchored, established a market on the shore, by erecting a number of houses with bamboo poles and mats, the women and children assisting in the work; so that a little village was built in a few hours, and carried away with ease, whenever they wished to remove.

Admiral Elliott was about this time obliged to resign his command, on account of ill health, and it rested with Captain Elliott to negotiate with Keshen, who did not appear very ready to fulfil the engagements he had entered into with the Admiral, although he continued to profess his intention of so doing. The Chinese have a maxim relating to the "Barbarians," which says, "when the territory of the sovereign is in danger, the people should make haste to deliver it: what would be the use of keeping faith with the enemy, thereby involving doubts and delays." The new governor, Keshen, was probably acting on this principle, and strengthening his forces to attack Chusan, while he detained the fleet at Canton, under pretence of making an amicable arrangement. At length, the English commander grew impatient at the delay; and on the fifth of January, 1841, sent word to Keshen, that if the treaty was not confirmed by eight o'clock on the morning of the seventh, hostilities would be renewed. No answer arrived, therefore on the morning in question, some of the Bogue forts were assaulted, and taken by storm, with dreadful loss on the part of the Chinese.

The Bogue, or Bocca Tigris, is a narrow pass, about forty-five miles from the mouth of the river, having the strong forts of Anunghoy and Chuenpee on one side, and that of Tycocktow on the other. Above these are the islands of North and South Wangtong; where the river is about two miles broad, that being the narrowest part of the Bogue; and these islands are strongly fortified. Beyond the Bogue forts the river expands considerably in width, being in some places as much as seven miles across;

but towards Whampoa it again becomes narrow, and, a little below that village, divides itself into two branches, from which numerous streams and canals run in all directions through many miles of paddy fields.

On these waters dwell thousands of families in boats, which may rather be called floating houses, for the poor people who inhabit them have no other homes. The river population of Canton is estimated at two hundred thousand, of whom the men go on shore in the day to work in the fields, or at any employment they can obtain; while the women earn a little money by carrying passengers in their boats, which they manage with great dexterity.

There are many of these dwellers on the waters, who gain their liveli-

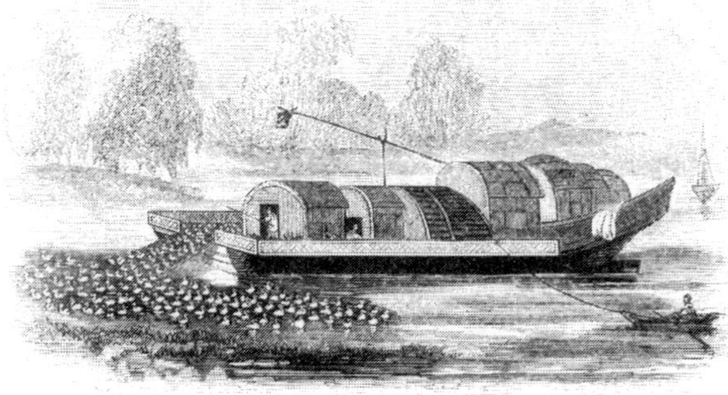

hood by rearing ducks. The boats for this purpose have on each side a compartment of basket-work, resting on the water, in which the ducks are kept at night, being sent out in the day to find their own food in the lakes and marshes. Each flock knows its own boat, and returns at the signal of

Painted by Piqua. On Stone by J. W. Giles

WHAMPOA_NEAR CANTON_THE ANCHORAGE FOR EUROPEAN SHIPPING.

London. Dean & Co. Threadneedle Street

the master, who stands on a platform to whistle back his feathered family, which is instantly seen swimming homeward. There are also other boats,

of a handsomer description, fitted up in very elegant style, and these serve as cafes, where Chinese gentlemen spend their evenings.

The appearance of a hostile fleet above the Bogue, caused great consternation among the inhabitants of the Canton river, who speedily removed their residences beyond the scene of danger. The forts first taken by the English were those of Chuenpee and Tycocktow, which were bravely defended by the Chinese and Tartar troops, hundreds of whom fell in the action; while many were destroyed by the burning of seventeen war junks, some of which were blown into the air by the firing of the powder magazines, and all on board of them perished. On the following day, a message was sent to Admiral Quan, chief in command at Anunghoy, demanding the surrender of that fort, on which he requested three days truce that he might communicate with Governor Keshen, on the subject; and this was granted. Keshen, who was now seriously alarmed, renewed the negotiation with Captain Elliott, promising to fulfil all the terms of the treaty, provided the Bogue forts were given up, and he also wrote to Elepoo, the governor of Ningpo, advising him to release the prisoners, as the only means of inducing the English to evacuate the island of Chusan. The forts were then abandoned, the captives were restored to their friends, and the British troops left Chusan and took up their quarters at Hong-kong, which they now considered their own, by the terms of the treaty, and on which island a provisional government was immediately formed, to which the inhabitants very readily submitted. The site of a new town was then fixed upon, and the Chinese proprietors received a compensation for their land, which was divided into building lots, and sold by auction; so that, in a short time, the town was actually in progress, a great many of the natives being employed in the work. In the mean time the Emperor, hearing that the English had met with still further success, sent to Ningpo, ordering that all the prisoners should be put to death; but this command fortunately did not arrive till two days after they had been sent away; and the only consequence that ensued from it was, that Elepoo was deprived of his office for his lenity.

Many were the changes that took place among the Chinese, during this war, both in their civil and military appointments; as every success of the English was sure to bring the displeasure of the Emperor upon some of his officers. In the meantime, Captain Elliott, finding there was no intention, on the part of the Chinese, to make any compensation for the opium, although this was a principal article of the treaty, proceeded again to the Bogue, where the Chinese had been busy in strengthening the fortifications. On the night before this second attack on the forts, which was made on the 26th of February, the heights of Anunghoy were covered with encampments, and thousands of lanterns were seen waving to and fro, in answer to the signal guns fired from the opposite fort, as a warning to the men to keep on the alert.

We will pass over the dreadful details of the second attack upon the Bogue forts, all of which were taken; and the brave old Admiral Quan, who highly distinguished himself on this occasion, was killed in the storming of Anunghoy, while leading on his men to repulse the foe. It was not immediately known that he had fallen, and his body not being recognised, was buried with the rest of the slain; but it was afterwards sought for and exhumed, at the earnest request of his relatives, who came with a flag of truce on the day after the action, to beg that it might be given up to them, and they carried it away with much sorrowing.

The Emperor was exceedingly grieved at the loss of the veteran, and gave proofs of the high estimation in which he had held him, by settling a handsome pension on his aged mother, and giving directions that his son, a young man about eighteen, should present himself at court, as soon as his mourning was over, to receive honours.

Keshen had already been degraded to a lower rank, and had received several angry letters from his Imperial master, to whom he addressed a most humble memorial in vindication of his conduct. He represented the great advantages possessed by the foreigners, owing to the superiority of their ships; stated that he had made enquiries for a cannon founder, that better guns might be cast, but that there had not yet been time to get them ready; and reminded his majesty that the war with the pirates, in the reign of his father, had lasted many years; and that it was with extreme difficulty they were conquered at last, although they had no better boats or guns than those in use among the Imperial forces. Yet with all the servility of a Chinese subject, he concluded his defence by owning that he had been guilty of disobedience, and deserved to die for not having performed impossibilities. The appeal was made in vain, but it was evident that the displeasure of the Emperor was excited chiefly by the correspondence maintained between the High Commissioner and Captain Elliott, which had probably been communicated to him with some false colouring, as the reply to the memorial was in these terms: "We cannot calmly put up with the insults of these rebellious foreigners, as you have done. Blinded and unwilling to see as you are, dare you still have the boldness to neglect our commands, and continue to receive their documents. Such proceedings pass the bounds of reason! Worthless that you are, what sort of heart is contained within your breast!"

These reproaches were accompanied by a hint of punishment, which was speedily followed by the arrest of the unfortunate offender, who was conducted to Peking in chains; and every member of his family was involved in his disgrace, according to the laws of China. His property, which is said to have been immense, was confiscated. He had several palaces, and extensive lands, besides many banking-houses in different cities. His wealth in gold, silver, and jewels, was also enormous; and among the valuables found in his houses were eighteen or twenty gold watches, two images of horses and two of lions, made of precious stones, a bedstead composed entirely of tortoise-shell, several crystal wash-hands basins, and a quantity of rich silks, broad cloths, and costly furs. All these treasures, a great number of female slaves, as well as several princely estates, became the property of the Emperor.

Orders were now issued for the raising of troops, in every province, to be marched down to Canton, that they might expel the enemy by force of numbers, and thousands arrived daily from all points; but they were mostly inexperienced, undisciplined villagers, unequal to contend with men accustomed to regular service; so that little was to be expected from their aid, although, in general, there was no lack of personal courage among them.

The Emperor had appointed his nephew, Yihshan, to the command of the armies, and had restored Lin to some of his former dignities, appointing him governor of Chekeang province. Orders for the extermination of the rebels, were repeatedly issued from the court, and promises of pardon were freely held out to all who had in any way committed themselves by holding communication with the barbarians, provided they would now make amends, by helping to destroy them; but in the meantime, every officer throughout the province, both civil and military, was deprived of his ball of honour. His Imperial Majesty also issued a mandate to the tea growers to destroy their crops, promising to make them full compensation for the loss; and this command was, to a great extent, obeyed, but not universally, some of the farmers being of opinion that crops were more valuable than promises.

The generals who conducted the armies were commanded to sweep every foreign sail from the seas, in order, as his Majesty expressed himself, to fill his Imperial mind with satisfaction; at the same time, warning his chief officers that they must expect to be severely dealt with, should they fail to exterminate the barbarians, or presume to make peace without his consent. In either case, the Emperor declared that he would himself take the head of his army, and make an end of English aggression.

Nothing could certainly be more impolitic than the threats of degradation and punishment launched against the generals in case of failure, as it naturally followed that they would use every means in their power to avoid the threatening doom; and thus they were led to send false reports of every military event of an unfavourable nature, so that the Emperor was never put in possession of the real facts, until circumstances rendered it impossible to conceal them from him any longer, which was not till the British forces were actually advancing towards Peking, in the middle of the following year.

At one time, about the commencement of 1842, the season being unfavourable for marching, the war was for a short time retarded, during which, Taou-kwang was so completely lulled into a belief that the foreigners had been brought to submission, that he sent tablets, on which were thanksgivings inscribed with his own hand, to be hung up in the temples, and the mandarins of every province were ordered to make sacrifices to Kwan-yin, the Goddess of Peace, for the restoration of that inestimable blessing. Yet during the very time whilst these rites were being performed, the English were in possession of Hong Kong, and several important cities, and were even preparing to invade the capital. These, however, were subsequent events. We may now, therefore, return to the approach of the Chinese armies towards Canton, and the renewal of hostilities. These were commenced by the Chinese, who, early in the month of May, broke through the truce that had been agreed upon after the capture of the Bogue Forts, by several hostile acts against the shipping in the river. At the same time, the British and Dutch factories were broken open by a large body of troops, and after having been completely plundered, were stripped of all their ornaments, and partly pulled down.

The losses of the English merchants on this occasion were very great, but those of Howqua, the rich Hong merchant, were still greater, for some fire junks sent against the British ships, having been drifted by the wind in a wrong direction, set fire to some of his warehouses, which were full of valuable goods; and before the flames could be extinguished, property to an immense amount was consumed.

It was now resolved to make a direct attack upon Canton; and while a part of the fleet, conducted by Captain Elliott, sailed up the river to the factories, to invest the city on that side, the rest of the ships, under the command of General Sir Hugh Gough, who had lately arrived from Madras, proceeded by another branch of the stream to a different point, and landed at a small creek, about two miles from the wall of the town, near which, on some heights, stood four fortresses, with guns mounted, and guarded by Tartar troops. These were all assailed at once, and taken by storm, the gallant defence of the Tartars costing many lives, and the people of Canton saw, with dismay, the British flag waving on the forts to which they had trusted for their safety. The firing from the walls of the city was continued all day, but at night all the principal inhabitants departed with their families, taking with them their plate, jewels, and other valuable property.

There is no doubt that Canton might then have been occupied by the English, without much or any opposition; but Captain Elliott preferred making terms with the authorities of that city, who, through the medium of Howqua, offered to treat for its ransom. The conditions proposed, and agreed to, were these. Six millions of dollars were to be paid, within seven days, for the use of the British government, besides a sufficient sum to indemnify those who had suffered by the plunder of the factories. The Imperial Commissioners, and all the troops, except those belonging to the province, were to withdraw to the distance of sixty miles from Canton; and the Chinese were to engage not to repair their fortifications, or erect any new ones, till the disputes between the two nations should be finally settled. This treaty was signed by Ke Kung, the governor, Yihshan, the Tartar commander-in-chief, and the Commissioners, on the day after the capture of the heights; and it was a great disappointment to the victors, just when they were preparing to take possession of the city, to receive a message from Captain Elliott, commanding them to stop all further proceedings.

The Tartar troops had scarcely marched out of Canton, when a new army, numbering apparently many thousands, appeared on the heights in warlike array, on which the English, who naturally suspected that treachery was intended, sent to require an explanation; but as the occurrence was as much a mystery to the ruling powers as to themselves, enquiries were instituted respecting the unknown troops, when it was ascertained that all the young rustics of thirty-six villages around Canton, had entered into a compact to deliver their country from the barbarians, and having armed themselves, had assembled to the number of about twenty-five thousand, for that purpose. Their valiant intentions were, however, frustrated by a peremptory order from the magistrates to disperse, and they returned quietly to their homes.

The despatches sent by Yihshan to Peking respecting what had taken place at Canton, were as far from the truth as can well be imagined. Not a word was said about the ransom money, but his Imperial Majesty was informed that the city having been in danger, and the people having begged for peace, the Commissioners had been induced to promise the barbarians one million of taels of silver for their opium, which, he said, was all they desired, and that when this demand should be complied with, they would be quite willing to withdraw to the outer waters, that is, beyond the Bogue. Thus the Emperor was kept in ignorance of the real state of affairs, while the forbearance of the British commander was purchased at the price of six millions of dollars, four of which were paid out of the treasury, and the rest by the Hong merchants, the share of Howqua being 820,000. When the greater part had been paid, and security given for the remainder, the British troops returned to Hong Kong. The arrangement made by Captain Elliott not being generally approved of, he was superseded by Sir Henry Pottinger, who arrived at Macao, in August 1841.

In the meantime, the mandarins of Canton, regardless of the treaty, were erecting new fortifications in many places along the river, and repairing those that had been injured; but the foreign trade was proceeding as usual, below Whampoa, a village about twelve miles from Canton, where the foreign trading vessels are usually anchored, and opium was again selling along the whole line of the coast.

The new British Commandant adopted a different line of conduct from that pursued by his predecessor, giving the Chinese authorities to understand that they must either accede to all the demands of the British government, or expect that very decided steps would be taken to force them into compliance. Not only did he require payment for the opium, but that

Drawn by E. Clayton from a Painting by Kipus — On Stone by J. W. Giles

AMOY, One of the Five Ports opened by the late Treaty to British Commerce.

London, Dean & Co. Threadneedle Street

other ports, besides that of Canton, should be opened to British trade; and he resolved not to terminate the war on any other conditions.

An expedition was immediately undertaken against Amoy, a strongly-fortified city and port, in an island of the same name, belonging to the province of Fokien, and situated, within a spacious bay, about half-way between Canton and Chusan. The town is large and populous, defended by stone walls and batteries, and has, from time immemorial, been a place of great trade, its merchants being classed among the most wealthy and enterprising in the Eastern world. It has a very fine harbour, with every convenience for loading and unloading ships, which can sail close up to the houses; and it also possesses a fine citadel, with a cannon foundry, and vast magazines for military stores in the suburbs, which are separated from the city by a chain of rocky hills, over which a paved road leads through a pass, with a massive gateway on the highest point. The streets of the city are narrow, but it contains several handsome temples, and houses belonging to the mandarins and merchants.

Stone cutter.

The fleet destined to attack this important place, consisted of thirty-four vessels, four of them steamers, which appeared off Amoy, on the twenty-sixth of August. The mandarins immediately despatched an officer with a flag of truce, to know why so many ships had come together, and what commodities they wanted. He was told they were not come to trade with the people of Amoy, which he probably knew perfectly well; and Sir Henry Pottinger sent a written answer, addressed to the chief commanding officer of Fokien, stating that the differences existing between the Chinese empire and Great Britain, made it his duty to take possession of the town, and to hold it until those differences should be settled; therefore, he intimated that, to save bloodshed, he would advise that it should be surrendered without resistance. The hint had the desired effect, and very little opposition was made; but despair caused several of the mandarins to commit suicide, which, in China, is not considered a crime, and is, therefore, often resorted to in times of difficulty and danger.

When the city was entered by the British troops, it was found in much the same state as Tinghae, on a similar occasion. The most respectable of the inhabitants had fled, and a great deal of property had been removed, but much had been necessarily left behind; and the streets were soon filled with plunderers, who, in spite of the efforts of the soldiery, contrived to appropriate a vast quantity of goods to which they had no claim. Leaving a garrison at Kolongsoo, a small rocky island, forming part of the fortifications of Amoy, the expedition proceeded to Chusan, which was speedily re-occupied, but not without the sacrifice of many lives on the part of the Chinese, who made an attempt to defend Tinghae, but were soon obliged to surrender; and this fine island was again governed by a British magistracy.

The next conquest was that of Chinhae, a large and opulent city at the mouth of the Ningpo river, the occupation of which was a preliminary step to the attack upon Ningpo itself. Chinhae stands at the foot of a lofty hill, and is inclosed by a high wall, about thirty-seven feet in thickness, over which may be seen the tall masts of vessels, gliding along a branch of the river that runs through the town. On the summit of the hill is the citadel, which, from its commanding position, is most important as a military station, being, as it were, the key to both Chinhae and Ningpo, the latter situated about fifteen miles up the river. This fortress is also surrounded by a strong wall, with massive gates, and on two sides, the height is so precipitous, that it is inaccessible, except at one point, where a narrow path winds from the sea, which skirts the base of the hill, and to this path there is no way by land. The citadel communicates with the town, by a steep causeway, to a barrier gate, at the bottom of the hill, where a bridge, over a moat, leads to one of the city gates; and when the British fleet arrived, every point was fortified with batteries, and guns mounted, while the hills were covered with encampments.

The taking of Chinhae was accompanied by some of the most frightful scenes of misery that were witnessed during the whole course of the war. The Chinese having prepared to make a vigorous resistance, the city and citadel were bombarded at once, and as the former was very densely peopled, numbers of the inhabitants were killed, even in their houses. Among the melancholy incidents of that dreadful day was, the bereavement of a poor man, whose four children were struck at the same moment, by a cannon ball. The distracted father was seen embracing their lifeless bodies in turn, and attempting to throw himself into the river, while his friends

NINGPO.— One of the Five Ports opened by the Late Treaty to British Commerce.

were holding him back. "These," remarked an officer who was an eye witness of this sad spectacle, "are the unavoidable miseries of war:" nor was it, on this occasion, a solitary instance of such calamities.

Chinhae was taken on the tenth of October; and on the following day, the fleet proceeded up the river to Ningpo, having left a guard of three hundred men in the captured city. The name of the river is the Tahee, and the country through which it runs is a highly-cultivated plain, intersected with numerous canals, and abounding with cattle, which is an unusual sight in China. The villages are numerous, and a large town is situated at every five or six miles along the river, while, in the distance, are seen ranges of lofty hills, forming the boundary of a very charming prospect. The whole province of Chekeang is luxuriant and beautiful, and contains an immense population, all the towns and villages being crowded with inhabitants. Numerous families also dwell on the waters, which are enlivened by verdure, as the poor people who lead this amphibious kind of life, cultivate little gardens on board their barges.

Hang-chow-foo, which, under some of the early dynasties, was the capital of the empire, is still one of the most wealthy and pleasant cities of China. It is supposed to contain a population equal to that of London, and is adorned with many elegant buildings. The shops are handsome, and well stocked, not only with native produce, but with British manufactures, particularly broad cloth, which is very much used in this and the more northern parts of China. The country around Hang-chow-foo is studded with ornamented villas, and lofty pagodas, and is beautifully diversified with hill and dale, the former covered to the summit with a variety of trees and shrubs, among which, the camphor and tallow trees are conspicuous, the one by their bright green, the other by their purple, leaves; and as Chekeang is one of the principal silk provinces, plantations of mulberry trees are found in every part.

The city of Ningpo, now a place of so much interest and importance to Great Britain, was taken without the least opposition on the part of the inhabitants, many of whom assisted the English to scale the walls, and open the gates, which had been barricaded, so that, happily, the terrible scenes that had occurred at Chinhae were not enacted on this occasion. Ningpo is a much larger city than Chinhae, and being in the immediate vicinity of the green tea districts, which are partly in Chekeang, and partly in Gan-hoey, one of the three divisions of the ancient province of Nanking, it is very conveniently situated as a trading station for British vessels. It has six arched gates, and is almost surrounded by water, the river running on one side almost close to the walls, and a canal, forming a boundary to the remainder of the city, with the exception of a small part of the suburbs. The ramparts are high, and so wide, that three carriages might be driven abreast on their summit, and the walls are strengthened by huge square buttresses on the inside.

The houses in Ningpo have generally two stories, the one raised above the other on pillars, each story having a separate tiled roof. All the good houses are within a small court, the latter paved with flag stones, and ornamented with flower-beds, and tanks for

gold fish. The principal entrance to these abodes consists of the usual triple doors, but those which form a communication between different apartments, are of many fantastic shapes, There are no glass windows, and when the English first arrived, there were no fire-places; but the officers very soon supplied that deficiency in the houses where they established themselves, and have thus introduced a convenience into China, which will probably become general among a people who are by no means indifferent to their personal comforts.

A curious incident, highly illustrative of the Chinese character, is related by one of the British officers, as having occurred during his residence at Ningpo. A paper was one day thrown over the wall, addressed to the English, containing, among other arguments, this singular appeal to their feelings, on the impropriety of remaining any longer in China. "You have been away from your country long enough; your mothers and sisters must be longing for your return. Go back to your families, for we do not want you here."

In the month of March, 1842, the Chinese made a desperate effort to recover the cities of Chinhae and Ningpo, which they entered on the same day, by scaling the walls; but in both cases, they were repulsed with considerable loss. At Ningpo, about two hundred and fifty soldiers were killed in the market place, when the remainder saved themselves by flight, scrambling over the walls in the utmost confusion. This attack appears to have been the result of a plan, concerted among the chiefs of the army and some of the governors, as a fleet of junks was sent just at the same time against Chusan, but equally without effect.

Having failed in their enterprises, the Chinese forces assembled at Tsekee, a town about eleven miles from Ningpo, where they formed an extensive encampment, and endeavoured to cut off the supplies that were carried every day, by the country people, into the city. This measure brought on an immediate engagement, and again the Imperial troops were put to flight, leaving above six hundred dead upon the field. For two months after this battle, hostilities were suspended, and the markets, as in time of peace, were plentifully supplied with poultry, fish, and very fine vegetables.

About this time, the Emperor removed to Zhehol for the summer, which gave rise to a report in the British army, that he had fled in dismay, on hearing of the preparations that were making for the invasion of the capital; but this mistake was soon discovered, as he haughtily refused to listen to the proposed terms of peace, and continued to issue orders for the total annihilation of the enemy, not being aware of the true state of affairs.

On the seventh of May, the British army left Ningpo, on its progress towards the north. The intention of the general was to proceed to Nanking, and take possession of that important city, as a prelude to the attack on Peking, provided the Emperor should persist in refusing to make peace on the terms demanded by the government of Great Britain. Between the mouths of the Tahee and Yang-tse-keang, or Ningpo and Nanking rivers, on the coast of Chekeang, stands the town of Chapoo, the chief port of communication between China and Japan. It is situated at the foot of a chain of wooded hills, which, on the landing of the English, were covered with Tartar troops, who fled without making any attempt to prevent the invaders from entering the city. The Tartar inhabitants of Chapoo, those who were able to bear arms being all soldiers, occupied a small division of the town, separated from that of the Chinese, by a wall, and built with the regularity of an encampment, where they dwelt with their wives and children, many of whom were made widows and orphans on that fatal day; for, unfortunately, when the soldiers fled from the heights, a party of about three hundred Tartars took refuge in a temple, to which they were pursued; and under the mistaken idea that, if they surrendered, no quarter would be given, they fired on the enemy, killing and wounding several British officers; an act of useless resistance that cost the lives of all, with the exception of about forty, who were made prisoners, but were subsequently released. Those who had sought safety in flight, on the first appearance of the British force, carried their families away with them; but most of the poor women whose husbands were killed at the Joss house, not knowing where to look for protection, and fully impressed with a belief that perpetual slavery would be their lot, should they fall into the hands of the foe, threw their helpless infants into the tanks and wells, and then destroyed themselves or each other. Many were saved by the timely interference of those they feared. From this, and many other scenes of horror witnessed during the war, it is evident that suicide is of more frequent occurrence in China than in any other part of the known world.

Soon after the capture of Chapoo, the fleet entered the river Yang-tse-keang, or the Child of the Ocean. This noble stream rises in Thibet, and flows through 2700 miles of country ere it reaches the sea, being the largest river in the world, except the Mississippi and the Amazon; and considering the innumerable canals which it supplies with water, to keep the country through which it passes under constant irrigation, the commerce carried on upon its bosom, the fruitfulness of its banks, and the depth and breadth of its waters, it may well claim the first place among the rivers of the globe. The right bank of the Yang-tse-keang is more picturesque than the left, on account of the chains of hills which rise behind each other, and which are covered with rich and varied foliage, not merely in the distance, but sweeping down to the banks of the stream; while the country on the other side is flat, and cultivated with rice, but rendered pleasing to the eye by many neat little villages. As the fleet sailed majestically up the river, the villagers flocked, in crowds, to the shore, to gaze at the novel spectacle of steam ships on the waters of China. On the twentieth of July, the fleet anchored at Chin-keang-foo, a strongly-fortified city, which, as regards its entrance by the Yang-tse-keang, is looked upon as one of the keys of the empire, and forms a barrier for the defence of the interior.

The river is, in this part, about a mile and a half broad, and near the shore rises the famous mountain of Kinshan, or Golden Island, the beauties of which are so highly celebrated by all Europeans who have had the good fortune to behold them. The town was garrisoned by Tartars, and the hills overhanging the river were covered with encampments of Chinese troops, who were in such numbers, as to present, at first, a very formidable appearance; but no sooner had the English set foot upon the shore, than they fled down the hills, and dispersed in all directions, so great was the terror now inspired by the sight of British soldiers. The Tartars, however, bravely defended the city, disputing every inch of ground, and firing incessantly from the ramparts, which were at length ascended by scaling ladders, and after some desperate fighting, in which many Englishmen were killed, the British flag was planted on the walls. Still the Tartars continued to resist with determined valour, fighting in the streets with their long spears, and firing with matchlocks from the houses, for several hours, till night came on, when they were obliged to give up the contest, and the inhabitants then began to make their escape from the city.

The taking of Chin-keang-foo is memorable for one of those extraordinary acts of individual resolution to which some would give the name of heroism, others, that of folly or madness. This was the self-sought fate of the Tartar general, who had made the greatest exertions to save the city, but who, when he found that the contest was decided in favour of the enemy, went into his house, and taking his accustomed seat in an arm chair, ordered his servants to set fire to the dwelling. His body was found the next day much burned, but retaining the sitting posture in which he had placed himself to meet the approach of death. Probably he had swallowed opium, to deaden his senses ere the flames reached him, as this is supposed to be not an uncommon practice. On the morning after the battle, the streets were found to be strewed with the dead; the houses were mostly deserted, those of the government officers were in flames; the shops were broken open and plundered; and female suicide was committed to a more fearful extent than even at Chapoo.

But let us leave this scene of horror, and proceed with the fleet to the famous city of Nanking, forty miles higher up the river. This ancient capital is still a large, populous, and wealthy city, and although exhibiting none of that splendour which depends on the residence of the court, is still superior, in many respects, to the present metropolis. It is the residence of a great number of literary men, and has many flourishing manufactures, particularly those of silk, and the cotton cloth which is known by its name. The city and its vicinity present many objects of attraction, among which, the porcelain tower still holds the first place. This celebrated work of art, and the temple to which it is attached, were built by the Emperor Yong-lo, ere he removed the seat of government from Nanking to Peking.

The pagoda is the most elegant structure of the kind that has hitherto been met with by Europeans in China, and takes its name from the tiles of white porcelain with which the solid brick-work of the building is covered, every tile being cast in a mould, with an indenture in the shape of a half cross, the bricks having a projecting piece of a similar form, which fits into the cavity. The tower consists of nine stories, and is remarkable for its correct proportions. Its form is octagonal, the angles being marked on each side by a row of tiles, red and green placed alternately. A light balustrade of green porcelain runs round each story, at every corner of which hangs a bell. The staircase is within the wall, and communicates with every floor. Each story forms a room with a painted roof, and contains a number of idols placed in niches; and each room has four windows, placed towards the four cardinal points. There are priests attached to this pagoda, to keep it in good order, and to see that it is illuminated at all festivals, the expenses being paid by the contributions of those who bestow money for such purposes in the hope of propitiating the deities.

It was about the middle of August, when the British fleet arrived within sight of Nanking, which was garrisoned by about fourteen thousand troops; and here another sanguinary conflict was expected, but happily this anticipation was not realized, for just as the attack was about to be commenced,

Drawn by B. Clayton from an original Painting by Piqua. On Stone by Dean & Co.

SHANGHAE. —— One of the Five Ports opened by the Late Treaty to British Commerce.

London, Dean & Co. Threadneedle Street.

a flag of truce was displayed, and the British general was informed that certain high Commissioners, deputed by the Emperor, were on their way for the purpose of negotiating a peace. These joyful tidings were speedily confirmed by the arrival of the three delegates, Keyning, an uncle of the Emperor, an elderly man of dignified manners, whose rank was denoted by his yellow girdle; Elepoo, the former governor of Chekeang, who has been already spoken of, and who was distinguished as a member of the royal family, by his red girdle; and a Tartar general, whose girdle was blue. The last, having been degraded for some offence, wore a cap with a white ball on the top, while the caps of his three attendant officers were distinguished by balls of a blue colour, denoting a superior rank to that of their master, who had not been deprived of his command, although lowered in point of dignity, a case of very common occurrence at the capricious court of the Celestial Empire. These high functionaries were conveyed on board the Cornwallis in a steam vessel, and opened the negotiations which terminated in a treaty of peace, which was most honourable to the English nation, and which was signed on the 29th of August, 1842.

As the British plenipotentiary had yielded nothing of his demands, all the concession was on the part of the Chinese government, which was thus placed in the novel position of being compelled to listen to the dictates of a foreign power, notwithstanding the vain-glorious boasting of a minister who in one of his despatches had said, "Shall a small nation dare to propose terms to the great central empire? such presumption cannot be borne!" The small nation did, however, propose terms, and the great central empire was obliged to accede to them.

The articles of the treaty were these: "Lasting peace and friendship to be preserved between the two empires. China to pay twenty-one millions of dollars, as an indemnification for the expenses of the war. The five ports of Canton, Amoy, Foo-choo-foo, Ningpo, and Shang-hae, to be open to the British, who should have the liberty of appointing consuls to reside in those towns; and regular tariffs of import and export duties to be established, so that the merchants might not be subjected, as they had been, to the impositions of the Chinese authorities." The island of Hong-kong was to be ceded for ever to the crown of England. All subjects of Great Britain, whether European or Indian, then prisoners, were to be released, without ransom or conditions of any kind. And lastly, the Emperor was to grant a free pardon to all those of his own subjects who had incurred penalties by holding intercourse with the British Officers.

The Emperor objected strongly to the opening of Foo-choo-foo, on account of its vicinity to the principal black tea districts; alleging that if the English shipped their tea at this port, instead of at Canton, the trade of the latter place would be ruined, and great numbers of his subjects thereby injured; but as the object of gaining access to this port was the very one that formed the ground of objection on the part of the Chinese government, namely, to avoid the inconvenience and expense of bringing goods four hundred miles for shipment; this point was insisted on, and eventually gained by the British plenipotentiary, who, as a security for the exaction of the treaty, announced his intention of keeping possession of Chusan and Koo-long-soo, until all the money should be paid, and the rest of the terms fully completed.

Foo-choo-foo, a place of considerable trade, and the capital of the province of Fokien, is seated on the banks of the Min, one of the great rivers of China. The country around is mountainous, and the scenery on the borders of the river is described as being very romantic and beautiful, resembling, here and there, the most picturesque parts of the banks of the Rhine; and as the climate is much more temperate than in the southern provinces, Foo-choo-foo will probably be more pleasant to the English as a place of residence, than Canton. The city stands on both sides of the river, the two parts being connected by a celebrated stone bridge, consisting of thirty-three arches, which is mentioned as a wonderful work of art, by the Jesuit writers of the seventeenth century. The liberty of trading to Foo-choo-foo is of the utmost importance to this country, as the black teas can be brought in boats direct to the ships from the farms where they are grown; and thus the enormous expenses of land carriage to Canton will be obviated. Shang-hae is one of the greatest commercial emporiums of eastern Asia, being advantageously situated for native trade, on the river Woo-sung, which flows into the mouth of the Yang-tse-keang, and thus communicates with the Great Canal, and the Yellow River. This port has a commodious harbour, and is frequented by trading junks from all parts of the empire. The streets are narrow, but many of them are paved with tiles, and although the shops are small, they are plentifully stocked with native commodities of all descriptions; and many of them contain English broad cloths and other European goods. The great advantage of Shang-hae, as a British station, is its easy communication, by water, with the interior provinces of the empire, and the populous cities on the Yang-tse-keang, and the Imperial Canal.

After the signing of the treaty at Nanking, the British ships began to leave the river, and by the end of October, the troops had all returned to

Drawn by R. Clayton from an original Painting by Piqua. On Stone by Dean & C°.

FOO CHOO FOO.—One of the Five Ports opened by the Late Treaty to British Commerce.

London, Dean & C°. Threadneedle Street

Drawn by B. Clayton from a Painting by Piqua. On Stone by Dean & C°.

VIEW OF VICTORIA TOWN — ISLAND OF HONG-KONG.

London. Dean & C° Threadneedle S^t

their several stations. Lord Saltoun was appointed governor of Hong-kong, where great improvements had been made since the British had been in possession of the island. The new town, the principal part of which is built on a hill, has made considerable progress, and many marine villas have been erected in the most picturesque situations by the English officers, for their own residence. A Baptist chapel, the first Protestant place of worship in China, was consecrated at Hong-kong on the 17th of July, 1842; and about the same time, a beneficent individual presented to the British authorities in the island, twelve thousand dollars, for the purpose of building a hospital for foreign seamen, either at Hong-kong, or any other of the British settlements. The donor is a wealthy Parsee merchant, largely connected with the British trade in India.

The peace so happily concluded at Nanking, was in some danger of being disturbed by intelligence which reached the British plenipotentiary, soon after his return to Amoy, of an atrocious act committed by the Chinese authorities at Formosa, who had put to death the crews of two vessels which had been wrecked some months previously on that island. The unfortunate men, amounting to above two hundred and eighty, thus cruelly deprived of life, were mostly natives of India, but subjects of Great Britain. There were also a few Europeans and Americans, six of whom were spared, on the supposition that they were of higher rank than the rest, and ought to be sent to Peking for execution; for it appeared that the Emperor had sanctioned the perpetration of this enormity, under a false impression that the ships had come to the island with hostile intent. Sir Henry Pottinger, on receiving the melancholy news, peremptorily demanded that all those who had been concerned in the transaction, should be degraded, and their property given up for the benefit of the families of the sufferers. The Emperor readily promised to investigate the affair, and make all the amends in his power for the cruelty and injustice of his officers, who will, no doubt, be severely punished, not only for their barbarity, but for having misrepresented the circumstances to their sovereign.

Not long after the sad event at Formosa, a serious disturbance took place at Canton, owing to the misconduct of some Lascars, which led to the assembling of a mob, and an attack on the British factory, which was plundered and set on fire. The English and American ladies were placed under the protection of Mingqua, the Hong merchant, who politely sent sedans to convey them to his factory, and even offered them an asylum in his house; but as the riots were speedily terminated by the arrival of Sir Hugh Gough, they had no occasion to avail themselves of Chinese hospitality, so that the unprecedented event of an English lady paying a visit to a Chinese family, has yet to be recorded among the curious events of the nineteeth century.

The ratification of the treaty of peace has been delayed in consequence of the sudden death of the High Commissioner Elepoo; but the monopoly of the Hong merchants is abolished, and there seems to be every reason to hope and believe that, in a short time, the social as well as commercial intercourse between Great Britain and China, will be so fully established, that the people of England will no longer be strangers in the Celestial Empire.

INSERT

FOLD-OUT

OR MAP

HERE!

INDIA.
English Miles
CABOOL
THIBET
HIMALAYA MOUNTAINS
Leh or Ladak
Cashmere
Peshawer
Attock
PUNJAB
Lahore
Umritsir
Mooltan
Lassa
DELHI
Delhi
Agra
Muttra
NEPAUL
Catmandoo
BHOTAN
ASSAM
BIRMAH
TIPPERAH
Indian Desert
DAODPOTRA
Beekaneer
Ajmeer
RAJPOOTANA
Hydrabad
Oude
Lucknow
Benares
Patna
R. Ganges
ALLAHABAD
Allahabad
BAHAR
BENGAL
Dacca
Moorshedabad
CALCUTTA
Gwalior
Kota
Oodeypoor
CUTCH
G. of Cutch
GUJERAT
Baroda
R. Nerbudda
Bhopaul
Indoor
Surat
G. of Cambay
KHANDEISH
BERAR
Nagpoor
GUNDWANA
Sumbalpoor
Cattack
R. Mahanuddy
Mths of the Ganges
ARUNGABAD
DECCAN
BOMBAY
Poonah
Sattara
Fort Victoria
Beejapoor
Hydrabad
HYDERABAD
Golconda
CIRCARS
Ganjam
Chicacole
R. Godavery
R. Kistnah
BAY OF BENGAL
Goa
Kurnool
Nellore
Pulicat L.
MADRAS
Arcot
MYSORE
Seringapatam
Mangalore
Laccadives
Pondicherry
Tranquebar
Calicut
Trichoor
Cochin
Madura
TRAVANCORE
Trivandrum
C. Comorin
GULF OF MANAAR
Palks Str.
Pt. Pedro
CEYLON
Trincomalle
Columbo
KANDY
Pt. de Galle
Maldives
INDIAN OCEAN

EARLY HISTORY.

It is universally believed that the rich, fertile, and extensive region known by the name of India, was one of the earliest civilized countries of the ancient world. It has never been, like China, a great monarchy united under one head, but has, from the most remote ages, been divided into many states, of which the early history is very uncertain.

The empire of the Hindus was probably founded as early as that of the Chinese, and, long before the Greek invasion, had attained to a high degree of prosperity, and made considerable progress in various arts. Several large kingdoms, under a well-regulated form of government, besides an infinite number of smaller states, were in existence many centuries before the Christian era; but there is no authentic history respecting their foundation, nor are there any records of their first rulers, except the romantic legends of the ancient poets of the land, which are full of fables. The Hindus, it is believed, were not the original people of the country, but colonists, who had wandered from some more western clime, and located themselves on the Banks of the Indus, where, at first, they occupied only a small tract of land, about one hundred miles to the north of the present city of Delhi. The period of their arrival is unknown, nor has it ever been ascertained from what country they came; but there is great reason to suppose that the first settlers were a company of priests, from whom descended the powerful order of Bramins, who established their religion with a form of government constituted by themselves, and gained an ascendancy over the barbarian natives by the influence of superior learning.

The surface of the country was, probably, at that time covered with extensive forests, and thinly inhabited by a few uncivilized tribes, whose origin is unknown. A broken chain of mountains, called the Vindya range, extending from east to west, formed a natural division of the country into two parts; all to the north of that chain receiving the name of Hindostan, all to the south that of the Deccan; and this distinction is still preserved by the natives, while the Europeans apply the term Hindostan to the whole of India. It appears that the north of the country was, for a long period, more advanced in civilization than the south, but as the Hindus became more numerous, they spread themselves southward, and gradually established the laws and religion of the Bramins all over India. Some have conjectured that the first strangers who formed a settlement on the Indus were an Egyptian colony, or if not so, that they had derived their knowledge of the arts they introduced into India, from the Egyptians. It has also been imagined that the Bramins were the wise men alluded to in the book of Kings, where we are told that, "Solomon's wisdom excelled the wisdom of all the children of the East country, and all the wisdom of Egypt." In all probability, these priests established themselves in India, with the view of becoming its chief rulers, as they brought with them a collection of sacred writings, called the Vedas, to which they ascribed a supernatural origin, and upon which all the ancient laws of the Hindus were founded. The people were taught to believe that these books came, by some miraculous means, from Brama, the supreme deity, who gave to the priests alone the power of explaining them, forbidding all men from seeking knowledge from any other source; and thus the Bramins, by the aid of superstition, became the sole instructors of the people, and obtained, in consequence, a most unlimited influence over them.

It is, therefore, evident, that the earliest form of government known in India, was that of a powerful priesthood; and it is supposed that the first code of laws promulgated among the Hindus, was compiled by the Bramins themselves about the ninth century before the Christian era. These laws, which are referred to as giving the earliest picture of the state of society among the Indian nations, were drawn from the Vedas, and framed with a view of maintaining the supremacy of the priests over all other classes, even that of kings. They are called the laws of Menu, and are said to have been the work of an ancient lawgiver, who, according to Hindu tradition, lived at the time of the Flood, from which he was miraculously preserved by the interposition of Brama; but the code affords in itself many proofs that it was composed at a period when the country was populous, and the people far advanced in the arts of civilised life, when the lands were in a high state of cultivation, and there were kingdoms governed by great princes; so that many centuries must have elapsed from the period of the Deluge, to have afforded time for such improvements; and thence it is inferred that the Bramins themselves composed these laws according to their own views respecting the best form of government to be established in the country.

The most important institution of this code was a division of the people into four distinct castes or classes, which were prohibited from intermixing either by marriage or occupation. The first class was that of the priesthood, who ruled over the political as well as the religious affairs of the state, and were treated with far greater respect than the kings, who belonged to the second order: their persons were held so sacred, that they could not lawfully be put to death, even for the greatest crimes; while any person who injured a Bramin, was punished with greater severity than for any other offence. The second was the warrior caste, called Kshatriya, which comprehended all the soldiers and rulers of the country; kings, princes, and magistrates. The third class, or Vaisyas, comprised the great mass of the people, as it included the husbandmen, merchants, and those who practised trades, except the lower order of mechanics, who belonged to the Sudra or servile caste, which was composed of servants and labourers. There were no slaves attached to the soil, but domestic slavery, which at a later period was universal over the whole of India, probably existed in those ancient times.

Besides the four principal divisions, the Vaisyas and Sudras were subdivided according to their avocations, every man being obliged to follow the trade or profession of his father, nor was it possible for him to alter his destiny, either by exertion of talent, or accumulation of property. The son of a jeweller was destined to be a jeweller, and the son of a husbandman inevitably became a farmer and nothing else; nor were the Bramins or Warriors at liberty to leave their respective classes for any other; but the Bramins were afterwards frequently employed as soldiers, like the Catholic monks of the middle ages; although no one could become a Bramin, unless born in that high caste. These rules have, with some variations, been preserved down to the present day, and have always exercised a direct influence over all the customs and manners of the Indian nation; as it was necessary to make a great number of laws with regard to the domestic habits of the people, in order to maintain the entire separation of the castes; for it may easily be supposed that, if the people had not been so restricted as to render it impossible for them to change their mode of life, without incurring severe penalties, many would have chosen other pursuits than those marked out for them by the accident of birth. Yet the ancient Hindus are represented as a happy and prosperous nation, living under a mild government, and free from most of the oppressions that usually accompany despotism.

The influence of the Bramins was, in those times, unbounded, for the kings were enjoined by the laws to select their ministers from among that class, to treat them with respect, and to learn from them; and the lands of a Bramin who died without male heirs, did not devolve on the king, like those of other persons, but were divided among the members of his order. The Bramins were the only physicians, the only judges, and the only teachers; it was deemed impious to act contrary to their will, and refractory princes were sometimes deposed by their authority. Yet they did not obtain this high consideration without much labour and self-denial, for they were obliged to submit to many severe penances, and lead a very austere life, in order to gain a reputation for that superior sanctity which has always been found the surest means of acquiring influence over a half civilized people. Even the Sudras, who, being a servile class, were considered unworthy of sacred instruction, so that all knowledge of the Vedas was kept from them, were taught to believe that by serving a Bramin faithfully, their souls would pass, after death, into a body of a higher caste; and by that means, they might hope to be admitted to higher privileges in their next state of existence.

The religious rites of the ancient Hindus were conducted with a degree of magnificence not excelled in any other part of the world. The temples were grand, and the ceremonies, particularly that of sacrificing, were imposing. The festivals were enlivened by music and dancing, and their splendour was generally increased by a gorgeous procession. The ancient religion of the Hindus was different from that which now exists. One supreme being was worshipped under the name of Brama, and the two gods, Siva and Vishnu, were also held in veneration as separate forms of

Vishnu. *Siva.* *Brama.*

the Chief Deity. They were considered as embodying the different attributes of one power, Brama being worshipped as the Creator of all things, Vishnu as the Preserver, and Siva as the Destroyer. The sun, moon, and stars, were also early objects of adoration; as were likewise the elements, and some of the rivers; among which latter, the Ganges was held the most sacred, and continues to be so to this day. The Bramins taught the doctrine of transmigration, which is still the prevailing faith of the Hindus, who believe that, between each state of existence upon the earth, they shall pass many thousands of years, either in bliss or pain, among the ever-blooming bowers of beneficent deities, or the gloomy abodes of evil spirits. They believe that Vishnu has already appeared in the world under nine different forms, the last of which was, that of the Sage Budha, worshipped by the Chinese, who came upon earth in the fifth century before the Christian era. Siva is represented as a God of Terror, dwelling amidst eternal snows on the summit of the Himalaya mountains, with his consort, the goddess Devi, to whom many temples in India are dedicated.

The simple religion which, at first, taught the people to adore one Divine power as the universal Creator, and other gods merely as personifications of his various attributes, in course of time degenerated into idolatry, by the practice of setting up numerous heroes as objects of adoration, and filling the temples with their images. Among the most celebrated of these were Rama and Crishna, two great warriors, the former supposed to have been the first king of Oude, the latter the first king of Magadha; and both are still worshipped in most parts of India. Each is adored by his votaries as one of the several forms of Vishnu, and the two great epic poems of Ramayuna and Mahabharat, which, together with the sacred books, constitute the chief authorities for the ancient history of India, celebrate the warlike exploits of those renowned heroes of antiquity. Rama was probably a great chief, who, having founded a kingdom in Hindostan, extended his dominions by conquest, and perhaps invaded the Deccan, then in a state of barbarism, inhabited by the original tribes, who were not of the Hindu race. Many fables are mixed up with the poetical history of Rama; tales are told of his warlike exploits, in which he is celebrated as the conqueror of the king of Ceylon, a terrible giant, who had carried off his queen, and kept her a prisoner in his castle. This the hero stormed, overthrew the giant, and rescued the lady. A festival, which used to be kept with great splendour, is still held every year in commemoration of this victory; and the character of Rama is so highly reverenced among the Hindus, that, in their customary salutation on meeting each other, they repeat his name.

As there were, in very early times, several independent states established in Hindostan, under the dominion of kings or rajas, all governed by the same laws, and subject to the same institutions, it is reasonable to suppose that the Bramins who made the laws, also took some part in the founding of the kingdoms, and helped to set up kings in them, still retaining in their own hands the greatest share of authority. Each kingdom was divided into military districts, every district being protected by a body of stationary troops, whose services were frequently in requisition against the neighbouring princes. Some of the earliest states established in the Deccan were possessed by the Bramins, and ruled by an assembly of that sacred order, the chief ruler being elected every three years; but, in course of time, they transferred the government to a military chief, still retaining the lands, which they let to men of the agricultural class, who were settled in colonies, under the same regulations as in Hindostan.

The most interesting feature of the Hindu government, and the most important, next to that of the institution of castes, was the establishment of townships, or village communities, which exist at the present day, in many parts of India, nearly in the same state as they did in ancient times. From the nature of the townships, it may be supposed that, when the people were separated into classes, the husbandmen were settled in villages, to each of which was attached a certain extent of land, to be cultivated by that community, every family taking an equal portion. They were not

Painted by J. R. Rawlins

On Stone by Dean & Co.

HEADMAN OF THE VILLAGE HOLDING HIS COURT.

London: Dean & Co., Threadneedle Street.

Page 263

placed there as vassals to toil for a feudal master, but were all freemen, and paid rents for their lands, amounting to about one-fourth of the produce collected by the headman, or chief of the village, appointed in those days by a superior, but whose office afterwards became hereditary. There seems at that period to have existed a sort of feudal system, since there were lords of large territories, answering to feudal fiefs, containing a thousand townships, who held supremacy over the lords of one hundred villages, subordinate to whom were the governors of ten villages, and these latter rulers appointed the headmen. The many revolutions that have taken place in the country at various times, have occasioned great alterations in this system, but every village has still its headman, and many of them are yet in the same state of happy simplicity which distinguished them in former days.

It is not exactly known by what tenure lands were held in India, or who were the actual proprietors of the soil. The kings were ostensibly the owners of all land within their dominions, except that belonging to the priests, and certainly derived a revenue from them; but it is supposed that, in many instances, other persons became the proprietors, by paying a fixed sum annually to the government, and receiving the rents for themselves of the farmers or ryots; but whether the latter ever were the owners of the fields they cultivated, seems a matter of uncertainty. They enjoyed, however, most of the advantages of landowners, for they were left in possession of three-fourths of the produce of their labour, and their farms descended to their children, being equally divided amongst the sons, who were bound to maintain their sisters as long as they remained unmarried.

The husbandmen never lived in isolated farms, but associated together in a village, which was sometimes surrounded by a wall, and defended by a little citadel; sometimes enclosed only by a fence for the protection of the cattle at night. The headman was looked up to as the father of the village, who regulated all its affairs, and administered justice in the manner of the ancient patriarchs, holding his simple court under a tree.

Village lands were parcelled out in a peculiar manner, being first divided into different qualities, some parts being more fertile than others, and not adapted for the same kind of produce; therefore every farmer took a fair share of the inferior with the good; and thus no one had greater advantages than another. The principal objects of cultivation were cotton, sugar, spices, corn, rice, and various other sorts of grain; the first of these productions supplying the material for the chief manufactures of the Indians, which were calicoes and muslins, famous in ancient as well as modern times for the beauty of their texture, and universally worn by both sexes.

The male costume of all ranks, consisted of two long pieces of white or chintz cotton, one wrapped round the waist, and hanging down below the knee; the other thrown across the shoulders, and occasionally over the head. The legs were bare, and very often the feet also, but most men had embroidered slippers, turned up at the points, which they put on when they went out. They wore long beards, which they dyed with henna or indigo, with the intention of making them red or black, according to fancy; but mistakes sometimes occurred in the operation, by which they were turned green or blue; and thus we read of the Indians dyeing their beards of various colours, although it is most likely some of the varieties were produced unintentionally. The dress of the women also was composed of two shapeless garments, differing, however, from those of the men, in being much larger, so that they reached to the ground. Both sexes wore necklaces, earrings, and bracelets, the value of such ornaments depending, of course, upon the rank of the wearer. The old Hindu dress is still worn in many parts of India, especially by the Bramins.

The state of female society in India during the early ages, affords one of the best proofs of the civilization and liberal government of the ancient Hindus. Women were not condemned to live in seclusion as they are in other Asiatic countries, neither were they treated as inferiors; one great reason of which might be that the Hindus did not give money for their wives, like the Egyptians and Chinese; but, on the contrary, received portions with them, which placed them on more equal terms with their husbands than in countries where they were in a manner purchased of their parents. They could hold property, and the fortune which a woman brought to her husband was always inherited by her daughters, and was secured to them by the laws of Menu, which expressly stated that the king should be the guardian of all widows and unmarried women, and that it was his duty to take care that their property should be protected from any encroachment. This law is referred to as a proof that the revolting custom afterwards practised by widows of burning themselves with the bodies of their deceased husbands, was unknown at the period when the code was composed; so that the odium of that barbarous rite does not rest with the early legislators, who, on the contrary, guarded the widowed female from oppression, and allowed her to contract a second marriage.

A Suttee is mentioned as a rare occurrence, by the Greek writers who attended Alexander in his expedition to India; but from that time, such dreadful scenes were often witnessed, and it is to be feared that the sacrifice was not always voluntary.

The commerce of India flourished at a very remote period, when it was carried on overland, chiefly with the Egyptians, who, for security, formed themselves into those large bodies called caravans, made laws for themselves, and chose officers to govern them on their journey. Providence had furnished them with an animal capable of carrying burthens across the hot sandy deserts, a service for which the camel seems expressly designed, since it is gifted with extraordinary strength, and requires but little food; while it possesses the singular faculty of taking at once a quantity of water sufficient to last for several days; so that where the horse would faint from thirst, the camel feels no inconvenience.

As a commercial country, India has, from the earliest ages, been an object of attention, and, on account of its wealth, of military depredation; and in the time of Darius Hystaspes, who gained possession of a small part adjoining his own dominions, the conquered territory formed the richest portion of the Persian empire.

It was more than a century before the Greek invasion, that Budha, the great reformer of the Braminical religion, appeared in India, where he devoted his life to the instruction of the people, and the introduction of a new system, with a view of lessening the power of the priesthood; a task he endeavoured to accomplish by denying the authority of the Vedas, and not admitting distinctions of caste. This celebrated sage, who was the son of some obscure Indian prince, and whose real name was Gotama, is worshipped by his votaries as Vishnu in his ninth earthly form. It is supposed that the religion he founded prevailed over the greater part of India, for many centuries, and that it did not entirely disappear from the Deccan, till about the tenth century of our era; since which time, the Braminical system has been introduced, which differs very materially from that originally established. Both Bramins and Budhists inculcated the doctrine of transmigration, and therefore interdicted the use of animal food, and the destruction of animal life, except for sacrifice.

The Budhist priests lived in communities, like the monks of Europe, and were forbidden to marry; whereas the Bramins had no monasteries, and were enjoined to take wives, whom they usually chose from their own caste, although they were not prohibited from forming alliances with the daughters of Kshatriyas; for a Hindoo, of any grade, might choose a wife from an inferior, but not from a superior caste.

The Budhists had temples excavated in the rocks, some of which are among the most interesting antiquities of India. The caves of Ellora,

which are about two hundred miles to the east of Bombay, consist of a great number of large and lofty apartments, decorated with columns and statues; and there is also an extensive excavated temple at Carlee, between Bombay and Puna, which resembles a Gothic church, having a vaulted roof, and colonnades running like aisles along each side. The principal monuments of ancient Hindu opulence and superstition are found in the Deccan; for, although the northern part of India was earlier and more highly civilised, it was repeatedly ravaged, and many of the finest specimens of native art destroyed, by the Mohammedans, long before they found their way across the Vindya mountains.

INVASION OF THE GREEKS.

IN the fourth century before the Christian era, Alexander the Great, having overrun the whole extent of the Persian empire, led his conquering armies to the shores of the Indus, spreading misery and desolation throughout the whole of the extensive country watered by the branches of that river, and called the Panjab.

Hindostan contained, at that period, three large kingdoms, besides a great number of petty states. The chief kingdom was that of the Prasii, which occupied the greater part of that immense plain through which the mighty Ganges takes its course. The capital of this empire was Palebothra, described by the Greeks as a magnificent city, eight miles in length, surrounded by a wall, with sixty-four gates, and fortified with more than five hundred towers. The modern city of Patna now stands on or near its site. The other large kingdoms occupied nearly the whole of the Panjab, and were ruled by the rival princes, Porus and Taxiles, the former of whom, after being subdued by Alexander, became the friend of that monarch, and assisted him to extend his conquests. The Indians used war chariots and elephants in battle. They wore armour, and their weapons were spears, long pikes, bows and arrows, the latter six feet in length.

Porus met the Greeks on the banks of the Hydaspes, the western boundary of his dominions, where he was defeated, and retired from the field severely wounded; but being pursued and brought before the conqueror, he conducted himself with so much dignity under his misfortunes, that Alexander seems to have been struck with admiration, and was desirous of displaying his own magnanimity to so great a prince, since he gave him back his kingdom, and requested his friendship, which the noble Indian did not withhold; and these illustrious allies conquered some of the smaller states, which were added to the dominions of Porus. Alexander made no permanent conquests in India, but he built a fort and constructed a harbour, at Pattala, on the banks of the Indus, supposed to be the modern Tatta, which became the seat of a considerable trade.

The advanced state of Hindu civilisation at this period, although it had not reached so high a point as was imagined until some errors had been dispelled by modern researches, was manifested by the great public works met with by the invaders in various parts of Hindostan, the most useful of which were excellent roads, furnished with mile stones, and houses of entertainment for travellers. When a king made a journey, he travelled in great state, with numerous guards and attendants, accompanied usually by the queen, and a train of females belonging to the court. He was carried in a palanquin on the back of an elephant, or rode in a chariot drawn by oxen. Over the head of the sovereign was borne a white umbrella, which, together with golden slippers, formed the insignia of royalty; while all the nobles had umbrellas of various colours carried over them.

All the elephants in the country were considered the property of the monarch within whose dominions they were found; and as these noble animals were generally trained to war, and always employed to increase the magnificence of religious and state processions, the power and grandeur of a monarch was often estimated by the number of elephants he possessed, as he was almost sure to have a corresponding number of horses and chariots. The elephant is found in the vast forests both of Hindostan and the Deccan; the camel, too, is an inhabitant of some parts of the country, particularly near the shores of the Indus; and the tiger is well known as a native of Bengal.

All Eastern nations have, from time immemorial, been fond of gorgeous display, a taste which none have had more ample means of indulging than the Indians, who, in all ages, have procured abundance of riches, by supplying other countries with the luxurious productions of their own. Their spices and perfumes were inexhaustible sources of wealth, while the diamond mines of Golconda and Visiapour have always been celebrated. It seems doubtful whether silk was a native production of India, but it is not mentioned as an article of wearing apparel, as the state dresses of princes were of muslin, embroidered with gold, and cotton was the staple commodity of the country. Silk, however, was cultivated and manufactured probably before the Christian era, though not to a great extent.

The principal food of the people consisted of fruits, and different sorts of grain, and milk. It was customary for the rich to plant orchards, and construct ponds for the public benefit; but although the trees frequently produced two crops in the year, and the farmers reaped two harvests from their fields, the miseries of famine were sometimes experienced, in consequence of the failure of the periodical rains, which generally fall for about four months, causing the rivers to overflow the country, which, by that means, is rendered fertile.

On quitting India, Alexander left a part of his army in Bactria, or Balkh, a country between India and Persia, where, about 250 B.C. a powerful Greek kingdom was established, which, there is reason to suppose from recent discoveries, extended, at one period of its existence, over all that now is comprised within the kingdom of Cabul. The Indians seem to have remained generally at peace with the Greeks of Bactria, and, probably, learned from them the art of coining money; for although they had been a commercial nation for many ages, it is very doubtful whether they had any regular coin before they came into familiar intercourse with the Greeks; or if they had, their coinage consisted of very rude specimens, such as bits of silver of irregular shapes, bearing a rough device intended to represent the sun, or moon. It is therefore imagined they used, as a medium of exchange, ingots of gold and silver, of certain weights, as was the custom of the Chinese.

The kingdom of Bactria flourished under its Greek sovereigns, till it was overthrown, about a century before the Christian era, by the Scythians, or Tartars, who established their barbaric rule over the greater part of that country to which the late war has given so much interest.

The invasion of Alexander had produced no material changes in the state of India, which, after his departure, remained almost undisturbed, except by the wars of its own princes, until the more dangerous intrusion of the Mohammedans led the way to great revolutions in every part of the country. During that interval, very little is known respecting the history of the Hindus, but there is little doubt that the ancient religion of the Bramins was subverted by the influence of Budhism, which is supposed to have prevailed over the whole of the Deccan, and of which, traces have been found in the most northern parts of Hindostan.

In the meantime, the trade of the country was greatly extended by the increasing demand for Oriental luxuries among the Romans, whose wants were supplied by the merchants of Alexandria, who, at this period, carried on their commerce by sea as well as by land. The principal manufacture of the Hindus was the fine muslin of Bengal, and they exported dying drugs, which produced more brilliant colours than those of any other country; but the chief commodities brought from India were jewels, spices, perfumes, sugar, cotton, and small quantities of raw silk. The merchants of Alexandria carried from Egypt, among the numerous productions of that country, presents for the kings to whose ports they traded, consisting of silver vessels, musical instruments, the wines of Cyprus, precious ointments, dresses of the finest fabric, and beautiful female slaves, skilled in the arts of dancing and playing on various instruments.

ARAB AND AFGHAN INVASIONS.

IT was soon after the introduction of the Mohammedan religion that the Afghans began to be famous in the history of India. They consisted of various warlike tribes, inhabiting the mountains of Ghor, and other hilly districts bordering on Cabul and Persia, where they had dwelt, from time immemorial, as an independent, semi-barbarous people, whose origin is unknown. They were not of Hindu race, and are supposed to have been fire worshippers, until the time of Mohammed, to whose religion they became early converts, and, in obedience to the laws of the Koran, propagated his creed by the sword, and frequently invaded the Hindu territories. The Arabs, too, having spread their conquests over all Persia, made frequent inroads into Cabul, which appears to have been, at that time, inhabited by Indians, and under the dominion of Hindu Rajas.

The history of India up to this period, is vague and uncertain. The great kingdoms that formerly existed had become divided into smaller states, and the whole country seems to have been composed of a multitude of principalities, without any one great leading monarchy among them. The chief share of power in Hindostan was possessed by the Rajputs, or warrior class of royal race, who were the most determined and most successful opponents of the Musselman invaders. The Rajputs all held lands by a feudal tenure, which bound them to perform military service for their respective princes, and thus they constituted a national militia, always being in readiness to take the field on any emergency. They were men proud of their noble descent, and celebrated in history for many of those romantic deeds of heroism, which it is difficult to determine whether to admire or condemn. The chief seat of the Rajputs was the kingdom of Ajmir, situated to the south-west of Delhi and Agra, between those provinces and the great Sandy Desert.

The first conquest of importance made by the Afghans was, a portion of the territory of Lahore, the capital of which, named Lahore, was a city of great antiquity in the Panjab, and became the residence of the first Mohammedan rulers in Hindostan. It is now the capital of the Sikhs, a new power that arose on the ruins of the Mogul Empire. The late ruler of Lahore, Runjeet Singh, was an ally of the British government in the early part of the Afghan war.

The invasions of the Arabs were, for a long time, confined to the west of the Indus, and were attended with varied success, until the beginning of the eighth century, when they began to make further inroads, and obtained possession of the province of Scind in the same year that the famous Arab general, Taric, crossed over from Africa into Spain, and commenced the rapid course of conquests that ended in the establishment of a Mohammedan empire in Europe.

The province of Scind was conquered by Mohammed Casim, a young warrior, who was sent with an army to besiege the port of Dewal, in consequence of the refusal of the Raja to indemnify some Arabian merchants for the seizure of one of their vessels. The invaders first attacked a fortified temple which stood close to the city, and was occupied by military Bramins, who made preparations for defence, but whose force was inadequate to contend against so formidable a foe. These unfortunate priests had fixed their sacred banner on the top of a high tower, which was no sooner perceived by the Arab general, than he used every effort to bring it down, rightly judging, that some superstition was attached to this standard, which was, in fact, regarded as the palladium of the place; and when it fell, the temple was immediately surrendered, for it was deemed useless by the besieged to hold out against the decree of fate, thus manifested in the fall of the banner. The Bramins were then required to renounce their idolatry, and embrace the religion of the Prophet; on which terms, the conquerors offered to spare their lives and property. But the Bramins, though vanquished, sternly refused to abandon their faith; and all of them above the age of seventeen, were cruelly put to death, while those who were younger, with many women and children, were carried away to be sold as slaves. Yet Casim is praised by historians for the humanity with which he generally treated the vanquished during his victorious career, nor is any other instance recorded of such severity as sullied his conquests at Dewal, where the city, as well as the temple, was given up to plunder, and numbers of the inhabitants were reduced to slavery.

The victor then proceeded towards Aror, the capital of the province, and was met by the Raja Dahir, with a large army, on the banks of the Indus, where a battle was fought, in which the Raja was slain, and his troops defeated. But this victory did not decide the fate of the capital, which was courageously defended by the widow of the deceased Raja, who, aided by a Rajput garrison, held out until a failure of provisions prevented the possibility of a longer resistance, when the siege was terminated by one of those desperate acts of self-sacrifice frequently met with in Hindu history. The women of the garrison raised funeral piles, which they ascended with their children, and lighted with their own hands; while the men, after performing many religious ceremonies, embraced and bade adieu to each other; then opening the gates, they rushed forth into the midst of the besiegers, and thus perished, fighting to the last moment. Aror, then a fine city, but now in ruins, was, after this scene of horror, occupied without further opposition, by the Arabs, but its peaceable inhabitants were not molested, as they paid, without opposition, the tribute imposed on them. The treasures of the late Raja were however seized, and his daughter, a princess remarkable for her beauty and captivating manners, was sent to the court of the Arabian calif, at Damascus. Little did Casim foresee the consequences of presenting the beautiful Indian to his sovereign, over whom she soon gained an almost unlimited influence, which she employed to effect the destruction of the conqueror.

In the meantime, Casim had reduced the whole of Raja Dahir's dominions to subjection, and gained the goodwill of the people by his moderation and conciliating manners. Several of the Hindu princes had become his allies, while all the cities that agreed to pay tribute had their privileges restored, and were allowed to rebuild the temples that had been destroyed. The prosperous career of the young Moslem chief was, however, suddenly terminated by the artifice of Dahir's daughter, who was bent on revenging the death of her father, and with that purpose, brought a false accusation against Casim to the calif, who was credulous enough to believe, on the word of the fair captive, that his faithful general had been guilty of an act of treachery that merited severe punishment; and, without investigating the case, he despatched an order for his instant death. The cruel sentence was executed, and the princess then exultingly declared the innocence of her victim, and the motive that had led her to practise the fatal deception.

The conquests of Casim were retained about thirty-six years, when a revolution in the Arabian government occasioned the expulsion of the Mohammedans from the province of Scind, which was recovered by its native princes, and many of the expelled Arabs found refuge among the Afghans. The cause of this revolution was the downfall of the first dynasty of Califs, that of the Ommiades, all the princes, except one, of that race having fallen victims to a cruel conspiracy, by which the family of the Abbassides gained possession of the throne. The contests that ensued between the respective adherents of the two parties in India, as well as in other conquered countries, caused so much confusion, that, in many cases, the people who had been subjected to the Mohammedan government, recovered their freedom, as they did in Scind, which long afterwards remained an independent state, ruled by its own sovereign.

It was about this time that monastic orders were first instituted by the Bramins, but so little is known respecting the earliest of these associations, that it is even doubtful whether they consisted solely of the priests, or whether persons of other castes were admitted into them, as they are now, Perhaps the religious communities of the Bramins were originally formed in opposition to the Budhists, who, there is every reason to believe, were the dominant priesthood in India at that time; as among the interesting antiquities of that country are many gigantic cave temples, in various parts of Hindostan, containing symbols of Budhism, with inscriptions bearing date as late as the tenth century.

The events relating to the long contest between the two great religious sects in India are involved in obscurity, nor is much known of the general history of the country during the middle ages, which has given rise to a conjecture that the Bramins, who ultimately triumphed over their rivals, destroyed all the records that might have proclaimed to posterity the subversion of their power.

The Bramins of that period differed from those of ancient times in regard to many particulars. Their authority was less absolute, and the religion they taught was more idolatrous. The sacred books of the ancient priests were disused, and others substituted, called the Puranas, which were more adapted to the new system; and although ascribed to the same origin as the Vedas, are known to have been composed by many learned Bramins at different times, between the eighth and sixteenth centuries. They contain a number of legends, and unconnected fragments of history, with instructions for the numerous religious ceremonies to be observed by the different castes, which were maintained as strictly as in former times. The punishment for breaking any of the rules was loss of caste, a sentence more terrible even than that of excommunication by the Roman pontiff, in the early days of Christianity; for the excommunicated Christian might be restored to his former state, by expiating his offence; but the unhappy Hindu who forfeited his station, became an outcast from society for ever, without a hope of regaining the position he had lost. The wretched men thus situated were termed Parias. They were aliens from their kind, forced to hide themselves in some cave or forest, not daring to speak to, or approach any human being; and so great was the horror of coming in contact with one of this degraded class, that no Indian would dress his food on a spot of ground over which the shadow of a paria had been seen to pass. Thus the loss of caste was, in those days, far worse than death; but, at present, like its corresponding sentence in the Catholic church, it is but little heeded, and may easily be avoided by a slight penance, or the payment of a fine. It is contrary to the Hindu laws for persons of different castes to eat together; and this was one of the crimes that brought the offender to the miserable condition of a paria.

MUSSELMAN CONQUESTS.

TWO hundred years had elapsed since the expulsion of the Arabs from Scind, when the Musselman arms were again directed towards India, which became the theatre of a long series of calamitous wars that ended in the subjection of the country to the Mogul emperors. The new invaders were the Turks, who had founded several states on the ruins of the Arabian empire, and had extended their dominions so near to the Indus, that some of the Hindu rajas grew alarmed at finding a Mohammedan government established close to their frontiers.

The city of Ghazni, near Cabul, had become the capital of a sovereignty founded by the Turkish governor of Chorasan, who from the condition of a slave, had been raised to that high office, but having revolted against the sultan his master, he seized on Ghazni, among the mountains of Soliman, and took possession of the whole tract of country between that and the Indus, where his authority was acknowledged by several Turkish and Afghan tribes. This chief left his newly-acquired dominions to a favourite, named Sebektegin, who had also been a slave, but had gradually attained to the highest rank in the army, and had been rewarded for his services by the hand of his sovereign's daughter.

Soon after the accession of Sebektegin, the Raja of Lahore, whose dominions were only separated from those of his Mohammedan neighbour by the Indus, entered the territory of Ghazni with a large force, hoping to crush the rising power of that infant state; but he soon found it was already strong enough to support itself, so that he was glad to retire without coming to an engagement, although he was only allowed to do so on condition that he should give up fifty elephants, and pay a certain sum of money to the new state. Having agreed to these terms, he returned to his kingdom; but when Sebektegin sent for the money, he refused to comply with the demand, and imprisoned the messengers; an insult which the chief of Ghazni revenged by invading Lahore, which was speedily subdued; and all the Afghan tribes within that territory tendered their allegiance to the conqueror. Such was the beginning of the Musselman conquests in India; and thus was opened a future path of glory for Mahmud, who succeeded his father, Sebektegin, in the year 997.

Mahmud, who assumed the title of sultan, was one of the greatest warriors of his time. His chief ambition was to extend his religion throughout the rich provinces of India, a task to which he was stimulated by a belief, cherished from his early boyhood, that he was entrusted with a divine mission to extirpate idolatry from the land of the Hindus. It was about four years after his father's death, that he marched from Ghazni at the head of his army, and crossed the Indus, where his passage was opposed by Sebektegin's old enemy, Jeipal, the Raja of Lahore, who was defeated and taken prisoner; but after a short captivity he was released, on condition of paying the same tribute that had been exacted by the late king of Ghazni. The unfortunate Raja, who had been despoiled of jewels to the amount of eighty thousand pounds, which he had about him when he was made prisoner, returned to his capital; but being dispirited and worn out with the toils of war, he abdicated in favour of his son. He then raised a funeral pile with his own hands, calmly ascended it, and kindled the flames, in which he perished.

The contest with Mahmud was regarded by the Indians in the light of a holy war, and a powerful confederacy of all the princes was formed for the defence of their religion, while the women gave up their jewels and golden ornaments for the support of a cause that was as dear to them as to their husbands and fathers; but all their efforts proved ineffectual against the conquering arms of the sultan, who dispersed their armies, and plundered their temples, the great depositories of the wealth of the country. After each campaign, Mahmud returned to his capital laden with spoil, and followed by trains of wretched captives doomed to slavery, leaving behind him scenes of misery and desolation, such as had never been witnessed in Hindostan until that unhappy period.

Among the many places of Hindu worship destroyed by this prince, were the temples of Nagarcot and Somnath, both containing immense treasures, and celebrated for their peculiar sanctity. That of Nagarcot was attached to a mountain fortress in the Panjab, connected with the Himalaya range, and besides having been enriched by the valuable offerings of a long line of Indian princes, all the wealth of the neighbourhood, consisting of gold, silver, and jewels, had been placed there for security during the wars; consequently, it proved an important prize to the invaders, who broke the idols, and carried off all the treasures. These precious spoils were exhibited by Mahmud, at Ghazni, on tables said to be of solid gold, on the occasion of his celebrating his triumph by a grand public festival, when the people of all ranks were feasted for three days, on an open plain, and alms were liberally distributed among the poor.

Temple of Somnath.

Mahmud had now extended his conquests over the whole of the Panjab, and his next scene of action was the mountainous country of Ghor, inhabited by Afghan tribes, where he was equally successful, and the chief of whom, to avoid the humiliation of making submission, put an end to his life by poison. The descendants of that great chief, about one hundred and seventy years afterwards, deposed the princes of the house of Ghazni, and became, in their turn, conquerors and rulers.

In the meantime, the city of Ghazni was growing into a great and splendid capital. The court was magnificent, for Mahmud was one of the richest monarchs in the world, and dispensed his ill-gotten treasures with a liberal hand. He founded and endowed a university at Ghazni, and granted pensions to men of literary talent, who were treated with great respect at his court. He also built a handsome mosque, and adorned the city with baths and fountains, while most of the great men erected palaces for themselves; so that Ghazni was one of the finest capitals in the east. Almost all the inhabitants were Persians.

The unjustifiable wars carried on by Sultan Mahmud in India were, no doubt, undertaken from a mistaken zeal in the cause of religion, aided, perhaps, by a desire of appropriating the wealth of the numerous shrines; for he was not oppressive in his government, but, on the contrary, was just towards his own subjects, easy of access, and ready to listen to any complaints. One day, a poor woman appeared before him in great distress, saying that a caravan had been attacked in a desert, within one of the states which had come into his possession by conquest, and that her husband was among those who had been killed by the robbers. The sultan said that he was sorry for her misfortune, but that it was impossible for him to keep order in so distant a part of his dominions; to which the woman fearlessly replied, "Then why do you take kingdoms which you cannot govern?" Mahmud, so far from being offended, dismissed her with a handsome present, and adopted measures for the future protection of the caravans.

During the space of twenty years, Mahmud had confined his invasions to the countries already mentioned, but his ambition increasing with his success, he determined to make an expedition to the Ganges, and after a march of three months, arrived before the Gates of Kanoj, the richest and largest city of Hindostan, having succeeded Palebothra as the capital of the states bordering on the Ganges. The Raja being thus taken by surprise, and totally unprepared for defence, came out with his whole family, to surrender himself prisoner, when the sultan magnanimously proposed to enter into a friendly alliance with him. After remaining at Kanoj a few days as the guest of the prince, he departed with his army to Mattra, one of the holy cities of the Hindus, which, for that reason, was plundered without scruple, and numbers of the inhabitants carried away for slaves. The magnificence of the temples at Mattra, which were all built of marble, astonished the sultan, who commanded his soldiers not to destroy them; but they were plundered of their treasures, and all the idols broken.

Many fine old cities were destroyed by the Mohammedans in this and succeeding wars, the sites of which are now only a matter of conjecture. The remains of ancient temples, coins of an early date, fragments of walls, pottery, and the numerous interesting relics of antiquity, lately discovered, buried, in some instances, far below the surface of the earth, serve to show that many a spot now deserted was formerly the abode of a vast population. The Afghan shepherds who feed their flocks on a wide plain not far distant from Cabul, frequently meet with evident tokens of former habitation, and the remains of a very ancient wall, about four feet underground, mark out the boundary of a city of immense extent; but there is no history extant to furnish us with the date of its existence, the condition of its inhabitants, or the cause of its being buried in the dust. The numerous coins of the early and middle ages found recently in various parts of Hindostan, prove the existence and duration of several states, and record the names of many of their sovereigns not otherwise known; but they throw no light on the general state of the country, nor do they afford any information with regard to the people for whose use they were coined.

Female Dancer.

The most celebrated exploit of Sultan Mahmud in India was, the conquest of the great temple of Somnath, near the southern extremity of the peninsula of Guzerat, at that time the richest and most frequented place of worship in the country. There were two thousand priests belonging to the shrine of Somnath, with a numerous train of musicians and female dancers, whose talents were called forth at all the religious festivals, which were conducted with the utmost joyousness; and all these were maintained out of the revenues of two thousand villages that had been granted by different princes, to support the grandeur of this splendid place of worship. The interior of the temple exhibited a specimen of Hindu magnificence, that was, no doubt, highly agreeable to the invaders. The great lamp was suspended by a chain of solid gold, and the pillars that supported the lofty roof were richly carved, and ornamented with precious stones, a greater proof of wealth than taste, but not less admirable on that account, in the eyes of Mahmud and his followers, who entered the spacious edifice after three days of almost incessant fighting, for it was strongly fortified and guarded, besides which, several neighbouring princes had come with their assembled forces to aid in its defence. At length the enemy prevailed, and the gorgeous temple was quickly despoiled by the rude hands of the Musselman soldiers.

It is related that the chief Bramins prostrated themselves before the conqueror, entreating him to spare the great idol, which was the grand object of their adoration, offering to purchase its safety by an enormous ransom; but Mahmud, who probably had a suspicion of the truth, ordered that the image should be broken in his presence, when the floor of the Temple was instantly covered with the gold and jewels that had been concealed within it.

In the meantime, the Raja of Guzerat had fled from his capital of Auhalwara, where Mahmud set up a new prince, who was to pay him tribute; and having thus enriched himself with the treasures of Somnath, and settled the affairs of Guzerat to his satisfaction, he set out on his return to Ghazni. The route by which he had arrived was now occupied by hostile troops, assembled to intercept his passage, and as his own army was much reduced both in strength and numbers, he sought to avoid a renewal of hostilities, by taking another road; but in so doing, he was obliged to cross vast deserts, where great numbers of his men perished miserably for want of water, and his own sufferings were so great, that he returned to his capital more like a fugitive than a conqueror. This was his last expedition into India, where his arms had been constantly directed against the religion rather than the people; and although there can be no doubt that the wars he forced upon the Indians were the occasion of much misery, yet there are few Eastern conquerors who are less accused of cruelty than Mahmud of Ghazni. He died in 1030, having named his eldest son, Mohammed, as his successor; but as that prince was of a very gentle disposition, his brother Masaud was chosen and proclaimed king, by the whole army, as well as by numbers of the people, with whom his warlike habits and bolder deportment had made him popular. The unfortunate Mohammed was deposed, and thrown into prison, where his eyes were put out by command of the usurper, who seized on the throne.

But the quarrels and wars of the princes of Ghazni have little connexion with the history of India, except that while their attention was engaged in other quarters, some of the Hindu Rajas took the opportunity of recovering portions of their dominions. The idol was set up again in the temple of Nagarcot, and the Hindus rose in arms against the Musselmans throughout the Panjab, where the whole country was long in a state of confusion, during which the sultans of Ghazni had removed their court to Lahore, which thus became the first capital of the Mohammedan empire in India. The successors of Mahmud kept possession of the throne till the latter part of the twelth century, when they were dispossessed by the Afghan princes of the house of Ghor, whose conquests in India were more extensive than those of Sultan Mahmud, by whom their mountainous country had been formerly subjected.

The Ghorian chiefs, who had re-established their independence, looked upon the sovereigns of Ghazni in the light of rivals, and were constantly engaged in a kind of desultory warfare with them. As the power of those princes declined, that of their opponents increased, till, at length, Khusru Malik, the last monarch of his race, was made prisoner by Mohammed Ghori, who took possession of his capital of Lahore and his throne, in the year 1187. This conquest was achieved by a cruel stratagem, which perfectly accords with our present ideas of the Afghan character. The young son of Khusru had fallen into the hands of Mohammed Ghori, who detained him for some time as a hostage, till he was prepared to execute the project he had formed; when, feigning a desire to make peace, he released the youth, and allowed him to depart for Lahore with a small escort. The sultan, to whom intelligence had been sent that his son was on the road, set off, as was expected, to meet him, too happy to think of treachery, when he suddenly found himself surrounded by a body of troops, was made captive, and kept in prison during the remainder of his life.

Some years before this event, the beautiful city of Ghazni was plundered and destroyed by the Afghans, all its superb edifices being demolished, except three royal tombs, one of which was that of Mahmud, a spacious building, surmounted by a cupola, and standing, at present, in the midst of a village. The modern town of Ghazni, one of the principal scenes of action in the late war, stands close to the site of the ancient city, the ruins of which overspread the adjacent plain; and near the citadel, on which the British flag was lately planted, are two elegant minarets, built by Sultan Mahmud, when Ghazni was in all its glory. It is still considered a place of great importance, on account of the strength of its fortifications, but it has no longer any claim to admiration as in days of old, when it was the splendid capital of a great kingdom.

About the time of the fall of the house of Ghazni, the celebrated Temple of Juggernaut was completed, at a town bearing the same name, situated on the sea coast, in the province of Orissa, and within the British presidency of Bengal, at the distance of about two hundred and sixty miles south of Calcutta. The principal street of Juggernaut is composed entirely of religious edifices, interspersed with luxuriant plantations, and at its end, on a high terrace, stands the temple of Juggernaut, or Vishnu. Juggernaut is famed as a place of pilgrimage, where, at some of the annual festivals, not less than one hundred and fifty thousand persons are sometimes assembled, of both sexes, and all ranks; for there is no distinction of caste within the precincts of this shrine, where every sect is admitted, and all worshippers are upon an equality. The chief temple, to which are attached fifty smaller ones, is built of red granite, and with its minor edifices, is enclosed with a stone wall, but is open every day, when the idol may be seen by those who go either to worship or to indulge their curiosity. The great idol, Juggernaut, or Vishnu, consists of a wooden bust, of immense size, with most hideous features; and two other monstrous figures are worshipped as his brother and sister. The shrine of these images is an inner apartment in the temple, surmounted by a high tower, which may be seen from a great distance, and is useful as a landmark to sailors.

The land for twenty miles around Juggernaut is considered holy ground, and held free of rent by the cultivators, on condition that they shall perform certain services for the temple, which is furnished daily with a large supply of rice, vegetables, clarified butter, milk, spices, and other viands, which are placed as a banquet before the Idols, by priests appointed for that purpose, and left for one hour, during which time the doors of the temple are closed, and the dancing girls belonging to the establishment sing and dance in a spacious apartment adjoining the shrine. At the expiration of the hour the food is taken away, and furnishes a real repast for the Bramins.

The grand festival of Juggernaut is held in March, when crowds of pilgrims arrive from all parts of India to worship the Idol, which is carried in state to another temple, where it remains four days, to receive the adorations of the people. The three images are removed on this occasion on large cars, that of Juggernaut having sixteen wheels, and a lofty dome, covered with woollen cloth of some conspicuous colour. The Idol is borne from the temple by a number of Bramins appointed for that purpose, and being placed on the car with many ceremonies, is drawn by the multitude, amid loud acclamations, to its destination, followed by a long procession, accompanied with drums, trumpets, and other noisy instruments. In former times, when Hindu superstition was at its height, it is said that numbers of devotees used to seek what they imagined to be a glorious death, by throwing themselves under the wheels of the chariot that bore the hideous object of their adoration. Self sacrifice has always been deemed a meritorious act among the idolatrous natives of India; and as it is well known that many precipitate themselves, at certain seasons, into the Ganges, the horrible spectacle representing the car of Juggernaut passing over the bodies of his misguided worshippers, may possibly be no fiction. At this festival, all castes are permitted to eat together. The influx of pilgrims is great at all times; and, among them, are frequently found poor creatures in a dying state, who make this painful journey not with a hope of being restored to health, but from a superstitious belief that future happiness will be the lot of him who breathes his last sigh within sight of the temple of Juggernaut.

Pilgrim.

THE PATAN, OR AFGHAN KINGS.

AT the period when the Turkish dynasty gave place to that of the Afghans, the principal kingdoms in India were those of Delhi, Ajmir, Kanoj, and Guzerat, all governed by Rajput sovereigns. The Rajputs were divided into clans, each under its own chief, whose name was borne by all his people, as among the Scottish highlanders; and every member of these associated bodies was bound to his own chieftain and to the rest of his clan by the strongest ties of mutual interest and support.

The Rajputs were the chivalry of India, romantic in their attachments, tenacious of their honour, and ever ready to engage in daring adventures. The friendships of those high-minded men were strong and lasting. It was a common occurrence for two friends to bind themselves by the most sacred vows to stand by each other, under all circumstances, until death; nor were they ever known to violate such an engagement, though it might involve the loss of liberty or even life. As the Rajputs claimed a descent from royalty, the pride of birth was one of their distinguishing characteristics, and was observable in their lofty bearing; yet the chivalric knights of Europe, in that romantic age, were not more devoted or respectful in their attentions to the softer sex, than the noble Hindus of the warrior caste.

A sort of feudal system was established among these warlike clans, as every soldier held lands on condition of performing military service for his chief; and the chiefs held their territories of the princes by the same tenure; and when, by the chances of war, or any other accident, a clan was obliged to change its locality, the new lands were distributed in the same proportions as the old ones had been.

Just before the accession of Mohammed Ghori, the kingdoms of Ajmir and Delhi had become united, in consequence of one of their princes dying without heirs, on which the other, who was related to him by marriage, succeeded to the vacant throne; and the sovereign of these extensive territories was Pritwi Raja, against whom the Afghan conqueror first led his armies, as a prelude to a grand design he had formed of subjecting the whole of Hindostan to his authority. The first battle terminated in favour of the Hindu Raja; but in a second engagement, a few years afterwards, he was totally defeated, and, being made prisoner, was put to death. His capital of Ajmir was entered in triumph by the victors, whose barbarous conduct towards the inhabitants, gave a sad foretaste to the unhappy Hindus of the horrors they were destined to experience in this new warfare. The conquest of Ajmir being achieved, Mohammed appointed to the government his favourite officer Kuttub, who had formerly been a slave, and who, in course of time, ascended the throne.

The new Viceroy did not fail to take advantage of his elevated position, but followed up his master's successes, and having subdued the surrounding country to a great extent, he gained possession of the city of Delhi, subsequently the splendid capital of the Mogul empire in India. The victories of the Mohammedans, in the immediate vicinity of his dominions, gave great alarm to the Raja of Kanoj, who assembled all his forces, and led them against the Viceroy Kuttub. The two armies met on the banks of the Jamna, where the Raja was slain, and the Hindus were completely routed; a victory that extended the Musselman empire over the greatest of the Indian monarchies, and opened the way into Behar and Bengal. A great number of the Rajputs of Kanoj emigrated with their families to Marwar, or as it is more frequently called, Joudpoor, a large state in Rajputana, where they founded a principality that is now in alliance with the British government.

The capture of Kanoj was followed by that of Benares, celebrated as the seat of Hindu learning, and esteemed the most holy city in all Hindostan. It is situated on the Ganges, extending about four miles along that river, and upon an embankment of considerable height, from which access to the water is obtained, by means of several handsome flights of steps, for the convenience of performing the frequent ablutions required by the Hindu forms of worship. The Bramin college was at Benares, and some thousands of Bramin families resided in the city, which contained a great number of Hindu temples, and was frequented by pilgrims from all parts of India. The plundering of the temples was an invariable consequence of a Musselman conquest, and few of the victories of Mohammed Ghori were unstained by those cruelties which are so much more revolting than the horrors of a battle field. That prince prosecuted the wars until he had extended his dominion over the whole of Hindostan, to the very confines of China; when, in returning from one of his campaigns, he was assassinated by a band of conspirators, who swam across the Indus, one night, when he was sleeping in his tent, which he had ordered to be placed close to the river, that he might enjoy the cool breeze from the water. Thus, after a reign of nineteen years, died Mohammed Ghori, a greater conqueror than Mahmud of Ghazni, though not so great a sovereign, but whose fame it had been his greatest ambition to eclipse. His death, which took place in 1206, was followed by quarrels and wars for possession of the Indian conquests, some of which were governed by Mohammedan viceroys, others by native princes, who had consented to pay tribute. At length Kuttub, the governor of Delhi, prevailed over all other competitors, and for a short time ruled as sovereign over the vast dominions of Mohammed Ghori; but his son, who succeeded at his death, was very soon compelled to relinquish the throne to Altamsh, who, like Kuttub, had been a slave in his younger days, but had risen by the favour of Mohammed, till at length he was appointed to one of the Indian governments.

The capital was now fixed at Delhi, a very extensive and magnificent city, supposed to have covered a space of ground equal to that occupied by the whole of London, as the ruins are still to be seen to that extent over the plain beyond the present city. In the time of Altamsh, was erected or finished a beautiful round tower, which is still standing near Delhi, called the Kuttub Minar, the highest column known in the world, being forty feet higher than the Monument in London. It is built in the form of a minaret, of red granite, inlaid with white marble, and crowned by a majestic dome.

It was in the reign of Altamsh, that the Mogul emperor, Zinghis khan, led his armies into the west of Asia, and pursued his victories to the shores of the Indus; but he did not cross that river; so that the states of Hindostan escaped, for a time, the horrors of a Mogul invasion.

The many revolutions that took place in the government, after the death of Altamsh, with the disputes and wars of the chiefs for the possession of the throne, render the history of this period extremely confused and uninteresting. The most remarkable event was the accession of a female sovereign, Rezia, the daughter of Altamsh, who was placed on the throne in consequence of a rebellion against her brother, Feroze, whose indolence and extravagance had given rise to popular tumults. The princess filled the throne with great ability, revised the laws, and made some salutary reforms in the administration. She gave audience every morning to the people, according to the custom of Eastern monarchs, to receive petitions, and redress grievances, when she always appeared in the habit of a sultan, and is highly extolled for the wisdom with which she decided such causes as were brought before her.

But it was not likely, in those times of anarchy, that a woman would be long suffered to occupy a position that was coveted by so many ambitious chiefs, and Rezia was deposed in less than three years, by the partizans of one of her brothers. The leader of this conspiracy was a nobleman, named Altunia, to whose care the sultana was confided; but instead of keeping her as a prisoner, he persuaded her to become his wife; and then asserted her right to the throne of which he had helped to deprive her, and went to war with his former confederates. Two battles were fought in this cause, the second of which proved fatal to the sultana and her consort, who were both made prisoners, and put to death.

Not long after this event, Nazir-u-din Mahmud, sometimes called Mahmud the Second, was chosen by the Omrahs, or nobles, to be their sovereign. Nazir was a very singular character. He took a pride in maintaining himself by the labour of his own hands, and, to that end, employed all his leisure time in transcribing valuable works, by which he earned sufficient money to pay all his personal expenses, taking care that they should not exceed the means supplied by his industry. His fare was as simple as that of a peasant, and usually prepared by his queen, who appears to have accommodated herself to her royal husband's eccentricities. Yet Nazir was much respected as a king, and was successful in repelling the invasions of the Moguls, who continued to harass the frontiers of the Panjab; but during the latter part of his life he left the management of

On Stone by Dean &c.

DOWLAT-A-BAD.

London, Dean & Co. Threadneedle Street.

affairs almost entirely to his vizier, Balin, who, at his death in 1266, succeeded, without opposition, to the throne.

The court of Balin, at Delhi, was famous for the many literary characters who resided there, as also for the number of Turkish princes who had sought refuge with the powerful sovereign of Hindostan, from the violence of the Moguls, whose inroads had driven them from their respective territories. Balin reigned twenty-three years, and was succeeded by his grandson, the last of his race, who was assassinated after a brief reign, when the Khiljis, a mountain tribe that had become identified with the Afghans, took advantage of the confusion that ensued, to raise one of their own chiefs to the sovereignty of Delhi.

Jelal, the new king, was a kind-hearted old man, whose convivial temper led him to treat his old companions with the same familiarity after he had been made king of a large empire, as when he was only the chief of a horde of mountaineers; and whose mild disposition rendered it so painful to him to inflict punishment, that the laws were seldom enforced; and the highways, in consequence, became infested with robbers, while the chiefs of petty states refused to pay their tribute. The king had a favourite nephew, Ala-u-din, a man of great ambition and energy, on whom he bestowed the government of Oude, allowing him to keep a large army at his command.

The power thus entrusted to this enterprising prince, proved the occasion of a new era in the history of India, since the first use he made of it was to invade the Deccan, a country till then but little known, having, from its remote situation, escaped the ravages of the conquerors of Hindostan.

The Deccan contained several large states, governed by Hindu Rajas. The capital of one of these was Deogiri, now Dowlatabad, a wealthy city on the borders of the Mahratta country, where Ram Deo Raja kept his court, a prince of such high consideration, that he was called 'King of the Deccan.' The conquest of Deogiri was the object which Ala-u-din had in view when he led his army into the Deccan, across the great chain of mountains that forms its natural boundary, and through vast forests scarcely penetrable. The Raja was not prepared to see a powerful enemy at his gates, for not even a rumour had reached him of the Musselman chief's approach. To defend the city was impossible, therefore he retired to the Hill fort, a place of great strength outside the walls, while the town was entered and plundered by the invaders, who would probably have destroyed it, if Ram Deo had not consented to cede some portion of his dominions to

Ala-u-din, and to pay him a large sum of money as a ransom for the safety of his capital. The victor then set out on his return, all his thoughts being bent upon raising himself to the throne; a project he speedily accomplished, by procuring the assassination of his good old uncle, who had been frequently warned of the danger of giving so much power to this ambitious and unprincipled chief.

Not long after the usurpation of Ala-u-din, an important victory was gained near Delhi over the Moguls, who appeared in terrific numbers, within sight of the capital, from which the inhabitants fled in the utmost consternation. This formidable army was, however, defeated with great loss, and the country again freed from the dreaded Moguls, who made no conquests in India until the time of Tamerlane.

Just before this invasion, the king had undertaken an expedition for the recovery of Guzerat, formerly conquered by Mahmud of Ghazni, but which had been lost by his successors. This extensive province, which now comprehends the northern districts of the British presidency of Bombay, was inhabited by Hindus, Mohammedans, and Parsees; the last, a people who, in the seventh century, emigrated from Persia, in consequence of a revolution in that country, and settled in the northern part of Guzerat, which is strongly fortified by nature with steep and craggy mountains, which render it on that side almost inaccessible. The Parsees were fire worshippers, and it is stated that many of them still adhere to their ancient religion. They are now a numerous, wealthy, and important class of the population of Bombay, extensively engaged in commerce, and connected with almost all the European mercantile houses in that part of India. Ala-u-din reconquered Guzerat, and took possession of the capital, from which the Raja escaped, with his only daughter, while his wife, Caula Devi, was made prisoner, and conveyed to the harem of the conqueror. The daughter, a princess of extraordinary beauty, had long been beloved by the son of Ram Deo, the Raja of Deogiri; but as her father, who was himself a Rajput, refused to bestow her on a prince of the Mahratta race, whom he deemed very inferior in point of rank, the lover had abandoned his hopeless suit.

It happened, some time afterwards, that Ala-u-din sent a large army into the Deccan, under the command of an able general, named Cafur, hoping to reduce some part of that country to subjection. Caula Devi, who had by this time, gained great influence over the king, entreated that he would desire his general to take some means, during the expedition, to recover her daughter, who was residing with her father, in one of the petty states of the Deccan, where he had taken refuge. An application was made to the fugitive Raja to give up the young lady to her mother, but as this request was not complied with, a party was despatched to take her by force, a consequence that had been foreseen by the Raja, who had provided against it, by giving a reluctant consent to her marriage with the son of Ram Deo, and sending her with an escort to the court of Deogiri. Cafur's people finding she was gone, divided into several parties, and set off by different ways, in pursuit of the fair fugitive, who was, at length, discovered in the Caves of Ellora, in the neighbourhood of Deogiri, which curiosity had induced her to visit, and whither her pursuers had been led by a similar motive. The attendants of the princess used their best endeavours to protect their charge, but the Mohammedans were the stronger party, and carried off their prize to Delhi, where she soon afterwards became the bride of the king's eldest son, whom she preferred to the prince of Deogiri, although he was a Mohammedan, and the son of her father's greatest enemy. In the meantime, Cafur was pursuing the wars in the Deccan, where he made many conquests, and acquired vast treasures by the usual violent means.

Hindostan remained at peace after the defeat of the Moguls, and, during the earlier years of the reign of Ala-u-din, enjoyed a high degree of prosperity; but the despotism of that monarch in the latter part of his life increased to excessive tyranny, and gave rise to many insurrections and secret conspiracies, which being discovered, subjected the people to still greater oppressions. The king forbade all private meetings, and carried this restriction so far, that no one was allowed to entertain his friends at his own house, without a written permission from the chief minister; and there were spies employed in all directions, to give information of any infringement of this order, which subjected the offender to imprisonment, and the confiscation of his property. The Mohammedan and Hindu nobles were alike objects of jealousy, while every class of people felt, more or less, the tyranny of the government, either by new exactions, or fresh restrictions. The rent of land was increased, and the farmers were prohibited from keeping more than a specified number of cattle, sheep, or servants; the prices were fixed for every article of food sold in the markets; the hours for opening and shutting the shops were regulated by law, and the slightest neglect of these, and many other rules, was punished with the utmost severity. It must, therefore, have been a cause of general rejoicing when Ala-u-din died in 1316, although his death was followed by five years of anarchy. The conquered part of the Deccan was in a state of insurrection, and the Musselman garrisons were expelled from all the cities; while Cafur seized on the government, having, according to some writers, imprisoned the late king's sons, and put out their eyes. The usurper was soon assassinated, and a younger son of Ala-u-din placed on the throne, but being a weak and vicious prince, he was deposed in a short time, and a new dynasty founded by Gheias Toghlak, the Mohammedan governor of the Panjab, who was proclaimed king at Delhi, in 1321.

The intermixture of Mohammedans with the Hindus had naturally produced some changes in the manners of the latter, in all those parts of India which had fallen under the authority of the conquerors. Many Indians had been converted to the faith of their rulers; and mixed marriages had created ties between the natives and the strangers that led to the adoption of new customs, especially with regard to the women of India, who, in the early ages, enjoyed much more freedom, and far greater privileges, than have been accorded to them in later times.

At this period, there were many sects of religious devotees among the Hindus, who lived upon charity, and obtained a reputation for sanctity, by making long pilgrimages, and imposing severe penances upon themselves. Among these were the Faquirs, who, at that time, were held in great veneration by the people, over whom they possessed an almost unlimited influence. They were every where received and fed, while their instructions were listened to with respect, and their austerities were regarded with reverence and admiration. These men were always met with in great numbers at Juggernaut, and other holy places, and contrived to turn their long journeys to some profit, by concealing in their long matted hair, and the cloths wrapped round them, such valuables as pearls, gold dust, and corals, with small quantities of the most costly spices and perfumes, in which they trafficked to considerable advantage between the sea-coast and the interior.

Among the changes effected by the Mohammedan conquests in India was, the introduction of the Turkish costume, which had become very general at Delhi, and was worn in most parts of Hindostan among the upper classes. The Brahmins, however, did not adopt the new style of dress; and even to this day, all strict members of their class clothe themselves in the ancient Hindu fashion.

INVASION OF THE MOGULS.

HE authority of the kings of Delhi over the Rajas of the country was held by a very uncertain tenure, since every change that took place in the government was a signal for the native princes to attempt the recovery of their independence. When Gheias Toghlak ascended the throne, the greater part of Bengal was in a state of revolt, and the new monarch, after having secured his frontiers against the invasions of the Moguls, proceeded to that province with a sufficient force to reduce the rebels to obedience. The expedition was successful, and Gheias was returning triumphant to his capital, when the accidental falling of a temporary pavilion, which had been erected by his son at a short distance from the city, for the purpose of receiving him with honour on his return, put a period to his existence, after a brief reign of two years. He was succeeded by the prince whose unfortunate attention had been the means of shortening the life of a very excellent sovereign, and also of exposing himself to the suspicion of a most detestable crime. This prince was Mohammed the Third, whose turbulent reign presents one continued succession of misfortunes, occasioned by his violence and folly; his conduct, on most occasions, evincing a degree of intemperance that bordered on insanity. Yet in the early part of his reign he gained popularity by his munificence, giving, liberally, pensions to the learned, and providing for the infirm and indigent by building hospitals and alms-houses on an extensive scale, and endowing them with funds for their support. But the benefits arising from these good deeds were counteracted by misgovernment, and the evils attendant upon the prosecution of the wildest dreams of ambition, by which his treasures were exhausted, and his armies destroyed.

Among these visionary schemes, the conquest of China was one of the most calamitous, as well as the most absurd, for although Kublai Khan had been dead some years, the Empire was scarcely less powerful and extensive than when it was under the dominion of that great prince. The consequence of Mohammed's folly was, that his army was met on the frontiers of China, and nearly annihilated by the superior forces of the Mogul Emperor; and those who survived the battle were cut off in their way back by hostile tribes of mountaineers; so that very few individuals of the many thousands that had been sent on that ill-advised expedition, returned to tell the fatal tale of its result.

The king had wasted so much money in various fruitless enterprises, that his resources began to fail, which led to the most ruinous consequences; for he attempted to recruit his treasury by issuing copper tokens, in imitation of the paper money instituted for the convenience of trade by Kublai Khan, in China. But the case was altogether different, for the Chinese Emperor was rich, and his credit good, so that his notes were taken without hesitation; whereas Mohammed being poor, his copper tokens, to which a nominal value was attached, were in reality worth no more than the intrinsic value of the metal; besides which, they could be very easily imitated; and forgery was committed to such an extent, that many persons, chiefly bankers and great merchants, made large fortunes by coining; while the manufacturers and traders, who were obliged to take the tokens at their nominal worth, in exchange for their goods, were entirely ruined. Insurrections broke out in every part of the country, but more particularly in Bengal, the greatest manufacturing province of Hindostan, where all the finest muslins and cottons had been made, from the earliest times, and where the silk manufacture was also carried on to a considerable extent.

The agriculturists suffered equally with the manufacturers, by the increase of their taxes, which became so intolerable, that in many districts they set fire to their villages, abandoned their fields, and took up their abode in the woods and jungles, where they built huts for their families, and lived by robbery. At length, the governor of Bengal headed a general revolt, and the whole of that extensive province was separated from the kingdom of Delhi, and remained a separate state for nearly two hundred years. Some of the Rajas of Southern India also recovered their independence, and re-established the ancient Hindu kingdoms of Carnata and Telingana, on the coast of Coromandel.

The Raja of the Carnatic founded a new dynasty, and fixed his capital at Bijayanagur, which stands near the fortress and town of Bellary, the head quarters of a British civil and military establishment in the ceded districts of Balaghaut. Bijayanagur was in the days of its grandeur a very extensive city, said to have been about twenty-four miles in circumference, but it is now not a third of that size; and in consequence of its ruined condition, a great part of it is uninhabited. It is very remarkably situated in a plain, enclosed by huge irregular masses of granite, of which immense blocks, in some places piled above each other to a considerable height, are scattered over the whole surface of the area that formed the site of the old city. Some of the streets communicate with each other by passages between these rocky fragments, and one of the principal thoroughfares is under a covered way formed by them.

The ancient battlements and gateways are still entire, and many temples, with choultries, or houses of entertainment for travellers, are seen on the most conspicuous eminences; the walls, pillars, and even the flat roofs of some of the ancient buildings being composed of granite. There is a temple dedicated to Rama, another to Crishna, and one in the centre of the city to Vishnu, in which there is a chariot cut out of a solid block of granite, on which the image of the god is placed on holidays. Most of the Idols in the numerous temples around Bijayanagar are of the same rough stone; some of them are colossal figures, from twelve to sixteen feet in height, but of very rude workmanship, being like most specimens of Hindu art, as regards sculpture, more remarkable for their gigantic proportions than for elegance of shape or skilful execution.

The tyranny of the sultan was augmented by the failure of his schemes and his losses of territory; and among other acts of oppression he transferred his court from Delhi to Deogiri, obliging all the principal inhabitants to remove to the new capital, the name of which he changed to Dowlatabad, or the Fortunate City. Here he completed the famous fortress that stands on an isolated mountain of granite, the outside of which is cut smooth and perpendicular, to the height of one hundred and eighty feet, so that there is no possibility of reaching the fort but by a winding passage cut within the rock. Delhi suffered materially in consequence of the compulsory removal of all the most wealthy and useful of its inhabitants, many of whom were ruined by this unwise act; but the city was afterwards restored to its former prosperity under the Mogul princes, and was the capital of their empire until its fall.

Mohammed died in 1351, when he was succeeded by his nephew Feroze, whose long reign was distinguished by a great number of useful public works, executed under his superintendence, and maintained by his munificence. They consisted of mosques, colleges, caravanseries, hospitals, and public baths, besides aqueducts, wells, and reservoirs for irrigating the lands.

It was this prince who constructed a fine canal running through the province of Delhi, from the river Jumna to that of Caggur, intended for the purposes of irrigation, but neglected after his death, and entirely disused until of late, when about two hundred miles of it have been re-opened by the British government, and thus contributed to fertilize a vast tract of country which before was lying waste. It also serves to float down rafts of timber from the mountains, and to turn mills for grinding corn, which were not used in India in the time of Feroze.

It was not long after the death of that prince, who had reigned thirty seven years, that the great Mogul chief, Tamerlane, already master of Persia and Transoxiana, entered Hindostan, and marched direct towards Delhi, which had again become the capital, leaving behind him the usual melancholy traces of his progress: smoking ruins, desolated fields, and deserted villages. Mahmud, the young king of Delhi, fought a battle with the Moguls near that city, but being defeated, fled to Guzerat, when the citizens immediately surrendered, and Tamerlane was proclaimed Emperor of India; but the submission of the people of Delhi did not save them from slavery, ruin, or death, for the fierce barbarian soldiers broke into the houses in search of plunder, and seized many of the women and children, whom they could always sell for slaves. These outrages being resisted, led to a general massacre, and the streets of Delhi presented a frightful picture of Mogul warfare. Tamerlane departed with the name of Emperor, but Delhi was for some time without any real head, and many chiefs who had been subject to its kings, took the opportunity of establishing their independence; so that when the government was restored in the capital, nothing was left to the monarch but the territories immediately surrounding it.

After the death of Timur, some of the former possessions of the kings of Delhi were recovered by the princes of the house of Lodi, an Afghan race, who occupied the throne during the latter half of the fifteenth and beginning of the sixteenth centuries, when Sultan Baber, a descendant of Timur became sovereign of the country that had been conquered but not ruled by his great ancestor, and established that powerful monarchy usually termed the Mogul Empire, in India. Baber was the grandson of a prince whose dominions comprised the whole of Cabul, Balk, Bokhara, and Samarcand, with several smaller states, which, at his death, were shared amongst many sons, one of whom, the father of the young hero in question, inherited a small but beautiful territory called Ferghana, in Independent Tartary, to which Baber succeeded, when he was only twelve years of age. It was not long before he was dispossessed of his inheritance by one of his more powerful relatives, when he sought refuge among the mountain tribes, and became the youthful leader of a small band of adventurers, who followed him in many a romantic enterprize, and by whose help he made several conquests, which he had not sufficient power to preserve. For some years he led a perilous life, and experienced numerous vicissitudes, sometimes being at the head of a gallant band, sometimes a solitary wanderer destitute of the means of subsistence, and often compelled to hide himself in caves or jungles from the pursuit of his enemies.

At length it happened that the throne of Cabul was seized by a chief who had no claim to it, which afforded Baber an opportunity for attempting to possess it himself, an adventure well suited to his enterprising disposition. Having succeeded in deposing the usurper, he ascended the throne of Cabul in the year 1504, and had reigned over that kingdom twenty-two years, when his attention was drawn towards Hindostan, in consequence of the disturbed state of that country, and the weakness of its government, which was harassed by constant insurrections. The Sultan Ibrahim was unpopular; the governors of some of the provinces had thrown off their allegiance, and several of the native chiefs were in rebellion, when Baber marched against Delhi, in 1526, where a battle was fought, in which Ibrahim was slain; and thus ended the last of the Afghan or Patan dynasties which had occupied the throne of Delhi for three hundred years. The city was immediately surrendered to the conqueror, as was also Agra, which had lately been the royal residence, and the King of Cabul mounted the throne of Delhi, and became the founder of the greatest empire ever established in India.

PORTUGUESE SETTLEMENTS IN INDIA.

IT was during the early career of Baber, that the Portuguese, whose great maritime discoveries were beginning to produce an important revolution in the commercial world, accomplished the long-desired object of finding a passage, by sea, to India; and they landed at Calicut, on the coast Malabar, in the year 1498.

The western coast of Southern India at this time consisted of Cambay and Calicut, the latter an extensive territory reaching from Bombay to Cape Comorin, and governed by a prince, called the Zamorin, or King of Kings, who was considered a very powerful monarch, in that part of the country, and who reckoned among his dependents, the princes of several tributary states. The Zamorin was a Hindu, but he had many Mohammedan subjects, for the merchants of Egypt and Arabia had long been in the habit of trading to Calicut, and many natives of those countries resided in the city. To them, the arrival of strangers who came for the avowed purpose of sharing in their lucrative commerce, could not be very agreeable, therefore they determined, from the first, to oppose them.

The leader of the European expedition was Vasco de Gama, who was

admitted to an interview with the sovereign, whose residence was a fortified palace or citadel, covering a large space of ground, surrounded by a wall, which enclosed extensive gardens and pleasure grounds. De Gama and his attendant officers, were carried in palanquins to the gates of the palace, where they were received by a venerable Bramin, who led them through several large halls to the state apartment, where the Zamorin was reclining on a low couch, placed on the dais, or raised part of the floor, which was covered with a rich carpet. On one side of the couch stood an attendant with a gold plate, containing the betel leaf, which is constantly chewed by Hindus of rank, who esteem it a great luxury; and on the other side was a large golden vase, placed there for the purpose of receiving the leaf when all its juice had been extracted, as it is never swallowed. The prince was dressed in a robe of fine white muslin, and a silk turban, both splendidly embroidered with gold. His arms and legs were without clothing, but were ornamented with a great number of costly bracelets, and his ears were adorned with long pendants of the finest diamonds. When the visitors drew near, he merely raised his head a little from the embroidered cushion on which it rested, and made a sign to the Bramin, that the chief was to sit down on the step of the dais, the rest remaining standing; for it is not customary among the Hindus to kneel to their princes, therefore strangers were not expected to do so. De Gama's credentials from the king of Portugal were very graciously received; but it was intimated to him that he ought to have brought a present, an omission he excused by saying, he had not expected to visit the dominions of so great a prince when he embarked on his voyage. The Zamorin appeared very much inclined to favour the views of the Europeans, by permitting them to form a settlement at Calicut; but the Mohammedans contrived to excite his suspicions that their ultimate object was to conquer the country, and he was led to sanction some acts of violence, which induced the commander, after loading his ships with spices, silks, and other produce of the country, to hasten his departure.

It was not long, however, before another expedition arrived from Portugal, under the command of Cabral, who reached Calicut in the month of September, 1500, and was met by a friendly message from the Zamorin, inviting him to land; but as he did not feel entire confidence in the good faith of a Hindu prince, he adopted the precaution of stipulating that four Bramins, of high rank, should be sent on board his ship as hostages; and, after some negociation, this demand was complied with. A building for the audience, which Cabral calls a gallery, was erected on the shore. It was hung with curtains of crimson velvet, and its floor was covered with carpets; and there the admiral, being duly prepared with presents, met with a most gracious reception, and, what was of still more consequence, obtained permission to build a factory at Calicut.

In the mean time, the hostages, who had evinced the utmost horror at being detained on board strange vessels, where they had no means of performing their customary rites, and who would not eat of the food offered to them, were soon reduced to such a deplorable condition, that they were removed from the ships, and were landed on an unfrequented part of the coast, that it might not be known they were released.

The factory was speedily erected, and the Portuguese began to trade with the natives; but the Mohammedans soon renewed their hostilities, and making a sudden attack on the new building, overpowered the inmates, many of whom were killed, whilst the rest sought shelter on board their vessels. The factory was completely plundered, and the Portuguese, after destroying several merchant ships belonging to the assailants, and firing on the town, which, being chiefly built of wood, was set on fire in many places, took their departure. Cabral at first thought of applying to the Zamorin for redress, but hearing that he had taken a large share of the spoil, concluded that he had countenanced the outrage. He therefore sailed away for Cochin, the capital of a small state on the coast of Malabar, governed by a native prince, who was then subject to the Zamorin of Calicut, but is now tributary to the British government in India.

Cochin is a beautiful and fruitful country, abounding in those rich productions of nature peculiar to an eastern clime. The villages are often embowered in groves of luxuriant mango trees and lofty palms; while the Ghaut mountains, which form the eastern boundary of the state, are covered with forests of teak, and other fine timber trees, from which the Raja derives a considerable part of his revenue. The teak, which is in great demand at Bengal, for ship-building, is one of the largest of the Indian trees, towering even above the tallest palm. Its leaves often measure twenty inches in length, and twelve in breadth, and it bears a small white fragrant flower. Mangoes and tamarinds are usually planted at the building of a village, as they help to supply the people with food, as well as to afford an agreeable shade from the intense heat of the sun. The people of Cochin cultivate rice in their well-watered valleys, and, like the Chinese, obtain two crops in the year. There were many Jews in the capital, which, next to Calicut, was the greatest trading city on the Malabar coast.

The king of Cochin, whose name was Triumpara, was a vassal of the Zamorin, but had long been desirous of shaking off his dependence on that prince, consequently, was very willing to form an alliance with any people likely to aid him in that design. But Cabral, on mature deliberation, determined to defer all hostilities with the Zamorin, and set sail for Lisbon, with an understanding that, if the king of Portugal should send out an expedition against Calicut, the Raja of Cochin might be regarded as an ally. A powerful fleet was immediately equipped for a new voyage to India, to demand redress for the injuries that had been sustained, and to establish, if possible, a permanent settlement. De Gama was appointed to the command, and on arriving at Calicut, declared he was come either to obtain satisfaction for the treatment his countrymen had experienced, or to avenge their wrongs; and sent a message to that effect to the Zamorin; but not receiving an answer so soon as he expected, he executed the latter threat in a barbarous manner, by putting to death fifty unoffending natives who had been seized on the coast.

It was by such disgraceful acts of cruelty as these, that the Portuguese frequently sullied their conquests in the east; for in those days, when the chief object of distant voyages was to obtain possession, by force, of newly-discovered countries, the greater number of those who engaged in such adventures were men of desperate fortunes and daring character, of whom there were vast numbers, both in Spain and Portugal. De Gama, however, did not succeed in effecting a settlement at Calicut, but was allowed to

Calicut.

build a factory at Cochin, where he left some troops to protect the King Triumpara, his faithful ally; and having captured several vessels, richly laden, he returned to Europe with the spoils.

As soon as the Portuguese were gone, the Zamorin resolved to punish his disobedient vassal, the King of Cochin, for having permitted the foreigners to establish a trading station in his capital, and with that intent he soon appeared with a large army at the gates of the city, on which the king hastily summoned his councillors, who advised him to make submission to the offended monarch, his liege lord; but Triumpara declared he would rather die than accede to the Zamorin's demands, which were to break off his alliance with the Portuguese, and deliver up all of that nation who had remained in Cochin.

Deserted by most of his nobles and chief Bramins, who had all fled in terror, the brave prince, with a small band of faithful adherents, defended the principal approach to his capital; but being overpowered by numbers, he at length gave up the contest, and withdrew to the little island of Vipeen, a place held sacred by the Hindus, to mourn over the loss of three sons who had fallen in the action. This unfortunate sovereign was restored to his throne by the great Albuquerque, who arrived with reinforcements from Europe, and soon forced the Zamorin to abandon Cochin; but Triumpara seems to have been disgusted with the cares of royalty, for, not long afterwards, he resigned his dignity to his nephew, and assuming the habit of a faquir, passed the rest of his life in solitude.

It is needless to enter into the particulars of the long struggle that ensued, or the horrors that attended the conquests of the Portuguese, who, in a very few years, were firmly established in the south of India, and in possession of the large maritime city of Goa, which they took in 1510, and where they formed a regular government, headed by a viceroy appointed by the King of Portugal; and this city has ever since been the capital of the Portuguese possessions in India. Goa was the chief city of a territory on the coast of the province of Bijapur, and was one of the states formerly attached to the crown of Delhi, but had become independent during the troubles that caused so many revolutions in the time of Mohammed the third.

The Zabaim was absent, engaged in war with a neighbouring prince, when the Portuguese led by the celebrated Albuquerque, attacked the city, which was surrendered without opposition, as the citizens had no efficient means of defence. The commander, who bore the title of Viceroy, acted with great moderation on this occasion towards the inhabitants, whose property was left untouched, and many of whom were permitted to retain their civil offices; while the Viceroy took possession of the palace, and assumed the character of a great potentate. The Zabaim made great efforts to recover the city, from which the intruders were at one time expelled, but they regained possession, after a desperate conflict in the streets; and in the end, the Portuguese supremacy was fully established.

Albuquerque kept his court with all the splendour of an eastern prince, and secured his conquest by erecting extensive fortifications around it. He exercised his authority with mildness, formed alliances with several of the native princes, and endeavoured to create a friendly feeling between his own people and those of the country, by promoting marriages between the Portuguese soldiers and the Hindu maidens, by which means, some of the principal Hindu families of Goa became attached to the Europeans. The brides were all obliged to embrace the Christian faith, and the descendants of these mixed marriages now form the greater part of the population of Goa.

Previously to the occupation of Goa, the Portuguese had made some conquests in the territories of the kings of Cambay and Guzerat, and built factories and forts on several parts of the coast; but they never obtained any possessions in the interior of the country, their real sovereignty being

Drawn on the Spot by T. T. Rawlins. On Stone by Dean & Co.

GOA, FROM THE UPPER CURTAIN.

London Dean & Co. Threadneedle Street.

on the seas, where they were sufficiently powerful, for more than a century, to keep all the trade of the east in their own hands; while they were enabled to repel the attacks of hostile princes, by the aid of those with whom they maintained friendly alliances. Among the conquests of the Portuguese, during the administration of Albuquerque, was that of Malacca, situated on the coast of the peninsula of that name, an important station, as being the centre of the commerce between India, China, and the principal oriental islands; a trade that is now possessed by Singapore, a British settlement at the southern extremity of the same peninsula.

Albuquerque died in 1515, to the great regret of all over whom his authority had extended; for although a great conqueror, he was a beneficent ruler, and had refrained from oppressing the vanquished by those exactions to which they were forced to submit under his successors. It was in the year following the death of Albuquerque, that the Portuguese made their first voyage to Canton; an important event in the history of the world, as being the commencement of a direct intercourse between Europe and China. Such was the state of affairs when Sultan Baber ascended the throne of Delhi, and became the founder of a line of sovereigns under whom the country reached its highest state of prosperity, and who ruled over a larger portion of it than had ever before been united under one head.

THE MOGUL EMPIRE.

THE very name of Mogul was so distasteful to the Hindu princes, as well as to the Patan omrahs or nobles, that Baber soon found it would be a difficult task to maintain the throne he had won; and, during his brief reign of five years, was constantly engaged in repressing the revolts of the numerous chiefs who united their forces against him. He had, therefore, but little leisure to organize any regular plan of government; but he succeeded in establishing his authority, by several signal victories, and reduced many of the hostile Rajput rulers to subjection; so that, at the time of his death, he was the acknowledged sovereign of nearly all the north of India. He was one of the most accomplished of the Eastern princes, being a poet, historian, and musician, of no ordinary merit; elegant, yet free in his manners, easy of access to his subjects, and fond of social enjoyments. He was so enthusiastic an admirer of the beauties of nature, that in the days of his adversity, when closely pursued by his enemies, he would pause in the midst of his flight to gaze on a beautiful landscape, or gather a simple flower; and his heart was so little corrupted by ambition, that amidst all his prosperity, his thoughts would often turn to the home of his boyhood, the lovely valley of Ferghana, with all the warmth of youthful affection; and there were moments, perhaps, when he would have given up all his brilliant conquests and his high station, to recover that one beloved spot, which had long since fallen a prey to the Usbek Tartars.

Baber was succeeded by his eldest son Humayun, a prince of great literary attainments, whose court was celebrated for the number of learned men who there found liberal patronage. Scarcely was he seated on the throne, when his brother, Kamran, who had been invested by his father with the government of Cabul, laid claim to that kingdom as his lawful inheritance; and it was ceded to him, with a large tract of country on the borders of the Indus: by which arrangement Cabul was separated from the crown of Delhi.

The new Sultan now turned his attention towards recovering some of the states that had formerly belonged to the kings of Delhi, and with that view invaded Guzerat, which, for nearly a century and a half, had been governed by its own independent sovereigns, and was one of the best cultivated and most fertile provinces of Hindostan, producing cotton, sugar-cane, indigo, flax, and grain of various sorts, in abundance; while, in many parts, the land that was not under culture, afforded rich pastures for cattle and horses. The cotton manufactures of Guzerat had long been in a very flourishing condition, and there was no part of India that carried on a more extensive foreign trade.

Surat.

Among the great commercial towns of this kingdom was Surat, famous for its manufacture of shawls, and one of the most ancient cities of Hindostan. It is also remarkable as being the first place in the Mogul dominions where the British East India Company obtained a settlement, which was for a long time their principal station. Another great port of Guzerat was Diu, the possession of which had long been ardently desired by the Portuguese, who had made several attempts to take it by force, but without success. At length, their wishes were accomplished by other means, for when the Sultan of Delhi went to war with the king of Guzerat, the latter entered into a negotiation with the Portuguese, offering to let them build a factory at Diu, provided they would assist him to maintain his dominions against the Moguls; to which they readily consented, and sent a body of five hundred men to aid the monarch and establish the new settlement. The invaders were speedily driven from the kingdom, and a factory was erected, according to agreement; but when Bahadur found that his allies were fortifying their building, he naturally became alarmed, and sent a remonstrance to their chief commander, Nuno da Cunha, who proposed to settle the difference at a personal interview. There is no reason to suppose that the Portuguese premeditated any act of violence; but it seems that, in the heat of the dispute that took place, the king was stabbed by one of the officers; and several of his attendants, as well as some Europeans, also lost their lives in the confusion that ensued.

This unfortunate circumstance led to the siege of Diu, a memorable event in the history of the Portuguese in India, who defended their fort for a long time against a host of besiegers, consisting of all the forces of Guzerat, aided by seventy Turkish galleys, carrying a great number of cannons, and having on board seven thousand troops, commanded by the governor of Cairo. This armament was sent by Solyman the Magnificent, who was sovereign of Egypt as well as Turkey, and whose interest it was to protect the trade of his subjects in India from the encroachments of the Europeans.

The siege of Diu is remarkable for the extraordinary courage displayed by the Portuguese ladies within the fort, who appeared in the midst of the soldiers, undaunted by the roaring of the cannon, lent their aid in repairing the works, carried away the wounded as they fell, and revived the drooping spirits of the defenders by their own enthusiasm. At length, reinforcements arrived from Goa, the fort was relieved, and the town of Diu was added to the Portuguese possessions.

While these events were taking place at Guzerat, the Sultan Humayun was engaged in wars with several chiefs, who were opposed to the Mogul government. The most formidable of these enemies was Shir-khan, an Afghan chief, who had raised a large force in Bengal, and, with all the treachery of the Afghan character, offered to make peace with the Sultan; but while the negociations were pending, suddenly attacked his camp, and put the whole army to flight, while Humayun himself narrowly escaped being made prisoner by swimming across the Ganges on his elephant. A second defeat obliged him to seek safety by a precipitate retreat, accompanied by a few followers, and the females of his family. His course lay through the Western district, towards the Indus, where, for three days, they could not find a drop of water to cool their parched lips, or a single tree to afford a temporary relief from the blazing sun, which no friendly cloud obscured, even for a moment. The appearance of a well, on the fourth day, was hailed with frantic joy; but in the rush to obtain the first bucket of water that was drawn up, some of the soldiers fell in and were drowned. Among the ladies who accompanied Humayun on this calamitous journey, was Hamida, his favourite Sultana, and the mother of the great Sultan Akber, who was born just as the fugitives had reached the other side of the desert.

It was usual for a father, on the birth of an heir, to distribute presents to those around him; but Humayun, who had nothing to give, broke a pod of musk and scattered its contents among his followers, wishing that the fame of his son might spread around like the odour of that perfume, a prayer in which all present heartily joined; and most amply was the wish accomplished in the brilliant career of one of the greatest princes that ever adorned an eastern throne.

In the mean time, the brothers of the Sultan had openly revolted, and Shir-khan had seized on the throne; while, to add to the distresses of this unfortunate sultan, his infant son was carried off from his camp, to serve as a hostage, in case of need. Surrounded thus by enemies, and overwhelmed with misfortunes, the unhappy monarch at length sought refuge in Persia, where he was received and magnificently entertained at the court of Shah-Tahmas, the reigning sovereign.

The reign of Shir-khan was a very short one, as he was killed by the accidental explosion of a powder magazine, about five years after his usurpation. Notwithstanding the treacherous manner in which he had obtained the throne, he proved an excellent sovereign, and ruled over a much larger extent of territory than was possessed by Humayun, as many of the princes who would not recognise the Mogul dynasty readily acknowledged the authority of an Afghan monarch; besides which, nearly the whole of Bengal was devoted to his interests before he ascended the throne of Delhi, and was, consequently, re-united to that empire. Shir-khan particularly distinguished himself by the formation of one of the finest high roads that was ever made in the world. It extended entirely across Hindostan, from the Ganges, in Bengal, to the Indus; and was bordered, on each side, along its whole extent, with fruit-trees.

Water girl.

It was one of the duties of an oriental sovereign to provide for the accommodation of travellers in his dominions; and many caravanseries had been built, trees planted, and wells dug, for that purpose; but this magnificent road far surpassed all other works of the kind, both for pleasure and convenience. The trees afforded shade as well as refreshment; and at every stage was a caravansera, where persons of all sects were lodged and entertained according to their peculiar habits, as, an instance, of which, attendants of different castes were paid by the government, to wait upon Hindu travellers, whose religion did not allow of their being served by Mohammedans. There were, also, mosques at regular distances, where provisions were given to poor way-farers; and at every two miles was a well or a fountain, which may be reckoned among the chief necessaries of a hot climate.

Shir-khan was succeeded by his son Selim, who reigned in peace nine years; but after his death, his son, a minor, was deposed by one of his uncles, whose bad government occasioned the defection of several chiefs; and again the Empire was dismembered, and distracted by civil warfare. In the mean while, Humayun, assisted by the Persian monarch, had been at war with his brother Kamran, from whom he recovered the crown of Cabul, and his little son Akber, then about three years of age. Kamran, after several attempts to regain possession of Cabul, took refuge among the Afghans in the mountains of Khyber, whither he was pursued; and after many adventures, was betrayed into the hands of his brother, who cruelly deprived him of his sight, and sent him to Mecca, where he soon died.

Humayun contented himself with the kingdom of Cabul, until the troubles that arose in Delhi, after the death of Selim, encouraged him to attempt the recovery of his former power. He marched into India, attacked the princes who were at war with each other for the throne, and eventually regained his capitals of Delhi and Agra; but he did not live to follow up these successes, a task that was left to his son Akber, who was but thirteen years old when his father died in 1556, a few months after his restoration to the throne of Delhi.

CUSTOMS AND MANNERS OF THE HINDUS.

THE Hindus, notwithstanding the many revolutions that had taken place in the country, and their intermixture with the Mohammedans, had preserved most of their ancient customs unchanged, but more particularly those that appertained to their religion, and some of their early political institutions, which, although not maintained perhaps in all their original purity, presented the same leading characteristics that distinguished them from all others in former times. Among these institutions were the townships or village republics, where the truest and most pleasing picture of Hindu life was to be found.

Amid all the changes that had taken place from time immemorial in the vast regions of India, the privileges of the townships had been respected, so that each village was a little independent commonwealth, governed by its own laws, and its own ruler, the elder, or headman, who was answerable to the lord of the soil for the rents paid by the ryots or cultivators for their holdings. The headman might be called the village mayor. He was the chief magistrate and judge; the commander in case of an attack; and to him belonged the right of levying such taxes as were necessary for keeping the temples in repair, for celebrating festivals, and for other public expenses. He was assisted by several subordinate officers, the chief of whom were the Accountant and the Watchman; the duty of the former being to keep the records of every thing relating to the lands, as the names of the ryots, the extent of their holdings, and amount of rents; with an exact account of all the payments and disbursements. This office was hereditary, as was also that of the Watchman, a very busy and important person, who might be called the head of the police, and had so many duties to perform, that he was usually assisted by his sons and other male relatives.

If any property were stolen, the watchman was bound to use every exertion to discover the thief, who was sometimes tracked through the country for many miles, the pursuit never being abandoned until he was traced to some other village, when it became the duty of the watchman of that community to take up the chase, which was thus continued until the robber was captured, for it was very seldom that these active officers missed their object. The watchman was expected to know the character of every inhabitant of the village, and to report to his superiors whatever might be wrong in their conduct.

It was also his business to overlook the fields, and watch the progress of the crops, as well as to see that the boundary marks were kept in proper order, for the fields were not separated by hedges or ditches, but their extent was usually marked by a tree, a pond, or a temple. The lands were allotted, as formerly described, each man taking a share of the inferior with the good; and the principal objects of cultivation were the same as in ancient times, with the addition of tobacco; which was, perhaps, introduced by the Portuguese, both in India and China, since there is no mention made of it in either country until after the discovery of America, where the plant was first found by the Europeans, and carried by them to other parts of the world.

Post-man.

Every village had its messenger or postman, and a certain number of useful artizans, as a smith, carpenter, potter, and such others as were required to supply the moderate wants of a rustic population; and to each little community was also attached a priest, an astrologer, a school-master, a bard, and a musician, who did not the less contribute towards the general happiness, by fostering the favourite superstitions of the simple people. All the Hindus believe in the existence of supernatural beings, and imagine that every village has its especial guardian genius, to watch over those whose virtues entitle them to such protection. The Bramins themselves inculcate the belief in good and evil genii, who often figure as principal characters in Hindu tales.

The villagers are described as living in happy unity among themselves, and, generally, in easy circumstances. They were strongly attached to the place of their birth, and if driven by warfare to remove to some other spot, would return when peace was restored, to settle again on the land of their fathers, even though all traces of their former habitations might have been destroyed, and their fields converted into a desert. The cottages, in some parts of the country, were constructed of bamboo, and thatched with the broad leaves of the palm; in others, they were built of clay, with flat tiled roofs; and, in many districts, had neat gardens, for the growth of vegetables. But the simple habits of the Hindus required so little furniture, that the house of a farmer seldom contained more than two or three mats, a handmill, some cooking utensils, an iron plate used for baking cakes, and a few dishes. The husbandmen arose at daybreak, and taking their breakfasts with them, set off with their cattle, to their respective fields, from which they did not return till evening. Their dinner was usually carried to them about noon, by their wives or daughters, whose chief employments were, to grind the corn, fetch water, cook, and spin. The cooking, which was always performed in the open air, or under a shed, consisted chiefly of baking cakes of unleavened bread, boiling rice, and preparing vegetables; for very little animal food was used by the people in general, and none by the Bramins.

The Indians, at their meals, help themselves with their fingers, and place their dishes on the ground, each man taking his meal alone; an unsocial custom that arose, no doubt, from the many rules to be observed with regard to different kinds of food, and the horror a Hindu feels of eating with a person whose caste is inferior to his own: a prejudice so deeply rooted, that any man would throw away his dinner untasted, if such a person only placed his foot on the spot where the meal was being prepared.

The evenings of the villagers, after their return from the fields, were spent in recreation with their families and neighbours; and they might sometimes be seen sitting in a circle under the trees, listening with delight to some wonderful tale related by the bard of the village, or, perhaps, by some wandering Faquir, or traveller, who had come to seek shelter and entertainment for the night; for whose accommodation there was always a

Wundering Faquir.

house maintained at the public expense; and a fund was also kept for the purpose of giving alms to religious mendicants. The monkish orders had become very numerous, and some of them had convents to which lands were attached; but a great number of the members subsisted entirely on charity, and were merely associated by certain rules which they made for themselves. Among these, were several sects of pretended devotees, who sought to obtain a reputation for sanctity by imposing on themselves, or seeming to do so, the most painful austerities; but their influence gradually declined, some of them were, in time, treated with contempt as impostors, while others inspired dread by their lawless deeds. To the latter class belonged the Nagas, who were at once monks, soldiers, and robbers, sometimes engaging, for pay, in the services of different princes, and sometimes forming themselves into large armed bands for the purpose of plunder. The personal appearance of these fanatics was forbidding in the extreme, for their clothing consisted merely of a coarse hempen cloth, tied round them, while their long shaggy beards and matted hair, hanging over their bare arms, gave them a wild and ferocious aspect. The Nagas were again divided into other sects, some of whom were worshippers of Vishnu, others of Siva, and desperate conflicts often took place between them.

The Emperor Akber, on one of his expeditions met, on the banks of the Ganges, two parties, who were about to dispute, with their swords, the possession of a bathing place. He humanely endeavoured to effect an amicable arrangement, but to no purpose; he therefore stopped to witness the battle, which was fought with great fury, many being killed on both sides; till, at length, one party gaining a decided advantage, the Emperor commanded his guards to interfere, to prevent more bloodshed; but, even then, the contest was given up with great reluctance.

As late as the year 1760, a still more violent affray took place at the great fair of Hardwar, where, it is said, some thousands were left dead on the field; but this is probably an exaggerated statement. Hardwar, or Ganga Dwara, meaning the Gate of the Ganges, is situated at the spot where that river issues from the mountains, and is a celebrated place of pilgrimage, besides being the seat of the greatest fair in India. The fair and religious

PILGRIMS AT THE SOURCE OF THE GANGES.

London, Dean & Co Threadneedle St

festival are held together, at the vernal equinox, on which occasion, not less than from two to three thousand persons are assembled; and every twelfth year, which is a sort of jubilee, the numbers are much greater; but the festivals generally ended in bloodshed, until Bengal was occupied by the British, in 1765; since which time, measures for preserving peace and good order have been successfully adopted.

There are no people in the world who pay so much attention to the ceremonies of their religion, as the Hindus, nor is there any country where places of worship are so numerous. No sabbath is observed, but holidays are frequent, and the temples are visited daily and hourly, by persons of both sexes, who carry offerings to the idols, and decorate them with garlands of flowers. The most devout perform their morning devotions on the banks of a lake or river, which is usually furnished with flights of steps, that the worshippers may descend to the water, to go through the customary ablutions which form a part of their religious rites. Parties of Bramins are constantly seen repairing to the temples; while, on every holiday, the roads and streets are thronged with religious mendicants, usually distinguished by a dingy orange coloured scarf, or turban; pilgrims bearing some symbol of the god they are going to worship, whose name they repeat aloud to every passer by; processions, with images borne on stages, elevated above the heads of the people, and representations of temples, chariots, and horses, accompanied by drums, cymbals, and other noisy instruments, and followed by immense crowds of the common people.

The native princes celebrated all the great festivals with extraordinary splendour, lavishing vast sums on gorgeous processions, and other costly pageants. The most magnificent of these spectacles was a dramatic performance, exhibited in the open air, at the festival of Rama, to commemorate the supposed victory of that deified hero over the giant king of Ceylon. On this occasion, a temporary building, erected on some large plain, represented the giant's castle, which was stormed and taken, by a band of warriors, led by one who personated Rama himself. It was customary for the prince, and all the great men of the province, to be present at this exhibition, which, after the mock combat, ended with fireworks, and a triumphal procession, described as the most magnificent spectacle ever witnessed even in the east.

The Hindus took great delight in shows and merry makings, especially in fairs, which were held generally once a year, in most of the towns and villages. Some of them were great commercial fairs, attended by merchants from different countries, but also resorted to for pleasure by the lower orders, for whose entertainment there were such amusements as are usually presented at an English fair. The Indians have a spring festival, called the Holi, which is celebrated in the villages with bonfires and sports, one of the favourite diversions of the revellers on this particular occasion being, that of throwing over each other a crimson powder, made up for the purpose into little balls, until every individual is so completely disguised that it is difficult to distinguish one from another, which causes abundance of mirth; and this game is played in the houses of the great with as much enjoyment as among the simple villagers.

It has always been customary among the Hindus to marry their children at a very early age, particularly the daughters; so that it was not unusual for a girl to become a bride when nine or ten years old, and sometimes the bridegroom was almost as juvenile. The young people, however, had more liberty of choice than in China; therefore it may be supposed that matrimony was often the result of mutual attachment. The nuptials were always performed at the residence of the bride's father, and consisted merely of a few simple ceremonies, such as tying the hands of the parties together with a blade of grass, and repeating certain sentences while the bride took seven steps across the floor, the seventh being considered the tie which rendered the union indissoluble. A dinner was usually given, and presents made to the guests, after which the newly-married pair were conducted in procession to their abode. If the bride were of high rank, she was literally covered with jewels from head to foot; and even females of the lower classes displayed gold and silver ornaments on such occasions, for the wealth of the Hindus, whatever may be their station in life, is invariably lavished on personal ornaments.

The suttee, or immolation of widows was a very prevalent practice at this period, but not universal, as was formerly supposed, and the victim generally acted by her own free will, often in opposition to the wishes of her relatives. But this was not always the case, especially among the families of princes and great Bramins, who were sometimes desirous of augmenting the solemnity of the funeral rites by a suttee, and would even employ force to gain their object. The emperor Akber made a law to protect women from so horrible a fate, and was fortunate enough to save the life of one lady, by riding some hundreds of miles, at his utmost speed, to the spot where he had been informed the sacrifice was to take place. The lady was the daughter-in-law of the Raja of Joudpoor, who, sanctioned by the Bramins of his court, had demanded of the reluctant widow this fearful proof of her affection for his deceased son, in order to increase the

Painted by B. Sewyn On Stone by Dean & Co

CEREMONY OF BURNING A HINDU WIDOW WITH THE BODY OF HER LATE HUSBAND

London, Dean & Co. Threadneedle Street. Page 204

pomp of the obsequies; but the Emperor happily arrived in time to prevent the ceremony, to the infinite joy and gratitude of the widow, but to the great disappointment of the Raja and priests, who considered that he had interrupted a most holy and meritorious act.

When the sacrifice was voluntary on the part of the woman, she was led to the pile by her female friends, amongst whom it was usual for her to distribute the ornaments which she wore, and to take leave of them as if she was setting out on some pleasant journey. A great number of Bramins were in attendance, whose exhortations and superstitious observances were calculated to produce that temporary excitement which enabled the victim to maintain a cheerful demeanour throughout the dreadful ceremonies. The scene was often rendered the more revolting by the circumstance, that the hand of a son was sometimes required to set fire to the pile on which his mother was about to perish in so cruel a manner. The British government has done much towards the abolition of this barbarous custom; and the humane endeavour to suppress it entirely has long been warmly supported by the most enlightened portion of the Indian population; but in some parts of the country, where the ancient superstitions still prevail in all their original force, a suttee is even now heard of occasionally.

The Hindus generally consume the bodies of the dead by fire, except those of the religious orders, which are buried in a sitting posture, with their legs crossed, as we see those of the idols. It is considered very unfortunate to die in a house, therefore when a man draws near his end, he is always carried out of doors, and laid on a bed of grass, usually on the banks of a stream, the Ganges being always preferred, if within reach. The funeral rites are performed immediately after death, when a pyre is raised, and decorated with flowers, and the deceased, after having been bathed, perfumed, and adorned also with fresh flowers, is laid upon it, having been conveyed to the spot, preceded by music. The pile is then lighted by the nearest relation, and scented oils, with clarified butter, are poured on the flames, the friends and relatives sitting on the banks of the stream to watch the burning. On these occasions, as well as at all other religious ceremonials, liberal presents are made to the Bramins, and alms given to the poor.

Tombs are seldom erected by the Hindus, except for those who are slain in any remarkable battle, or for widows who have devoted themselves to death; but rites to the dead are performed every month, in any lonely glade, or on the banks of a stream, whither the relatives of the departed bring offerings of rice cakes and clarified butter, which they set down on the edge of the water, invoking the manes to come and partake of them.

At this period, the domestic manners of the great were probably influenced, in a higher degree, by those of their Mohammedan conquerors, than at any former period. Women of rank never went abroad without being closely veiled, or shut up in a covered palanquin; but since the fall of the Musselman empire, they have not adhered very strictly to this custom, although they have still their separate apartments, and do not mix in society with the opposite sex. They were attended by great numbers of female slaves, whose condition was, in general, superior to that of free servants, as they were considered a part of the family, and often treated by their mistresses in the light of humble friends, as we similarly find them represented in most eastern tales.

The towns of India were, in general, populous, and full of shops, which were always open to the street, and sometimes consisted only of a small booth or verandah, in front of the dwelling. The customers stood outside in the street while they made their purchases. The upper part of the house was usually let to a private family, as the shopkeeper only came to their place of business in the morning, and returned home at sunset. The greater number of them were confectioners, fruiterers, grain-sellers, druggists, and braziers; but there were also many dealers in cloth, silks, shawls, and stuffs, of various descriptions, who kept their goods in bales, to preserve them from the dust. The streets were, in general, unpaved, narrow, and crowded; the houses high, and built of brick, stone, or other material, according to the part of the country in which they were situated. In the houses of the Hindu nobles, the interior wood-work was richly carved; but there was no furniture, except a thin cotton mattress spread over the floor, covered with a white cloth, on which, at their entertainments, the guests satin rows, opposite to each other, around the room, while the master of the house was seated at the upper end, raised above the rest by a second mattress, covered, perhaps, with a carpet of embroidered silk, and, if he were a prince or great chief, a high embroidered cushion formed his musnud, or throne. A quilted silk curtain supplied the place of a door, and the apartment was lighted at night by torches, held by men, on occasions of ceremony; though for ordinary purposes, brass lamps were used. Entertainments were very rarely given, except at weddings, and a few of the great festivals, when it was customary to hire female singers and dancers, parties of whom were continually roaming about the country.

It was the custom among the Indians to offer presents to their guests, such as shawls, bracelets, ornaments for the turban; or, on a first introduction among people of rank, the gift was frequently a handsome sword, a horse, or even an elephant, which last was considered as the most complimentary.

The carriages used in India were of various kinds. Palanquins, carried by bearers, were the most general, but the principal inhabitants in some of the cities rode in a vehicle resembling what we call a chaise-cart, covered with fine cloth or silk, and drawn by two small buffaloes. The howdahs were of various forms, some being like pavilions with silk curtains; others, like chairs; while some were merely flat cushions; so that any seat fixed on the back of an elephant was called a howdah.

There was also a state conveyance called a naulkeen, which bore some resemblance to a throne, and was carried with poles; but this was never used by any other than sovereign princes, or their representatives.

Mango tree.

THE EMPEROR AKBER.

AS Akber was yet too young to take the government into his own hands, it was entrusted, during his minority, to a Turkish nobleman, named Behram, who had been his father's most valued friend, and who succeeded in maintaining the throne for the young monarch against the princes of the late reigning family. Behram was an able minister, but fond of absolute authority; therefore not very ready to bring forward his royal charge, who was kept for some years under more restraint than suited a high spirit, impatient of control.

Akber was handsome in person, courteous in manners, and gifted with all those princely qualities that are sure to render a monarch popular. Skilled in all manly exercises, and courageous even to madness, he delighted to exhibit his prowess, in taming wild horses and elephants, or in braving the dangers to which huntsmen are exposed in the east, from the ferocious nature of the animals they chase. Tiger-hunting was the favourite sport of the young sultan, who, when engaged in this perilous pastime, was ever the most daring of the party, and in the eagerness of pursuit, was frequently separated from his train; the only times, perhaps, when he found himself perfectly at liberty. It was on one of these occasions that he executed the bold project of freeing himself from a state of tutelage that was becoming every day more irksome to him. Galloping off alone to Delhi, he took possession of the palace as sole master, and issued a proclamation, declaring that he intended, from that moment, to take the government into his own hands. Finding plenty of friends to support him, he sent a formal dismissal to the regent, who was so incensed at being thus unexpectedly deprived of office, that he revolted, and collecting a body of troops, attempted to make himself master of the Punjab; but being defeated by the royal army, he repaired to court, and kneeling at the foot of the throne, solicited pardon for his rebellion; which was graciously accorded. The sultan then offered a government of some importance to the humbled minister, who, however, declined the proffered favour, on the plea that he desired to expiate his fault by making a pilgrimage to Mecca. Having received the royal permission, he set out on his journey, but never reached the holy city, as he was assassinated on the way, by an Afghan chief, in revenge for the death of his father, who had fallen in battle against the Moguls.

The empire of Delhi, at this period, comprised only the country around that city, and Agra, with the territory called the Punjab, which includes all the land watered by the five great branches of the Indus, and constitutes the kingdom of Lahore. These dominions were too limited to satisfy the aspiring mind of the young Sultan, who, from the earliest period of his reign, seems to have formed the grand design of uniting the whole of India into one vast monarchy. With this view, he judiciously endeavoured to conciliate the Hindus, by bestowing offices of state, without distinction, on the native, as well as Mohammedan nobles; and he formed an alliance with one of the greatest of the Rajput families, by marrying the daughter of Bahara-mal, the Raja of Jeipur, a powerful state in Rajputana. The capital of this state was one of the handsomest cities of Hindostan, being embellished with many fine buildings, amongst which was a magnificent palace, built entirely of white marble, and surrounded by beautiful gardens. This building is said to have been the work of an Italian architect, employed by a predecessor of Bahara-mal, in the fifteenth century.

But it was not by conciliatory measures alone, that a country containing so many independent states, was to be brought under subjection to one ruler; therefore Akber very soon appeared in the field, and, in a few years, had largely extended his dominions on every side. The Rajputs, who held a great many principalities, made a desperate struggle to maintain their independence; but the arms of the Sultan were uniformly victorious, and that once-powerful class of men, as their governments were overthrown, and their princes made subjects to the Mogul empire, mingled, by degrees, with the mass of the people, and were known, in after times, rather as agriculturists than warriors. The chiefs of the conquered states were always treated honourably, and enrolled amongst the nobles of Delhi, while their territories were united to the empire, and placed under its regulations; so that, in course of time, one uniform system of government was established throughout the greater part of Hindostan.

Akber distinguished himself no less as a legislator than a conqueror. He made many beneficial laws, and relieved the people from a great number of burthensome taxes, which had been imposed by different princes to support either their wars or their extravagance. Among the most oppressive of these were a capitation tax, and a toll levied on pilgrims going to any of the holy cities; both of which were abolished by the sultan, who was blamed by some of his councillors for encouraging the idolatry of the Hindus, by allowing them to make their pilgrimages toll free. Akber, however, silenced these objections, by saying that he held it a sin to place obstacles in the way of any man's devotions, whatever might be his mode of performing them; and as long as he occupied the throne, this indulgence was continued to the Hindus; but the tax was afterwards revived, and has only lately been abolished by the British government in India.

As so many imposts were removed by Akber, it became necessary to increase the rents of land, which were raised to about one-third of the produce, and usually paid in money; but if any husbandman thought he was rated too high, he was allowed to claim the right of paying in kind, and was thus protected from extortion on the part of the collectors. Wherever Akber established his sway, he made great reforms in the courts of justice, which had long been very badly regulated, and, in many places, had become altogether inactive. They were now revived in every city; judges and cazis appointed; the laws restored; the severity of the penal code was greatly mitigated; and the use of torture entirely prohibited.

In the meantime, the Sultan was steadily and successfully pursuing the object he had in view. The great kingdom of Guzerat, which had been in a state of anarchy ever since the assassination of Bahadur, was finally subdued, and annexed to the Mogul dominions, in 1573; so that, in twenty years from the date of his accession, Akber had made himself absolute sovereign of all the country then known by the name of Hindostan. Among the many conquests achieved by this great prince was, that of Cashmere, a small but beautiful province, situated in an extensive plain among the Hindu-cush, a chain of the Himalaya mountains. A long succession of Hindu princes had ruled over Cashmere previously to the fourteenth century, when the last of them was superseded by one of those Turkish adventurers who, about that period, founded so many petty states; and the country was ruled by his successors until the invasion of Akber, when it was annexed to the empire of Delhi; and a jaghir, or feudatory estate, in Behar, was granted to the vanquished king, on condition that he should furnish a certain number of troops to the Emperor, in the manner of a feudal vassal. There were many such feudatories during the sway of the Moguls; and to them was first applied the title of Zemindar, a Persian word, meaning a holder of land, and since used to designate those high officers or agents, who are answerable to the government for the revenues derived from the lands.

Cashmere is described as the most enchanting spot in all Asia. It consists of a broad luxuriant valley, clothed with perpetual verdure, and watered by gentle cascades falling from the mountains. Fruits and flowers abound in this delightful country; and the rose of Cashmere, the theme of many a poet's song, is held in high estimation by the natives, who, at the time of its appearing in all its beauty, are accustomed to celebrate an annual festival, called "the Feast of Roses." Cashmere contained several large towns, besides a great number of pleasant villages; and being considered by the Hindus as a holy land, was full of temples, dedicated to various idols, and was resorted to by pilgrims from all parts of India. The celebrated shawls of Cashmere are made from the wool of the goats of Thibet, and this manufacture was so flourishing under the Mogul dynasty, that the number of shawl looms constantly at work in the province, is said to have amounted to forty thousand; though at the end of the last century there were not half that number, and now they are reduced to less than three thousand; yet the manufacture is as good as it was in former days. The making of a pair of shawls of the best kind, which are worth from two to three hundred pounds, will occupy fifteen men for eight months.

As long as the Mohammedan sovereigns ruled in India, and the princes and governors of provinces held courts scarcely inferior in splendour to that of the capital, there was also full employment for manufacturers of gold and silver stuffs, rich silks, fine muslins, jewellery, and goldsmith's work; but since the fall of the empire there have been no wealthy potentates to encourage those branches of industry, which declined gradually, until some of the most beautiful were entirely lost. Cashmere became the favourite summer residence of the emperors of Delhi, one of whom constructed the famous gardens of Shalimar, where, erected on arches over a lake, were several elegant saloons, to which the great men of the court resorted, to take sherbet, coffee, and other refreshments.

Soon after the conquest of Cashmere, Akber turned his arms against the Afghan tribes of those mountainous regions beyond the Indus, where the British armies have been lately engaged. The nature of the country gave great advantages to its inhabitants, who were accustomed, from their earliest boyhood, to wander among the intricate passes of the mountains, until they were acquainted with every path and winding, and knew exactly at what points an enemy might be intercepted. The way across the Khyber hills, which stretch from the banks of the Indus, and from the western side of the fertile plains of Peshawer, lies through many a narrow defile, while the Hindu-cush on the north of the plain are intersected by fine broad valleys, thirty or forty miles in length, with others branching out on each side, and all terminating in deep glens, hemmed in by the rugged mountains, or lost in the wilds of some pathless forest.

The first expedition sent by Akber into the Afghan country entirely failed, for his troops were beset in the most difficult passes, and cut off by thousands, so that the army was nearly destroyed. Still he did not abandon the hope of subduing that nation, and pursued the war for fifteen years, at the end of which time, he was obliged to content himself with a very imperfect conquest, for although most of the Afghan chiefs were brought to make submission, and a tribute was imposed on them, their subjection was rather nominal than real, and the authority of the Emperor extended but little beyond the city of Peshawer, which he greatly enlarged, and beautified with mosques, and other fine buildings. In the meantime, he had become master of Scinde, an extensive country, through which the Indus takes its course, and which contains, among other populous cities, those of Hyderabad and Tatta, the latter of which became, under the dominion of his successors, one of the most opulent commercial and manufacturing towns of Hindostan. The prince of Scinde had, in his armies, a

Afghan soldier.

number of Portuguese soldiers, and a band of natives, dressed in the European fashion, who were the first Sepoys in India. After the loss of his territories, he was made a noble of Delhi, and the large province of Scinde was thus added to the Mogul empire.

The victories of Akber were never stained with the cruelties that had disgraced those of former conquerors, for the army had been newly modelled, and the soldiers being all paid, were not permitted to plunder the towns, or sell the prisoners as slaves. They had, therefore, no motive for seizing and carrying off the peaceable citizens, which used to be done to a frightful extent. In most cases, too, the condition of the people was improved by the introduction of the new laws; and the whole country, when thus united under one government, was in a far more flourishing state than at any former period.

About the end of the sixteenth century, the attention of Akber was called towards the Deccan, under the following circumstances. The king of Ahmednagar had just died, and as he had left no direct heir to the throne, the succession to it was disputed by four claimants, one of whom having obtained possession, requested the aid of the Moguls to asssist him in maintaining it. The Emperor sent two armies, by different roads, into the Deccan; but ere they had reached their destination, the chief to whose succour they had been dispatched, had been deposed by one of the rival parties, headed by Chand Sultana, a celebrated heroine of Indian history, who assumed the sovereign authority, as Regent for her nephew, Bahadar Nizam Shah. The Moguls laid siege to the city, which was defended by the spirited princess with all the ability of a brave and experienced commander. She wore armour, directed all the operations, and, on one particular occasion, saved the city from being entered through a breach, made by the explosion of a mine, by standing at the opening alone, armed with a sword, until the alarm had been given, and assistance had arrived.

The Moguls, at length, being weary of the contest, abandoned the siege; but hearing soon afterwards, that the Sultana had been killed in a revolt, they took advantage of the confusion caused by that event, to storm the town, when the young king was made prisoner, and sent to the Hill fort at Gwalior; but it was not till after the death of Akber, that the conquest of Ahmednagar was completed.

The court of Akber was the most splendid that had ever been held in India; and his own style of living was of that sumptuous character, that the mere description of it may seem to partake of exaggeration. His hunting establishment is said to have consisted of five thousand elephants, and double that number of horses, which were also used in war; and when he marched in person at the head of his armies, he was provided with an equipage that enabled him to surround himself, even in a desert, with all the pomp and luxuries of his imperial palaces. Whenever the army encamped, a vast space was enclosed by screens of red canvass, ornamented with gilt globes and spires, forming a wall, within which were erected a great number of splendid pavilions, richly furnished, some of which were used as rooms of state, some as banquetting halls, others for retirement or repose; while an inner enclosure contained the apartments of the ladies, all fitted up in the most costly and elegant manner. This inclosure, as we are told, occupied an area of full five miles in circumference.

The birthday of the Emperor was an occasion on which there was always a grand exhibition of wealth. It was celebrated by the court in an extensive plain, near the capital, which was covered with superb tents, that of the Emperor, of course, surpassing all the rest in the splendour of its decorations, the carpets being of silk and gold tissue, and the hangings of velvet, embroidered with pearls. At the upper end was placed the throne, on which Akber sat to receive the homage of the nobles, who were presented with dresses, jewels, horses, elephants, or other gifts, according to their rank. But the most extraordinary display of the munificence, as well as the riches of the Emperor, was made on his causing himself to be weighed in golden scales three times, the first balance being of gold pieces, the second of silver, the third of perfumes, all which were distributed among the spectators that crowded the plain. He also threw, in sport, among the courtiers, showers of gold and silver nuts, and other fruits, for which even the gravest of the ministers were not too dignified to scramble; and these were worn as favours for the rest of the day.

The favourite residence of the Emperor was at Futtehpur Sikri, a town which he built himself, in the province of Agra, where his spacious palace of white marble, and a magnificent mosque near it, are still standing in good preservation, although the town itself is nearly deserted. The walls and citadels of Agra and Allahabad were erected by this prince, who ornamented them in the Indian style, with turrets, domes, and battlements, and each gateway was a stately edifice that would have formed a noble entrance to a royal palace. Allahabad, now so well known as an important British military station, is a very ancient city, and derives a peculiar sanctity from its situation at the confluence of the Ganges and the Jumna, which causes it to be frequented by pilgrims, who repair thither for the purpose of bathing at the sacred spot where the waters meet. Agra was the chief seat of government during this and the succeeding reign, and was greatly embellished by Akber with many fine buildings; but, as in most Hindu towns, the streets were narrow and unpaved, while the houses had a very gloomy appearance, being five or six stories high, and built chiefly of brick, with very small windows, placed at a great height.

Among the architectural works of the Emperor Akber was a splendid mausoleum, erected, at Delhi, in honour of his father, Humayun. It is a vast edifice, of white marble, surmounted by a dome of the same material, and standing on a high terrace; so that it is visible at a great distance, and forms a magnificent feature in the landscape; but its once beautiful gardens are gone to decay, like most other monuments of the former wealth and grandeur of Hindostan.

It was during the reign of Akber, that the first Christian missionaries were received at the court, to which they were invited by the Emperor himself. They were sent by the Portuguese government from Goa, and resided at Agra fifteen years, where they were treated with great respect, and allowed to hold discussions on the subjects of religion with the priests of other persuasions, in the presence of the Emperor, who was accustomed, on a Friday evening, to assemble all the most learned men of his court, for the purpose of holding discussions, when Mohammedans, Christians, Jews, Bramins, and Fire Worshippers, were all allowed to give their opinions without restraint, and to support them by argument. This enlightened sovereign instituted many public schools, both for Hindus and Mohammedans, where every boy was educated according to his prospects in life, and the circumstances of his parents; but most Hindus of rank had their children instructed at home by Bramins, who taught them usually to read and write in several languages, of which there were not less than ten spoken in various parts of India.

During the latter years of the reign of Akber, the Portuguese power in the Indian seas had been almost superseded by that of the Dutch, in consequence of the tyranny of Philip of Spain, who had prohibited the commerce between Holland and Lisbon; thus unintentionaly forcing the Dutch to go to India for their spices and silks, instead of procuring them, as heretofore, in the capital of Portugal, which was the great European mart for Indian commodities. The Dutch obtained several naval victories over the Portuguese, and, about the time of Akber's death, were in possession of the Spice Islands, and had fully established their supremacy on the seas of India.

But a far more important circumstance as regards the history of that country, was the incorporation of a British East India Company, by Queen

Elizabeth, in the year 1600, when the English began to make voyages to the Indies, where, for a long time, they met with very little success, owing to the opposition of the Dutch and Portuguese, who, though enemies to each other, were equally interested in keeping such formidable rivals as the English out of the field. It was not, therefore, till after the death of Akber that any settlement was gained by the English, or permission to trade to India granted to them by the Emperor, who, at that time, was usually styled in this country, the Great Mogul.

Akber died in the year 1605, having reigned forty-nine years. He was buried at Agra, where, over his remains, a splendid tomb of white marble

The Gate of Akber's mausoleum.

was erected, which was of such vast dimensions, that, in 1803, it was occupied by a whole regiment of British dragoons, who made it their quarters for some time after the conquest of that territory.

JEHANGHIR.

HE Emperor Akber was succeeded by his son, Selim, who assumed the presumptuous title of Jehanghir, or Conqueror of the World; and, although not equal to his illustrious father in ability, was a great sovereign, under whose dominion the empire lost none of its power and splendour. The early part of his reign was distinguished by his marriage with one of the most beautiful and talented women that ever appeared in the east, the celebrated Nur Jehan, who is better known, in tales of fiction, by the name of Nur Mahal, or the Light of the Harem.

The life of Nur Jehan is full of romantic interest. Her father, the son of a Persian nobleman, had been reduced by a series of misfortunes to a state of poverty, that induced him, at length, to leave his native country, in the hope of obtaining some employment in India. Accompanied by his wife and family, he joined a caravan that was going to Delhi, and on the way, in the city of Candahar, was born the future empress of the country to which her parents were journeying to seek a livelihood. The distressed condition of the mother and child excited the compassion of a rich merchant, belonging to the caravan, who showed great kindness to the whole family during the rest of the journey, and, being a man of some consideration, had influence enough to obtain for the father a subordinate employment at the court of the Emperor Akber. The little girl, who had been the unconscious cause of her father's introduction to so good a friend, soon began to attract notice by her extraordinary beauty, and as she grew older, was almost constantly with the ladies of the harem, where Selim used frequently to see her, and was no less fascinated by her sprightly wit, than by the graces of her person.

The attachment is supposed to have been mutual: but the young lady, whose father had been raised to a high post at the court, was already affianced to a Persian officer, in the service of the Emperor, who conferred on him a large estate in Bengal, and hastened the marriage, for the purpose of removing the dangerous beauty to a distance from her royal lover. The prince also married, but as it was allowable for him to have as many wives as he pleased, he had no sooner come to the throne, than he determined to obtain his first love, whose absence had produced no change in his affection; and, with that view, he induced the viceroy of Bengal to devise some pretext for placing the husband in confinement for a few days, during which the lady might be carried off from his house, and conveyed to the capital. The Viceroy accordingly sent for Shere Afkun, the husband, who, having a suspicion that some wrong was intended, concealed a dagger in his dress, which he drew forth on the first symptom of violence, and stabbed the viceroy to the heart. The guards instantly rushed forward, and struck down the assailant with their scymetars. His death, therefore, which ensued immediately, was the consequence of his own rashness, and not the contrivance of the Emperor; although it appears that his wife was not, at first, satisfied of that fact, since it was a long time before she would consent to marry Jehanghir, notwithstanding her early attachment. At length, however, being convinced of his innocence, she gave him her hand, and the nuptials were celebrated with great splendour.

Few women, perhaps, ever enjoyed so high a consideration at a Mohammedan court, or took so large a share in the government, as Nur Jehan, Her ascendancy over the Emperor was unbounded; he consulted her on all affairs of importance; her name was even associated with his on the coin; and his chief happiness seemed to consist in exalting, and surrounding her with honours such as appertain to a reigning sovereign. Nur Jehan made a good use of her influence; and her father, who was raised to the office of Grand Vizier, was one of the best ministers that ever ruled at the court of an eastern prince.

In the early part of the reign of Jehanghir, an English captain, named Hawkins, who had been sent out by the East India Company, landed, in the autumn of 1608, at Surat, where he had an interview with the Viceroy, who, after raising many objections, gave him permission to dispose of his cargo, but told him he must not bring any more goods to the ports of India, or attempt to establish a factory on the coast, without the permission of the Emperor. The captain soon discovered that this viceroy was leagued with the Portuguese to prevent the English from obtaining a settlement in the country. He therefore determined to make a journey to Agra, and see the Emperor himself. On his arrival in that capital, he was immediately admitted to an audience, for Jehanghir was so easy of access, that, it is said, he had a cluster of golden bells hung in his private apartment, and attached to a chain outside the palace gate. These bells might be rung by any person, who wished to see him out of the regular hours of public business; a plan he adopted to prevent the attendant officers from refusing to admit a petitioner.

Captain Hawkins presented a letter from his sovereign, James the First, which was translated to Jehanghir by one of the Portuguese Jesuits, of whom there were several at the court. The Emperor was highly pleased with the British officer, invited him every day to the court, conversed with him freely in the Turkish language, and treated him for some time with distinguished favour. At length, however, he suffered himself to be persuaded that if he encouraged the English to trade to his dominions, the Portuguese, who, he was told, were a richer and more powerful nation, would cease to visit his ports, and he would thereby lose all the advantages derived from the commerce of that people, which produced a considerable revenue to the government. In consequence of these representations, the Emperor did not grant the request contained in the letter of King James, but dismissed the captain in rather a summary manner; at the same time issuing a mandate, by which the English were forbidden to return to his dominions.

Some of the states of the Deccan were, at this time, in rebellion, and most of them ill-governed; in consequence of which all that part of India was in a very disturbed and disorderly state during the whole of the reign of Jehanghir, whose son, Shah Jehan, was engaged for several years in suppressing various insurrections. In consequence of these wars between the Emperor and the native princes, many of the towns bore signs of devastation in almost every part.

In the meantime, the English continued to make voyages to different ports, but with very little success, until the year 1615, when a regular embassy was sent to the court of Jehanghir, conducted by Sir Thomas Roe, who landed at Surat, and proceeded at once to Ajmir, where the Emperor was then residing. This gentleman, who remained for some time at the court of Jehanghir, obtained, with difficulty, his majesty's permission for the establishment of an English factory at Surat, which was immediately erected, and a regular trade opened with this port, the first British station in India.

The Envoy was greatly surprised at the familiar manners of the sovereign, and the publicity with which he was surrounded. In the morning he might constantly be seen at the windows of the palace, before which a crowd regularly assembled; and in the afternoon, he always took his seat in the Durbar, or hall of audience, where he held both a council of state, and a court of justice, which was open to every one.

The palace of Ajmir overlooked an open plain, on which combats of wild elephants and tigers were frequently exhibited for the amusement of the Emperor, who evinced great delight in witnessing them. The princes and nobles of Hindostan also derived much enjoyment from these barbarous spectacles, and on most grand occasions, entertained their guests with similar conflicts, for which purpose a temporary theatre was erected, of bamboo, bound tightly together, and high enough to prevent the escape of the tiger, whose opponent was usually a buffalo, which, in its wild state, is a very fierce and powerful animal.

As Jehanghir advanced in years, his life was embittered by the rebellion of his son, Shah Jehan, who had great reason to apprehend that the Emperor, acting under the influence of his Empress, Nur Mahal, intended to nominate the husband of that lady's daughter as his successor to the throne. It was with a view of counteracting this design, that he openly raised his standard in opposition to that of his father, and seized on the provinces of Bengal and Bahar, from which he led a body of troops, to secure the fortress of Allahabad; but the Emperor had sent out an army, under the command of Mohabat Khan, to intercept his march; and a battle took place, near Allahabad, where he was defeated, and obliged to seek shelter in the Deccan. All his former adherents now deserted him; and finding that there was no hope of establishing his claim by force, he wrote a humble and repentant letter to his father, who replied to it, by demanding that he should send his two sons, Dara Sheko and Aurengzebe, as hostages for his future good behaviour. The young princes were, accordingly, sent to their grandfather; but before the monarch had granted a pardon to his rebellious son, his own career was brought to a close, his death being preceded by some remarkable events.

Mohabat Khan, a nobleman of great talents, and the chief commander of the army, had incurred the displeasure of the Empress, whose unbounded influence over her husband empowered her to ruin any individual who might be imprudent enough to excite her enmity. Mohabat, who, after his victory over Shah Jehan, had remained in occupation of Bengal, was very much astonished at receiving an order from the Emperor to repair immediately to his camp, to answer certain charges brought against him, which he knew to be utterly false. Still it was necessary to obey the summons; and he set out, attended by a guard of five thousand Rajputs, on whose fidelity he could safely rely. Immediately before his departure, he had betrothed his daughter to a youth of noble family, without applying to the Emperor for his consent, as was customary among the Mohammedan nobles; and Jehanghir, who was in no frame of mind to overlook such an offence, vented his wrath on the unoffending bridegroom, whom he caused to be beaten almost to death, having previously seized the dowry he had received from Mohabat. The indignant father-in-law determined to revenge the insult, proceeded, at once, with his army of Rajputs, to the tents of his royal master, who was encamped on the banks of the Hydaspes, but had sent his troops over the river, intending to follow in the course of the day. The monarch was reposing on a couch, when a rude noise disturbed his slumbers, and starting up, he saw himself surrounded by armed men, and recognizing Mohabat Khan, exclaimed, "Traitor, what means this?" Mohabat, kneeling before him with a look of deep humility, declared that no treason was intended, but begged that his majesty would rise and mount his elephant, that the people might see that he was safe; and as Jehanghir had no means of resistance, he was obliged to comply, and rode in the midst of the soldiers, by the side of Mohabat, to the tent of that chief, who had thus boldly made him a prisoner.

No sooner was Nur Mahal informed of the capture of her lord, than she set out, in disguise, to join the army on the opposite side of the river; and although the bridge was guarded by Mohabat's troops, she was allowed to cross, as the guards had been ordered to let any persons pass that way, but not to let them return. The beautiful Amazon now appeared, mounted on an elephant, and armed with a bow and arrows, at the head of the Imperial troops, leading the way to storm the bridge; but the Rajputs, expecting this movement, had destroyed it, and easily drove back those who attempted to swim the ford, amongst whom was the Empress herself. The deliverance of the Emperor was, however, shortly accomplished by the contrivance of Nur Mahal, but he died very soon afterwards, and Shah Jehan, with the powerful support of Mohabat Khan, took possession of the throne, in the year 1627.

SHAH JEHAN.

THE splendour of the Mogul Empire was never so great, even in the time of Akber, as during the reign of Shan Jehan, whose taste for profuse expenditure exhibited itself in every possible form. He built new palaces in all the principal cities, and lavished vast sums of money on shows and festivals. His retinue was more numerous, and his whole establishment on a grander scale than that of his predecessors; and, altogether, he was perhaps the most magnificent sovereign, with regard to wealth, that ever reigned in India. The most brilliant specimen of his extravagance was the celebrated Peacock Throne, resplendent with diamonds, which is supposed to have cost six millions sterling. It took its name from its principal ornament, a peacock, with a spreading tail, the colours of which were represented by different kinds of precious stones. This glittering appendage to the court of the Great Mogul, is subsequently mentioned among the rich spoils of the Persian conqueror, Nadir Shah.

Soon after the accession of Shah Jehan, Mohabat Khan, who had been appointed governor of the Deccan, was commanded to display his military talent in repelling an invasion of the Uzbeks, who had entered Cabul, and after having ravaged the country, had laid seige to the capital. He succeeded in putting these barbarians to flight, but he had scarcely performed this service, before a serious insurrection in the Deccan obliged the Emperor to take the field in person. There was a great chief, named Khan Lodi, who had held a high military command under Jehanghir, to whom he had been faithfully attached, but was now suspected of aiming to establish an independent principality for himself. The Emperor, however, thought it would be prudent to keep on friendly terms with him, as he was very popular in the Deccan, and, with that view, sent for him to the court, where he was honourably received, and lived for some time with his family at Agra, surrounded by a great number of retainers. He probably entertained some doubts of his own security, which were, at length, confirmed by an anonymous communication, warning him to keep on his guard, as the Emperor only waited an opportunity to imprison him on a false charge. Khan Lodi speedily assembled his forces, and marched openly out of the city, at the head of two thousand Afghan warriors, accompanied by twelve of his own sons, and the ladies of his harem, in their howdahs, mounted on elephants.

This proceeding was, naturally, treated as an act of open defiance, and the royal troops were marched off in pursuit of the daring chieftain, who was compelled to give battle, but was defeated. He saved himself, however, though with difficulty, by swimming over a river, and concealed himself among the woods of Gondwana, from which, he opened a correspondence with Nizam Shah, the king of Ahmednagar, who promised to assist him. The three great kingdoms of the Deccan had recovered their ancient limits, and Ahmednagar, the most extensive of them, joined the Mogul dominions: therefore the Emperor put himself at the head of his army, and entered the Deccan in formidable array. Nizam Shah and Khan Lodi met him near Dowlatabad, where a battle was fought, in which the Emperor was victorious, and Lodi fled towards the Afghan country; but being overtaken by his enemies, he made a desperate stand with his few

Khan Lodi overpowered.

followers, and bravely defended himself until he fell, covered with wounds, when his head was cut off, and sent as a trophy to the Emperor.

One of the most powerful adherents of Khan Lodi during this war, had been Shahjee, a famous Mahratta chief, and the father of Sevajee, the founder of the Mahratta empire. The country of the Mahrattas was a mountainous region south of the Nerbuddah river, defended on the west by the Ghauts, and a narrow strip of land between these mountains and sea, called the Concan. Some parts of this tract are very rugged, and almost inaccessible, on account of the thick forests, and mountain torrents rushing down the sides of the steep rocks; but, in other places, it is fertile, and produces rice, hemp, and cocoa nuts. The sides of the mountains are mostly covered with large trees, but the summits are barren and rocky, and only to be reached by the winding paths, and rude flights of steps, leading to different fortresses; the approaches being guarded by towers and massive gateways, erected by the princes who have ruled over the country at various times. The Mahratta chiefs were not sprung, like the Rajputs, from a noble race, but were originally Sudras, of the same caste with their own people, and derived their consequence from having long filled the ancient hereditary offices of heads of villages. After the Mohammedan conquest, lands were bestowed on many of these persons for military service; so that almost every Mohammedan prince had his feudal vassals among the Mahratta chieftains, who furnished him with a certain number of troops, according to the extent of his jaghir, or fief. Hindu titles were frequently bestowed with the lands, such as those of Rajah, Naick, Rao, and others of less importance; so that a race of Mahratta nobles was created, who, in the time of Shah Jehan, began to be distinguished in history.

Trained to military exercises from their early years, the young Mahrattas were taught to regard learning as a pursuit better adapted to Bramins than to soldiers; and as few of them could either read or write, every great chief kept in his employ a number of Bramins, as writers, and men of business, some of whom managed his estate and private affairs, while others were employed in public transactions, and often sent on embassies, in which capacity they were called Vakeels.

The women in the Mahratta country were treated with great respect, and are often found taking a considerable share in public affairs, when the death of a husband, or the minority of a son, made it desirable that they should do so; and, for this reason, widows were, in most cases, dissuaded from sacrificing themselves on the funeral pile. At the death of her husband, therefore, a lady of rank generally laid aside the veil which, during his life, she had always worn, as it was considered undignified to appear unveiled in the presence of men, except where the lady was required to supply the place of the absent chief.

During the greater part of the sixteenth century, the Mahrattas were held under supremacy by the two chief sovereigns of the Deccan, the kings of Bijapur and Ahmednagar, particularly by those of Bijapur, a distinguished race of princes, known as the Adil Shah dynasty. The capital of that once great kingdom is now in ruins; but its splendid mosques, mausoleums, and palaces, although falling into decay, are among the grandest works of art that are met with in southern India. Among these, the tomb of Ibrahim Adil Shah, who was reigning when the Portuguese took the town of Goa, holds a distinguished place, both for its immensity, and the elegance of its structure. Ibrahim Adil Shah entrusted the affairs of his government chiefly to the Mahratta Bramins, whose general influence was thereby greatly increased; and he numbered among his vassals some of the most powerful chiefs of the country. The kings of Ahmednagar had also their vassal chiefs, amongst whom, the greatest was Jadu Rao, who held a jaghir for the maintenance of ten thousand horse soldiers, and had, like all other men of wealth and influence, a vast number of followers and dependents. One of these was Malojee Bhonslay, the head of a small village near Doulatabad, who, through the patronage of Jadu, had obtained a command in the armies of the sovereign of Ahmednagar, but still was classed among the retainers of Jadu Rao, until a singular incident placed them on very different terms with each other.

It was customary among the Hindus for all great men to invite their dependents to their houses to celebrate the festival of the Holi, on which occasion they were at liberty to take their children with them; and Malojee Bhonslay went, in the year 1599, accompanied by his son, Shahjee, a fine boy, about five years of age, to the residence of his patron, Jadu Rao, to enjoy the festivities of the season. The noble countenance of the young Shahjee attracted the notice of Jadu, who seated him on his knee, and calling his own little daughter to him, a child of three years of age, he asked her playfully if she would have that pretty boy for her husband, to which she readily assented, and threw some balls of red powder at him, which caused much laughter among the company. But great was the surprise of the little lady's father, when Malojee, rising, appealed to all present to bear witness that their chief had affianced his daughter Jeejee to Shahjee Bhonslay; and none could deny the fact, although every one was sensible that he had done so only in jest.

For some time, Jadu would scarcely believe that Bhonslay was serious in his pretensions, and his wife was extremely incensed, both at the presumption of the dependent, and the folly of her lord, in having degraded himself so far as to match his daughter, even in sport, with the son of a person so much beneath him. The ambitious Malojee, however, resolved to carry his point; and, with that view, must have turned his attention, in the first instance, to the accumulation of wealth, as he became very rich in the course of a few years. This rapid acquisition of riches might have excited much astonishment among a people less given to superstition than the Hindus, but Malojee solved the mystery to their satisfaction, by affirming that the goddess Devi had appeared to him in a dream, and pointed out a spot where a great treasure was concealed; at the same time declaring, that one of his family was destined to be a king. Whatever might have been the means by which Malojee acquired his riches, he made a good use of them, by constructing wells, and tanks, and other useful public works. He also increased the number of his cavalry, and eventually obtained, at the court of Ahmednagar, the title of Raja, with a considerable jaghir, comprising two forts, with their districts, and the village of Poonah, afterwards the capital of the country. Jadu Rao was no longer averse to the marriage of Shahjee with his daughter Jeejee Bye. The nuptials, therefore, were celebrated, and with great pomp, the king himself honouring the feast with his presence. The word Bye added to a name in India, means lady: thus Jeejee Bye signifies the Lady Jeejee.

It has already been stated, that Shahjee Bhonslay was one of the partizans of Khan Lodi, but after the fall of that chief, he tendered his services to the new Emperor, Shah Jehan, from whom he received fresh grants of land in return. Sevajee, his son, the celebrated founder of the Mahratta empire, was born just before the rebellion of Khan Lodi, in the same year that Shah Jehan ascended the Imperial throne. His father and mother then lived very happily together; but when he was about three years of age, Shahjee, with a view of strengthening his family connections, took another wife, at which Jejee was so much offended, that she left him, and went to reside with her own relations, taking with her the little Sevajee, who was her favourite child, and leaving his elder brother with his father. Sevajee was married at the age of seven, on which occasion both his parents were present, and a partial reconciliation took place between them.

Shahjee, who was going upon some distant expedition, then placed his young son under the care of his head Bramin, who built a large house at Poonah for the Lady Jeejee, and took care that the youth should be instructed in all fitting accomplishments, such as horsemanship, hunting, and military exercises, all of which were eminently suited to his taste. He was also fond of listening to the romantic tales and ballads of the country, from which he imbibed that daring spirit of adventure for which he was afterwards distinguished. His fondness for such fictions, even when he had passed the days of boyhood, frequently led him into great dangers, as he would venture, in disguise, among his deadliest foes, to be present at a Kutha, which is a popular amusement among the Mahrattas, consisting of recitations, songs, and tales, related by professional story-tellers. The favourite companions of the young chieftain were the leaders of some of the neighbouring hill tribes, in whose exploits he was often suspected of taking an active part; nor could the admonitions of his guardian Bramin restrain his adventurous spirit, or detach him from such lawless associates.

In the meantime, several revolutions had taken place in the kingdom of Ahmednagar, the king of which had been assassinated; and, in the confusion that ensued, Shahjee had taken possession of the throne, the true heir, an infant, having been made prisoner by the Imperial forces. The usurper was speedily dethroned by Shah Jehan, who once more took the field in person, and put an end to that monarchy, which was thus annexed to the Mogul dominions, in the year 1637, when Shahjee entered the service of the Emperor. The kingdoms of Bijapur and Golconda were reduced to subjection shortly afterwards, but were not extinguished like that of Ahmednagar, as Shah Jehan contented himself with making their kings tributary to the Mogul empire.

Shah Jehan built the new city of Delhi, which far surpassed the old one in point of magnificence. The palace was a noble structure, and was well protected by a deep moat and strong walls. It stood on a spacious esplanade, approached by a wide handsome street, through which flowed the famous canal of Ali Merdan Khan, a grand work, executed by a Persian of that name, in the reign of Shah Jehan. Ali Merdan had been the governor of Candahar, under the Shah of Persia, whose tyranny having driven him to revolt, he gave up the city to the Mogul Emperor, and took refuge at the court of Delhi, where he distinguished himself very highly by his great talents, in constructing useful public works, of which the canal still bears ample testimony. This fine aqueduct conveyed the waters of the Jumna in a pure state, from the point where the river leaves the mountains, to the city of Delhi, a distance of one hundred and twenty miles. The water which it furnished was not only the drink of the inhabitants, but the source of vegetation in the beautiful gardens around the capital. At a later period, during the troubles that attended the decline of the Mogul empire, the canal was so entirely neglected, that it became choked up with rubbish, and the luxury of good water was unknown at Delhi for a very long period; until the British government undertook the beneficial task of clearing the canal, which was re-opened in 1820, when the whole population of the city went out rejoicing, to meet the stream, throwing into it sweetmeats and flowers.

Source of the Jumna.

The gardens of Shalimar, celebrated in Moore's "Lalla Rookh," were constructed by the Emperor Shah Jehan, than whom no prince was ever more fond of luxurious pleasures. Every summer he passed some months in the lovely vale of Cashmir, where with music, dancing, feasting, and excursions by land and water, he beguiled the time in a constant succession of varied enjoyments.

One of the most splendid works of Shah Jehan was the Taj Mahal, the tomb of his favourite Sultana, at Agra. It stands on a stone terrace, on the banks of the Jumna, and is surrounded by extensive gardens. It is built entirely of white marble, and has a large cupola and four elegant minarets. The tomb itself is in the centre of a circular hall, under the dome, and is formed also of white marble, enclosed with an open screen of mosaic, which is wrought into wreaths of flowers of the most exquisite workmanship, and formed of agates, jaspers, lapis lazuli, and various coloured marbles. This elegant memorial of the dead is kept in repair by the British government.

When Shah Jehan had made himself master of so large a portion of the Deccan, he introduced there the same system of assessing the lands, and collecting the revenues that had been established by Akber, throughout northern Hindostan, where its good effects had been sensibly felt by the agricultural population.

The peace of the Deccan was not of long continuance. It was first disturbed by the king of Golconda, Abdullah Shah, who had for some years, paid his tribute regularly, till, in consequence of a quarrel with his vizier, a popular minister named Mir Jumla, he became involved in a new war

Drawn by R. Tayler. On Stone by Dean & Co.

THE TOMB OF THE FAVOURITE SULTANA OF AKBER KHAN, AT AGRA.

London, Dean & Co Threadneedle St.

with the Emperor. The misunderstanding between the king and Mir Jumla, arose from some offence given by Amin, the Vizier's son, to the monarch, who carried his resentment so far as to dismiss the father from his office. Mir Jumla considering himself wronged, applied to Prince Aurengzebe, one of the Emperor's sons, who was governor of the Deccan, and who warmly interested himself in behalf of the deposed minister. Influenced by him, Shah Jehan sent an order to the king to reinstate Mir Jumla in his former appointment; but instead of doing so, the angry Abdullah confiscated his property, and sent his son to prison.

Shah Jehan being indignant at this contempt of his imperial command, instructed Aurengzebe to enforce the obedience of his refractory vassal, on which the prince, without declaring his intention, made a sudden and most unexpected attack on Hyderabad, the capital of Golconda, at the very time when Abdullah, who was aware of his approach, was preparing an entertainment for him, little suspecting that he had any hostile intent. The city was plundered and set on fire, while the surprised monarch fled in the utmost consternation to a hill fort, some miles distant, from which he despatched orders for the release of Amin, and the restoration of Mir Jumla's property. But these concessions did not satisfy the prince, who imposed a large increase of tribute, and demanded the hand of Abdullah's daughter, with an enormous dowry, for his son, Sultan Mohammed. Mir Jumla did not return to the court of Golconda, but remained with Aurengzebe; and when that prince became Emperor, he was his chief minister.

About this time, Shah Jehan was seized with so serious an illness, that his recovery was deemed hopeless; and his four sons, who were all aspirants to the imperial throne, began to devise the best means for realizing their respective pretensions. Aurengzebe, the youngest of the four brothers, was a man of remarkably mild temper, but cautious, designing, and a perfect master of the art of dissimulation. Dara Sheko, the eldest, was, on the contrary, open-hearted, impetuous, and rash, even to folly. The other two princes, Sujah and Morad, of whom the former was viceroy of Bengal, the latter of Guzerat, were bold, ambitious leaders, but were not equal to Dara Sheko, in spirit, or to Aurengzebe in policy. Each of the four raised an army, and they went to war with each other, while their father was yet alive. The crafty Aurengzebe pretended, at first, to resign in favour of his brother Morad, who thus was induced to join his forces to those of the dissembler, and the two together defeated Dara and Sujah in succession; but while Morad was rejoicing over his fancied success, he was made prisoner by a contrivance of Aurengzebe, who invited him to a supper, and made him drink wine till he was quite insensible, when he was carried off to the citadel, and put in chains. He was afterwards removed to Fort Gwalior, where he died.

Fort Gwalior, the great state prison of those times, stands on an isolated rock, in the province of Agra, near the town of Gwalior, subsequently famous in the history of British India; and in modern times, the residence of the powerful Mahratta chief, Scindia, whose palace occupies one extremity of the hill fort.

The imprisonment of Morad was not the worst of the many crimes by which Aurengzebe raised himself to the throne of the Mogul empire. Taking advantage of his father's advanced age and the weak state to which his late illness had reduced him, he compelled the unhappy monarch to sign his own abdication; and although a palace was assigned for his residence, and he was treated with the utmost respect during the few remaining years of his life, and solaced by the affectionate attentions of a favourite daughter, still he was, in reality, his son's prisoner, and obliged to submit where he alone had the right to command.

And now let us return to the Mahrattas, whose great hero, Sevajee, now nearly thirty years of age, had been slowly but surely laying the foundation of an empire, which was destined to rival that of the Mogul princes. The first acquisition of importance made by the young chief was, the fort of Torna, a stronghold about twenty miles south of Poonah, where he soon collected a large band of mountaineers, ready to follow him in any bold enterprise. His first care, however, was to strengthen his fortress, and in digging among some ruins, he discovered a large treasure in gold; a piece of good fortune which, with true Hindu superstition, he attributed to the liberality of his favourite goddess Devi, and thence augured well for the success of his plans, the ultimate object of which was to raise himself to the rank of an independent prince. He employed his treasure in building another fort, on a mountain about three miles distant, to which he gave the name of Raighur; and as it was very strongly fortified, it became the chief depositary of all the treasures he obtained by plunder, and, with the town attached, was long regarded as the Mahratta capital.

For some years, Sevajee pursued his designs so quietly, that the government of Bijapur, to which he was lawfully subject, did not take much notice of his aggressions, from which no danger was apprehended; but when he began to plunder rich towns, and carry away their treasures to his castle of Raighur, the king, Mohammed Adil Shah, thought it necessary to interfere; and finding that Sevajee paid no attention to his commands, he sent for his father, Shahjee, to remonstrate with him on the subject. Shahjee protested he had no power to control the actions of his son, or prevent his encroachments; but the king mistrusted him; and on receiving news that Sevajee had openly revolted, and seized a convoy of royal treasure in the Concan, he imprisoned Shahjee in a stone dungeon, which was so built up as to leave only a small aperture for the admission of food; and the captive was told that, if his son did not submit within a given time, the opening would be closed for ever.

As soon as Sevajee was made aware of the horrible situation in which his father was placed, on his account, he applied to the Emperor, Shah Jehan, who gladly received the offer of his services, gave him a high command, and sent an order to Bijapur for the release of Shahjee, who was liberated from the dungeon, but detained, under restraint, at the court of Bijapur, for nearly four years, during which time Sevajee refrained from making any very serious aggressions. No sooner, however, had his father been restored to liberty, than Sevajee returned to his former course, and even invaded the territories of the Mogul empire, just at the time when the illness of Shah Jehan gave rise to the war among his sons, which ended in the usurpation of Aurengzebe. Sevajee had, by this time, made himself master of the whole of the Concan, with its numerous forts, some of which had been taken by force, others by stratagem; of which the following is an example.

It was customary for the villagers in the neighbourhood of hill forts, to supply a quantity of grass and palm-leaves to thatch the houses within the fortress, and to carry in the loads themselves. A party of soldiers, disguised as peasants, one day appeared at the gates of a certain fort, with the usual tribute, and were admitted, without suspicion; when throwing down their burthens, they snatched their swords and matchlocks from the bundles of grass they had carried, and falling on the astonished garrison, captured the place with very little trouble.

Soon after Aurengzebe had mounted the throne of Delhi, Sevajee renewed his depredations in the kingdom of Bijapur, where Mohammed Adil Shah had just been succeeded by his son, a youth of nineteen, who sent out a powerful army against the invader, under the command of an able general, named Afzul Khan, a haughty Musselman noble, who looked upon the Mahrattas as barbarians, and their chief as a foe scarcely worthy of his attention. Sevajee was under some alarm at the approaching danger; and, in order to gain time, sent an ambassador with offers of submission, to which Afzul was the more inclined to listen, as he thought it desirable to avoid a war in so wild a country. He therefore appointed one of his Bramins to negotiate with the chief, and state the terms on which his submission would be accepted. This treacherous Bramin was won over, by bribes and promises, to enter into a plot against his master, whom he persuaded to give a meeting to the rebel chief, saying that the latter was so completely humbled, that he was willing to surrender, on any terms, provided he should be assured of the king's pardon, by Afzul himself. Afzul agreed to grant him an interview, and was imprudent enough to consent to go unattended to a certain spot appointed for the meeting, as the Bramin said that Sevajee was afraid otherwise to trust himself without a guard, which, under the circumstances, it would not be proper to bring with him. The result was such as might have been expected. Afzul, leaving his escort at some distance, proceeded in his palanquin, accompanied by only one attendant, to the place of meeting, habited

in a thin muslin robe, with no arms but his sword; while Sevajee had put on a shirt of mail under his cotton tunic, had concealed a dagger in its folds, and had also armed his left hand with a steel instrument used among the Mahrattas, called a tiger's claw, which has three sharp crooked blades, and being fastened on two fingers, may be entirely hidden in the hand. Having thus prepared himself for the deed he meditated, and performed his devotions, he knelt at the feet of his mother, to beg her blessing; and then slowly descended from the hill to meet his victim.

Afzul Khan advanced a few paces towards him, expecting some mark of homage, when the treacherous chief sprang suddenly, like a tiger, on his prey, fixed his steel claws in his breast, and in an instant had dispatched him with his dagger. Then, on a given signal, his men rushed down from several secret paths, and were led on, without delay, to attack the Musselman troops, who were waiting, not far off, for the return of their commander, and being unprepared for such an assault, were easily overcome. Those who resisted, were killed; but those who surrendered, were well treated, and received into the service of Sevajee.

AURENGZEBE.

THE reign of Shah Jehan terminated with the usurpation of Aurengzebe in 1658. The new Emperor, during the first years of his reign, had to maintain his seat on the throne by force of arms against his two brothers, one of whom, Shuja, having lost a decisive battle, disappeared from Hindostan, where he was never heard of afterwards; a circumstance that for several years caused the Emperor considerable anxiety, as he was in constant expectation of the return of the fugitive, strengthened, perhaps, by the aid of some foreign power.

Dara Sheko was still more unfortunate. Deserted by his troops, and pursued by his enemies, he was doomed to witness the death of a beloved wife, occasioned by fatigue and suffering; and was, soon afterwards, betrayed by a pretended friend, into the power of his brother; whose conduct towards him is a stain on his character that no time can efface. The captive prince, after having been paraded in chains through the streets of Delhi, was publicly beheaded, and his sons afterwards met with a similar fate.

Aurengzebe for some time affected to despise the power of the Mahrattas, whose chief he contemptuously styled the mountain rat; yet he well knew that Sevajee was a dangerous foe; and in 1662 he appointed his uncle, Shaista Khan, to the command of an army which he was about to send into the Mahratta country, for the purpose of taking all the forts, and reducing the daring chief to subjection. Shaista Khan, after some fighting, gained possession of Poonah, where he chose for his own quarters the house which had formerly been the residence of Jeejee Bye, and in which Sevajee had passed his childhood. The chief, who had spies in all directions, was soon informed of this circumstance, which led him to plan and execute a plot that is still related with great exultation by the Mahrattas, as one of his cleverest exploits.

Two Bramins, devoted to his interest, gained over one of the Khan's soldiers, a Hindu, who obtained permission to celebrate a marriage in the usual manner, with a procession. Sevajee had brought with him a band of chosen men, whom he mixed amongst the crowd assembled on the occasion, and contrived to introduce three or four of them at a time into the cavalcade, according to the plan concerted. Having thus joined the procession, they by degrees detached themselves from the party, which had not assembled for any real wedding, and proceeded to the house occupied by the Mogul commander, every part of which was so well known to Sevajee, that he led the way silently through a back passage, and thus surprised the occupants, who were cut down before they had time to see who were their assailants. The khan, however, saved his life, by making his escape through a window. The retreat of the Mahrattas was so rapid, that they were beyond reach of pursuit ere the horrible scene that had just been enacted was known in the Mogul camp; and Sevajee, with his daring band, were seen ascending to their fort, at twelve miles distance, amid a blaze of torches, which they had lighted to display their triumph. The Mogul invasion was altogether unsuccessful, and the army was eventually withdrawn from the country.

Not long after the events above narrated, the Mahratta chieftain undertook an expedition against the rich city of Surat, which, for six days, was plundered by his barbarian troops, who carried off an immense booty to Raighur, chiefly the property of the citizens; for although they made great efforts to force the English and Dutch factories, they were not able to succeed, on account of the gallant manner in which they were defended. The English distinguished themselves very highly on this occasion, not only by saving the property of the East India Company, but in assisting the inhabitants of the town, who would have suffered to a greater extent, but for their generous protection. Aurengzebe, in return for their services, granted them a perpetual exemption from a part of the customs exacted from the merchants of other nations trading to Surat.

The frequent incursions of the Mahrattas, and the arbitrary exactions of the Emperor's officers, had long made it desirable for the English to have some place of their own, which they might fortify against such aggressions; and, about two years before the plunder of Surat, the wished-for opportunity was afforded by the marriage of Charles the Second, who received with his bride, Catherine of Portugal, the island of Bombay, with its dependencies, as a part of her dowry; and it was thus that the crown of Great Britain obtained its first territorial possession in India. The island, however, did not yield a sufficient revenue to pay the expenses of the establishment formed upon it; and about six years afterwards, its entire sovereignty was made over to the East India Company, who, in 1687, transferred the presidency of their other settlements from Surat to Bombay, which has, from that time, been the capital of their dominions on the western side of the peninsula.

In the mean time, their possessions on the eastern side were rising into importance. They had an extensive factory at Masulipatam, the chief emporium for the cottons and muslins of Bengal; and another at Hoogley, a considerable city on the river of that name, connected with the Ganges, where the Portuguese, Danes, and Dutch also had settlements. While the English were thus gradually increasing their power and possessions in India, the French, after having made some unsuccessful attempts to establish factories at Surat and other ports, formed a permanent settlement at Pondicherry, on the coast of Coromandel, which they purchased in 1672, of the King of Bijapur; and this was their capital at a later period, during their struggle with the English for supremacy in India.

Shahjee Bhonslay died soon after the Mahratta attack on Surat, when Sevajee immediately assumed the title of Rajah, and began to coin money in his own name, which was equivalent to a declaration of independent sovereignty, and was therefore regarded as an open act of rebellion by the Emperor, who sent out so powerful an army against him, that he found it expedient to make peace by giving up half his territories, and consenting to hold the rest as a jaghir or fief of the empire. In return for these concessions, Aurengzebe made a grant to the chief of a portion of the revenue derived from certain districts under the government of the king of Bijapur, which he was to collect himself; and this grant gave rise to the claim made and enforced by the Mahrattas, in later times, to the well-known contribution of the chout, which afforded them constant pretexts for invading foreign possessions.

Aurengzebe was at this time engaged in a war with the king of Bijapur, and Sevajee, as the holder of a jaghir, was bound to assist him. On this occasion, Sevajee performed some signal services for the empire, and was, in consequence, invited to court, whither he repaired, naturally expecting to receive some signal mark of favour; instead of which, to his great surprise and indignation, he was treated with coldness and contempt by the haughty sovereign, who scarcely deigned even to notice his presence. Sevajee, burning with resentment, allowed some violent expressions to escape him; which being repeated to Aurengzebe, led to the imprisonment of the chief, whose escape is one of the many extraordinary adventures of his eventful life. Under a pretence of being ill, he was visited by a Hindu physician, who was soon made a partner in the plot, and who secured some confederates among the Bramins, to whom Sevajee, still feigning sickness, sent daily large baskets of provisions to be distributed among the poor.

These charities excited no suspicion, as it was very usual for rich men, when ill, to give alms, and make presents to Bramins; therefore, the baskets, after having been once or twice examined, were suffered to pass without enquiry. At length he ventured to trust himself in one of these hampers, the bearers having been bribed not to complain of its unusual weight; and he was thus safely conveyed to the house of a Bramin, who was in the secret, and had prepared a disguise and a horse; by the aid of which, he reached his own capital, before his escape was known at Delhi. Shortly afterwards, he concluded a fresh treaty of peace with Aurengzebe, who granted him a new accession of territory in Berar, and acknowledged his title of Rajah.

Being now a more powerful prince than either the king of Bijapur or of Golconda, he demanded tribute of both these monarchs; who, to avoid a contest with so formidable a foe, were obliged to submit to this humiliation. Hitherto Sevajee had been considered more in the light of the chief of numerous banditti, than as the head of a powerful state; for his government had as yet assumed no regular form, and his whole attention had been engrossed by the conquest of forts, and the accumulation of treasure; but he now began to make those regulations which have given him a place in history as the founder of a great empire. His chief minister, called the Peishwa, was a Bramin of high rank, and all his civil officers were of that caste. A Superintendent, who was always a Bramin, was appointed over every two or three villages, to see that the cultivators were not oppressed by the headmen, and that their rents were proportioned to the state of the crops: the amount paid to the government being equal to about two-fifths of the produce.

The army was also well regulated, and many Bramins were attached to it as accountants. The soldiers, who found their own arms and habiliments, generally wore cotton drawers and a tunic, with a shawl round the waist, and a turban. They were armed with swords, shields, and matchlocks, added to which, the horsemen carried long spears. The chiefs wore necklaces of gold or silver, and large ear-rings; but the Mahrattas prided themselves principally on their moustachios, which they allowed to grow to an enormous length, and which gave them a very ferocious appearance. The

Mahratta chief.

soldiers were all well paid, and therefore were not entitled to any share of plunder, which, by Sevajee's laws, was the property of the state; and was brought at stated times to his Durbar, or treasury, when honours and rewards were bestowed on those who brought the most; so that the wealth of the chief was constantly increasing.

In the year 1674, he was solemnly enthroned at Raighur, as an independent sovereign, with all the pomp that attended the inauguration of the Mogul Emperors. On this occasion he was weighed against pieces of gold, which were afterwards distributed among the Bramins, and assumed several grand titles, one of which was Raja Siva, meaning the Lord of the Royal Umbrella, one of the chief ensigns of regal dignity. At this ceremony was present a British ambassador, who had been sent to the Mahratta court for the purpose of obtaining some commercial privileges from the new sovereign, who concluded a treaty, by which the English were allowed to build factories at four places within his dominions, and to trade, on certain conditions, to all parts of them.

The wars between the Mahrattas and Moguls were, nevertheless, very injurious to the British trade in India, as both powers had fleets of galliots, which engaged, repeatedly, in the harbour of Bombay; and either party would have taken the British factories, had they not been resolutely defended. In the meantime, Amin, the son of Mir Jumla, whose quarrels with the king of Golconda, it may be remembered, first introduced him to the notice of Aurengzebe, was appointed to the government of Cabul, where he engaged in wars with the Afghans, who about this time set up a king, and coined money in his name. Great efforts were made to keep these warlike tribes in subjection; and so anxious was the Emperor to prevent them from becoming an independent nation, that for some years he took upon himself the chief conduct of the war; but he never gained any real authority over the Afghan country, and was obliged, in the end, to rest satisfied with the nominal submission of some of the chiefs, and to terminate the war on conditions that were but very imperfectly observed.

About this time, Aurengzebe began to adopt a very harsh line of conduct towards the Hindus, whom he excluded from all public offices, and prohibited from worshipping their idols with shows and festivals, according to their ancient customs. Edicts were issued against public dancers and singers, of whom there were great numbers attached to the temples; and even the poets and astrologers were forbidden to exercise their vocations. These orders, although but little attended to, revived all the ancient hatred of the Hindus towards their Mohammedan conquerors, which had been almost extinguished by the judicious government of former rulers; but as most of these new rules could be evaded, none of them caused such universal discontent as the revival of the capitation tax, which was the more obnoxious, as it made an invidious distinction between Mohammedans and Hindus; thus marking the latter as a conquered people.

The general abhorrence of this measure was evinced on the Friday following its announcement, at Delhi, by the assembling of vast crowds of the lower orders in the streets, as the Emperor, according to custom, was going in procession to the mosque. He was saluted with loud murmurs on every side; but instead of giving ear to the complaints of his subjects, as his great ancestor, Akber, would have done, he angrily commanded his guards to force a passage through them, when horses and elephants were pushed forward among the dense throng, and numbers of persons were trampled to death.

The arbitrary and unfeeling conduct of the Emperor, on this occasion, produced the intended effect of enforcing the payment of the tax, but it raised up a host of enemies to the Mogul dominion, among the whole body of the Rajputs, who had, till then, been the faithful supporters of the throne. Aurengzebe soon became aware of the disaffection of the Rajputs, but his temper was too haughty to admit of his adopting any conciliatory measures; and he was unwise enough to add fuel to the flame, by acting in an oppressive manner towards the widow and infant sons of the deceased Rana of Oudipur, the chief of the Rajput princes. The Rana died at Cabul, and the lady immediately after his funeral obsequies, set out for India, with her children, to secure the inheritance of her eldest son; but as she had no passport, she was stopped at the Indus by the Mogul authorities, who refused to let her cross the river. The soldiers who formed her escort, in defiance of the Emperor's officers, carried their royal charge over a ford, but they were overtaken, and the whole party conveyed as prisoners to the camp of Aurengzebe, who ordered that the Ranee and the young princes should be kept in close confinement. His Rajput troops, indignant at the insult thus offered to the family of one of their own chiefs, contrived the escape of the captives, who reached their own territories in safety; but this open act of disobedience, with other manifestations of hostile feeling, drew upon the Rajputs the resentment of the Emperor, who sent bodies of soldiers into their country of Ajmir, to burn their villages, destroy their crops, cut down their fruit-trees, and carry off the women and children for slaves.

These inhuman orders were but too faithfully executed; and from that time, Aurengzebe was held in detestation, not only by the Rajput race, but by all Hindus, especially in the Deccan, where the people began to look with hope to the rising power of the Mahrattas, as a means of delivering them from the government of the Moguls.

Sevajee was now dead. His loss was deeply mourned by his people, who admired him as a warrior, and respected him as a sovereign. With the exception of the murder of Afzul Khan, few crimes or acts of inhumanity are laid to the charge of this great chief, even by his enemies, who allow that he possessed extraordinary talents and many virtues. At the time of his death, his possessions, both in treasure and territory, were immense; the former amassed by plunder, the latter extended partly by

grant, and partly by conquest. He left two widows, one of whom manifested her affection and constancy by sacrificing herself on the funeral pile; while the fate of the other was still more dreadful, as, in consequence of the jealousy of Sambajee, the eldest son and successor of her deceased husband, she was put to a lingering death.

Raja Ram, the son of this unfortunate lady, was preferred to his elder brother, by the Bramin ministers, who wished to place him on the throne; but Sambajee, supported by the soldiers, arrived in the capital before they had effected their object; and having sent his brother to the fort, and put his father's widow to death, he imprisoned some of the Bramins, and gave orders for the execution of all other persons who had declared in favour of Raja Ram, but who were not protected, like the Bramins, by their sacred profession. But even this security was of no avail in the case of Amajee Dutto, a Bramin of high rank, who held the office of Public Recorder; for he, with some others, was condemned to be trampled to death by elephants, for engaging in a new conspiracy in favour of Raja Ram.

The Rajputs, owing to the hostile measures adopted by the Emperor, had induced his youngest son, Akber, to join in an insurrection, by promising to place him on the throne. The young prince at the head of an army of seventy thousand men, advanced towards his father's camp; but just as the royal troops were on the point of giving battle to the insurgents, several chiefs, not Rajputs, who had joined in the rebellion, suddenly deserted, with all their followers; which so materially lessened the forces of Prince Akber, that the project of dethroning the Emperor was abandoned, and the prince fled for safety to the Mahratta court, where he was well received by the new monarch, Sambajee, who afforded him protection for several years.

It was on the arrival of Akber at the court, that Amajee Dutto, who was already in confinement for the attempt to exclude Sambajee from the throne, contrived to send proposals to the fugitive prince, offering to aid him in mounting the throne of Delhi, provided he would espouse the cause of Raja Ram. Akber declined the proposition, and Amajee was executed in the barbarous manner before-mentioned, in consequence of the discovery of his intended treason. To cause the death of a Bramin is considered as the height of impiety among the Hindus, who speak of such an act with the utmost horror and detestation; therefore, the Raja rendered himself extremely unpopular by enforcing the law against Amajee Dutto; besides which, he proved himself, in all respects, a very unworthy successor of his illustrious father.

During his reign, which lasted only nine years, the Emperor Aurengzebe was engaged in prosecuting his favourite object of extending the Mogul empire over the whole of the Deccan, by the conquest of the two kingdoms of Bijapur and Golconda. He conducted the war in person, besieged, and took the capitals, and made prisoners of the kings, both of whom died in captivity. The fine city of Bijapur, no longer the metropolis of a wealthy state, was speedily reduced to its present deserted condition, but its noble mosques, the ruins of its palaces, its lofty walls of hewn stone, and the grand mausoleum of Mohammed Adil Shah, the dome of which is said to be larger than that of St. Paul's Cathedral, afford existing proofs of its former grandeur, although they are now mingled with dwellings of the meanest description, as is the case with other noble relics still existing in different parts of India.

The camp of Aurengzebe, during these wars, is described as having surpassed even that of the Emperor Akber in magnificence; and the immense wealth of the sovereign may be inferred from an anecdote related of one of his royal prisoners, Abel Hussein, the last king of Golconda. This unfortunate monarch, while yet a prisoner in the camp, ere he had been sent to finish his life in the fortress of Doulatabad, heard one day a favourite Hindu air performed by one of the imperial band, which gave him so much pleasure, that he said to some one near him, he wished he had a lac of rupees to give the musician. The wish was told to the Emperor, who immediately sent the desired sum (ten thousand pounds) to Abel Hussein, requesting that he would gratify his inclination.

The two great governments that had hitherto preserved order in the south of India being thus overthrown, many of the Zemindars who had been subject to them, took advantage of their fall to declare themselves independent, and were always ready to assist the Mahrattas against the Moguls, who were now commencing that struggle for power which was continued until the downfall of the Mogul empire.

Not long after the conquest of the Deccan kingdoms, Sambajee was made prisoner by a stratagem of the Moguls, who carried him off from a summer-house, in which he was enjoying himself with a small party of friends, to the camp of the Emperor, who had him put to death in a most cruel manner. Raja Ram was then released from his long imprisonment, and declared regent during the minority of the late Raja's infant son, who was residing with his mother, Yessoo Bye, at Raighur.

Much of the open country of the Mahrattas was now in possession of the Moguls, who took some of the forts, and at length besieged the capital, where most of the great chiefs were assembled. It was defended for several months, when the fort was surrendered, and Yessoo Bye, with the young Raja, were made prisoners, and conveyed to the imperial camp, where they were received with great kindness by the Begum, or Princess Sahib, a daughter of Aurengzebe, whose amiable attentions consoled them during many years of captivity. The Emperor himself grew very fond of the noble boy, whom he married to the daughters of the two highest chiefs in his service, one of them being Sindia, an ancestor of the late distinguished prince of that name. On the occasion of these marriages, which were celebrated with great splendour, the Emperor bestowed on the young bridegroom several large districts in jaghir, and restored to him a famous sword, called Bhowanee, which had belonged to his grandfather, Sevajee, and is still preserved in the country as a valued relic of that chief.

After the capture of Raighur, the Regent escaped to the Carnatic, where, in consequence of the captivity of his nephew, he was proclaimed Raja, and the war proceeded with still greater fury than before.

The Mahrattas never engaged an enemy in the open field, but were constantly on the watch for opportunities of making unexpected attacks, and cutting off parties of stragglers; while large bands, under different leaders, made predatory excursions through various parts of the country, levying contributions on the inhabitants under the name of chout, which, as already mentioned, was originally a grant from Aurengzebe to Sevajee, of a portion of the rents of certain villages in the kingdom of Bijapur, but was now levied by every Mahratta chief, wherever it was possible to enforce it. The habits of the soldiers, and their mode of warfare, remind us of those of the Scottish Highlanders in former times. They never encumbered themselves with baggage, nor did they use tents, but each man carried with him a coarse blanket, a bag of millet, and an empty bag for plunder. They slept on the bare earth, with their arms and horses beside them, so that they were ready, at any instant, either to make an attack or a retreat.

The regular armies of the Moguls, superior as they were in discipline and numbers, contended to great disadvantage against enemies, whose movements were so rapid, whilst their own were constantly impeded by supernumerary accompaniments. Their camp followers, consisting of women, merchants, cooks and servants, of all kinds, frequently amounted to ten times the number of soldiers; and the habit of carrying with them all the luxuries to which they were accustomed, created a necessity for a long train of elephants, oxen, camels, and wagons, all heavily laden, especially when the Emperor's moveable palaces formed a part of their burthen.

Raja Ram died in the year 1700, leaving two sons, Sevajee and Sambajee, the mother of the elder being the celebrated Tara Bye, a very clever woman, who, for many years, exercised the authority of a sovereign princess, and carried on the war with great ability against Aurengzebe, during the rest of his life, not fixing her residence in any particular place, but moving about from fort to fort, according to circumstances.

The Emperor, although more than eighty years of age, persevered in his fruitless endeavours to crush the growing independence of the Mahratta nation. But the empire of the Moguls was fast declining, and several of the provinces were overrun by the enemy, particularly that of Guzerat, where many villages were plundered, and set on fire, and a great part of the country laid waste.

The province of Guzerat is separated from Marwar on the north-east, by a range of mountains, in which is Abboo, or Abboo-gush, a mountain lake,

surrounded by many ancient religious edifices, built of marble and stone; this place is held in high veneration by the Hindus, who found a safe asylum here from the persecutions of their Mohammedan conqueror, on account of the difficulty of the mountain-passes, and the ferocity of their inhabitants. Abboo is particularly rich and fertile, and abundantly produces the vegetables of the tropical, as well as of the northern, climates. The Mohammedans destroyed the richly sculptured temples in the plain, using the materials for erecting their mosques and cities.

In the mean time, the English, whose possessions and influence on the eastern coast of India had considerably increased, had been several times engaged in direct hostilities with the Moguls, and Aurengzebe had threatened to expel them from his dominions. They were occasionally supported by some of the Rajas, from whom they obtained grants of territory, in return for aid against the Imperial authority; yet the Emperor was too well aware of the importance of the British trade, to make any attempt to put into execution his threat of expulsion, and even confirmed the cessions of the Rajas, on making peace with the English, who, in 1648, obtained a grant of the three connected villages of Chutanattee, Govindpore, and Calcutta. These new possessions being fortified, received the name of Fort William, in honour of the King of England, William the Third.

The death of the Emperor took place in 1707. He died in his camp at Ahmednagar, at the advanced age of eighty-nine, in the fiftieth year of his reign. Aurengzebe was remarkable for the simplicity of his habits and manners, which he constantly maintained amid the splendour of the most magnificent court in the world. An English envoy, sent on a mission to Delhi, about ten years before the Emperor's death, on being introduced into the imperial presence, was surprised to see a little old man, with a long silvery beard, dressed in plain white muslin, standing in the midst of a group of Omrahs, whose rich robes, sparkling with jewels, formed a striking contrast to the unostentatious appearance of their sovereign.

BAHADUR SHAH.

AS soon as the death of Aurengzebe became known, his eldest son, who was governor of Cabul, was proclaimed Emperor in that city, while his brother Azim was elevated to the imperial dignity in the camp, where he took the command of the army. The first act of the latter was to release the Mahratta prince Saho, hoping, by this measure, to convert the Mahrattas into friends, and obtain aid from them against his brother, who was marching from Cabul at the head of a large army, to assert his right to the throne. But the contest was speedily decided; for the two brothers

Cabul.

met near Agra, where a battle was fought, in which Azim was slain, when his troops submitted to the conqueror, who was immediately acknowledged at Delhi, and assumed the name of Bahadur Shah.

Saho proceeded to his own country, sending letters to Tara Bye, to intimate his approach, but the lady not being willing to resign her authority, affected to believe that he was an impostor, and assembled all the ministers and chief officers from whom she exacted an oath of fidelity to her son. There were many, however, who took up the cause of the true heir, and a civil war ensued, which lasted several years, for Tara Bye would not give up the contest, until she was compelled to do so by the death of her son, who was of weak intellect, and had never been able to conduct the government himself.

This event took place about five years after the return of Saho, when Tara Bye was immediately removed from the elevated position she had so long occupied, and Sambajee the younger son of Raja Ram, was placed at the head of the state, or, more properly speaking, at the head of his party. This party was eventually overthrown by that of Saho, who had been enthroned at Satara, where he had appointed ministers, and assumed all the ensigns of royalty, his authority being acknowledged in several extensive districts. The chief supporter of Saho was a Bramin, named Balajee Wiswanat, the hereditary accountant of a village in the Concan, a man of great ability, both in civil and military affairs. His services in the war were rewarded by Saho with the office of Peishwa, or prime minister; and the government was left almost entirely to his management, while the Raja pursued his favourite amusements of hunting, hawking, and fishing, for which he had acquired a taste, during his residence at the Mogul court.

Thus was laid the foundation of that power afterwards usurped by the Peishwas, who became, in time, the real sovereigns of the Mahratta empire.

About this time, another people began to figure in the history of India. These were the Seiks, till then known only as a religious sect, founded in the time of the Emperor Akber, by Guru Nanik, a Hindu philosopher, whose own principles were those of a deist, but whose chief doctrine was that of universal toleration.

After the death of Akber, the Seiks were persecuted by the Mohammedans, and their leader was put to death. The tyranny with which they were treated, implanted among them the deepest hatred towards the Mogul government, and the Musselmans generally, till it became a part of their religion to destroy, to the utmost of their power, that detested race. Their original country was Lahore; but they had been expelled from that province, and had now established a sort of religious and military commonwealth among the mountains, under a chief named Govind, who, with a view of increasing the number of his subjects abolished all distinctions of caste, so that all who entered the fraternity might eat together of the same food, and were freed from all the restrictions which the obligation of preserving the castes unmixed imposes on other Hindus. The Seiks, however, paid great respect to the Bramins, and worshipped the Hindu gods, and they scrupulously obeyed the superstitious enactment which forbids an Indian killing a cow, even to save a family from starving.

By the regulations of Govind, every chief was destined to be a soldier at his birth, or his admission into the order. Their distinguishing marks were a blue dress, and long hair and beard, and every man was to carry steel about him in some shape. At that period the Seiks were violent fanatics, and carried on their war against their oppressors with a ferocity that has seldom been surpassed.

During the reign of Bahadur Shah and his immediate successors, the most horrible scenes were witnessed in the Punjab, where the inhabitants of whole towns fell victims to the relentless fury of these frenzied warriors, whose numbers were, however, insufficient to secure any permanent advantages, until a later period. The Seiks are, now, the greatest independent power in India, but their character is much changed, and retains no traces of the fanaticism that led them to commit so many crimes, and rendered the name of Seik odious as well as terrible, in the early part of the last century. Bahadur Shah, reigned only five years. His death was followed by a dispute among his sons, who all aspired to the vacant throne, which fell to the lot of the eldest, Jehandar Shah, two of his brothers having been slain in the contest.

The reign of Jehandar was brief, for scarcely was he seated on the throne, when his nephew, Farokhsir, the son of one of the princes who had lost their lives in the preceding quarrel, raised an army at Allahabad, and proceeded to Agra, where a battle was fought, in which the Emperor was defeated; and being afterwards betrayed into the hands of the victor, was put to death by his command.

FAROKHSIR.

THE new Emperor, a weak indolent prince, owed his elevation, in a great measure, to the exertions of two brothers, Houssein Ally, and Abdullah Khan, who were Seiads or descendants of the prophet, the former of whom was made commander-in-chief, and governor of the Deccan, while the latter ruled the court in the capacity of Vizier. It was soon obvious that these two ambitious men had only placed the young prince on the throne for the purpose of getting all the authority into their own hands; and the factions that in consequence divided the state, tended to hasten its downfall.

The Mahratta rulers were watchful to avail themselves of every circumstance that afforded an opportunity of advancing the interests of their nation at the expense of the declining empire; and although the Raja Saho had acknowledged himself a vassal of the throne of Delhi, his people did not refrain from invading the Mogul territories, and some of their chiefs seized on several villages within the Emperor's dominions, which they converted into forts, where they maintained bands of freebooters, who issued forth from these strongholds to plunder the surrounding country. They waylaid travellers, robbed the caravans, and committed so many depredations, that the high roads to Surat, both from Hindostan and the Deccan were rendered impassable for all peaceable subjects.

At length, Houssein Ally, who had vainly attempted to clear the road from the south by force, opened a negotiation with the Peishwa Balajee, who demanded, as the price of peace, that the Mogul government should confirm Saho in all the former possessions of his grandfather Sevajee; and that he should have the right of levying the chout over the whole of the Deccan; that is, of taking one-fourth of the revenue; besides which, he demanded a farther contribution of one-tenth of the remaining three parts for hay and corn money; with some other concessions, in return for which the Raja was to pay a tribute of ten lacs of rupees to the Emperor, and to furnish him with fifteen thousand horse soldiers. He was also to be responsible for the conduct of his people, and to indemnify the subjects of the Emperor for all losses that might be sustained by any violation of the peace by the Mahratta chiefs. The Emperor, however, refused to sign this treaty, in consequence of which Houssein Ally joined the Mahrattas; and the combined armies proceeded to Delhi, to enforce their demands. The vizier, who favoured the views of his brother, had his partizans in the city, where a violent tumult ensued, and Farokhsir being seized by the two Seiads, was imprisoned and put to death, having occupied the throne only six years.

The short reign of this prince is remarkable for the cruel policy adopted with regard to the Seiks, whose ferocious chief, Bandu, being made prisoner, was conveyed to Delhi, with seven hundred and forty of his followers, who were all beheaded; while their wretched leader was tortured to death. After this fearful tragedy, the unfortunate Seiks were hunted down like wild beasts, by the Mogul troops, until they were supposed to be totally annihilated; nor did they appear again, in any numbers, for a very long period.

During the reign of Ferokhsir, the English obtained new privileges and additional grants of territory, in consequence of the medical skill of an Englishman, who was one of an embassy sent from Madras to the court of Delhi, at a time when the Emperor happened to be very ill. The gentleman in question speedily restored him to health, for which service three villages were granted to the English in the neighbourhood of Madras, with the liberty of purchasing in Bengal thirty-seven townships, and of conveying their goods through the province, free of duty. The Nabob, however, being opposed to any extension of their influence, contrived to deter the owners from selling the townships; so that no advantage was, for some time, reaped from the Emperor's permission on that head; but they availed themselves of his leave to carry on a free trade in Bengal, by which Calcutta soon became a place of considerable importance.

About seven years after the death of Farokhsir, the Company was allowed to establish a court of justice, consisting of a mayor and nine aldermen, at each of the three presidencies, Madras, Bombay, and Calcutta.

MOHAMMED SHAH.

AFTER the murder of Farokhsir, two princes of little note were successively raised to the imperial throne; both of whom died within a few months; when Mohammed Shah, the son of Jehandur, was proclaimed Emperor, in 1719. The absolute authority assumed by Houssein Ally and Abdullah Khan, which rendered the Emperor an object of mere pageantry, excited great dissatisfaction; and a conspiracy was very soon formed against Houssein, who was assassinated in the street, by a person who stopped his palanquin, on pretence of having a petition to present to him. Abdullah, on hearing of this event, collected all his forces and hastened towards Delhi, with the intent of deposing Mohammed Shah; but he was met by the imperial forces, who defeated and made him prisoner, and he shortly afterwards died of the wounds he had received in the battle. The Emperor, thus relieved from the control of the Seiad brothers, was declared sole master of the empire, and entered his capital in splendid procession.

Grand Mosque at Delhi.

The people were greatly rejoiced at this revolution, and for several days the city of Delhi presented one continued scene of festivity. Letters of submission, and professions of loyalty, greeted the new sovereign, from all quarters. The Raja Saho despatched an envoy to the court, to perform homage before him; and the heads of the European factories sent embassies, with congratulations, and wishes for his long and happy reign. His reign was indeed long, but it was very far from being happy; for the unfortunate monarch was doomed to witness the ruin of the empire, and the sad fate of its magnificent capital, an event that gives a mournful celebrity to his name, and marks his reign as the most calamitous era of the Mogul dynasty.

One of the first acts of Mohammed Shah was to ratify the treaty with the Mahrattas, which Farokhsir had refused; and not long afterwards, the Peishwa Ballajee died, bequeathing his power, wealth, and dignities, to his son, Bajee Rao, the greatest of all the Bramin rulers. The new minister, who governed absolutely, without any interference on the part of the Raja, sought out men of talent to fill all the high offices, without regard to the obscurity of their origin; and these became the founders of the great Mahratta families of modern times. Among these were Holkar and Sindia, whose names are well known in the present day, both of whom were raised from humble employments to the rank of military chiefs.

Sindia was a relative of the chief of that name, whose daughter was one of the wives given by Aurengzebe to Saho, during his captivity at Delhi. The lady, who had never been released, was dead, and the family had sunk into such abject poverty, that the individual who attracted the notice of Bajee Rao, held, at first, a very undignified post in the great man's household, one of his duties being that of carrying his master's slippers.

The object of the Peishwa was, to attach to his service a number of bold enterprising men, who might aid him in carrying into effect his design of extending the Mahratta power and territory in Hindostan. Aware of the weakness of the Mogul government, he seems even to have meditated its final overthrow. "Now is our time," said he, "to drive strangers from the land of the Hindus, and to gain immortal renown. Let us strike at the trunk of the withering tree, and the branches must fall of themselves." By such forcible arguments he persuaded the Raja to sanction the invasion of the northern provinces, and he granted permission to Holkar, Sindia, and other chiefs, to levy the chout in Guzerat, Malwa, and other northern provinces.

About this time, another rival power sprang up in the south of India, where a new independent monarchy was established by Nizam-ul Mulk, a Mohammedan officer who had been appointed to the vice-royalty of the Deccan, by Mohammed Shah, and who throwing off his dependence on the empire, founded the sovereignty usually called the dominions of the Nizam, or Soubehdar of the Deccan, and fixed on the city of Hyderabad as his capital.

The success that attended the Mahrattas in the north, at length emboldened the Peishwa to demand of Mohammed Shah the grant of a jaghir, comprising the extensive territory of Malwa, with a large portion of country south of the river Chambal, including the holy cities of Benares, Allahabad, and Mattra, places of great importance, on account of the revenue derived from the pilgrims who frequented them.

The Chalees Satoon, or the Forty Pillars, is a pavilion attached to the

palace of Allahabad, and was erected by the Emperor Akber; it is built of grey granite and freestone. The fort of Allahabad is favourably situated on the point where the rivers Ganges and Jumna unite. The numerous vessels to be seen on these rivers, particularly on the former, give great animation to the scene. The buildings in general, here, are in the Mohammedan style. Allahabad is five hundred miles westward of Calcutta, and eighty-three from Benares.

Mohammed refused to make the grant demanded by the Peishwa, on which Bajee Rao appeared before the gates of the capital, at the head of a numerous force, with a view of intimidating the Emperor; but retired, without proceeding to any act of greater hostility than the plunder of the suburbs. For some time, however, he continued to carry on a very harassing warfare in the Mogul territories, until the Emperor was forced into compliance with his exorbitant demands.

It was at the very time when this concession was made to the Mahrattas, that the Mogul empire was invaded, and its capital taken by the great Persian sovereign, Nadir Shah, at this period the most warlike of all the eastern princes. He was an usurper, who, having raised himself to the throne of Persia, in 1736, went to war with the Afghans for the recovery of Candahar. This city had formerly belonged to Persia, but was then in possession of the Ghilzies, the most powerful of the Afghan tribes, who inhabited the country around Candahar, which they had formed into an independent state in the year 1708, when they revolted from the Persian government. The occupation of the Ghilzie country, which he reduced to subjection, brought Nadir Shah to the frontiers of the Mogul empire; yet it was not until after he had taken Cabul, and was actually advancing towards Delhi, that the Emperor, and the people of that devoted city, aroused themselves to a sense of danger. Mohammed Shah then hastily assembled his forces, and met the invader about one hundred miles from Delhi, where he sustained a total defeat, and was obliged to repair in person to the Persian camp, to make submission to the conqueror; a sad humiliation for a successor of the great Akber.

The two monarchs rode side by side to the capital, where Nadir, assuming the right of conquest, distributed his troops in various parts of the city, to the infinite disgust of the inhabitants, who bore the intrusion and exactions of the enemy with gloomy discontent, until a report was raised that Nadir Shah had died suddenly, when the suppressed fury of the populace burst forth, and great numbers of the Persians were put to the sword. In the midst of the tumult, Nadir rode forth from the palace gates, expecting that his presence would overawe the people, and put a stop to their violence; instead of which, their disappointment at seeing him alive, only added to their rage; and the Shah then gave the fearful command, which devoted to ruin that magnificent city which had so long been the pride of the eastern world.

When the order had been issued for a general massacre of the unfortunate inhabitants of Delhi, Nadir Shah retired to a little mosque in the grand bazaar, where he sat for hours in solitude, while the work of death and destruction was going on around him. Many parts of the city were in flames, and the number of human beings sacrifced on that dreadful day, is said to have amounted to fifty thousand. At length, the wretched Emperor forced his way into the presence of the destroyer, exclaiming with tears streaming down his cheeks, "Spare my people;" and the command that was instantly given to shed no more blood, was as promptly obeyed as that which had caused it to flow in such frightful abundance.

Having thus so far depopulated the great capital of the Mogul empire, and laid it partly in ruins, the Shah proceeded to take possession of all its moveable treasures. Gold and jewels, rich stuffs of every description, elephants, horses, camels, and the celebrated peacock throne of Shah Jehan, were carried off by the conquerors; and so general was the plunder, that many persons suspected of having concealed their wealth, were put to the torture, to make them confess where it was hidden. Then Nadir Shah reinstated the humbled monarch on his throne, and wrote to the chief princes of India, to announce his restoration. One of these letters was addressed to the Raja Saho, and another to the Peishwa Bajee Rao, desiring that they would obey all the commands of Mohammed Shah, whom he now regarded as his brother, therefore should return with his army to punish any disobedient vassals. Bajee Rao immediately sent a large present in gold to the Emperor, with a letter of submission, which were acknowledged by a splendid present in return, consisting of a complete dress, a pearl necklace, jewels for his turban, a horse, and an elephant. The presents made by an inferior or vassal prince to his superior, are received as tribute, and termed his Nazzir.

Not long after the invasion by the Persians, Bajee Rao died, and was succeeded in his high office by his son, Ballajee Rao, under whose able government the power of the Mahratta nation continued to increase, and the authority of the Peishwa entirely superseded that of the Raja.

Just at the time of Bajee Rao's death, which happened in 1740, some affairs of great importance, in regard to the progress of the British empire in India, were taking place in the extensive territory of the Carnatic, one of the subordinate principalities of the Deccan, subject to the Soubehdar Nizam-ul Mulk, who was nominally a vassal of the Emperor, but in reality, an independent prince, and, as already stated, the great rival of the Mahratta sovereign, with whom he was obliged to share the revenues of the greater part of the Deccan. The Carnatic war was ostensibly undertaken to support the rights of certain Indian princes; but might, with more truth, be called a struggle between the English and French for supremacy in India, where it was now evident the Mogul dominion was drawing to a close.

The circumstances which led to the war were these. The Raja of Trichinopoly, one of the numerous tributary states of the Deccan, died in 1736, leaving one son, an infant, whose mother, according to Hindu usage, assumed the government as regent. It frequently happened, however, on the death of a Raja, that many of his male relatives would come forward as claimants for the throne, and endeavour to set aside his sons by force, as was the case in the present instance, when the widow had to maintain the rights of her child against a rival, whose superior force gave him every chance of success; therefore the princess gratefully accepted an offer of assistance from Chanda Sahib, son-in-law of the Nabob of Arcot, which was the capital of the Carnatic. Not doubting his sincerity, she allowed him free access to the citadel, which he treacherously seized, and confined the princess in a prison, where she soon died.

It was by these dishonourable means that Chanda Sahib became Raja of Trichinopoly, a place of great strength and importance; and he was supported in his usurpation by the French; but the neighbouring Hindu Rajas, not liking to see a Mohammedan in possession of a throne that had always been occupied by a Hindu, applied to the Mahrattas to assist them in displacing him. A Mahratta army accordingly appeared on the frontiers of the Carnatic, a few weeks after the death of Bajee Rao, and invested the city and fort of Trichinopoly, where the usurper defended himself for several months. At length, however, being compelled to surrender, he was sent captive to Satara, the capital of Raja Saho, where he was detained, a prisoner at large, for several years. During his captivity, Chanda Sahib kept up a correspondence with the French governor of Trichinopoly, who paid a part of the ransom for which he was liberated, in 1748, the same year that witnessed the succession of another prince of the race of Akber to the imperial throne of the Moguls.

But before entering upon the wars in the Carnatic, it will be necessary to relate some other events that took place before the death of the Emperor Mohammed Shah. A tribe of Afghans called the Rohillas, from the name of their chief, had lately founded a new state in the Doab, or tract between the Ganges and the Jumna, the confines of which approached within a hundred miles of the capital. This principality had attained to considerable importance at the time of the Emperor's decease, and its affairs were afterwards intimately connected with the general history of the country; but an event of still greater consequence was, the establishment of the kingdom of the Afghans, now sufficiently famous under the name of Afghanistan. The founder of this state was Ahmed Shah Abdalla, the son of an Afghan chief, whose tribe had been for some time settled in Herat, when that province was invaded and conquered by Nadir Shah. Ahmed having surrendered himself, was received into the service of the Shah, to whom he remained faithful until the death of that formidable prince, who was assassinated in the year 1747, when Ahmed Abdalla left the Persian army, in which he had obtained a high rank, and returned with a great number of his tribe to Herat, where he was soon proclaimed king of the whole Afghan nation.

The confusion that followed the assassination of Nadir Shah, afforded the new sovereign an opportunity of extending his dominion; and with that view, he invaded the provinces of Lahore and Moultan, where very little opposition was made to his arms, and he soon found himself monarch of a vast territory beyond the Indus, including Cashmere, Cabul, Candahar, Balk, and Scinde. Ahmed changed his name from Abdalla to Durani, by which appellation his tribe was from that time distinguished. Encouraged by his rapid successes, the conqueror raised his eyes to the throne of the Moguls, and boldly advanced towards Delhi; but his march was stopped by the imperial army, headed by Prince Ahmed, eldest son of the Emperor, who obtained a complete victory over his Afghan namesake, which checked the ambitious views of the latter, who was obliged to retreat to Cabul. The victor then returned triumphantly to the capital, where he was greeted as Emperor, Mohammed Shah having just breathed his last. This event happened in the month of April, 1748, and was shortly followed by the deaths of the other two most potent sovereigns of India, Nizam-ul Mulk, Soubehdar of the Deccan, and Saho, king of the Mahrattas.

AHMED SHAH.

AHMED SHAH succeeded to the throne of his ancestors, and to the title of Emperor; but the former was divested of its previous splendour, while the latter was a mere nominal dignity, to which but little glory or authority was now attached. The Mogul power had ceased to be paramount in India, where several nations were contending for that supremacy which was eventually obtained by Great Britain. The English had long been bent on acquiring sovereignty as well as lands, in India; and their interference in the quarrels of the native princes had always that object in view.

On the death of Nizam-ul Mulk, who had reached the extraordinary age of one hundred and four years, the government of the Deccan was assumed by his second son, Nazir Jung, whose eldest brother, Ghazee-ud-din, held a high post at the court of Delhi. The deceased sovereign, however, had left a numerous family; and one of his grandsons, Mirzafa, chose to dispute the title of Nazir Jung to the throne of the Deccan, on pretence that Nizam-ul Mulk had disinherited him for rebellion, and had expressed a wish that he, Mirzafa, should be his successor. The pretender was joined by Chanda Sahib, who had returned, as already stated, from his imprisonment among the Mahrattas, and had been for some months collecting troops for the purpose of making an attempt to obtain the sovereignty of the Carnatic, as his father-in-law, the late Nabob, had died during his captivity, and the government had been bestowed by Nizam-ul Mulk on an individual of a different family, whose right to keep possession Chanda Sahib considered himself entitled to dispute. Mirzafa and Chanda Sahib being thus engaged in similar enterprises, agreed to assist each other; and the French became their able and willing allies, in the expectation of increasing their own power and possessions, should they succeed in making these two princes rulers of the Deccan; in which case, their superiority over the English, who supported the opposite parties, would be fully established.

The sovereign of the Carnatic, or, as he was more usually styled, Nabob of Arcot, was killed in an engagement with the allies at Amboor, on which the victors marched to Arcot, which was surrendered without opposition, and Chanda Sahib assumed the sovereignty. Arcot is a very ancient town, about sixty-eight miles to the west of Madras, and, at the period alluded to, contained a fine palace and citadel, of great extent, which are now in ruins.

When Chanda Sahib took possession of Arcot, Mohammed Ali, the son of the late Nabob, fled to Trichinopoly, a city of great importance, on account of its strong fortifications, as well as its extent, the walls being six miles in circumference. The French were desirous of besieging this place without delay, but the princes chose to indulge their vanity, by making a grand display at Arcot; after which, they proceeded in state to Pondicherry, the principal French settlement, where the new Nabob made a formal grant to the French, in return for their services, of eighty-one villages in the vicinity of that town.

The next object was to assist Mirzafa in deposing his uncle, Nazir Jung, but Chanda Sahib wanted money, which he determined to extort from

Drawn by T. J. Rawlins. On Stone by Dean & Co.

TOWN AND FORT OF TRICHINOPOLY.

London Dean & Co. Threadneedle St.

the Raja of Tanjore, one of the tributary princes of the Deccan, who had for some time neglected to pay his tribute, in consequence of the unsettled state of the country. Tanjore, which had constituted a part of the dominions of the Mahratta chief, Shahjee, and descended in the family of his eldest son, had never been entirely subdued by the Mohammedans; and there the old Hindu institutions and edifices were preserved in greater purity, perhaps, than in any other part of India. Every village had its temple, with the lofty gateway of massive architecture prevalent in ancient Hindu structures, where large establishments of Bramins, musicians, and dancing girls, were maintained; and on all the high roads, as well as in the villages, were choultries, or houses for the refreshment of travellers. This district was noted for the frequency of the suttee, a practice that has happily become almost obsolete. The capital of Tanjore is a large fortified city, of the same name, consisting of two distinct parts, one of which contains the palace, an old building, with several high towers; the other, a celebrated temple, of singular construction, esteemed one of the finest specimens of architecture in India. It contains a gigantic figure of a bull,

in black granite, sixteen feet long, and above twelve high, supposed to be of great antiquity.

The Raja of Tanjore not being prepared for the invasion of Chanda

Sahib, was obliged to make a compromise, agreeing to pay a sum equivalent to nine hundred thousand pounds; but he had no intention of fulfilling his engagement, if he could by any means evade it, therefore he endeavoured to gain time, by sending instalments of plate and jewels, on the plea that he could not immediately raise the money, hoping that, if he could contrive to delay matters long enough, assistance might arrive: nor was he mistaken; for Nazir Jung, who was perfectly aware of the design against him, had applied both to the English and the Mahrattas for aid, and entered the Carnatic with an army strengthened by those two powerful allies. Fortune now turned again. A battle was won by Nazir Jung, which obliged Chanda Sahib to seek an asylum at Pondicherry, while Mirzafa was taken prisoner, and placed in strict confinement. Soon after this victory, however, Nazir Jung lost his life in a rebellion of his own people, instigated by the French, who liberated Mirzafa, and placed him on the throne of the Deccan, at the end of the year 1750.

The revolution thus effected in the government of southern India, for a time, gave the French great advantages over the English in that country. A large accession of territory was granted them; and although Mirzafa soon lost his life in an insurrection, they maintained their influence, by raising to the vacant dignity his youngest brother, Salabat Jung.

In the meantime, Mohammed Ali, whose cause was supported by the English against Chanda Sahib, had by their aid retained possession of Trichinopoly; and so long as he held that fortress, the Nabob could not feel himself entire master of the Carnatic. It was also of the utmost importance to the English that they should keep a position of such strength; therefore, it was at this time the chief scene of the war in the Carnatic. Chanda Sahib laid close siege to the city, which must in the end have fallen, had it not been saved by the gallantry of a young British officer, Captain Clive, whose enterprising spirit prompted him to plan and execute a daring scheme for the relief of Trichinopoly. This was to make a direct attack on Arcot, the Nabob's capital, with a view of diverting his attention, and drawing his troops from the besieged city; and at his own earnest request, the Presidency of Madras gave him permission to undertake the expedition, with five hundred men, of whom three hundred were Sepoys; and with this little army, Captain Clive set forth towards Arcot. The attack was so sudden and unexpected, that the garrison fled in dismay, without making the slightest effort to defend the fortress, which was immediately occupied by the assailants, who were thus in possession of the city.

This exploit entirely changed the tide of affairs in the Deccan. Chanda

Sahib, as was expected, sent the greater part of his forces from Trichinopoly, under the command of his son, who entering Arcot, besieged the fortress, which the British commander defended, for seven weeks, with his few men, against a host of foes. At length, finding that the numbers of the enemy were daily increasing, he resolved to make a bold effort to disperse them, and went out with the greater part of his garrison, when an engagement took place in the streets; and although he was obliged to retire again to the fort, the loss of the enemy had been so great, that they quitted the town in the night, and being pursued by the British commander, who was reinforced by a body of Mahrattas, and a fresh detachment of troops from Madras, they were totally routed; and thus the adventurous expedition of Captain Clive was crowned with complete success.

The adherents of Chanda Sahib now began to desert him in such vast numbers, that he was, at length, driven by despair to accept an offer of protection from the Raja of Tanjore; but when he arrived at the court of that treacherous prince, instead of finding the asylum he expected, he was loaded with chains, and thrown into a dungeon, where he was soon put to death.

This event made the English masters of the Carnatic. Mohammed Ali was declared Nabob, and Captain Clive was rewarded for his services by a higher rank in the army. The French, however, still carried on the war, on pretence that the Subehdar of the Deccan had granted to them the sovereignty of the Carnatic, which was one of his dependencies; but the English contended that the Subehdar, being himself an usurper, whose title to the throne had never been recognized by the Emperor, he had no right to dispose of the principality in question, which belonged to their ally, Mohammed Ali. The French again laid siege to Trichinopoly, which was so ill supplied with provisions, that the inhabitants, in number about four hundred thousand, were obliged to leave the city, carrying away with them such property as they could conveniently move, and most probably burying a great quantity of treasure in the earth, which was a common practice amongst the natives of India in time of war. The siege of the deserted city, which was defended by only about two thousand men, composing the garrison, lasted more than a year, during which the Emperor, Ahmed Shah, was deposed, and his place supplied by a prince, who afterwards became a pensioner of the British government. Thus, while the French and English were quarrelling for the future empire of the Deccan, other parts of Hindostan were also the scenes of many important events, which have now to be related.

The settlement of the Rohillas in the Doab, and the establishment of the kingdom of Afghanistan, immediately before the accession of Ahmed Shah, have already been noticed. The new Emperor, or rather his vizier, Sufder Jung, was very soon engaged in wars with the Rohillas, who proved such formidable foes, that he was induced to solicit aid from the Mahrattas, which was granted by the Peishwa, Ballajee Rao, on condition that his troops should be paid for their services, by being authorized to levy contributions in the Rohilla country, which, in consequence of this permission, was so completely ravaged, that, for many years afterwards, the melancholy traces of this ruinous warfare were visible through its whole extent. The Rohillas, at length, agreed to give up the country, except a few villages for the maintenance of their chiefs; and, for awhile, peace was restored.

In the meantime, Ahmed, of Durani, the king of the Afghans, had invaded the Panjab, and obtained the cession of that province from the Emperor, who was glad to keep his capital free from invasion, on any terms. Sufder Jung, however, on his return from the Rohilla war, was very much displeased that any treaty had been concluded without his knowledge; and the dissentions that arose in consequence were carried to such a height, that the city of Delhi became a scene of warfare between the two factions that divided the court; for the Emperor had grown weary of submitting to the control of his overbearing vizier, who was, in the end, deposed by the leader of the opposite party, Ghazee-ud-din, a grandson of Nizam-ul Mulk, whose father, a powerful Omrah of the same name, had died on an expedition undertaken for the purpose of expelling the usurper, Salabat Jung, from the throne of the Deccan.

The Emperor had little cause to rejoice in the triumph of Ghazee-ud-din, whose presumption exceeded even that of the fallen minister, and whose ambition knew no bounds. Anxious, therefore, to rid himself of one whom he saw he had every reason to fear, he resolved to make him a prisoner; but as he could not accomplish this object without the assistance of some of the nobles, he entrusted his intentions to them; in consequence of which, Ghazee became aware of the plot, which he frustrated by seizing, and putting out the eyes of the unfortunate monarch, who was then deposed, and a great-grandson of Aurengzebe raised to the throne, by the title of Alamgir the Second.

In effecting this revolution, which took place in 1754, Ghazee-ud-din was assisted by the Mahrattas, whose history has now to be traced through the brief period of the reign of Ahmed Shah. The Raja Saho, who died shortly after the accession of that prince, having no heir to succeed him,

Tara Bye, although upwards of seventy years of age, resolved, with all the spirit and ambition of earlier days, to make an effort for the recovery of her former authority. She had, therefore, just before the Raja's death, brought forward a youth, whom she declared to be her grandson, saying, that he was born, soon after her son's decease, in the fort of Panalla, to which place the widow and herself had both been sent; and that, to save the child from assassination, she had contrived to have him conveyed secretly to a place of safety, and brought up in obscurity. Saho believed the tale, and acknowledged the boy as his heir; but Tara Bye was disappointed in her hopes of being proclaimed regent, as the Peishwa, Ballajee Rao, was no less bent upon usurping the sovereign authority than herself, and had more power to effect his object. He proclaimed the youth as head of the Mahratta states, by the title of Raja Ram, and took the government into his own hands, granting lands to the most influential of the chiefs, in order to secure their support. Almost the whole of the fine province of Malwa, so famous for the produce of opium, and the annual revenue of which was estimated at not less than one hundred and fifty lacs of rupees, being equal to one million and a half sterling, was divided between the two great chiefs, Holkar and Sindia, the latter of whom dying about this time, was succeeded in his wealth and honours by his son.

The Peishwa fixed his residence at Poona, which, from a small village, had become a large town, and might, from that time, be called the capital of the Mahratta empire. He was, at this period, in alliance with the English; and when Salabat Jung was placed by the French on the throne of the Deccan, he joined in an expedition to expel that usurper, undertaken by Ghazee-ud-din, the father of him who dethroned Ahmed Shah. Before Ballajee departed on this enterprise, he attained the grand object of his ambition, by inducing Raja Ram to resign all pretensions to the supreme authority, which, from that time, was openly assumed by the crafty Bramin, who assigned to the young prince a splendid maintenance, with a separate establishment at Satara.

The wars of the Mahrattas were invariably pursued with the object of increasing their own wealth and territory, therefore they paid little regard to the question of right or wrong, but always took the side that seemed to offer the widest field for plunder, under the name of tribute, of which they claimed a vast amount of arrears, in virtue of the treaty made in the reign of Ferokhsir, and confirmed by Mohammed Shah, giving them liberty to levy chout over the whole of the Deccan. This imprudent agreement was an abundant source of misery to the agricultural population of the country; for whenever a village resisted the demand, the headman and principal persons were seized, and compelled, by threats and torture, to pay the amount claimed; so that the Mahratta plunderers always returned home laden with treasures. Nor did they confine their exactions to the tribute money, for the people were compelled to furnish them with supplies of all kinds. Every morning, at day-break, parties of Mahratta soldiers on small active ponies, set out in different directions from the place of encampment, and riding into the villages, helped themselves, without ceremony, to hay and corn for their horses, tore down wood from the houses for fuel, and dug up grain from the pits, where it had been hidden by the inhabitants, all which they carried back to the camp; thus living in plenty on the spoils of the villagers. Yet those amongst the Mahrattas who have not followed the profession of arms, but have been content with the simple enjoyments of the husbandmen, are described as a remarkably kind, moral, humane, and hospitable people.

In the meantime, Tara Bye had taken advantage of the Peishwa's absence to renew her schemes for obtaining the regency. She endeavoured to persuade Raja Ram to assert his supremacy, and place her at the head of the state; but the young man, being devoid of ambition, refused to involve himself in troubles and dangers, for the sake of gratifying her love of power. His moderation, however, cost him dear; for the angry lady reproached him with his want of spirit, declared he was not her grandson, and finally made him a prisoner in the fort of Satara, where he was confined in a damp stone dungeon, and fed on the coarsest food, for nearly eight years, when the death of his persecutor restored him to liberty. The prison of this unfortunate young man, whose health and spirits were entirely ruined by his long confinement, is still shewn in the fort of Satara. The cause of Tara Bye was espoused by many that were opposed to the government of the Peishwa; but on the return of Ballajee Rao, she was persuaded to give up her claim, being allowed, however, to retain the control of the young Raja, on whom she seemed resolved to revenge herself for her disappointed hopes. The Peishwa consented to this arrangement with apparent reluctance, but was, probably, not sorry to be relieved from even the shadow of a rival, without incurring the odium of injustice.

Such was the state of affairs in the Mahratta Empire, when Ahmed Shah was deposed, and Alamgir the Second was placed on the tottering throne of the Moguls.

THE FALL OF THE EMPIRE.

FAMOUS for his heroism, at this period, was Ahmed of Durani, king of the Afghans, one of the greatest warriors of his time. He was active, bold, and enterprising; but would, probably, have confined his ambition within the limits of the kingdom he had established, had it not been for the outrageous conduct of Ghazee-ud-din, who provoked an invasion of the Mogul dominions, by attempting, partly by force and partly by stratagem, to re-annex the provinces of Lahore and Moultan to the empire. These territories had been entrusted by Ahmed to the government of a woman, the widow of the late viceroy, an Afghan noble, whose daughter had been betrothed in childhood to Ghazee-ud-din.

This engagement afforded the latter a pretext for entering the country without exciting suspicion of his hostile intentions, and he was received with joy by the mother of his affianced bride, whose pride was gratified by the prospect of being so nearly allied to the grand vizier. But the poor lady very soon discovered that she was the victim of a plot to deprive her of her rank and liberty, for she was carried off to Delhi as a prisoner, while the vizier assumed the government of the provinces.

Ahmed, enraged at this outrage, set forth at the head of a large army, towards Delhi, and that unfortunate capital was again subjected to all the horrors experienced at the time of Nadir's invasion; for although the gates were opened almost unresistingly, and Ahmed was himself far from being inclined to cruelty, yet he could not prevent his troops from taking the fullest advantage of the capture of the city. From Delhi, the conquerors proceeeded to Mattra, which they surprised in the midst of a religious festival, when a dreadful scene of bloodshed ensued; for this being one of the holy cities, its rich temples were eagerly broken into, and plundered of all their treasures, while those who endeavoured to defend them, were cut down, unsparingly, by the hands of the merciless invaders.

On his return to Delhi, Ahmed made peace with Alamgir, and formed an alliance with him, by marrying one of his daughters, and contracting another to his son, Timur, whom he appointed governor over the whole of the Panjab, including the provinces of Moultan and Lahore, which Ghazee-ud-din had been obliged to surrender. He then gave the military command at Delhi, to a Rohilla chief, in order to protect the Emperor from any violence that might be offered by his vizier; and having thus succeeded in recovering his territories, increasing his wealth, and establishing a decided superiority over the Mogul sovereign, he returned to his own capital.

While these events were passing at Delhi, the English, in conjunction with the Mahrattas, destroyed the famous piratical state, that had existed for more than half a century, on the western coast of India, to the great injury of the British trade of Bombay. Its first chief, Conajee Angria, a man of low birth, had distinguished himself, in the time of Sevajee, by his services against a band of pirates that infested the shores of the Mahratta country, and had been promoted by degrees, in reward for many valiant exploits, till he had become admiral of the fleet, and governor of Severndroog, a strong fortress, standing on a high precipitous rock on the coast of the Concan.

Not long after Angria had obtained the government of Severndroog, some dispute arose between him and the Mahratta chief, which led him to revolt; and as he was popular among the men he had been accustomed to command, he was soon master of the whole fleet, and about sixty leagues of the coast; which, after some negociation, he was allowed to retain, on condition of paying a small annual tribute to the Mahratta government. Conajee Angria, and others of his family after him, carried on the trade of professed pirates, their strongholds being Severndroog, and the no less impregnable hill fort of Gheriah, situated on another insulated cliff, where these formidable chiefs reigned as absolute sovereigns over their own territories, and aspired to the sole dominion of the Indian seas. The English and Mahrattas had several times united their forces to extirpate the corsairs, but without much prospect of success, until the year 1755, when Severndroog was captured by Commodore James; and in the following year, Gheriah was stormed and taken by Colonel Clive, who, by this important victory, put an end to a power which had so long been a check to European commerce in that part of the world. Toolajee Angria, the ruling chief, surrendered himself after the capture of Gheriah to the Mahrattas, and passed the rest of his life in captivity. The two forts were also given up by the English to their allies, according to the terms of an agreement entered into before the war.

It was just after the fall of the pirate state, that Ghazee-ud-din made an alliance with the great Bramin chief, Ragoba, brother of the Peishwa, and commander of the forces, for the purpose of recovering his former power at the Mogul court. It was the policy of the Mahratta government to aid in any enterprise that tended to accelerate the downfall of the imperial power; therefore, the chief hastened with a numerous force, to the assistance of the vizier, who, thus powerfully supported, entered Delhi, where he soon obtained possession of the palace, and assumed unlimited control over the Emperor. Not long afterwards, he caused the unhappy and degraded monarch to be assassinated, and placed on the throne a grandson of Aurengzebe, who assumed the title of Shah Jehan; whilst Shah Alum, the son of the late Emperor, was sheltered by Shujah-ud Dowlah, the Nabob of Oude, by whom he was placed at the head of a confederacy against the English, in the well-known warfare of Bengal.

The Mahratta power had, by this time, reached its greatest height. Ballajee Rao remained absolute sovereign of the country, and his dominions, exclusive of numerous tributary states, extended from the Indus and Himalaya mountains to the southern extremity of the peninsula, including the whole of Guzerat, of which province the Mahrattas had lately completed the conquest. The civil administration was conducted by a cousin of the

Peishwa, who was called the Bhao; and the command of the army was given, as already seen, to his brother, Ruganoth Rao, better known by the name of Ragoba; and thus Ballajee confined all power to his own family.

The melancholy fate of the Emperor Alamgir the Second, and the confusion that invariably attends a revolution thus violently effected, now afforded a prospect to Ballajee Rao of realizing the long-cherished hope of establishing the Mahratta dominion over the whole of Hindostan. Ragoba had been occupied, since the restoration of Ghazee-ud-din, with the conquest of Moultan and Lahore, of which he had gained possession, with the assistance of the Seiks, who had been long hidden in the mountains, but were now beginning to appear again in great numbers.

The invasion and occupation of these provinces naturally led to a war with Ahmed of Durani, to whom they had belonged; and he therefore hastened to the aid of the Rohillas, through whose country the Mahrattas had to pass in their way to Delhi, the possession of which was the grand object of their ambitious views. The timely assistance of the Afghans obliged the Mahrattas to retreat, but not before they had destroyed as many as one thousand three hundred villages, and reduced the whole country to a piteous state of desolation. Great preparations were then made for a new campaign, under the conduct of the Bhao; which serves to show the increased wealth and refinement of the Mahrattas, whose taste for luxury seems, at this period, to have equalled that of the Moguls in the days of their glory. Their spacious tents were lined with silks and broad cloths, and surmounted by gilded ornaments; each suite belonging to the officers being enclosed by screens of coloured canvas. Trains of elephants, horses superbly caparisoned, gay banners, and all the splendid accompaniments of an Indian army, were displayed on this occasion, and the principal officers wore cloth of gold.

All the great Mahratta chiefs were engaged in this expedition. Delhi was stormed; and although its inhabitants were not treated with the barbarity that stained the triumphs of Nadir Shah and Ahmed of Durani, the

Painted by T. J. Rawlins   On stone by Dean & C.

CANNAMORE FORT — SETTING IN OF THE MONSOON.

London Dean & Co. Threadneedle Street

Bhao used his right as a conqueror to deface, for the sake of their valuable ornaments, the palaces, tombs, and shrines, which even the Persians and Afghans had spared. The silver ceiling of the hall of audience was torn down and coined into rupees, of which it is said to have yielded seventeen lacs.

Ghazee-ud-din, and his protegee, Shah Jehan, whom he had dignified with the imperial title, had escaped, and the Bhao proposed to proclaim as Emperor, Wiswas Rao, the son of the Peishwa; but this design was frustrated by the approach of the Afghans, headed by their intrepid King, Ahmed, who had been for some time detained on the frontiers of Oude, by the Monsoon. As soon as the rains had ceased, he marched towards Delhi, and disposed his army in such a manner that the Mahrattas were entirely surrounded. His next measure was to intercept their supplies, for which they depended chiefly on the Banjarras, or camp dealers, a class of men whose trade was to furnish armies with provisions in time of war, and who were by no means scrupulous as to the means of obtaining the corn and cattle which they brought into the camps, so that the country people suffered constantly from their depredations.

Frequent skirmishes took place in the neighbourhood of Delhi, but Ahmed still delayed coming to a regular engagement, thinking to obtain an easier victory, if he first reduced the strength of the enemy by famine. All day long, this active chief was on horseback, riding about in all directions, to reconnoitre; and at night he kept watch, to prevent a surprise, sometimes saying to his officers, "Do you sleep; I will take care to arouse you, in case of danger."

In the mean time, the Mahrattas, pent up within the city, and suffering severely for want of food, were begging to be led out, to risk an engagement, in the open field; and the Bhao at length yielded to their entreaties. An obstinate battle was fought near the town of Panniput: it lasted from day-break till two in the afternoon; when the Mahrattas having lost their commander, and most of their great chiefs, gave way, and left the Afghans masters of the field, who followed up their victory by pursuing and cutting to pieces all who had not fallen in the fight; so that the Mahratta army was totally destroyed; and few were the families throughout the nation that had not to mourn the loss of friends and relatives killed on that fatal day. The Peishwa's son was among the slain, and it was supposed that the Bhao also fell; but as his body was never found, some believed that he had withdrawn from the field, to end his days in religious seclusion. This celebrated battle took place on the 7th of January, 1761.

The Peishwa was so much affected at the news of the defeat, that he retired to a temple he had erected in the environs of Poona, where he died in a few months. His death was sincerely lamented by the people, especially the rural population, whose condition had been materially improved, during the period of his reign.

Under former rulers, the rents of villages had often been farmed by petty chiefs, who paid a certain sum to the government, and took the chance of the crops, to gain or lose by the bargain; but this arrangement subjected the peasantry to great oppression, as these persons seldom contented themselves with the share of the produce which the law allowed them, and there was no redress for the injured parties; farming of rents had therefore been abolished, and such regulations made, as effectually prevented the collectors of revenues from exacting more than was due from the husbandmen.

Under the auspices of Ballajee Rao, many improvements were introduced into the courts of justice; the army was well regulated; and in every respect the Mahratta nation was better governed, and more prosperous than at any former period.

Ballajee Rao was succeeded by his second son, Madoo Rao, whose uncle, Ragoba, took the chief management of affairs, as the young Peishwa was but seventeen; and at the close of the same year died Tara Bye, at a very advanced age; an event that released from his dreary prison, the royal captive, Raja Ram, who, with ruined health, and broken spirits, resided quietly at Satara, where he was considered in the light of a prisoner at large, nor did he ever attempt to interfere with the politics of the state. Ahmed of Durani, after the victory of Panniput, returned to Cabul, and the empire of the Moguls being left without any acknowledged head, was thus virtually ended.

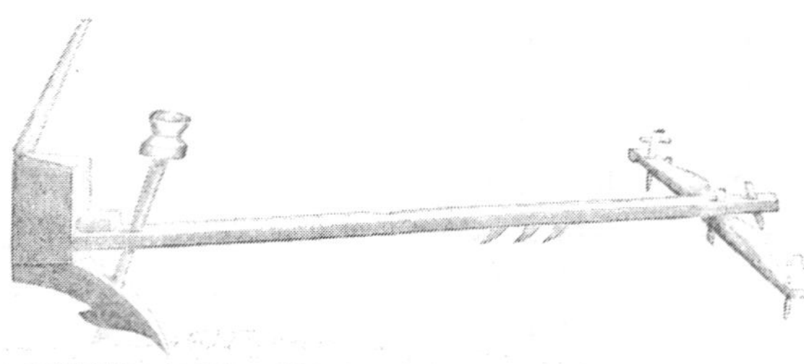

Indian Plough.

ESTABLISHMENT OF THE BRITISH EMPIRE IN INDIA.

WHILE the foregoing events were passing in the north of India, the great question was decided whether the French or English were to be the future lords of the country. The issue of the contest was, for some time, doubtful; but the British arms at length prevailed; and a few days after the great battle of Panniput, the French capital of Pondicherry, was surrendered to Colonel Coote; and the hopes of France, with regard to extending her dominion over the east, were thus terminated. During this war, Count Lally, the French general, laid siege to Madras, which was bravely defended for two months, when the arrival of a British squadron with fresh troops, relieved the town, and forced the enemy to retire.

Madras was, at this period, the capital of the British possessions in India. Its territory extended five miles along the shore, and was about one mile

Black Town of Madras.

in breadth. The English division of the town, called Fort St. George, did not contain more than fifty houses, besides the warehouses of the Company, and two churches, the one Protestant, the other Roman Catholic. The wall and batteries separated this division from the part inhabited by Armenian and Indian merchants, who were, in general, very wealthy. This portion of the city, together with a space allotted to the poorer natives, was called the Black Town, and the European part was called the White Town. Many of the natives, both in the city and district, were weavers in the employ of the East India Company.

Madras is not very well situated as a trading capital, on account of the difficulty of approaching it by sea, as it possesses no harbour or inlet of any kind to break the violence of the surge, which rolls heavily upon the coast at all seasons of the year, particularly from October to January, when ships can neither arrive nor depart, on account of the storms and typhoons that prevail during the whole of that period. Even at the most favourable season of the year vessels usually anchor a mile or two from the shore, and their cargoes are conveyed to land on a kind of raft, called a catamaran, which is constructed of three flat pieces of timber, eight or ten feet long, tied together, the middle one being longer than the others, and curved upwards at the ends. It is pushed through the surf by a man, with a paddle, who is often washed off, but is so well practised in his calling, that he leaps on again in an instant. The catamarans are quite safe when a boat, or any other vessel, would be inevitably lost. The regular boats

Madras Roads, with the manner of hauling the boats through the surge.

of that coast are wide, deep, and of a clumsy form, and are made of planks, fastened together with strong cord. They are rowed with ten or twelve paddles, the boatmen keeping time to a monotonous, but not unpleasing, song. The city has been greatly enlarged and improved, as will be noticed hereafter.

The next transaction of which we shall speak in the complicated history of India, are the wars with the native princes, which led to the important conquests of Bengal and Mysore, by which a company of British merchants became the powerful sovereigns of a vast empire. The English authorities in Bengal had been opposed from the beginning by the viceroys of that province, until the time of Aliverdi Khan, a prince of great skill, both in civil and military affairs, who had successfully protected his dominions from the inroads of the Mahrattas, and was ruling at the time of the defeat and capture of the pirate Angria. Aliverdi was a friend to the English and their trade. He allowed them to dig a moat round Calcutta, to protect that city from predatory attacks, and granted them many privileges, by which they were enabled to improve their settlements in Bengal.

Aliverdi died in 1756, when he was succeeded in the office of Nabob, or governor, by his grand-nephew, Suraja Dowlah, a narrow-minded tyrannical prince, who had always disliked the Europeans, and very soon found a pretext for commencing hostilities. The English had so long enjoyed the protection and friendship of Aliverdi Khan, that they were but ill prepared for a war with his successor, therefore, when he appeared before Calcutta with a force that made resistance hopeless, all the women and children were sent at night on board a vessel, to be conveyed to a place of safety, while the council assembled to deliberate on the means of warding off the threatened danger. So great was the alarm, that all the rest of the ships sailed away at day-break, with the English governor, and some others, who were selfish enough to secure their own retreat; thus depriving those who remained of their only means of escape.

It was immediately made known to Suraja Dowlah that the fort would be surrendered; whereupon, his troops marched in, and took possession. The Nabob entered soon afterwards, accompanied by his vizier, Mir Jaffier, and although he had promised that no violence should be offered to the garrison, amounting to one hundred and forty-six individuals, he ordered that they should be all confined till the morning, in a small dark room, called the Black Hole, scarcely eighteen feet square, where, during a night of the most horrible suffering, one hundred and twenty-three human beings died of thirst and suffocation, while the few who survived were found either in a state of stupefaction or frighful delirium. It appears that the Nabob had not anticipated the fatal consequences of confining his prisoners in the Black Hole, yet he evinced neither pity nor remorse when informed of the dreadful catastrophe, but merely desired that the English chief, meaning the governor of the fort, if still alive, should be brought before him. Mr. Howell, the gentleman who had assumed that office after the flight of the governor, was accordingly supported, more dead than alive, into his presence, when Suraja allowed him to sit down, and desired that a glass of water should be given to him; but not a word of regret was uttered by the unfeeling prince for the calamity of which he had been the cause.

The following anecdote will afford an instance of the dread in which this tyrant was held. One of the Hindu guards set to watch the prison on that fearful night, was willing, for a large bribe, to represent to him the horrible situation of the sufferers, and beg that they might be placed in a larger apartment; but the Nabob was asleep, and the soldier had not the courage to disturb him, although strongly tempted, both by interest and humanity, so to do.

Calcutta was very soon retaken by Colonel Clive, who also sent an expedition to the rich city of Hoogly, about twenty-five miles higher up the river, which was taken and plundered. The rage of Suraja Dowlah at these successes, was unbounded. He laid siege to Calcutta, but soon finding there was no prospect of regaining possession of it, he consented to make peace, on terms sufficiently favourable to the English.

These events occurred in the early part of the war with the French; and as it was thought not improbable that the Nabob of Bengal might, under the circumstances, be disposed to afford aid to any power opposed to the English, Colonel Clive was induced to enter into the views of the vizier, Mir Jaffier, who aspired to the sovereignty of Bengal, which he proposed to obtain, by deposing his master. The British government at Calcutta sanctioned this treasonable conspiracy, on condition of deriving considerable advantages in case of its success. This was the occasion of the famous battle of Plassey, fought on the twenty-third of June, 1757, and won by the British, the event of which, decided the future fortunes of India. The victory, however, was much facilitated by the desertion of Mir Jaffier, with a great part of Suraja's troops, according to the plan which he had concerted with his allies.

The Nabob, who had remained in his tent during the engagement, no sooner heard of the defection of his vizier, than he mounted a camel, and fled towards his capital, Moorshedabad, a city on the Ganges, now gone to decay. Here the unfortunate prince soon found that a tyrant must not expect to meet with friends in his misfortunes. He left the city in disguise, and hired a boat, intending to proceed up the river as far as Patna; but when he arrived at Raj-mahal, the boatmen declared they would go no farther till the next day, nor could he prevail on them to alter their resolution. In this distress, he sought concealment for the night in a deserted garden of this once splendid city, which, before the time of Aliverdi Khan, had been the residence of the Viceroys of Bengal; and here he was seen and recognized, in the morning, by a man whom he had formerly treated with unjust severity, and who now revenged himself, by betraying the unhappy fugitive to his enemies. His fate was speedily decided. He was delivered into the hands of his late vizier, who had already assumed the rank of sovereign, and being shut up in a remote apartment of the palace, was there put to death in the night, by assassins sent for that cruel purpose.

The English received from the new sovereign of Bengal an immense sum of money, with a large accession of territory around Calcutta, and the right of taking possession of all the French settlements and factories in the province.

Scarcely, however, was Mir Jaffier seated on the throne of Bengal, when an unexpected rival appeared in the person of the Mogul prince, Shah Alum, the son of the Emperor Alamgir the Second, who, it may be remembered, had taken refuge at the court of the Nabob of Oude, and now came forward, supported by that prince, to assert his claim, as Soubahdar of Bengal, Bahar, and Orissa, a rank that had been bestowed on him by his father. It was about this time that the unfortunate Alamgir was assassinated, when Shah Alum was immediately proclaimed Emperor by his partizans at Delhi, with the sanction of Ahmed, of Durani, who by the event of the battle of Panniput, was then master of that city. The conqueror placed the government, during the absence of the Emperor, in the hands of a chief of the Rohilla nation, after which he returned to Cabul; nor did he ever again interfere with the affairs of India.

The new Emperor, having entered upon the war in Bengal, did not return to Delhi to take possession of the throne, but he assumed the imperial title, and nominated as vizier his friend, Shuja-ud-Dowlah, the Nabob of Oude, the son of Sufder Jung, who, under the Emperor Ahmed Shah, had enjoyed the same dignity.

Oude is an extensive plain, situated between the Himalaya mountains and the river Ganges. The soil is very fertile, producing sugar, cotton, indigo, opium, and many kinds of grain. In the time of the Mogul Emperors, Oude was one of the richest territories of Hindostan, and after the breaking up of the empire, was, for a considerable time, a wealthy and powerful state, until the misgovernment of its rulers led to a different condition of affairs, and the people, from being oppressed, neglected the cultivation of the land; the laws were disregarded; and the whole country, at length, became a prey to disorder and anarchy. At the time, however, of Mir Jaffier's usurpation of Bengal, Oude was in a very flourishing condition, under the dominion of Shuja-ud Dowlah, whose father, Sufder Jung, having been deposed by Ghazee-ud-din, had retired to his government of Oude, where he died shortly afterwards. Shuja, as already stated, afforded Shah Alum an asylum from the violence of Ghazee-ud-din, and assisted him to undertake the war in Bengal, which lasted several years, and ended in the subjection of that country to the British government.

Mir Jaffier died before the conclusion of the war, and was succeeded by his son, Nujeen Dowlah, who was so entirely dependent on the English, that the latter were considered by the natives as the real sovereigns of the country. The Emperor placed himself under their protection, and the Nabob of Oude, after sustaining several defeats, gave up the hopeless contest, and repaired to the British camp at Allahabad, to make the best terms in his power. The distinguished British officer, then Lord Clive, who had just been appointed to the government of India, proceeded to Allahabad to arrange matters with the vanquished princes, when Shuja-ud Dowlah was permitted to resume his government, with the title of Vizier of the Empire, in return for which he became a valuable ally of the British government in India. The Emperor, with the revenues of two of the conquered districts for his support, continued to reside under the protection of the English, in the hope that they might eventually be induced to furnish him with an army, without which he could not venture to return to Delhi, where great confusion reigned, and the sovereign authority was a subject of contention. The English, however, had no intention of aiding him in this particular; therefore, the disappointed prince at length applied to the Mahrattas, who espoused his cause, and, in 1771, placed him on the throne of his ancestors.

HYDER ALI.

NO name is more celebrated in the history of India, particularly as regards the connection of that country with Great Britain, than that of Hyder Ali, King of Mysore. The fall of the Mogul empire, and its consequent want of a supreme head, had emboldened many a daring adventurer to muster around him a lawless band, composed of men who were at once soldiers and robbers, and, by their aid, to seize upon some petty state, and set himself up as an independent sovereign. Hyder Ali was one of these chiefs. He was a Mohammedan, of obscure origin, who had served under one of the native princes, in alliance with the French, at the famous siege of Trichinopoly, and had enriched himself by a regular system of robbery, pursued on a most extensive scale. Besides pursuing the usual predatory excursions of such freebooters, who constantly plundered the villages, and seized convoys of horses, grain, and cattle, Hyder's men would carry off money, plate, jewels, and wearing apparel, and even stop the women and children, to despoil them of the ornaments they wore.

After some time, Hyder Ali found himself at the head of an army, consisting of fifteen hundred horse, and five thousand foot soldiers, with a train of elephants, camels, and all other warlike appendages of a great chief. Flushed with success, his ambition was directed towards the possession of a kingdom. The state on which he had fixed his views was Mysore, a territory of Southern India, nearly equal in size to the whole of England, possessing a delightful climate, and in a high state of cultivation. Mysore had, from time immemorial, been governed by Hindu Rajas, who since the Mohammedan conquests, had been tributary to the Emperors of Delhi, but had, like other princes, availed themselves of the weak and troubled state of the empire, to withhold the tribute, and assume an independence which, in the days of the more powerful Emperors, they were not able to maintain. As the dominions of the Raja bordered close upon the country of the Mahrattas, he was glad of the assistance of great military chiefs, to repel the invasions of that people, and Hyder Ali, whose plan was to raise himself, by degrees, to the sovereignty, performed such signal services against them, that he was appointed commander of the Mysorean army, and, after a time, became chief minister at the court, although he could neither read nor write.

Palace of Mysore.

It would be tedious to trace the various artifices by which the bold adventurer reached the point at which he aimed: suffice it to say, that, after meeting with some reverses, he succeeded in deposing the Raja, and seating himself on the throne of Mysore, about the time that the English completed the conquest of Bengal. He then began to extend his territories on every side, by invading and conquering those of the neighbouring princes, and augmented his treasures by the plunder of their capitals.

Among the important conquests by which Hyder Ali established a large and powerful kingdom in the south of India was, that of Calicut, so famous in the history of the Portuguese, and ruled, as at the time of their first landing in India, by a prince, called the Zamorin, who, to avoid falling into the hands of the victor, set fire to his palace, and perished in the flames.

The rapid successes of Hyder Ali naturally alarmed the other potentates, especially Nizam Ali, Soubahdar of the Deccan, and Madoo Rao, the ruler of the Mahratta country. Nizam Ali had succeeded to the sovereignty of the Deccan in 1760, by the murder of his brother, Salabat Jung, and, after some warfare with the English, had made peace with them, on condition that they should pay him an annual tribute for a certain territory along the Coromandel coast, called the Northern Circars, to which the Emperor had given them a title, but which had always formed a part of the viceroyalty of the Deccan. Besides having agreed to pay tribute for the peaceable possession of this tract of country, the British government had also consented to furnish Nizam Ali with auxiliary forces when required; and as he claimed the performance of this promise when about to join the Peishwa in an invasion of Mysore, the English became involved in a war with Hyder Ali, although they had no direct quarrel with that prince. They were not unwilling, it is true, to seize the opportunity of checking the progress of a rising power that might interfere with their own views of supremacy over India; and, in 1767, hostilities were commenced. Tippoo Saib, son of Hyder Ali, then a youth not more than seventeen years of age, highly distinguished himself by his courage and ability during this war, which was carried on, with varied success, for about two years, the advantage being generally on the side of Hyder Ali, who had bribed the Mahrattas to withdraw from the confederacy, and was thus relieved from the most numerous portion of his foes. At length, seeing no immediate prospect of success, Nizam Ali and his English allies concluded a treaty of peace with Hyder, by the terms of which, all parties were placed, with regard to possessions, in exactly the same position in which they had stood before the war.

No sooner had peace been restored to Mysore, than a new invasion of the Mahrattas exposed the people of that country to fresh scenes of misery and desolation. Madoo Rao conducted the army in person, and took several strong fortresses, but, in the midst of the campaign, was obliged, in consequence of ill-health, to give up the command, and return to Poona; nor was he ever again well enough to take an active part in the wars. In the war still carried on in Mysore, his place was supplied by Trimbuck Rao, a great chief, who was so successful, that Hyder Ali was eventually obliged to purchase peace by the cession of a great part of his northern dominions, and the payment of fifteen lacs of rupees, or one hundred and fifty thousand pounds, with the promise of an equal sum at a future period, not specified; by which he well understood that, if he desired to preserve his territories from the ravages of the Mahrattas, he must pay a large price for their forbearance.

Soon after the conclusion of this treaty, died the Peishwa, Madoo Rao, in the twenty-eighth year of his age. He had been highly respected, and much beloved as a sovereign, having been mild and equitable in his government, and especially famed for protecting the poor from oppression, and upholding equally the rights of all classes. His widow burned herself on his funeral pile. He was succeeded by his brother, Narrain Rao, a young man, scarcely seventeen, who was assassinated in the following year, in consequence of an insurrection of the troops, who forced their way into the palace, where two of the leaders killed the unfortunate youth in the arms of a faithful old servant, who, in trying to save him, shared his fate. It was suspected by many, that the ambition of his uncle Ragoba, who succeeded to the vacant dignity, had led to the untimely death of the young Peishwa; but although there is sufficient reason to believe that Ragoba had authorized the seizure and imprisonment of his nephew, the crime of the murder appears to have rested with his wife, who is supposed to have altered a written order from her husband to the conspirators, by erasing a word that meant, to seize, and substituting one that signified, to kill.

Ragoba was proclaimed Peishwa; but his accession was opposed by a certain party in the state; and Hyder Ali took advantage of the confusion that ensued, to make an effort for the recovery of the districts wrested from him during the late war. Ragoba hastened to defend the conquered territories, but being soon recalled by the news of a violent insurrection, he made peace with Hyder, by restoring some of the provinces he had lost. The Peishwa, whose authority was far from being fully established, was now very anxious to obtain the support of the British government, which was promised to him, on condition that he should cede to the East India Company the important island of Salsette, with some smaller islands contiguous to Bombay, together with the port of Bassein, and some other territories in Guzerat, all which had belonged to the Portuguese until the year 1750, when they were expelled by the Mahrattas, who had held them ever since.

The acquisition of these islands was a point of the greatest importance to the English, because they guarded the entrance to the spacious harbour of Bombay, the most commodious port in all India. It was even then famous for its dock-yard, and was well adapted to become the mart for the supply of the interior of that part of the country, and the great emporium of the trade with China, Persia, Arabia, and the Red Sea. Besides the protection which it afforded to Bombay, Salsette secured the principal trading entrance to the Mahratta country, which is said to have been supplied, at that time, with woollen cloths, and other staple commodities of Great Britain, to the amount of fourteen lacs of rupees annually. Salsette is remarkable for its cave temples, the largest of which was converted into a church by the Portuguese, and contains a colossal statue of Budha, nearly twenty feet in height. The East India Company had long been negociating with the Mahratta government for the cession of the islands, and, just before the death of Madoo Rao, had appointed a resident envoy at the court of Poona, in the hope of forwarding this desirable object. The difficulties in which Ragoba was involved after the death of his nephew, at length opened the way to the treaty, by which the valuable port and islands adjacent to Bombay, came into the possession of the English.

In the meantime, the ministers at Poona continued to treat Ragoba as an usurper, and to carry on the government in the name of the infant son of Narrain Rao, born some months after the murder of his father, who had left a young widow to lament his fate. The English, who were bound, by virtue of their treaty with Ragoba, to place him at the head of the Mahratta states, prepared for an attack on Poona; but the difficulties they met with on their march were so great, that, instead of putting their ally in possession of the capital, they were obliged to turn back without reaching it; a movement that brought upon them the whole force of the enemy; and an action took place, in which they sustained great loss. This was the cause of what is usually termed the first Mahratta war, for the opposite party, elated with success, demanded the surrender of all the places ceded by Ragoba; and thus the English were involved in a quarrel respecting their own affairs, instead of acting merely as the champions of the Bramin chief.

On Stone by Dean & Co

A STREET IN BOMBAY.

London, Dean & Co Threadneedle St.

The most remarkable event of this war was, the capture, by the English, of the famous hill fort of Gwalior, formerly the state prison of the Mogul empire, but, at that time, in possession of the great Mahratta chief, Sindia, within whose dominions it was situated. With the exception of the conquest of this fortress, very little advantage had been gained by the English, when they found it expedient to make peace with the Mahratta government, in consequence of a new war with Hyder Ali, the king of Mysore. Ragoba being thus deprived of his principal supporters, accepted the terms which they had made for him, and retired, on a liberal pension, to a pleasant spot on the banks of the Godavery, where he soon died.

Hyder Ali had some cause to be dissatisfied with the conduct of the English, who had neglected to fulfil several articles of the treaty concluded at the end of the last war, by which they had engaged to aid him in defending his dominions from the Mahrattas; a promise to which they had paid no attention; and he had, in consequence, been several times exposed to great difficulties and dangers from the invasions of that people. He resolved therefore to renew the war as soon as he was in a condition to do so; and in the month of June, 1780, departed from his capital, Seringapatam, to join his army assembled on the frontiers, which exhibited the finest show of native troops ever seen in the south of India, amounting to more than eighty thousand men, and provided with above one hundred pieces of cannon. At the head of this host he entered the Carnatic, and marched direct towards Màdras, where his approach was first announced by columns of smoke and flame, that were seen ascending from the burning villages. The English were in the utmost consternation, for it was impossible for them to bring their troops together, which were dispersed over the country in small detachments, and the principal roads were occupied by the enemy. Two divisions, however, succeeded, though with great difficulty, in joining each other, and when united, formed a little army of between three and four thousand men, Europeans and Sepoys; but these were furiously attacked by the Mysoreans, and all cut to pieces, with the exception of about two hundred, who were made prisoners, and conveyed to Seringapatam, where they were thrown into dungeons, in chains, and scarcely allowed sufficient of the coarsest food to keep them alive.

Hyder was a barbarian in warfare. A terrible instance of his cruelty was exhibited during the invasion of Calicut, when he offered a reward of five rupees for every human head that should be brought to him, and sat in state to receive, and pay for, the dreadful trophies, of which, it is said, above seven hundred were presented to the merciless conqueror without exciting in him the least signs of remorse, till a soldier appeared, bearing two heads so remarkably beautiful, that he was touched with pity, and gave orders to stop the massacre.

After the defeat of the British troops, Hyder laid siege to the city of Arcot, which was surrendered; and he then invested several of the strongest towns in the Carnatic. Arcot was still considered the capital of the Nabob, Mohammed Ali, whose sovereignty continued to be acknowledged by the presidency of Madras, which was now subordinate to that of Bengal. In the latter presidency, the British government was supreme, and all the civil officers of the interior were appointed by the Governor General, who resided at Calcutta; consequently, that city had become the capital of the British dominions in India. Warren Hastings, who was then Governor-General, on hearing of the successes of Hyder Ali, sent Sir Eyre Coote, a veteran officer of the highest military reputation, to stop the career of the invaders, whose ravages had converted the country into a desert; so that when the British forces marched from Madras under the conduct of General Coote, they were obliged to carry with them all kinds of supplies, as though they were about to cross the deserts of Arabia, instead of marching through an inhabited country. The expedition was, on the whole, successful. Hyder Ali, and his warlike son, were forced to abandon the places they were besieging, and at length sustained a total defeat at Cuddalore, where the two armies came to a regular engagement.

About this time, Lord Macartney, whose name is known in the history of China as ambassador to the court of the Emperor Kien-long, having been appointed governor of Madras, arrived in India, bringing news of a war between England and Holland. In consequence of this intelligence, the English made an immediate attack on the Dutch settlements on the coast of Coromandel, and the important station of Trincomalee, in the island of Ceylon, which were, in turn, surrendered to the assailants; and the Dutch were thus expelled from every possession which they had held in India, except that of the island of Java.

The war with Hyder Ali, who had received aid from the French, was still prosecuted, with varied fortune, until his death, which happened in the year 1782, he being then above eighty years of age. Although an usurper, he had not been an oppressive ruler. He had not interfered with the customs of the Hindus; he had left the Bramins in possession of their lands; and the revenues which he had exacted from the farmers were so light, as to leave them the means of living in comfort. During his wars in the Carnatic,

Hyder made captive great numbers of the lowest class of field labourers, many of whom were slaves, and formed them into colonies in the most uncultivated districts of his dominions, where lands were assigned them, and orders given by that judicious prince, that they should not be called by the name that marked them as men of inferior caste, but that they should be termed cultivators.

Hyder Ali founded the city and fortress of Bangalore, which, in his time, was a place of great importance, on account of its numerous manufactures, and its trade with the neighbouring states; but in the reign of Tippoo, who did not rule with the moderation of his predecessor, the inhabitants of Bangalore suffered greatly, in consequence of being prohibited from trading with Arcot and Hyderabad, the capitals of the Carnatic, and the dominions of the Nizam, that being the title by which the Soubahdar of the Deccan was then generally distinguished.

TIPPOO SAIB.

HYDER ALI was succeeded by his son, Tippoo, a prince equal to his father in ambition and military talent, but far inferior in policy, and a violent persecutor of the Christian natives, who were numerous in all those parts of India where the Portuguese had held settlements, owing chiefly to the exertions of the Jesuits, who had spread the Christian faith to a considerable extent among the villagers on the coast of Malabar.

For some time after his accession to the throne of Mysore, Tippoo maintained the war against the English, till the news of a peace between Great Britain and France occasioned the secession of his French allies, and led to a treaty with the British, concluded in March, 1784, by which all conquests were to be mutually restored, and the Indian prince was to set at liberty all the prisoners confined in the different fortresses of Mysore.

Tippoo Saib was now the most powerful prince in all India. He assumed the title of Padsha, which had hitherto been only used by the Emperor, as it signified supreme ruler; and, from that time, his name was substituted for that of Shah Alum in the public prayers; and thus even the nominal supremacy of the Mogul sovereign, which had, till then, been acknowledged in Mysore, was entirely set aside, and Tippoo was called Sultan. His capital was Seringapatam, a mean-looking town, situated on an island formed by the river Cavery, which is there a broad and rapid stream. The island is about three miles in length, rocky and barren, and was probably chosen by Hyder for his chief residence, on account of its insular advantages, and the ease with which it might be fortified. The famous fort of Sri Ranga was built by Tippoo, and contained his chief palace, a large edifice, enclosed by a high wall. His apartments were on one side of a large square, from which a private passage, strictly guarded, led to the Zenana, or part of the palace appropriated to the ladies, who were carefully concealed from all eyes, save those of their royal master. Many of these were the daughters of Bramins and native princes, who had been made captives in infancy, and brought up in the Mohammedan religion, ignorant of their parentage, and of the world beyond the walls which surrounded them. The Sultan had two other palaces, with fine gardens, on the island. One of them was situated at the extremity, opposite to Sri Ranga, and was an extremely elegant building, near which stood the mausoleum of his father.

The Zenana.

In the old palace of Seringapatam, resided the family of the late Raja of Mysore, who had been deposed by Hyder Ali. That prince had left no children, but had adopted as his son a young relative, who had been brought up under the care of his widow, both being strictly confined to the palace, which was suffered to fall into a very ruinous condition. Tippoo was so anxious to destroy every vestige of the old government, that he pulled down the palace and temples of Mysore, the ancient capital, and removed the stones to a neighbouring height, where he commenced building a fortress, which was never finished. One of the great faults of this prince seems to have been the inconsiderate manner in which he undertook great and expensive works, without the means or leisure to complete them; yet the peasants were compelled to labour at such profitless employment, to the detriment of themselves and their families. On the whole, however, the dominions of the Sultan are said to have been well governed, highly cultivated, and in the enjoyment of a great degree of prosperity.

The people of Mysore were divided into no less than twenty-seven castes, as every trade was kept distinct, and its members were obliged to observe certain rules, especially as regarded intermarriages, and the manner in which food was to be cooked and eaten. Each caste was distinguished, according to the custom of the Hindus, by a particular mark on the forehead, made with white clay; so that the laws might not be so liable to transgression through any mistake of the person; and every class had its chief, whose office was hereditary, and whose duty it was to punish those who did transgress, by expelling them from the society to which they had belonged, a terrible sentence in ancient times, but not much regarded at the present time, when the payment of a small fine can always obtain pardon for the culprit.

The trades and manufactures were numerous in all the large towns of Mysore, and weekly fairs were held, which the neighbouring farmers usually attended, to sell their produce. The trade of some of the cities, however, was depressed by the bad policy of the Sultan, who filled his warehouses with large stores of goods, which he obliged the merchants to take at enormous prices, and, at the same time, prohibited all commercial intercourse with the states governed by the English, or in alliance with them. His high pretensions, and encroachments on the territories of his neighbours, gave rise to a powerful league against him, formed by the Mahrattas and the Nizam, who, in 1786, advanced towards the Toombuddra, the chief barrier between them and the Sultan's dominions.

In the meanwhile, Shah Alum had remained on the throne at Delhi, where he had been supported, amid the factions that agitated the court, by Sindia, the great Mahratta chief, to whom he had given the command of the Imperial army, and the entire government of the provinces of Delhi and Agra; so that what remained of the sovereign authority, was, in reality, exercised by Sindia, who had previously extended his power and possessions by conquests, over the princes of Rajputana. The Mahrattas might, therefore, be said to have been masters of the empire at the time of the confederacy against Tippoo, who was not slow to meet the combined armies on his frontiers; but although he gained some advantages, he was the first to propose terms of peace, and even agreed to restore some conquests that he had made, having, it is supposed, reason to suspect that the English were about to join the enemy.

About this time, there arose a formidable insurrection against Sindia, and the imperial government of Hindostan, headed by a Mohammedan noble, named Ismael Beg, and Gholam Kawdir, a Rohilla chief, who gained possession of Delhi, drove out the Mahratta garrison, plundered the palace, and having dethroned the Emperor, and treated his family, wives, sons, and daughters, with the greatest indignity, the ruffian chief put out the eyes of the unhappy monarch with his dagger; an act of barbarity that so shocked his ally, Ismael Beg, that he withdrew his troops, and joined the Mahratta army that was approaching to the relief of the capital. Gholam Kawdir, who had fled from Delhi, was pursued, overtaken, and put to death, by order of Sindia, who replaced the now sightless Shah Alum on his throne with great pomp, but annexed the provinces of Delhi and Agra, with the greater part of the Doab, to his own dominions.

This immense accession of power to a sovereign chief, already so powerful, could not be viewed with indifference by the English; but their attention was more immediately called to the proceedings of Tippoo, who recommenced hostilities, by the invasion of Travancore, a small independent state, forming the western part of the southern extremity of India, the Raja of which was a faithful ally of the British government. This little kingdom was defended by a barrier wall and moat, extending along the whole length of its frontiers, and, in one part, intervening between the territories of the Sultan and the state of Cochin, which he had made tributury by conquest. It was on account of its vicinity, that Tippoo was desirous of gaining possession of Travancore; and he made it a ground of complaint, that the Raja's wall obstructed his free passage into his vassal kingdom of Cochin, and also that the prince had afforded refuge to the Nairs, or nobles of Malabar, who had fled to his territories. This they had done for the sake of protection against the Sultan, who was notorious for his barbarous treatment of the conquered Hindus, unless they consented to abandon the worship of their idols for the Musselman faith. He made a boast of the numerous temples he had destroyed; and he imprisoned great numbers of the refractory natives in different fortresses. On one occasion, it is said that two thou-

THE MERCHANTS OF CALICUT SEIZED AND CHAINED TO A BARREN ROCK BY ORDER OF TIPPOO SAIB.

sand Bramins drowned themselves, to escape the cruel persecution with which they were threatened; and many families fled from their houses to seek shelter in the forests among the mountains.

Among the many acts of cruelty committed by Tippoo Saib, may be mentioned that which he practised on the merchants of Calicut, from whom he exacted a heavy tribute, much greater than they could pay; and in default of their compliance with his demand, he caused them to be torn from their families and chained to a barren rock, in sight of their homes, where they were left to perish.

The first attack on Travancore was repulsed with great loss to the Sultan, who escaped himself, with great difficulty, on foot, among a crowd of fugitive soldiers; but a second attempt was more successful, the barrier wall was demolished, and the whole country overrun and laid waste, by the Mysorean army, who made numbers of the unhappy natives prisoners and carried them away into captivity. The English sent assistance to the Raja, and entered into an alliance with the Nizam and the Mahrattas, for the purpose of lessening the power of Tippoo Saib. The war was commenced by the English, who, during the first campaign, recovered the whole province of Malabar from the Sultan, whose troops were driven from every fortress they had held.

The treaty between the allies stipulated, that all conquests should be equally shared, and that those Zemindars who were formerly dependent on the Peishwa or the Nizam, should be restored to their several territories, on paying a sum of money, to be divided among the confederates; after which payment, the Zemindars were to be tributary to their respective princes, as before.

Early in the year 1791, Lord Cornwallis, governor of Madras, took the command of an expedition into the kingdom of Mysore, and laid siege to the strong fortress of Bangalore, built by Hyder Ali. It contained a handsome palace, with extensive gardens, laid out in a rather formal manner, with straight walks dividing the grounds into square plots, each plot being filled with one particular kind of tree or plant, and the sides of the walks bordered with cypress trees. The rest of the buildings within the fort were chiefly huts, for the accommodation of the garrison, and magazines for military stores.

The first care of the Sultan, on the approach of the invaders, was to send off all the ladies of his harem, under a strong escort, to Seringapatam; and the time he lost in making arrangements for their safe removal, afforded the British army an opportunity of taking up an advantageous position close to the walls of Bangalore. The town was stormed, and taken, after a desperate conflict in the streets with the Sultan's troops, who were eventually driven out with frightful bloodshed; and this victory was immediately followed by the capture of the fortress. Tippoo was not personally engaged in these actions: he was hastening to the relief of the fort, when met by a crowd of fugitives, who announced its fall, with that of the city, to the dismayed monarch, who retreated towards his capital to provide for its defence. Thither he was followed by the English, who however, suffered much distress from want of supplies; for he had made a complete desert of the country through which they had to pass, by driving away the inhabitants, and burning the villages; so that neither grain nor cattle could be procured; and by the time the allied army had reached Seringapatam, it was in a very exhausted condition. Notwithstanding, a battle was fought on the banks of the Cavery, the result of which was decidedly favourable to the English; but the troops were so weakened by want of food, that Lord Cornwallis was obliged to give up his intention of besieging Tippoo in his capital, and he returned to Bangalore.

In this expedition, he had been joined by the troops of the Nizam, a predatory host, who, under no sort of control, traversed the country in search of plunder, on horses as uncouth in appearance as themselves. Each man was armed, equipped, and mounted, according to his own fancy; and they were so entirely undisciplined, that they were of no use whatever to the British commander, who would rather have been without such unruly auxiliaries. In his retreat, however, he was met by a large division of the Mahratta army, under the command of two celebrated chiefs, Hurry Punt and Purseram Bhow, whose appearance was hailed with joy, as their ample stores afforded a seasonable relief to the famished soldiers.

With the aid of this powerful reinforcement, Lord Cornwallis captured some of the droogs, or hill fortresses, on which the Indian princes were accustomed to place their chief dependence for defence against their enemies; and among those which were taken were, Nundidroog, Ootradroog, and Savendroog, the name of the last signifying the Rock of Death, from its difficult ascent, being almost perpendicular, and above half a mile in height, surrounded for several miles by a forest, or jungle, so thick as to be scarcely penetrable. Every accessible part of the mountain was guarded by walls and massive gateways, and on the summit were erected two citadels, with a wide chasm between them, which greatly increased the danger to the assailants.

After these exploits, Lord Cornwallis advanced again towards Sering-

Drawn by B. Clayton. On Stone by Dean & C.

THE LAST EFFORT OF TIPPOO SAIB AT SERINGAPATAM.

London Dean & Co. Threadneedle St.

apatam, expecting to be joined by General Abercrombie, who had been actively engaged, for above a year, in Malabar, and the adjoining districts. Tippoo was encamped with his whole army, in front of the capital, his position being strengthened by numerous fortifications, when the enemy appeared on a range of heights before him. Trusting to his strong encampment, he was unprepared for immediate action, thinking that the English would not venture an attack; but as the British commander was of opinion that prompt measures were requisite, he resolved to come to an engagement without delay, and to commence by surprising the camp under cover of the night. The event answered his expectations; for the suddenness of the attack occasioned such confusion, that great numbers of the Sultan's troops escaped in dismay, by crossing the river into the island, and Tippoo himself provided for his own safety in the same manner, while many took advantage of the panic to desert the army, and return to their homes. The battle was renewed at day-break and lasted till evening, when the Sultan, who had been losing ground every hour, was obliged to withdraw within the walls of the city.

Among the deserters were several thousand men, who had been forcibly enlisted in the territory of Coorg, a small state, bounded by the Ghauts, through which lay the direct road into Malabar. It is a wild, woody country, famous for the number of elephants found in its forests, and was first annexed to the kingdom of Mysore, by Hyder Ali, who exacted tribute from the Raja. Soon after the accession of Tippoo, the people of Coorg made an attempt to recover their independence, when the Sultan marched into their country with a large force, and treated the inhabitants with such barbarity, that his name was held in detestation by them; and, therefore, it was not surprising that the soldiers of Coorg should forsake his standard on the first opportunity.

The desire to return to their native villages was, perhaps, more ardently felt, on account of a happy change that had taken place in the country. While Tippoo was engaged in warfare, the captive Raja of Coorg had contrived to make his escape from the fort in which he was confined, and reached a forest in his own dominions, where he was joyfully received by a band of freebooters, who had maintained themselves in the woods by robbery, rather than submit to the new government. By the aid of these men, the prince made known his return to numbers of his subjects who were also living in exile; and he was soon at the head of an army sufficiently strong to drive the Musselman garrison from the forts, and clear his territories from those detested enemies. Being once more in possession of his own dominions, he was glad to obtain the friendship and alliance of General Abercrombie, who was thus enabled to pass through Coorg peacefully with his army to join Lord Cornwallis, whose camp he reached a few days after the battle of Seringapatam.

Tippoo was now so fully sensible of his danger, that he opened a negociation with the English, in the conviction that he should be obliged to make peace with them on their own terms. The conditions they offered were, that he should cede one half of his dominions to the allies, that is, to the Nizam, the Mahrattas, and the English, who should be privileged to take the portion nearest to their respective territories; that he should pay down a sum equivalent to four millions sterling; and that he should send his two sons as hostages to the British camp. The haughty Sultan assembled his chief officers in the great mosque, and read these proposals to them, when they all agreed that his best course was to secure peace, even on these hard terms; and the treaty was signed accordingly, in February, 1792.

The parting with the two young princes, was a severe trial to the whole of the royal family. The youths rode forth dressed in white muslin robes, wearing round their necks several strings of large pearls, mixed with jewels, and mounted on elephants richly caparisoned. The walls were crowded with spectators to witness their departure, and Tippoo himself stood with his people, to take a farewell look of the beloved children whom he was compelled to confide to the care of his enemies, uncertain what sort of treatment they might experience. The chief Vakeel, who accompanied them, was instructed to take them direct to the tent of Lord Cornwallis and, in delivering them into the hands of that nobleman, to recommend them to his paternal care. They were received with the utmost kindness, and created a great degree of interest, by the graceful dignity of their demeanour, in which were blended the politeness and reserve that distinguish the manners of oriental courts. They remained about two years in the English camp, when, all the conditions of the treaty having been fulfilled, they were sent back to their father.

In consequence of this peace, the Mahratta territories were extended to the Toombuddra rivers; the dominions of the Nizam were enlarged southward to the Pennar; and the English added to their possessions several detached portions of the ceded districts, including a considerable part of the Malabar coast, by which they acquired the once powerful state of Calicut. The cession of Coorg was also demanded, and obtained, after a violent opposition on the part of the Sultan, who was only brought to comply, by the fear of seeing his children sent off as prisoners into the

Carnatic, and the war renewed. He was thus disappointed of the revenge he would have taken on the Raja and people of Coorg, who were now safe under the protection of the English.

About this time, died Sindia, who left his extensive realms to his grand-nephew, Doulat Rao Sindia, a youth only fifteen years of age.

The Mahrattas were not, at this period, such as they were in the days of Sevajee; but they were still a military people. Some members of every peasant's family were soldiers; and in many of the villages, a fourth part of the inhabitants were men trained to arms, who were always ready to serve when occasion required; and such an occasion presented itself during the few years of peace with Tippoo, when a dispute arose between the governments of Poona and Hyderabad, which caused a declaration of war; and thus the two potentates, Nizam Ali and Madoo Nurrain Rao, so lately friends and allies, took the field as enemies. The troops of the Nizam made so sure of success, that they were constantly heard to boast how they would plunder and burn down the city of Poona; and the minister declared in a public assembly, that he would banish the Peishwa to Benares; while the dancing-girls in all the temples, daily celebrated the triumph of the army in their songs. But the result was very different from that which had been expected, for the Mahrattas gained so decided a victory in a pitched battle fought at Kurdla, on the Mahratta frontiers, that the Nizam, who commanded in person, was obliged to take shelter in a small fort, where he was soon surrounded by the enemy, so that he had no chance of escape, except by agreeing to the terms proposed by the victors; who, as usual, exacted, besides money, a large cession of territory, comprising, among other valuable acquisitions, the fort of Dowlatabad.

The Peishwa, who, it may be remembered, was the son of the murdered Narrain, was yet scarcely twenty-one years of age, and had always been kept under strict control by the chief minister, a Bramin, somewhat advanced in years, named Nana Furnuwees, whose ambition was to keep all the authority in his own hands. The family of Ragoba had been in confinement ever since the death of that celebrated personage; and when the war broke out with Nizam Ali, the two sons of Ragoba, Bajee Rao and Chimnajee Appo, were sent to the hill fort of Sewneree, where, even after the close of the war, they remained in captivity.

The melancholy fate of these young men excited the deepest sympathy. Bajee Rao, in particular, was greatly beloved by all who knew him, being liberally gifted by nature with those attractive qualities that are sure to make friends. In him were combined a graceful person, handsome countenance, gentle manners, and the most winning address, with mental accomplishments rarely found in a Mahratta, while he also excelled in the bodily exercises which are held by that nation in so much esteem. The young Peishwa, who was too high-minded to feel jealous of the praises he often heard lavished on his cousin, was anxious to procure his release, and make him his companion; but this desire was opposed by the wily minister, who was not, like his master, free from jealousy. It happened, however, that Bajee Rao became acquainted with the Peishwa's friendly disposition towards him; on which, he commenced a clandestine correspondence, which had all the charms of romance for both the young men, whose mutual attachment was strengthened by the opposition of Nana, who, at length, discovered their secret intercourse, to which he immediately put a stop by the most vigorous measures. The friend who had been the bearer of their letters and messages, was imprisoned; the Peishwa was compelled to submit to the bitterest reproaches; and Bajee Rao was more closely watched and guarded than before.

The effect of this harshness on the mind of Madoo Rao, led to a catastrophe that could scarcely have been contemplated. For several days, he shut himself up in a private apartment, refusing to take his accustomed seat in the Durbar, or attend to any public business; and was, with difficulty, persuaded to bear his part in a religious festival, at which he was expected to appear in procession with his troops, and to receive the chiefs and ambassadors at court. These ceremonies were evidently irksome to the unhappy prince, who, two days afterwards, threw himself from a high terrace of his palace, and died from the wounds he had received in the fall. His last wish was that Bajee Rao should succeed him; but Nana Furnuwees, naturally dreading the elevation of a prince whom he had treated so harshly, called together an assembly of the great chiefs, and proposed that Yessooda Bye, the youthful widow of the late Peishwa, who was yet but a mere child, should be considered head of the state until some boy should be selected by the council for her adoption. One of the ministers who attended on the part of the young chief, Sindia, objected to this arrangement; but his judgment was overruled, and the plan acted upon. Bajee Rao, who was informed of all these proceedings, then contrived to open a correspondence with Sindia, and to engage him in his cause.

The minister was now so much alarmed at the prospect of Sindia's enmity, that he thought it would be even safer for himself to release Bajee, and acknowledge him as Peishwa, trusting, by submission, to induce him to forget all that had passed. The event answered his expectation; but Sindia and his minister, offended that Bajee Rao should have availed himself of other means than those which they had offered, to enable him to obtain possession of his dignity, determined to revenge themselves for the slight, by siding with the other party. With this view, Bajee was induced, by some artifice, to visit Sindia's camp, where he was detained as a prisoner, whilst his brother, Chimnajee, was, against his will, formally invested with the dignity of Peishwa; but Bajee Rao soon contrived, by his insinuating address, to win back the favour of the young chief, and was restored in a few months; this took place at the close of the year 1796.

One of his first acts was to get rid of the prime minister, Nana Furnuwees, who was treacherously seized, in returning from a visit of ceremony to the Peishwa, and carried away in custody, with several other persons of distinction who had accompanied him, while some of their attendants were killed, and the rest dispersed. This outrage produced a violent tumult at Poona, where all the ministers of Nana's party were arrested, and confined in the palace, while their adherents mustered in a body, and fought with the soldiers who were sent to sieze all property in the houses of the prisoners. Much blood was shed on this occasion, but the Peishwa's faction triumphed, and Nana was sent to the fort of Ahmednagar.

Soon after this, a still more dreadful scene occurred at Poona. Sindia had recently married the daughter of a chief named Ghatgay, and had bestowed upon him the high office of Dewan, or collector of the revenues. Ghatgay had made some objections to the match, because he held his own family more noble than that of his proposed son-in-law, but he had at length consented, on certain conditions, one of which was that he should be made Dewan; and, accordingly, the marriage was solemnized with great splendour. The procession on such occasions, with the superb presents made to the guests, involved Sindia in expenses so enormous, that he was afterwards distressed for money to pay his troops, and applied to Bajee Rao for a certain sum he had agreed to pay on his restoration. The Peishwa replied, that he had not the money, but that Sindia was at liberty to levy contributions, to the amount required, on the rich inhabitants of Poona; and the chief, accordingly, sent his Dewan for that purpose. It is believed that Bajee Rao, in giving this permission, had no forethought of the cruelties to which it might probably lead; and as he was absent from the capital, he was not aware of the consequences until it was too late to prevent them.

Ghatgay, whose name is still mentioned with horror by the people of Poona, began to execute his mission by inflicting tortures on the imprisoned ex-ministers, until they gave up a vast amount of property which they had concealed in different places; and when this had been seized, the rich merchants and bankers were forced, by similar barbarity, to contribute vast sums towards the payment of the debt contracted by the Peishwa, who cannot be exonerated from the charge of flagrant injustice, in allowing Sindia to levy the contributions, however guiltless he may have been of the inhuman proceedings of the Dewan, who invented a new mode of torture, by tying his victims on a heated gun, until the required sum had been extorted from them. One of the nobles, a relative of Nana Furnuwees, expired under this dreadful treatment, rather than submit to the extortion; and several others were so injured, that they never recovered from the effects of the Dewan's cruelty.

In the meanwhile, the great Revolution had taken place in France, and Tippoo Saib was holding a correspondence with the Directors of the French Republic, with a view of obtaining efficient aid to enable him to expel the English from India, succeeding in which, he and the French were to divide the whole country between them; but instead of the large force he expected, a few men, not exceeding one hundred, were sent from the Mauritius; and as much publicity had been given to Tippoo's proceedings, the British government judged it necessary to renew the war. The Marquis Wellesley, then Governor of India, made immediate preparations for that purpose, and a new treaty was concluded with the Nizam, who agreed to dismiss a number of French troops in his service, and to receive in their stead six battalions of English sepoys, who, with the rest of the troops furnished by him for the approaching war, were placed under the command of the present Duke of Wellington, then Colonel Sir Arthur Wellesley. The Mahrattas were bound, as well as the Nizam, by the terms of their former treaty with the English, to aid them in all wars with the Sultan of Mysore; but Bajee Rao, who had proved but a weak ruler, was persuaded by Sindia to wait till he saw which side would be likely to be successful; therefore, no assistance was rendered from that quarter.

The war was not of long duration. After two or three indecisive actions, the British forces were once more encamped before Seringapatam. Tippoo, who was unprepared for the sudden movement that had brought the enemy so soon to the walls of his capital, and was fully impressed with the conviction that it must inevitably fall, called his chief officers around him, and asked them what they had resolved to do in this emergency. "To die with you!" was the unanimous reply of these brave men, who were destined to fulfil their promise to the very letter; for there were few who survived the dreadful day that witnessed the fall of their sovereign.

The town was closely besieged for the space of one month, when, on the fourth of May, 1799, the final attack was made that completed the conquest of Mysore, and terminated the career of Tippoo Saib. General Baird, who conducted the assault, had, during the former war with the Sultan, suffered a long imprisonment in the gloomy dungeons of the Sri Ranga, the walls of which he now mounted as a conqueror. Tippoo fell in the thickest of the fight, wounded by three musket balls. His sabre was still grasped in his hands, when a soldier attempted to take off his richly embroidered sword belt, on which the dying Sultan made an effort to lift the weapon he held, and wounded the soldier, who instantly shot him through the head, not knowing who he was; and it was not till some hours afterwards, that his body was found, and recognized.

In the mean time, strict search had been made for him in the palace, where his two elder sons were found in a private apartment, seated on a carpet, surrounded by numerous attendants. They were not then aware of the death of their father, and were, with some difficulty, persuaded to order that the gates of the palace should be thrown open to the victors, who, they were told, would otherwise take the building by force. The unfortunate princes were then led forth as captives, yet with the respectful sympathy which their exalted rank and recent misfortunes excited, and were conducted into the presence of General Baird, who endeavoured, by the kindest assurances, to relieve them from, at least, the dread of personal danger.

The body of the Sultan was carried to the palace, and the next day was buried, with military pomp, in the magnificent sepulchre of the Lall Bang, erected by Hyder Ali on the island of Seringapatam.

The Lall Bang.

BRITISH GOVERNMENT.

THE fall of Tippoo Saib placed a large kingdom at the disposal of the Governor General, the Marquis Wellesley, who took in full sovereignty, for the East India Company, the coast of Canara, the district of Coimbetoor, the passes of the Ghauts, and Seringapatam; thus securing the whole sea coast of southern India, with a free communication across the country. A large tract was assigned to the Nizam adjoining his dominions, and a portion of the conquered states was offered to the Peishwa, on condition that he should allow British troops to be stationed within his territories; but as these terms were rejected, the profferred share was withheld, until circumstances induced Bajee Rao to consent to an arrangement by which his independence was virtually lost.

When the Governor General had taken possession of all he thought fit to appropriate, it was resolved to form what remained into a native kingdom, and restore the family of the former Rajas, whose representative was a child not more than six years of age, who was taken to Mysore, and there installed with as much ceremony as the ruined state of the place would allow; for as it was intended to make Seringapatam a British military station, the ancient capital was fixed on as the future seat of government, and the re-building of the fort and city, which, as before stated, had been destroyed by Tippoo, was immediately commenced.

The new town of Mysore is much handsomer than that of Seringapatam. It stands on an eminence, and is surrounded by a wall of earth. The streets are regular, and the white houses are interspersed with trees and temples. The fort contains the palace, with the houses of the principal merchants and bankers. A British resident was appointed at the court, for whom a good house was erected on a rising ground near the town; and in this officer was vested the actual government of the state, for the Raja was, in reality, a mere dependent of the British rulers in India.

The princes, and other members of the family of the late Sultan, were removed to Vellore, a town and fort of considerable extent about eighty miles from Madras, where they were maintained in a style befitting their rank, but were not allowed to go beyond the fortress, which was strongly garrisoned with Europeans and Sepoys. Tippoo had been very popular among the military chiefs of Mysore; therefore, it is not surprising that some attempts should have been made to restore his family to the throne. In the year 1806, a formidable mutiny broke out among the native troops at Vellore, when all the Europeans of the garrison were barbarously massacred. More than six hundred of the insurgents were made prisoners, some of whom were shot, others sent to penal settlements, and the rest gradually set at liberty; but this rebellion caused the removal of Tippoo's sons to Calcutta, as there was great reason to believe that, if they had not been personally concerned in it, the ultimate object of the outbreak was that of effecting a revolution in their favour, and of placing the eldest prince on the throne.

About the time of the conquest of Mysore, the Nabob of Surat, who, like many other princes, had established his independence, in consequence of the fall of the Mogul Empire, died; and his successor, whose title was disputed, purchased the support of the English, by surrendering to them the administration of his dominions, both civil and military, in return for which, he received the empty name of sovereign, with a pension for his maintenance. It was under similar circumstances that Tanjore was added, at the same period, to the British dominions, and its Raja to the list of royal pensioners.

The attention of the British government was now directed towards acquiring an ascendency over the Mahrattas, the only rival power remaining in India. It may be remembered that, when the sovereign authority was first assumed by the Bramin minister, under the title of Peishwa, he bestowed grants of land on many of the chiefs, and that the greatest of these were Sindia and Holkar, between whom the whole province of Malwa was divided. For some time, these chiefs were equal in power; but Sindia, by degrees, obtained a decided superiority, which he preserved until the rise of a chief of the house of Holkar, named Jeswunt Rao, an adventurous leader, who proved a formidable rival to Doulat Rao Sindia, whose villages he frequently plundered in the course of his predatory excursions. Sindia and the Peishwa united their forces to check the inroads of the daring chieftain, and a desperate battle was fought near Poona, in the month of October, 1802, when Holkar gained a complete victory, and the Peishwa fled, first to the fort of Singurh, and then to Bassein, leaving the city in the hands of the conqueror.

It was in consequence of this event that Bajee Rao was induced to conclude the famous treaty of Bassein, by which he deprived himself of all pretensions to the rank of an independent prince, and gave to the English a decided supremacy in the Mahratta states. A large British force was to be permanently stationed at Poona, and maintained there by the revenues of certain districts ceded for that purpose; and the Peishwa, moreover, bound himself not to engage in hostilities with other states, or to negociate with any other power, without the consent of the British government; and on these conditions he was restored, by the aid of a British army, to his throne.

The dissatisfaction felt by many of the Mahratta chiefs, but more especially by Sindia, at the influence thus obtained by the British nation in the government of the country, led to the war which transferred what may be termed the Empire of India, from the Mahrattas to the English, who became masters of Delhi, and took once more under their protection the now aged and powerless prince who still bore the title of Emperor. The British commander, General Sir Arthur Wellesley, had vainly endeavoured to come to an amicable arrangement with Sindia, but the hostile feelings of that chief were so manifest, that a declaration of war was inevitable; and two armies were at once employed against him; one in the north, under the command of General Lake; and the other in the south, under General Sir Arthur Wellesley, who gained a complete victory over the Mahrattas, commanded by Sindia in person, on the plains of Assaye, in the month of September, 1803. General Lake was equally suceessful in the north; and, a few days before the battle of Assaye, had taken possession of Delhi, after defeating the enemy within sight of its walls.

The people of Delhi regarded this event as a deliverance rather than a misfortune, as the government of Sindia had by no means been popular. The British general, on entering the once splendid capital of the Moguls, requested an audience of the Emperor, Shah Alum, who received him under a torn and faded canopy, the miserable remnant of former state. The countenance of the aged and sightless monarch was impressed with a deep and settled melancholy, and his whole appearance bore evident tokens of neglect; therefore, he had reason to rejoice in a victory, which, though it only restored him to a semblance of power, yet rescued him from the control of those by whom he had been despised and ill-treated, and who had allowed him but a very scanty portion of those comforts by which the infirmities of old age may be alleviated. His condition was now materially improved. He was again surrounded with the semblance of a court; he was treated with the respect due to majesty; the government was conducted in his name; and the form observed, of obtaining his sanction for every measure adopted by the new rulers.

The conquest of Delhi was followed by that of Agra; soon after which, a treaty of peace was concluded with Sindia, who ceded the large territory of the Doab, with some provinces beyond the Jumna, and the two cities of Delhi and Agra, with all right of control over the person of the Emperor.

Town and fort of Agra.

He also gave up his maritime districts in Guzerat to the English, and some extensive possessions in the Deccan to the Peishwa and the Nizam. This peace was concluded in 1803; and, by a subsequent treaty in 1805, he made some farther cessions to the British government; in return for which, he obtained the important fort of Gwalior, which became his residence, and the capital of his dominions.

The influence of British authority was, by this time, extended over the greater part of India, not only by conquest, but by protective treaties with the native rulers, who were glad to purchase security by consenting to maintain a body of British soldiers within their dominions, who were to guard them from foreign aggression, but not to interfere with the internal government. It is, however, obvious that the presence of a military force superior to his own, must have reduced every prince in whose territory it was stationed, to a state of complete subjection.

The next step taken by the East India Company was, to require that certain districts in each protected state should be assigned for the maintenance of the troops; and, at length, the princes were obliged to resign the civil administration, with all the revenues, and to accept from the Company a pension just sufficient to support the pomp of royalty. Among these pensioners were, the Emperor himself, the Nabob of Bengal, the Nizam, and the King of Mysore.

The general condition of the people was materially improved by the new system of government; for, as the revenues of India are derived almost entirely from the land, the cultivators had been subjected to many oppressions that were removed by their new masters. The collection of the revenues has always been, and still is, the principal feature of the government of India; and in making fresh regulations with regard to the assessment of villages, great difficulties arose out of the fact, that it is a doubtful point who are the real proprietors of the soil. The Mogul sovereigns had assumed the lordship of all the lands over which they ruled, so that the Emperor was called Lord of the land in some parts of the country, and the native princes in others; while the ryots, or cultivators, had some claim to the ownership, because they occupied their farms by inheritance, and, according to the ancient laws, could not be ejected as long as they paid the dues. There were also certain lords, called Zemindars, who held districts of their several governments, for which they paid a fixed sum annually, and thus became entitled to the rents of all the villages within their Zemindaries. This system was chiefly prevalent in Bengal, and was not altered in that presidency by the British government; but the Zemindars were restrained from oppressing the ryots by arbitrary exactions, being obliged to fix the rent, and give a bond that it should not afterwards be increased. Much of the landed property in Bengal, however, was transferred to new masters, in consequence of the Zemindars being sometimes unable to keep their contract with the government; in which case, the lands were seized, and sold.

In the south of India, under the Madras presidency, the ryots are treated as the owners of the lands, and the rents are collected, as in ancient times, by the headman of the village, who transmits them to the chief magistrate of the district, an office usually held by a Bramin, whose duty it is to make a circuit, once every year, to ascertain the state of every district within his jurisdiction. When this officer has received the rents from all the headmen of his district, he sends the amount to the European collector, of whom one is appointed by government to every ten or twelve districts. Under this system, the government takes a certain share of the produce, or its value in money; and the cultivators are protected from oppression, by being allowed an opportunity, once a year, of stating to the chief authority any grievances of which they may have to complain. This is towards the time of harvest, when the native collectors are summoned by the English government to settle their accounts, and give an exact statement of the condition of the villages, the extent of each farm, the value of its stock, and the nature of the crops. The farmers are then assembled, and the accounts read to them, in order that they may correct any mis-statements. If any man thinks that he has been unjustly used, he is at liberty to make his complaint; and when all disputes are settled, each receives his lease for the following year.

In Bombay, the lands are farmed either to the headman of the village, or to an association of the ryots, who contract with the government for a certain sum annually, and take the chance of profit or loss.

The great mass of the people of India are cultivators, but the mode of agriculture has not yet been much improved; and the implements used in husbandry are of a very primitive construction. Nevertheless, owing to the fertility of the soil, the spontaneous productions of the country are most numerous, and two crops are yielded yearly; one in September and October, the other in March and April.

In most parts of India, the soil is so extremely fertile and easy of management, that a simple wooden plough (see page 316) is sufficient to turn up the earth, and render it fit to receive the seed. The plough is drawn by oxen, which are harnessed to the two wooden pegs in front; the husbandman follows to guide it, and holds in one hand the upright pieces of wood intended for that purpose, whilst, with the other, he pours the seed into the mouth of the funnel at the top. The seed runs out through an opening at the lower part of the funnel, and is, by this means, thrown into the furrows made by the ploughshare, which has immediately preceded it.

Machine for drawing water for irrigating land.

In Indian cultivation, the greatest attention is requisite in irrigating the soil, the water for which is raised from wells by a simple mill constructed by the natives for that purpose, and is worked by oxen, which walk round a circle, in the same manner as the horse in a common English mill; the ranges of buckets are, by this means, set in motion, and have been so constructed, that they turn over when they reach the top, and pour their contents into a trough, by which the water is conveyed to any distance. The buckets then come down empty, in order to be refilled from the well beneath.

Among the numerous and valuable products of Hindostan is, the indigo plant, which is cultivated to a great extent in Bengal, where there are from three to four hundred indigo factories, some of which belong to natives, but the greater number to Europeans. The indigo factors are, in general, very wealthy, as the trade has much increased since the revolution in St. Domingo, which used to supply all Europe with that commodity. It is now exported from Bengal in large quantities, to France, Holland, and Germany.

Sugar, which is used by the Hindus in almost every thing they eat or drink, is so generally cultivated, that almost every village has its little plantation of sugar-cane, and a coarse kind of sugar is also extracted from the palmyra, and cocoa-nut tree. Sugar is produced in nearly every part of Hindostan, but that of Bengal is the best, and its manufacture is carried on largely at Benares. Another staple commodity is tobacco, immense quantities of which are required for home consumption, as it is used by all classes of the people. Coffee is raised in Malabar, where the first coffee plantation was established in 1823. Cotton is grown abundantly in all its varieties, the most beautiful being the fruit of a lofty tree, covered first with crimson flowers, which, in falling off, leave a pod filled with cotton of a lighter and more silky quality than that of the common cotton shrub. The manufacture of cotton goods, however, has greatly declined, in consequence of the introduction of goods from Manchester and Glasgow, which have superseded the native manufactures as clothing for the generality of the people. The chief silk districts are in Bengal, but the silk is inferior to that of China, where more care is bestowed on its culture. It is sold in cocoons by the farmers to the agents of the East India Company, who have large factories for reeling it on the simple Italian principle.

Oil mill.

Oil is used in India for many purposes, and is expressed from different kinds of seeds, by a mill of simple construction, which is kept in motion by an ox, which is harnessed to it; the seed, or other material, is placed in a kind of trough or hopper in the centre, from which the oil is drawn off through a small aperture in the side.

In the neighbourhood of Ghazepore, a British station on the Ganges, roses are cultivated for the purpose of being made into rose water, and the perfume commonly known by the name of otto (or more correctly, attar) of roses.

KINGDOM OF CABUL.

WHILE the English were extending their empire in the east, Bonaparte had become Emperor of France; and although that great potentate was sensible that the last remains of French influence in India had been annihilated by the fall of Tippoo, yet he manifested a disposition to restore it, and with that view sent an embassy in 1808 to the court of Persia, where it was favourably received by the reigning sovereign, Futteh Ali Shah. This movement induced the British government to send a mission to Persia to negotiate a treaty by which the danger of a French invasion of the British territories, on that side, might be obviated; and an ambassador was also despatched to the court of Cabul, as the road from Persia to Hindostan lay through the country of the Afghans, to whose history it will now be proper to return.

After the battle of Panniput in 1761, it was expected that the Afghan monarch, Ahmed Shah, would have assumed the title of Emperor, at Delhi; but he wisely returned to the kingdom he had founded for himself, which comprised all the fine provinces beyond the Indus, with the rich vale of Cashmere, and the territories of Balk and Herat. These together formed the great monarchy of Cabul, or Afghanistan.

The Afghans had never been governed previously by a king; yet the good policy of Ahmed Shah enabled him to conciliate the many different tribes that constituted this warlike half-civilised nation. He did not interfere with their customs: so that each tribe formed, as before, a distinct commonwealth, divided into several clans, each of which was headed by a chief, who bore the title of Khan. The superior of a whole tribe is sometimes called Sirdar, a military title, meaning general. The Afghan chiefs possess but a very limited authority over their people, who look upon them rather as magistrates than rulers, and are governed more by the laws and customs of their tribe, than the will of their chief. Each tribe has its own territory, where the people live in villages, and the khans in small forts, generally destitute of furniture, and of all that, in a more advanced state of civilisation, is necessary to ensure even a moderate degree of comfort The Afghans of the plains cultivate the land, and the khan takes a share of the produce as rent; but the peasants are not his vassals, nor has he any more authority over them than a Scottish laird has over his tenantry. If he possess flocks and herds, they are kept at distant pastures, under the care of shepherds, who dwell in tents, and form a numerous class of the population.

Afghan shepherd.

The present city of Candahar was built by Ahmed Shah, and was the seat of government during his reign, when it was a rich and populous capital. It is a regularly built town, with four wide bazaars, which meet in the centre, where they form a handsome market-place, which is covered with a dome, and one of them leads to the palace or citadel, where the king chiefly resided. As long as the court was held at Candahar, most of the great khans had houses in that city, and its trade flourished in proportion to the wealth and consequence of its inhabitants; but when Timur removed the seat of government to Cabul, Candahar became a town of secondary importance.

The true Afghans never engage in trade. All the shopkeepers, artificers, and merchants, are of other nations, many of them Hindus, who pay a small tax for the privilege of exercising their several professions, and observing the customs of their religion, which they are allowed to do, with the exception of that of exhibiting their idols in public; and, in consequence of this restriction, no Hindu festivals are held in Afghanistan.

During the vigorous goverment of Ahmed Shah, regular courts of justice were held in all the great cities of Cabul, and they were kept in order by an efficient police; but the country has suffered so much since that time, from the effects of civil war, and the want of a powerful head, that all these good regulations have fallen into disuse, and the kingdom of Cabul is no longer what it was in the days of that great prince with whom it rose, and with whom it fell.

Ahmed Shah died in 1773, and was succeeded by his son, Timur, a prince of great talent, but deficient in the policy that had maintained his father's influence over a people so difficult to govern as the Afghans. He was ambitious of possessing absolute power, and thus made enemies of those chiefs whose friendship had been the main support of Ahmed's throne. Under these circumstances, it is not surprising that the country should have been disturbed by frequent insurrections during the reign of Timur Shah, which lasted twenty years, and that some of the states which had been conquered and made tributary by his father, should have taken advantage of the unsettled state of affairs to attempt the recovery of their independence. Among these was Sinde, a wild, and in some parts, a barren province, ruled, in the time of Ahmed, by a prince of Persian origin, named Abdoolnubbee, who, in consequence of his tyranny, was deposed soon after the accession of Timur, to whom he fled for protection.

The revolution that deprived Abdoolnubbee of his principality, was effected by the Talpoores, a warlike tribe, who constituted the military population of the country, and have kept possession of it ever since, subject to the king of Cabul; for Timur, after several vain attempts to restore the deposed sovereign, accepted the submission of the rebels, and consented to invest their chief with the government, on condition that he should continue to pay the customary tribute; which he promised to do. Some time afterwards, three brothers agreed to divide the country amongst them; and it was long governed by three military chiefs, who received their investiture from the king of Cabul, and ruled in his name, under the title of Ameers, or commanders of Sinde. Their numbers have since increased; and at the commencement of the late war in India, the province was found divided into a number of petty principalities, of which every chief bore the title of Ameer, and was a military despot.

The death of Timur Shah, which took place in 1793, was followed by a civil war; for as there was no fixed rule of succession with regard to the throne, several of his sons came forward as claimants, the fourth of whom, Shah Zeman, having the strongest party among the Sirdars, was proclaimed, and placed by force on the throne. It is said that his success was owing to his mother, who gained the support of a powerful khan, the father of the grand vizier, by sending to him her veil; an expedient sometimes adopted by females of high rank, when they would implore the aid of him to whom the token is sent. It would seem, therefore, that a feeling allied to a spirit of chivalry existed in Afghanistan, and that knights were not wanting to fight in a lady's cause.

The ceremony of Zeman's coronation was no sooner over, than an ambassador arrived at Cabul from Tippoo Saib, who offered splendid bribes to the new monarch, to induce him to join in the wars against the English; but Zeman had plenty of employment at home, for several of his brothers were in arms, for the purpose of depriving him of the throne, and the whole province of Cashmere was in rebellion. It is needless to enter into the particulars of the wars that ensued among the brothers, one of whom, Prince Mahmud, was defeated in battle; and another, Prince Humayun, was made captive, deprived of sight, and put in confinement for the rest of his life. Mahmud, after wandering about in exile for some time, attended by a few faithful followers, was induced to return by the news of a rebellion, headed by the famous Futteh Khan, which ended in his own elevation to the throne, and the imprisonment of Shah Zeman, whose eyes were put out, according to the barbarous practice so common among the eastern nations.

The brief reign of Mahmud was marked by the anarchy that usually attends the success of a military adventurer, and in less than three years, he was deposed by his brother, Shuja-ul-Mulk, who ascended the throne of Cabul in the year 1803. Shah Zeman was immediately released, and has ever since lived in a style befitting his rank, under the protection of the British government.

Shah Shuja maintained the sovereignty during the space of six years, but he had not ability sufficient to restore order to the state, or power to the government, which was so weak, that every discontented chief was able to raise a rebellion, knowing that, in case of failure, he could escape punishment by seeking shelter in the midst of his clan. The most dangerous of these was Futteh Khan. He was a powerful chief of the Durani tribe, and his influence might have supported Shuja on the throne, if that monarch had been wise enough to have secured his friendship by granting him certain appointments that had been held by his father; but this favour was refused, and the indignant chief retired from court, and offered his services to Mahmud, the ex-king, who, by his aid, was in a few months restored to the throne of Cabul, and Shah Shuja was obliged to leave the kingdom, and seek safety in the British dominions.

It was just before the dethronement of this ill-fated monarch, that the English, as before stated, having some reason to apprehend an invasion of the French by the way of Persia, sent a mission to Cabul, with a view of engaging the government of that country to oppose such an attempt, if it should be made. When the embassy arrived in the early part of 1809, Shah Shuja, who had already commenced the war with his brother Mah-

Afghan lady in her riding dress.

mud, was holding his court at Peshawer, a wealthy and populous city of Cabul, situated in an extensive and fertile plain, surrounded by mountains, and studded with villages, orchards, and mulberry groves. Like other oriental cities, Peshawer is a busy, crowded place, with narrow streets, full of shops, and thronged with men of all nations, in every variety of costume.

One of the peculiarities of this, and other towns of Cabul, is, that wheel carriages not being used in that country, the ladies ride on horseback in the streets, wrapped in a thick white veil; and as they sit on their horses in the same fashion as gentlemen, they always wear a huge pair of white cotton boots for riding.

The court was held at that time with great splendour. When the ambassador was admitted to an audience, he found the King seated on a superb throne, dressed in a green tunic embroidered with flowers of gold, interspersed with precious stones, and wearing a breast-plate of diamonds. On his head was a crown, covered entirely with diamonds, and radiated like the crowns of the ancient kings. He wore round his neck several strings of large pearls, and on his arms bracelets of emeralds, with a diamond called the Coni Noor, which is known as one of the largest in the world. The hall, which was open on all sides, was supported by pillars, a fountain played in its centre, and it was covered with rich Persian carpets, round the edges of which were small mats, of silk and gold, for the nobles to stand on, all of whom were dressed in cloth of gold, the usual state dress of that period at the court of Cabul. The embassy was most graciously received, but the king was then preparing to set out on the unfortunate campaign that ended in his loss of the crown, and as the British government was not inclined to interfere in the affairs of the state, the embassy returned to India.

Shortly afterwards, Shah Shuja, having been defeated, fled from his kingdom, and, after many misfortunes, placed himself under the protection of the English, who granted a pension for his support, and allowed him to reside at the frontier town of Loodiana. Mahmud again took possession of the throne, but the government was left to the chief minister, Futteh Khan, who ruled, according to his own pleasure, in the name of the king. By the aid of the powerful chief, Runjeet Singh, who had lately established a new kingdom in the Punjab, Futteh Khan recovered the province of Cashmere, and also gained a victory over the Persians, who had laid siege to Herat, to enforce a demand of tribute made by the Shah of Persia. But the successful vizier sullied his victory, and accelerated his own ruin, by plundering the palace, and even the harem of the governor, who was a brother of the king; on which Prince Kamran, Mahmud's eldest son, in revenge for the insult offered to his uncle, caused Futteh Khan to be imprisoned, and deprived of sight; and, soon afterwards, he was put to death, by command of the ungrateful monarch whom he had placed on the throne.

The death of the vizier threw the whole country into confusion, for Mahmud was again deposed, and a series of wars followed, which terminated in the breaking up of the empire into several petty principalities, of which the most important, that of Cabul, was seized by Dost Mohammed, a younger brother of the unfortunate vizier, Futteh Khan.

The usurpation of this prince was the cause of the late war in Afghanistan, which was undertaken by the British Governor General with a view of restoring the exiled monarch, Shah Shuja, to his throne; but other, and more important events that occurred in India during the long interval between the flight of Shuja and his restoration, now claim attention, and will be related under, what may be termed, the reigns of the British Governors of India.

MARQUIS OF HASTINGS.

THE Governor General of India held his court with all the state of a sovereign prince, at Calcutta, where a magnificent palace had been built by the Marquis Wellesley. The extensive plain, in the front of which this edifice was erected, was adorned with a great number of handsome detached mansions, which were the residences of the principal English families, and were placed in the midst of large gardens. The city had also been greatly enlarged and improved; or, it may be said, that a new city had been added to the old one. The latter was called the Black, or native

Drawn by B. Claxton

On Stone by Dean & Co.

CALCUTTA.

London Dean & Co. Threadneedle St.

town, while the new part was distinguished as the European quarter, and consisted of fine streets and squares, formed of elegant buildings, mostly detached from each other, but having a communication by stone terraces, and being shaded by a variety of luxuriant trees. Between the Black town and the European quarter, were many dwellings in the eastern style, built within inclosed courts, and inhabited chiefly by wealthy merchants, some of whom were natives of Bengal, others Parsees, or Armenians. Besides the government house, the new town boasted of several other fine

The Government House.

public buildings, among which were two large churches, a town house, and a court house, to which was afterwards added a theatre; and Calcutta had, in a short time, become an extensive, gay, and populous capital.

The Marquis of Hastings succeeded Lord Minto as Governor General of India, in 1813, and continued to exercise the vice-regal authority for nearly ten years, during which he did much for the benefit of the native population, by promoting education, projecting and executing many useful public works, and suppressing those predatory hordes already mentioned under the name of Pindarries, who had become the scourge of the whole country. The Pindarrie chiefs held lands in the dominions of Holkar and Sindia, both of whom had large bodies of these desperadoes attached to their armies, for whose maintenance they had granted portions of territory on feudal tenure, which gave them a degree of consideration, notwithstanding their bad character. They did not belong to any particular caste or tribe, but seem to have consisted of the worst of almost every nation in India; and, when not engaged in the service of the native princes, roamed about the country in large bands, of from two to three thousand, for the purpose of obtaining plunder, for which end, they did not scruple to commit the most revolting outrages. Some were well mounted, and armed with spears and matchlocks; but the greater number were supplied but indifferently with horses and arms of any description; and every man depended on his own resources for obtaining food, both for himself and the animal on which he rode. Their costume was as varied as their equipments; but all were distinguished by a ferocity of aspect that corresponded with their mode of life.

The sufferings experienced by the helpless villagers, when so unfortunate as to be visited by a party of these marauders, were most severe. Their houses were ransacked, and set on fire, the women and children were often murdered, and the men subjected to the most excruciating tortures, to make them confess where they had concealed either money or ornaments.

For some years, the Pindarries confined their ravages to the provinces of Malwa, Rajputana, and Berar: but, after a time, they began to make incursions into the territories of the Nizam and the Peishwa, but still refrained from visiting the British possessions. They were accompanied in all their expeditions by their wives, who rode on small horses or camels, and were no less rapacious and cruel than themselves; and after every predatory excursion, they returned home to share the spoils, when the elephants and palanquins were given up to the chief, but the rest of the ill-gotten treasure was equally divided, and publicly exposed for sale at a kind of fair held for that purpose, where the women sold the goods, while the men amused themselves with smoking, and playing at various games. It is stated, that these fairs were always numerously attended, although the nature of the business transacted at them was perfectly well known. At the time when the Marquis of Hastings arrived in India, the Pindarries mustered a force of not less than forty thousand cavalry, so that there was no chance of putting a stop to their depredations, but by a regular war of extermination. As they had not, however, up to that period, begun to infest the British possessions to any extent, the attention of the Governor was not directed towards any immediate measures for their subjugation.

But there was another predatory horde, called the Ghoorkas, inhabitants of the mountainous regions of Nepaul, who were nominally subject to the Emperor of China, but were governed by a prince of their own tribe. These people had seized on some territories belonging to the British government, which they refused to give up, and had been guilty of some violent outrages during a negociation with the English; so that a war with them was inevitable. The prince of Nepaul applied for assistance to the Chinese Emperor, Kea-king, who gave orders that an army should be sent to his aid; but when he became acquainted with the cause of the war, he declared that the Ghoorkas were in the wrong. He therefore refused to assist them, and revoked his orders for sending the troops.

A Goorka chief.

The English were very unsuccessful in the early part of this contest, partly owing to the inability of their commanders, partly to the nature of the country in which it was carried on. The fact, however, that they had sustained several defeats, became known to the Mahrattas, who considered this as a favourable opportunity to make head against them; and Sindia lost no time in forming an alliance with some of the Rajput princes, and with Runjeet Singh, the powerful ruler of the Seiks, who had long since assumed the title of King of Lahore. The Seiks had been gradually increasing in numbers since the fall of the empire, both in the Punjab, and the country between the Sutlej and the Jumna, which, about the year 1770, had fallen under the dominion of a confederacy of Seik chieftains, one of whom was the grandfather of Runjeet Singh.

Runjeet was about twelve years old, when the death of his father left him in possession of a large territory, of which his mother assumed the government during his minority; and being an ambitious, unprincipled woman, she entirely neglected the education of her son, as a means of retaining her own power; so that the boy was not even taught to read or write. She became, at length, so unpopular, that she was assassinated, some say with the connivance of her son, who assumed the government at the age of seventeen, a short time before the fall of Tippoo Saib. It happened that Runjeet had performed some service for Shah Zeman, king of the Afghans, who, in return, invested him with the government of Lahore; and after the dethronement of that monarch, Runjeet asserted his independence, and, with the general consent of the Seiks, took the title of King of Lahore, and soon established his authority over the whole of the Punjab.

The Seiks were not, at this period, the barbarous fanatics which they had been in former days; but they were still a military nation, and but little civilised. They suffered their hair and beards to grow to a great length, and wore high turbans; but, with the exception of a large scarf, which persons of distinction usually displayed, thrown negligently over one shoulder, they did not encumber themselves with much clothing. Their arms were bows and matchlocks, the bow being so necessary an appendage to a man of rank, that on paying a visit of ceremony, he always had a finely ornamented one in his hand, and an embroidered quiver at his side.

Runjeet Singh being anxious to keep on friendly terms with the British government, concluded a treaty with an envoy sent to his court for that purpose, by which he agreed not to attempt to extend his territories to the east, beyond the boundary of the Sutlej river; but this treaty did not limit his ambition in other directions; and during the civil wars of the Afghans that followed the dethronement of Shah Shuja, he made great additions to his kingdom, both on the south and the west. The unfortunate Shuja, when he fled from Cabul, had at first sought shelter at Lahore, where he was detained for some time as a prisoner, and compelled to give up all his jewels; so that Runjeet Singh became the possessor of the famous diamond, Coni Noor, which signifies "the mountain of light." The murder of Futteh Khan, and consequent breaking up of the Afghan monarchy, opened the way for the further aggrandizement of the king of Lahore, who crossed the Indus, and possessed himself of Peshawer; soon after which, he became master of the beautiful valley of Kashmere. He was, therefore, a powerful monarch, and might, in conjunction with Sindia and the Peishwa, have proved a formidable foe, had not the British, by the termination of the Nepaulese war in their favour, found more leisure for watching and counteracting the hostile movements of the Mahrattas.

Bajee Rao had given his entire confidence to an unworthy favourite, named Trimbuckjee, who had an inveterate hatred to all Europeans; and in that spirit, instigated his master to pursue a most dishonourable course of conduct towards his English allies. At length, it happened that a Bramin, ambassador from one of the Indian courts to that of Poona, was assassinated by order of Trimbuckjee, in defiance of a guarantee for his safety given by the British government; and for this outrage, it was intimated to the Peishwa that he must either give up his minister as a prisoner to the English, or prepare for a war. He chose the former alternative; and Trimbuckjee was confined in the fortress of Tannah, in the island of Salsette, from which he soon contrived to make his escape, and began to organize large bodies of Mahrattas and Pindarries, just about the time when the inroads of the latter into the British territories had determined the Governor General to take active measures for their total extirpation.

The first step was to disable the Peishwa from giving them any support; and as he was in no condition to resist the British power, he was compelled to sign a fresh treaty, by which he made such concessions as deprived him of all claim to be regarded as the head of the Mahratta states. Sindia was, at the same time, required to enter into an engagement to assist in the warfare against the Pindarries; and as he saw no other way of avoiding a war with the English, he was obliged to comply. Holkar, who had been the chief patron of the Pindarries, was dead, and his son, a mere youth, had not the same influence that had enabled his father to protect those lawless bands; so that they had but little chance of making a successful resistance. Their lands were surrounded; the passes by which they might have escaped, were guarded; and parties of them that were dispersed over the country were pursued, and great numbers of them were killed in the skirmishes that took place; while those who escaped, either perished in the jungles, or fell by the hands of the peasantry, who did not fail to use this opportunity of avenging themselves for the sufferings they had endured from these freebooters, who had long been so terrible to them.

The result of the Pindarrie war freed the country from a race of most formidable robbers; for those who survived, adopted a new course of life, and devoted their attention to agricultural pursuits; so that, in time, the Pindarries, who still retained their name, were only known as industrious farmers.

While the war was still going on, the Peishwa had been secretly plotting against the English, with a hope of recovering all he had lost by the treaty of Poona. Bribes had been even offered to the Sepoys to induce them to desert from the British army; and, when there could no longer be any doubt that the Bramin prince was preparing for hostilities, a body of English troops was ordered to proceed at once to Poona. On hearing of this movement, Bajee Rao collected all his forces on the plain near his capital, where a desperate battle was fought; and the Mahrattas, though greatly superior in numbers, were driven from the field. The English then marched into Poona without opposition, and the Peishwa made a hasty retreat. He soon, however, rallied his forces; but was again defeated at Korygaum: and this second victory decided the contest.

Bajee Rao, finding there was no hope of re-establishing his authority, surrendered himself to the English, who allowed him to fix his residence at Beithoor, a place considered holy by the Hindus, in the neighbourhood of

Cawnpore, a British station within the territory of Oude. Thither the fallen potentate was conducted under a suitable escort, a liberal pension being allowed for his support: and thus ended the Bramin dynasty. It was then resolved to restore the house of Satara to the throne, and the Raja, Pertab Sing, was enthroned with much ceremony, on the eleventh of April, 1818; but his territory was limited to a tract extending from Poona to Goa, not including the city of Poona, which, with the rest of the Mahratta country, was annexed to the British possessions in India, and an English resident officer was appointed to every district, invested with the powers of judge, magistrate, and collector of the revenues. The subordinate offices, were conferred, with liberal salaries, on natives. All the principal stations were occupied by a strong military force, and great numbers of the irregular native troops that had served under Bajee Rao, were enlisted in the British service, and became good and faithful soldiers; for it is one of the peculiarities of the Hindu troops, that they serve with fidelity the master who pays them, without any scruples on the score of patriotism; which is a sentiment unknown among a people who have always been subject to foreign dominion, and care little who governs them, provided they are protected, fed, and clothed.

Hill village.

In making the new regulations, great care was taken not to shock the prejudices of the natives by any unnecessary interference with their laws and usages; while those who had suffered loss of property or employment by the change of government were, as far as possible, provided for; and the villagers conciliated by the protection afforded them against the hordes of banditti, from which mountainous countries are seldom free.

The greatest enemies to the establishment of British ascendancy in the Mahratta country were the Bramins, who naturally opposed a revolution that destroyed the supremacy of their order, and thereby deteriorated their influence generally. Several insurrections broke out, headed by men of that class, some of whom, being seized, were put to death by a military execution; after which the country was gradually tranquillized, and the benefits of the new system of government were sensibly felt. The farming of revenues, one of the greatest sources of oppression in India, was abolished, and the collection, of the rents left in the hands of the hereditary headmen of the villages, who were the government agents, as in the Madras presidency. The holders of jaghirs or feudal estates were to be left in possession of their lands, so long as they showed no disaffection towards the new rulers of the country.

The administration of the Marquis of Hastings, was a period of considerable improvement in India. It was under the auspices of this highly talented nobleman, that the great canals which have perpetuated the names of Ali Merdan Khan and the Emperor Feroze Shah, were re-opened; and a new one, since finished, was projected, to run through the country east of the Jumna. The famous canal of Ali Merdan Khan, and the ceremony of its opening, have been already described. It passes through Delhi, and by means of an extensive aqueduct, supplies the Emperor's palace with constant streams of fresh water. In the space between the hills near Delhi and the palace, there are innumerable channels under ground, which conduct the water to the houses of the nobles, as well as to each division of the city; so that the whole community are bountifully supplied with it. Numerous mills have been erected on both these canals.

Many tracts of jungle have since been cleared and brought under cultivation, and the land has altogether become more valuable. The Governor General also formed a new road, two hundred miles in length, from the commercial town of Mirzapore, on the Ganges, to that of Jubbulpore on the Nerbudda; a most useful work, since the generality of the roads in central India are impassable for wheel carriages during the greater part of the year, so that, on a failure of the crops, the poor people were sometimes reduced to a state of starvation, because there were no means of sending supplies from the more fertile districts, an evil that is remedied to a great extent by the new road of Mirzapore.

The establishment of schools for the instruction of natives was begun by the Marquis of Hastings; and the Hindu College at Poona was instituted during his government.

LORD AMHERST.

THE Marquis of Hastings, in 1823, was succeeded in the government of India, by Lord Amherst, who had been employed, a few years previously, to conduct an embassy to the court of Peking, on the subject of the grievances sustained by the British merchants at Canton. India was, at this period, in a state of unusual tranquillity, owing to the wise and successful measures of the late Governor General; but scarcely had Lord Amherst assumed the control of affairs, when the English became involved in a war with the Burmese, which originated in the following circumstances.

In the province of Arracan, belonging to the Burman empire, were extensive tracts of country cultivated by a race of people who were held in bondage by the sovereign, who was styled King of Ava. These slaves having long suffered under the most oppressive treatment, had, during the latter part of the eighteenth century, begun to emigrate in vast numbers, seeking shelter in the British territories, where they were reduced to the greatest distress, and many perished from want; until the government of Calcutta took their case into consideration, and resolved to settle them on the waste lands of Chittagong, a province adjoining Arracan. In the meantime, provision was made for the relief of their immediate necessities, until, by degrees, they were established in villages constructed by themselves, and had cleared tracts of forest land for cultivation.

Many complaints were made, from time to time, by the Burmese government, respecting the protection afforded to the refugees, who were claimed as slaves of the state; but the British rulers did not think themselves justified in expelling, by force, a large body of people who had come to them for shelter from oppression; nor would it have been easy or politic to have done so, as they amounted to many thousands of families, who had cleared and were cultivating a vast deal of land, previously unproductive.

Many and violent were the disputes that arose at various times between the British government, and the court of Ava, respecting the emigrants; but no serious hostilities occurred, till after the arrival of Lord Amherst, at Calcutta, when the Burmese, without any previous declaration of war, took possession of a small island, near Chittagong, belonging to the English, and committed other acts of aggression, which obliged the British authorities to send an army into the Burman empire. A war was thus commenced, which lasted about two years, and was carried on entirely within the dominions of the King of Ava, who was obliged, in the end, to make peace on such terms as were dictated by the English, who acquired by the treaty a large addition of territory on the eastern coast of the Bay of Bengal.

Burmese war-boat.

The details of this war, like those of most of the previous wars in India, possess very little general interest; but one of its important results was, the annexation to the British territories of the extensive province of Assam, of which the right of sovereignty was transferred by the King of Ava to the English. Assam is an immense plain, watered by many large rivers, and situated between India and China. It is bounded on all sides but the west by chains of lofty mountains, and bears a great resemblance to China, in its general features.

Much of the country is under rice cultivation, but there are large tracts covered with timber trees, some of which are so large, that they will admit of being hollowed into barges of a considerable size, and these vessels are very numerous, as all carriage is by water. Elephants, Rhinoceroses, and all the animals common to the forests in the neighbourhood of the lower Ganges, are also found in the forests of Assam. It is supposed that the original inhabitants came from China, and were, at some distant period, a numerous and wealthy people, as the remains of cities and temples, now overrun with tangled shrubs, indicate the former existence of a large population.

The Emperor Akber conquered Assam, which was then added to the Mogul Empire; but the frequent floods, the inroads of the mountaineers, and the wars of the native chiefs, reduced the country, in time, to a most deplorable state; and it fell under the dominion of the Burmese, who treated the inhabitants with so much cruelty, that they gladly seized the opportunity of this war to place themselves under British protection; and thus the country of Assam was added to our eastern empire. The people consist of Hindus, Mohammedans, and a few Christians, descended from the Portuguese. They are, in general, exceedingly poor, and many of them are slaves. The soil and climate of Assam are favourable for the growth of the tea-plant, which is already cultivated there to some extent, by a company formed for that purpose.

After the successful termination of the Burmese war, the Governor General made a visit to the court of Delhi, to settle a point of some importance, which was, the relative position in which the British government and the Emperor were to stand, in future, with regard to each other. Hitherto, the sovereign of Delhi had been left in possession of the nominal supremacy over all the other powers in India; but it was now thought a fit time to assert the independence of British authority; and the powerless monarch, Akber the Second, had no alternative but to acquiesce in a measure that deprived him of the last shadow of imperial dignity; still he was painfully alive to this additional humiliation, and sent an embassy to represent his case at the court of England, in the hope of being restored to his former rank, as superior lord of India, but the mission was unsuccessful. The ambassador, on this occasion, was the Raja Rammohun Roy, a Hindu, distinguished for his high rank, talents, and knowledge of English literature.

During the administration of Lord Amherst, an expedition was sent to Bhurtpore, one of the upper provinces, for the purpose of restoring to the throne the rightful heir, an infant, whose place had been usurped by his cousin, Doorjun Sal. The enterprise was both difficult and dangerous, on account of the strongly-fortified position of the city, which is seated in the midst of a plain, surrounded by an extensive forest, approaching nearly to the edge of a wide moat, that could, at any time be filled with water from a neighbouring lake. The town was also defended by a wall, flanked with strong towers and bastions; and the citadel was inclosed by a separate wall and moat. The siege of this celebrated fortress, which had hitherto been considered as impregnable, was commenced on the 23rd of December, 1825; and it was taken by storm, on the 18th of the following month; when Doorjun Sal was made a captive, and conveyed to the fortress of Allahabad, where he occupied a suite of apartments assigned to state prisoners of rank, and was allowed to receive English visitors.

The young Raja thus recovered his inheritance; but, according to the terms stipulated, his dominions were placed under the protection of the British government.

LORD WILLIAM BENTINCK.

LORD AMHERST was succeeded in the government of India, in 1827, by Lord William Bentinck, whose administration was distinguished by several acts of great importance, one of which was, the suppression of those fearful associations of assassins known under the name of Thugs.

The Thugs had existed in India for more than twenty years. They were organized into a regular brotherhood, and bound to each other by certain mysterious rites, which gave to their society, in their own eyes, at least, the character of a religious order, if the word religious may be thus profaned. The object of the confederacy was to rob and murder travellers, not by attacking them openly, in the usual manner of banditti, but by assuming various disguises, and inducing people to join them for the sake of company.

It appears strange that, although every body had heard of Thugs, few persons gave credit to the rumours that were spread abroad from time to time, of the numerous murders committed by them; for the disappearance of travellers in India does not occasion much surprise, nor lead to any enquiries, as the peculiar customs of the Hindus expose them continually to such casualties. From time immemorial, it has been customary for men to make long pilgrimages on foot; and of the thousands who leave their homes in the course of a year for that purpose, it is not surprising that many should perish from some one of the various accidents to which all wayfarers are subjected, in traversing the plains of central India. Robbers are numerous, tigers are frequently encountered in the jungles, and often the weary wanderer can find no better place of repose for the night, than the ground, where he is exposed to the dangers of malaria, or the bite of some venomous reptile.

These were causes sufficient to account for the loss of those who, after their departure from home were never heard of again; nor was it till the attention of the British authorities was called to the fact of many bodies being found in the wells of the Doab and Bundelkund, that the truth was brought to light. A murder was traced to a party of persons in the ordinary guise of travellers. They were apprehended, and one of them, on a promise that his life should be spared, made the dreadful disclosures that enabled the government to take immediate steps for the suppression of a fraternity whose crimes are unequalled in the annals of any country in the world.

By the confession of this miscreant, it appeared that the Thugs formed separate societies, each having a superior, who was obeyed by all the rest. They used secret signs, like freemasons, by which they could recognise each other, and usually lived in the villages, engaged apparently in the same pursuits as the rest of the inhabitants. By this means, they had opportunities of learning who were going on journeys, and what property they would have about them. Information was then given to the superior, and a plan laid to entrap the unsuspecting victim; the most common method being for two or three persons to join him on the road, and enter into conversation, when they pretended to discover that they were going to the same place as he was, and would invite him to become one of their party. Towards evening, they would sit down with him to drink and smoke; when, on a given signal, only understood by the initiated, a noose was suddenly thrown over the head of the unfortunate traveller, who was strangled in an instant. The body was then robbed, and thrown into a well, or a grave that had been prepared for the purpose. These murders were not always single; but parties of four or five, or even more, were often despatched at once, and the bodies hastily buried.

Such was the diabolical system that had been carried on to an enormous extent, for above twenty years, when it was discovered as before mentioned; and vigorous measures were adopted for the apprehension of the Thugs, who were conveyed to Sangor, the capital of the Nerbudda districts in central India, and the place appointed for their trial. Numbers of them, betrayed by their former companions, were taken in the villages in which they resided, by parties of Sepoys sent for that purpose, accompanied by those who had given the information, and whose presence was necessary to identify the culprits.

Great was the horror of the villagers on such occasions, to find that some of their intimate friends and neighbours were no other than Thugs; and happy were they to see these wolves in sheep's clothing marched off to the prisons of Sangor. Property to an immense amount was usually found in their houses, consisting of such valuables as were likely to have been taken from travellers. All that could be identified, was restored to the families of the unfortunate individuals from whom it had been taken, and the rest was sold for government; and the proceeds were employed in the erection of two new prisons, at Saugor.

By the end of 1836, above two thousand Thugs had been brought to trial. Many were hanged, some imprisoned for life; and others transported to penal settlements; but although their associations were thus, in a great measure broken up, it is to be feared they are not, even yet, totally subdued in some of the wildest parts of the country.

Another great benefit conferred on the Hindu population, about this time, was the abolition of the rite of suttee, throughout all the territories under British authority. This humane measure was strongly opposed by a numerous class of the natives, whose prejudices were in favour of ancient customs; but happily, there were many who, more enlightened, warmly applauded the act that prohibited the burning of widows; and it is to be hoped that the efforts which are made to bestow the blessings of education on the people of India, will lead, in time, to the extinction of this revolting sacrifice, even in the independent native states.

Lord William Bentinck was a great friend to the diffusion of knowledge among the Hindus, who are in great measure indebted to his benevolent exertions for their present improved state. Under the auspices of that excellent nobleman, many schools were instituted in various parts of India, where the pupils were provided with translations of the best English works on history, geography, mechanics, and other useful branches of knowledge; but in the year 1835, it was resolved that the English language should be the medium of instruction throughout the country; and since that time, English has been studied at the more remote courts of Hindostan, and English tutors have been engaged to educate the sons of many of the rajas. Runjeet Singh, the ruler of the Punjab, consented to the establishment of an English school at Lahore, his capital; and some of the princes of Rajputana followed his example.

It was during the administration of Lord William Bentinck, in 1833, that the expiration of the Company's charter, produced a material change in the commercial affairs of India, by depriving that body of all its exclusive rights, as a trading association, and abolishing the restrictions that had hitherto prevented private individuals from holding lands in the British possessions, or trading to the interior without a license.

The monopoly of the China trade was abolished by the new charter, which was granted for twelve years, but the government of India was left in the hands of the Company. About the same time, two of the native princes, the King of Mysore, and the Raja of Coorg, were deposed, on account of their bad government, and their territories annexed to the British dominions.

Up to this time, the British empire in India had been divided into the three presidencies of Bengal, Madras, and Bombay; but in consequence of these acquisitions of territory, a fourth presidency was established for the north-west provinces, including Delhi and Agra, the seat of which was

Palace of Allahabad.

at Allahabad, where the Governor resides in the ancient fortress of the Emperor Akber.

Each presidency has its separate army, but the Governor-General is commander-in-chief of the whole; and he has authority to make peace or war, and to direct the military operations in any part of the country. The number of European troops stationed in India, is about thirty thousand, of whom two thirds are Queen's regiments, and the rest in the pay of the East India Company; but the main body of the Indian army is composed of native troops, or sepoys, whose numbers vary according to exigencies, but generally average above two hundred thousand men. Most of the Hindu sepoys in the Bengal army are men of high caste, principally Rajputs and Bramins, but there are also many Musselman soldiers in all the regiments, and all are at liberty to observe the ceremonies of their religion, which is, no doubt, one great means of preserving their attachment and fidelity. When old or disabled, the sepoy retires on a pension to

CHITTAPORE ROAD, CALCUTTA.

his native village, carrying with him his soldier's uniform, which he proudly displays on all festive occasions.

In 1835, Lord William Bentinck resigned the government of India, and Lord Auckland was appointed to succeed him, but did not arrive at Calcutta until the following year. In the mean time, the administration was conducted by Sir Charles Metcalf, who distinguished himself by abolishing the strict censorship to which the press had, till then, been subjected.

The progress of publication in India, within the last thirty years, has been very considerable. In 1814, there was only one newspaper, which was printed at Calcutta, and called the Calcutta Gazette; whereas there are now daily and weekly papers printed at every large British station, besides a great number of magazines and other periodicals, both in the English and native languages; and many of the printing offices are managed entirely by natives.

LORD AUCKLAND.

HINDOSTAN had never been in a more tranquil state than at the time when Lord Auckland arrived at Calcutta in 1836, invested with the high functions of Governor-General of the British eastern empire. All then appeared to promise a continuance of peace, and the uninterrupted progress of those improvements so steadily and effectually pursued by his predecessor; but the calm was not of long duration; and the attention of the government was soon engrossed by the affairs of Cabul, which led our armies, for the first time, across the Indus, and replaced on the throne the long-exiled monarch of that kingdom.

Before the commencement of that war, a revolution had occurred in the kingdom of Oude, a considerable state, dependent on the Government of Bengal, but ruled by its own sovereign, whose court is the only one now existing in Hindostan, that retains any of the splendour formerly exhibited by the Indian princes.

It may be remembered that, after the conquest of Bengal, Sujah Dowlah, the Nabob Vizier of Oude, surrendered himself to the English, on certain terms; and was restored to his former dignity, on condition that he should enter into a lasting alliance with the British Government.

Soldier of the King of Oude.

The territory of Oude, under the able management of that prince, formed one of the most important states into which the Mogul Empire had been divided; but the successors of Sujah governed with less ability; and in 1798, a disputed succession called for the interference of the British authorities, who placed on the throne Saadat Ali, one of the claimants, who in return for this service, agreed to disband the greater part of his army, and employ British troops for the protection of his dominions. By a subsequent treaty, he surrendered the valuable provinces of the Doab and Rohilcund; so that the Ganges became the boundary of his state, and his dependence was completely secured by the establishment of the important military station at Cawnpore, on the Ganges, about six hundred miles from Calcutta, and not more than fifty from Lucknow, the capital of Oude.

The cantonments at Cawnpore extend nearly six miles along the bank of the river; and the European residents, independent of the military, are numerous, some of them being shopkeepers, others makers of gloves and saddlery, for both of which manufactures, Cawnpore is especially celebrated. The principal civil officers, such as the judges and collectors of revenue, live in magnificent style, according to the Indian fashion, being surrounded with a numerous train of domestics; as every man's consequence, in India, is estimated by the number of servants belonging to his establishment.

Cawnpore is considered rather a gay station, as it can boast of a theatre for amateur performances, handsome assembly rooms, and a good race-course; and it also has the advantage of being sufficiently near to the famous city of Lucknow, to admit of excursions thither, at all seasons of public festivals and court ceremonies, which far surpass, in grandeur, any thing now seen at Delhi.

The Nabob-vizier, or ruler of Oude, although in reality dependent on the British Government, was nominally a vassal of the Emperor, until the year 1819, when, with the sanction of the Governor General, and Council of Calcutta, he assumed the title of king, and became, to a certain extent, an independent sovereign; since he was permitted to conduct the internal government of the country, free from any direct control or interference; He was, however, still obliged to maintain British troops in his capital, and to receive an English resident on terms of equality at his court, so that he was kept in check, as the slightest act detrimental to the British interests would have been immediately reported to the authorities at Calcutta.

The country of Oude possesses natural advantages that are not exceeded in any part of India. Its level surface is watered by innumerable streams that fertilize the soil, which, when carefully cultivated, as it was under its former rulers, produced rich crops of wheat, cotton, sugar, opium, indigo, and other valuable products; but the mode of taxation had become so oppressive, that the people had no encouragement to industry, and were miserably poor, while much good land that might have been tilled for their benefit, was lying waste.

Under the government of Saadat Ali and his successor, the kingdom was divided into sixteen districts, the revenues of which were farmed to private individuals, who paid a certain sum annually to the king, and collected the rents from the tenants for their own benefit. There was no check on their exactions, consequently they extorted from the cultivators much more than was legally their due; and it was owing to this oppressive system, that many men who, under a better form of government, would have been employed in the useful labours of the field, betook themselves to a less honest but more lucrative occupation; and thus the whole country was overrun with Thugs, and robbers of all descriptions.

Such was the state of Oude, for many years, till Lord William Bentinck took some very decided steps towards remedying these evils, by making preparations for transferring the civil administration to English officers, which certainly would have been done, had not the king introduced some reforms calculated to relieve the people, in a great degree, from the heavy burthen of taxation by which they had been oppressed.

In the year 1837, the death of the sovereign occasioned a violent commotion in the capital of Oude, as it was generally believed that two young men, whom he had declared to be his sons, had, in reality, no claim to such relationship. The British government, therefore, which had long been the arbiter in all questions of importance, set aside the doubtful claims of the young men, in favour of Nusseer-ud-Dowlah, the uncle of the late monarch, a prince rather advanced in years. A violent disturbance ensued in the capital, in which the queen mother took an active part. The gates of the palace were forced; the new sovereign, with all the English officers who were there, were seized by the insurgents, headed by the queen in her palanquin; and one of the young princes was formally installed. But the party of Nusseer-ud-Dowlah triumphed, in the end; and he remained King of Oude, under the protection of the British government.

The city of Lucknow, like many Indian towns, looks well at a distance, from the imposing appearance of its numerous cupolas and minarets; but the streets are, in general, narrow, dirty, and crowded, except in that quarter where the palace and the houses of the great are situated. Some of these are very handsome buildings, partaking of both the European and Oriental style of architecture; and many of them are furnished in the English fashion, of which the late king was a great admirer. One of his palaces, on the river Goomtee, about nine miles above Lucknow, was quite an English residence, and to this quiet retreat he was in the habit of making excursions, in a small steam-boat, constructed for him, in 1819, by an English engineer, the first steam vessel known in India.

The state processions of the late King of Oude are described as rivalling those of the Mogul Emperors, in the days of their glory; and his court, on occasions of ceremony, as presenting an almost equal display of barbaric splendour. His state carriage is of English construction, and is drawn by eight black horses; and his Paulkee, a sort of throne, on which he sometimes appears in processions, is of wrought gold, and is carried by bearers, habited in scarlet vests and fine turbans, profusely ornamented.

The Mohammedan festivals are celebrated at Lucknow, with great magnificence; and the Europeans attached to the court are usually entertained by his majesty with a combat of wild beasts, and a dinner in the English style, with the accompaniment of dances performed by certain female dancers, called, in India, Nautch girls; without whose presence, an entertainment would be considered dull and insipid.

KINGDOM OF CABUL.

THE events of the Afghan war, in which so many English families were deeply and personally interested, are so familiar to every one, that a detailed account of that unhappy contest would only be a repetition of an oft told tale. A very brief sketch may therefore suffice for the present purpose. The exiled King of Cabul, Shah Shuja, who had continued to reside at the British station of Loodiana, about two hundred miles to the north of Delhi, constantly occupied himself in vain attempts to recover his throne; while the ambition of Dost Mahommed's brothers, and the successes of Runjeet Singh, kept the whole country in a state of anarchy. Kamran, the prince who had compassed the death of Futteh Khan, and was the bitterest enemy of Dost Mahommed, still retained the government of Herat, and having involved himself in a war with Persia, had increased the confusion, by bringing the Persians into Afghanistan.

This war was of some consequence to the British government, on account of the influence exercised at the court of Persia by the Russians, who might possibly, have availed themselves of any conquests made by the Persians near the frontiers, to send their armies into the Indian territories. On the other hand, it was the interest of Dost Mahommed to secure the friendship of the Persian monarch, and not to prevent him from proceeding against Prince Kamran; but he was also anxious to put a stop to the encroachments of the Seik ruler, Runjeet Singh; and, with that view, applied for aid to Lord Auckland, the Governor General of India, who considered this application as affording him a favourable opportunity of opening a commercial intercourse with the countries west of the Indus, and securing the free navigation of that river to British merchants. An envoy was despatched to

Runjeet Singh at Peshawar, to negociate a peace between that great prince and the King of Cabul, which might have been concluded, but that Dost Mahommed was not satisfied with such concessions as Runjeet was willing to make; and as there was great reason to believe that he was playing a double part, by corresponding secretly with the Persians and Russians, the British governor withdrew his interference with regard to the Seiks, and resolved to depose the monarch whose conduct was so dangerous.

This determination was, naturally, a preliminary step towards the restoration of Shah Shuja, who, while he was in power, had cordially entered into the views of the British government with regard to Persia; and, on these grounds, war was declared against Dost Mahommed, and two armies were prepared for the invasion of his kingdom, one to march from Bengal, the other from Bombay, and to form a junction with the forces of Shah Shuja, at Shikapore, a large commercial town, fifteen miles west of the Indus.

The route of the Bombay troops lay through the territories of the Ameers of Scinde, who refused to grant them a free passage, although there was a treaty of friendship subsisting between them and the British rulers of Hindostan. It was, therefore, necessary to force a way, and the two principal cities, Hyderabad and Kurrachee, were attacked, and taken without much trouble, as very little resistance was offered. The Ameers were so much alarmed at these easy conquests, that they not only accelerated the march of the army, but agreed to a new treaty, by which Scinde was added to the subject states, and the troops pursued their way to the place of rendezvous.

The whole army was assembled at Shikapore in the early part of March, 1839, and began to move towards Candahar, through a wild mountainous country, beset by fierce marauding tribes of Belooches, and suffering severely from want of water and provisions. After many dangers and distresses, however, they reached Candahar, from which the governor, a brother of Dost Mahommed, fled, leaving the city to be occupied by the British forces. Shah Shuja was here formally reinstated as King of Cabul; and, a few weeks after this ceremony, which was performed on the open plain, in the midst of the troops, the army proceeded to Ghazni, the celebrated capital of the early Musselman conquerors, which was stormed and taken, after a desperate conflict with the Afghans, who defended the town with the utmost bravery.

About this time, the death of Runjeet Singh deprived the English of a powerful ally, and the eastern nations of one of their greatest rulers. This illustrious prince, the founder of a vast empire, which, like that of Ahmed, of Durani, was destined to fall with him to whom it owed its rise, died in

June, 1839, and was succeeded by his son, Kurruch Singh, who survived him but a few months. The funeral obsequies of the latter were celebrated with the sacrifice of one of his wives; and on the same day, his son and successor, Nehal, was accidentally killed by the falling of a beam, as he was passing under a gateway on his elephant. This event gave rise to much confusion in the state, as there was no direct heir to the crown; and one party supported Dhian Singh, who had been Runjeet's chief minister; while the opposite faction proclaimed Shere Singh, another prince of the family.

Such was the state of affairs in the Punjab during the early part of the Afghan war, consequently, the Seiks were too much occupied with their own troubles, to afford that efficient aid which had been expected from the friendly alliance that had subsisted between the British government and the late monarch, Runjeet Singh.

Fortress of Ghazni, with the two Minars.

In the mean time, Dost Mahommed had taken refuge in Bokhara, where he was treacherously thrown into prison by the King of that country, who seems to have had no other object in so doing, but to force him to surrender his jewels, which are of immense value. He contrived, however, to effect his escape, by bribing one of his guards, who undertook to procure him a fleet horse, and to guide him beyond the frontiers. The plan was successful, and the fugitive prince, after several hair-breadth escapes, reached a place of safety, and began to assemble friends around him, with a view of expelling his rival, and the British, from Cabul, of which he had the greatest hopes, as he knew that Shah Shuja was unpopular, and that nothing but the power of those who had placed him on the throne, could keep him there. A detachment had been left for the protection of the monarch in the capital, but the main body of the army had returned to their several stations, consequently, Dost Mahommed flattered himself with hopes that their absence would be favourable to his success; but he was disappointed; for, after having twice attacked the protecting force, he was made prisoner, and given up to Sir William M'Naghten, the British resident at Cabul. He was then sent to Calcutta, where he was received by the Governor General with the respect due to his rank, and although a captive, was treated as a distinguished guest, until he obtained permission to retire, with his family, to Loodiana, where the house was assigned to him that had so long been the residence of Shah Shuja. That monarch seemed to be now fully re-established, and his capital for some time remained tranquil; but the protective force, which was stationed about five miles from the city, was frequently engaged in skirmishes with some of the mountain tribes, who were in the habit of plundering the mails on their way from Calcutta to Cabul, and committing various kinds of depredations.

Cabul is a large walled city, inhabited by people of many nations. The houses, which are only two stories high, are mostly built of wood, or unburnt brick, and are mean in appearance; but the great bazaar, since destroyed, was one of the largest and most elegant in all the east. It was built by the famous Ali Merdan Khan, in the time of Aurengzebe, and was the great emporium of the trade of central Asia; but it exists no longer, having been destroyed by the British before they quitted the country at the conclusion of the war.

In the month of April, 1841, General Elphinstone assumed the command of the British army at Cabul, which, at that time, was perfectly tranquil, and its inhabitants peacefully engaged in their various occupations. The ladies of many of the British officers had accompanied their husbands, and were residing with them in the city, some of them having their children with them. The privations they suffered, even under the most favourable circumstances, were very great, among a people to whom the comforts of European life are utterly unknown; but to these inconveniences were soon added the horrors of an insurrection, which broke out on the second of November, caused, as it was afterwards discovered, by a seditious letter addressed by one of the Ghilzie tribe to some of the most influential chiefs

On Stone by Dean & C°.

BAZAAR AT CABUL IN THE FRUIT SEASON.

London Dean & C°. Threadneedle St.

at Cabul, informing them that it was the intention of the British envoy to seize, and send them all to London. A general tumult ensued. The houses of all the British residents in the city were furiously assailed, and several distinguished officers, among whom was Sir Alexander Burnes, lost their lives in the confusion. The revolt increased to such an alarming height, not only in the capital, but also among the tribes of the surrounding country, that it was thought advisable to endeavour to make terms with the leaders, the principal of whom was Akber Khan, the favourite son of Dost Mahommed. The conduct of Akber during the whole of this war, afforded a striking illustration of aristocratic manners among half-civilised nations, the courtesy of a prince being strangely mixed with the ferocity of a barbarian in his intercourse with his enemies.

In the meantime, Shah Shuja had kept himself closely shut up in the Bala Hissar, the palace and citadel of Cabul, which was partly garrisoned with British troops, where he anxiously awaited the result of the insurrection. It soon, however, became apparent that the revolt was not confined to the capital, but was general all over the country. The situation of the British was one of extreme peril, being in want of supplies of all kinds, and surrounded by hostile tribes of warlike barbarians, who occupied all the roads by which assistance might be sent. The nearest British station was six hundred miles distant; the road to any place lay through mountainous passes, many miles in length, choked up with snow, and beset by the enemy, while the soldiers were already falling victims to the severity of a Cabul winter, which was more especially fatal to the Sepoys, who, bred in the sultry climate of India, were utterly incapable of enduring the rigour of such a winter, the ground in Cabul being covered with deep snows during five months of the year. Under these circumstances, the British envoy, Sir William M'Naghten, resolved on making terms, if possible, with Akber Khan, who gave him a meeting on the plain, where a long conference took place relative to a treaty of peace, which was concluded, on condition that Shah Shuja should abdicate the throne of Cabul, and Dost Mahommed be reinstated. The British troops were to be withdrawn from the citadel, and join the rest of the army at the cantonments, and Akber himself undertook to escort them thither, to protect them from the Ghilzies, and other tribes that were hovering about the neighbourhood. During this movement, some signs of treachery on the part of the chief spread dismay amongst the already dispirited troops, who were fired upon ere they had reached the cantonments.

It was now that the increasing distresses of the army indnced Sir William

M'Naghten to give Akber a second meeting. The interview, which took place outside the city, terminated fatally to the envoy, who, in full confidence of Akber's sincerity, repaired to the spot, accompanied by only a very small retinue. After a short conference, Akber betrayed the treachery of his intentions, by provoking a misunderstanding, when, attempting to seize Sir William M'Naghten, and to make him prisoner, a scuffle ensued: Sir William was shot by the hand of Akber, and two or three other officers were also sacrificed at the onset of the chiefs, while the rest of the party were carried off as prisoners.

The place of the murdered envoy was supplied by Major Pottinger, who renewed the negociations with Akber; and it was finally arranged that the British army should be permitted to leave Cabul, and proceed to Jellalabad, a small fortified town between the capital and Peshawer, then held by General Nott.

The retreat of the British from Cabul may well be compared to that of the French from Moscow, but was, if possible, more calamitous, owing to the vast number of women and children who encumbered the army, adding greatly to the miseries of those who had no means of protecting them from the inclemency of the weather, or the cravings of hunger. Their way lay through the rugged narrow defiles of Khoord Cabul, Tezeen, Jugdullock, and Khyber, the latter of which gives its name to a mountain tribe, who had long been in the habit of receiving an annual tribute, or black mail, from the government of Cabul, for the free transit of the pass; but as this tribute had been unwisely discontinued by Shah Shuja, the Khyberries had become the fierce and implacable enemies of that monarch and his supporters; so that it was only through the influence of Akber Khan that the British troops could hope to march through the Khyber pass in safety. To depend on this wily chief, was a desperate alternative, yet, under the existing circumstances, it afforded the only means of avoiding certain destruction; therefore, it was resolved rather to brave the dangers of a retreat, than to remain with the wretched prospect of perishing for want of food and clothing.

The march was commenced on the sixth of January, 1842, and no sooner had the cantonments been evacuated, than the Afghans rushed in, and set fire to them, carrying off every article that had been left. This hostile movement was followed up by the pursuit of the retreating army, and, notwithstanding the treaty made with Akber, the baggage was seized, and those who attempted to defend it, were cut down by the well-armed and mounted barbarians, large bands of whom kept hovering around. It ought to be borne in mind, that the fugitives were not all soldiers, but that many were women and children, and that the mere camp followers were more than double the number of the troops, whose difficulties were considerably increased by the care of so many helpless persons.

British troops en route from Cabul.

The circumstances attending the annihilation of that unfortunate army will long be remembered. Some perished miserably in the snow; others were made prisoners; but the greater number fell in the narrow passes of the mountains, under the murderous attacks of the Ghilzies, Khyberries, and other barbarous hordes, whom Akber had promised to restrain from violence. From the very commencement of the march, the chief had kept near the army, for the purpose, probably, of taking advantage of every circumstance that might arise, but contriving, at the same time, to preserve such an appearance of good faith, that many believed his intentions were friendly, until undeceived by subsequent occurrences. His first act was to get into his power some of the principal officers, and their families, which he did, by presenting himself, about three days after their departure from Cabul, offering to take the ladies and children back under his own protection, as the only means of saving them from the fierce hordes by whom they were surrounded. The invitation was extended to such of the officers as chose to return, and was accepted by those who were wounded, or whose wives were about to become the guests or captives, they knew not which, of a barbarian prince. They were conducted to one of those small forts already mentioned as the residences of the khans, or heads of tribes, where the accommodations were so rude and scanty, that an English peasant's cot might be termed a luxurious abode, compared with the dwelling of an Afghan nobleman. Three dark hovels, utterly destitute of furniture, were allotted for the use of the Europeans, who were almost stifled with the smoke of a wood fire, which could only find vent through the doorway. Food for the whole party was furnished in one dish, without a single knife, fork, or spoon, and the only place of repose was the floor, spread with sheepskins; yet these were the best accommodations the place afforded; nor does it appear that the chief himself was better lodged or entertained; so that, according to the customs of the country, the prisoners were well treated. Among the number, were Lady Sale and the widow of Sir William M'Naghten, with about seven other ladies, most of whom had their children with them, and were consoled by the presence of their husbands. The new envoy, Major Pottinger, and General Elphinstone, were also among the captives, the latter having gone to Akber's camp, in the hope of inducing him to exert his influence in restraining the mountain tribes that cut off the retreat of the army through the passes. This the chief promised to do, but detained the general as a hostage for the performance of certain articles of the treaty, while the unfortunate army was left to its fate.

Akber soon removed his prisoners to the strong fort of Buddeeabad, near Tezeen, belonging to his father-in-law, a Ghilzie chief, on the way to which, they had to pass the Khoord Cabul pass, where they beheld, with horror, the remains of many hundreds of those who had left Cabul with them only a few days previously, and whose sufferings had been terminated by the most painful deaths. The fort of Buddeeabad, destined to be the abode of the prisoners for three long months, is situated in a narrow valley, enclosed by lofty precipitous hills, and fortified with a wall and ditch. Akber, who had assumed the title of Sirdar, paid great attention to their comforts, as far as circumstances would permit, and they were allowed to correspond with their friends at Jellalabad, where General Sale was then in command, who sent them clothing, letters, and newspapers, the value of which, to persons thus situated, may be well understood. General Elphinstone, whose health had sunk under the pressure of anxiety and misfortune, died soon after his melancholy journey to Tezeen, and his body was sent to Jellalabad for interment.

In the mean time, the inhabitants of Cabul were divided into several factions, each of which set up a different claimant for the throne. The assassination of Shah Shuja in March, 1842, who was shot by one of the chiefs as they were riding together, close to the city, gave still more room for contention; and, amid the confusion that ensued, Futteh Jung, the eldest son of the murdered monarch, obtained possession of the citadel. He soon made terms with Akber, who became vizier; in which capacity he ruled, for some time, with absolute sway at Cabul, and, at length, imprisoned his royal master, in consequence of having intercepted a letter, written by Futteh Jung, and addressed to General Pollock, containing proposals by no means suited to the views of the vizier. Futteh Jung had repeatedly desired that the prisoners should be given up to him, a demand which Akber had decidedly refused to comply with. The monarch, therefore, had written to the English general, urging his speedy advance, promising to aid in liberating the captives, and crushing the power of Akber Khan. The vizier had no sooner discovered this correspondence, than he placed Futteh Jung in confinement, from which, however, he soon escaped, by means of a hole in the roof of his prison, and fled to the British camp; but his friendly intentions towards the English had nearly proved the ruin of those who were in the power of Akber, who put a stop to all intercourse between them and their friends at Jellalabad, and declared that, the moment he should hear of the approach of British troops, he would send them all to Tartary, and make slaves of them. They had been removed from the fortress at Tezeen, to one about three miles from Cabul, where they were now kept in horrible suspense as to their ultimate fate.

In the meantime, Ghazni had been recovered by the Afghans, and nine British officers made prisoners, who, at the latter end of August, joined their companions in misfortune at Cabul. All were then sent off under a strong escort, they knew not whither, or with what intent, and continued their journey for seventeen days, through a beautiful country, where the lanes were overshadowed by mulberry trees, and the finest fruits were seen in profusion around; but the scene had no charms for the heart-sick, dispirited travellers, who were lodged at night in different forts, well guarded, and, by day, pursued their weary way in ignorance of their ultimate destination.

General Nott was, at this time, marching towards Ghazni, and General Pollock towards Cabul. Akber, therefore, true to his threat, sent orders to Saleh Mahommed, the chief who had the charge of the prisoners, to convey them all to Kholoom, on the borders of Tartary, where, had this command been obeyed, slavery would have been their inevitable doom; but, fortunately, Saleh Mahommed had his own reasons for acting a more friendly part, and offered, for a large reward, to effect their escape. It is needless to say with what joy the proposal was accepted; and as many chiefs in the neighbourhood were well disposed towards the English, the execution of the plan was the less difficult. Secret messages were conveyed to the British generals that they might send troops to meet the fugitives, who, on the sixteenth of September, commenced their perilous flight, knowing that instant death awaited them should they be recaptured. The event was propitious; and, on the twentieth of September, the captives found themselves once more at liberty, and under the protection of their friends and countrymen. The English were again in possession of Cabul, and had retaken the city of Ghazni, which they had reduced to ruins, bringing away with them, among other spoils, the beautiful sandal wood gates of the ancient temple of Somnath, carried off from that celebrated place of worship by Mahmud of Ghazni, as a trophy of his conquests. They had since formed the entrance to the tomb of that great conqueror, and are still in excellent preservation.

Akber Khan had endeavoured to prevent one division of the British forces from reaching Cabul, by intercepting them in the valley of Tezeen, where a battle was fought, which ended in his total discomfiture, and he was compelled to seek safety in flight, while the British army proceeded triumphantly to the capital, where Shah Poora, a younger son of Shuja, had been proclaimed King, Futteh Jung having withdrawn to the British territories.

Lord Ellenborough, who had succeeded Lord Auckland as Governor General, in the early part of 1842, now resolved, as the release of the prisoners had been accomplished, to interfere no farther in the affairs of Cabul, and to allow Dost Mahommed to return with his family, as soon as all the troops had left the country. The last division recrossed the Indus early in November, 1842, and the deposed monarch, his wives, daughters, and other members of his household, were conducted with the respect due to their rank, to the frontiers of Afghanistan, of which country he has since resumed the government.

Bazaar in Bombay.

ARTS AND CUSTOMS.

THE termination of the war was celebrated by the Governor General with great public festivities at Ferozepore, the capital of a small state lately acquired by the East India Company, in consequence of the death of an aged princess, who died without heirs. Ferozepore was, under the Mogul emperors, a city of considerable importance, being advantageously situated for commerce near the Sutlej, which communicates with the Indus; and as the passage of the latter has been secured, for the purposes of trade, by the recent conquest of Scinde, Ferozepore has a fair prospect of being restored to all its former prosperity. Steam vessels now ascend the Indus, and proceed by the Sutlej a distance of nine hundred and fifty miles, to that city, where the population has been lately much increased by fresh settlers, desirous of benefitting by the newly-opened trade. A fair has been established, the city enlarged and improved by the erection of several handsome bazaars; and it is anticipated that Ferozepore will shortly become one of the chief commercial towns of India.

The administration of Lord Ellenborough has thus been distinguished by the opening of the Indus to merchant ships of all nations, and also by another vast benefit, that of the abolition of slavery throughout the British dominions in India, whereby another important step in the moral and social condition of the people has been attained. There is, however, still one great bar to the perfect civilisation of the Hindus. Christianity has hitherto made but a very limited progress among them, so that notwithstanding the unceasing efforts of European missionaries, the great mass of the Indians are idol worshippers, and retain most of the customs appertaining to idolatry, so that their domestic habits cannot materially differ from those of their forefathers, since almost every act they perform has some reference to the superstitions of their religion. The number of converts has always been small, and is likely to be increased only as the minds of the people become more enlightened; an effect that must naturally result from the educational system so successfully pursued by the British government, the benefits of which are extended to both sexes.

All the cities esteemed holy by the Hindus are still visited, at particular seasons, by crowds of pilgrims, who are only restrained from the excesses which formerly disgraced their worship, by the influence of British authority. The temple of Juggernaut is still the most frequented, and immense sums of money are lavished on the maintenance of a numerous establishment in honour of its hideous idol, the expenses of which are paid chiefly out of the revenues derived from the temple lands. The tax on pilgrims has lately been abolished. The Hindu festivals are usually observed with great gaiety; but the splendid spectacles and processions that used to be exhibited by the native princes, have since degenerated into paltry shows for the amusement of the rabble.

The progress of education, added to their increased intercourse with Europeans, has greatly modified the scruples of the Hindus with regard to caste, especially among the higher orders, whose prejudices appear to be giving way, by degrees, to more enlarged views. The lower classes adhere generally to the superstitions of their creed, but the castes are now so numerous, and the distinctions frequently so slight, that it is very difficult for them to keep the line of separation.

The domestic arts of the Hindus are many and various, for there is scarcely any trade that is not practised by them; and almost every considerable town is famous for some particular art or manufacture. Thus, Patna, a wealthy city on the Ganges, and the great mart for opium, is cele-

Weaver and Loom.

brated for its table linen and wax candles; Benares, for its rich brocades; Monghir, another town on the Ganges, for steel and iron goods; Calcutta and Moorshedabad for curious and elegant toys, while Delhi surpasses all other cities for the ingenuity of its goldsmiths and jewellers. The manufacture of paper has been improved, of late years, by the introduction of a steam-engine, at Serampore, the capital of the Danish settlements in India; and great improvements have also been made in the mechanical arts.

Delhi is the famous mart for the shawls and superb embroidery of India. The modern city is called by the natives Shahjehanabad, from the Emperor, Shah Jehan, its founder, who built the imperial palace, which is enclosed by a wall of red granite, a mile in circumference. The celebrated gardens of Shalimar, laid out by the same Emperor, at a cost of a million of money, are now destroyed. Beyond the site of these gardens, to the south, extending for some miles, are the ruins of the ancient capital, exhibiting the remains of its once splendid palaces, mosques, and minarets, which form a singular contrast to the new suburb of European villas and cantonments. The British resident occupies the palace that formerly belonged to Ali Merdan Khan, but which has been modernized for the sake of convenience. The streets of Delhi are hot, crowded, and dusty. English carriages are in use there, and are seen intermingled with the sedans, palanquins, and little chaises, drawn by bullocks, which are common in many of the cities of India; besides which, elephants, camels, and horses, gaily caparisoned, are continually passing. It is the custom for all great men, when riding out in state, to have their titles proclaimed aloud before them; and the approach of the Emperor is announced by kettle drums, when all persons dismount as the cortege goes by. The shops of Delhi exhibit all kinds of European goods, and confectioners are numerous; for among the arts in which the Indians excel, may be reckoned that of making an infinite variety of sweetmeats, all composed of sugar, flour, molasses, and spices, for they never use any fruit in them except the cocoa nut.

All the towns of India are very much infested with beggars, who are chiefly mendicants of the religious orders, and present a most disgusting sight, from dirt, and scarcity of clothing; for the holiness of these fanatics appears to be estimated by the wretchedness of their outward appearance, and people bestow alms on them accordingly. Benares is the great resort

Benares.

of these idle, useless beings, who are there sure of constant donations from the multitudes of pilgrims that are always going to and from the holy city, as also from the numbers of wealthy individuals in the decline of life, who repair thither in hopes to expiate their sins by giving away large sums in indiscriminate charity. Benares is a British station, but the cantonments are at Secrole, some little distance from the city, and about five hundred miles from Calcutta.

The mode of travelling in India renders all long journeys extremely tedious, difficult, and dangerous. The conveyance is by means of a kind of litter, called a palanquin, carried by men, who are changed, like post horses, at every ten or twelve miles, there being regular post-masters at certain towns and villages, who take care that a fresh set of bearers shall be in readiness when wanted. The usual number of these is twelve: eight to carry the vehicle, which is slung on poles; two for the luggage, and two to act as torch-bearers. They are generally found honest and faithful to their trust, but have sometimes been known to abandon their charge in cases of danger, particularly on the appearance of a tiger, the dread of all travellers in the unfrequented parts of the country.

Tiger hunting has always been a favourite sport in India, and used to be conducted with great pomp, and on a very grand scale, by the native princes, whose retinue sometimes consisted of twenty thousand persons. The chase of the wild hog is also an Indian sport, in which the Europeans take great delight, and in the pursuit of which, they frequently rouse a tiger from his lair.

Elephants are caught in their wild state, by being hunted into an enclosure, prepared for the purpose, which is surrounded by a strong fence and deep ditch, to prevent their escape. These ponderous creatures are found in all the forests and jungles of the southern and eastern provinces, and are taken by the natives, who assemble for that purpose in large bands, furnished with fire-arms for their own protection, and with all kinds of noisy instruments to frighten the animals, who are thus driven towards the enclosure, which they are induced to enter, by the fruits, and other tempting baits that are within it, full in view. A whole herd is thus sometimes drawn into the enclosure, the entrance of which is then closed upon them;

Trapping elephants.

and they are tamed by degrees, being securely fastened to the trees, and fed by their mahouts, or men who are to be their drivers, whose business it is to tame, and render them fit for service. Each elephant thus learns to obey his own mahout, although he would, perhaps, be refractory under the guidance of any other driver. Most of the great men keep elephants, which are almost as common in the streets of an Indian city, as horses are in London.

The natives of India, whether Hindu or Mohammedan, attach importance to a grand equipage, and a numerous body of attendants; and these outward signs of dignity are so essential to persons holding official situations, in order to secure to them a due share of respect, that it is often necessary for an English family to keep an establishment of from twenty to thirty servants; an arrangement that is indeed scarcely to be avoided on another account; for the greater number of these serving men are Hindus, who are very careful to observe the rules of caste in one point, that of not interfering with each other's duties; so that every trifling occupation is allotted to some particular individual, who will perform that one and no other. The expense, however, of keeping so large an establishment, is not very great, as the wages of native servants are small, and they furnish themselves with food and clothing; for no Hindu would eat of a dish that had been set before a Christian. They live chiefly on rice and vegetables, and sleep in huts near their master's house. Almost all the household duties are performed by men, such as dusting the rooms, making the beds, sweeping the floors, and a variety of offices that usually fall to the lot of women in Europe, the only female domestics employed in English families being ladies' maids and nurses. Owing to the religious prejudices of the Hindus, the cooks and men who wait at table, are always Mohammedans.

Hindu farm-yard.

The Indian system of husbandry has already been noticed. The farms are, in general, small, and the wealth of the farmer is usually estimated by the number of his bullocks. The staple food of the people is rice, but potatoes have been introduced into every part of the country, and very excellent wheat is grown in the northern and western provinces.

Indian thrashing.

The thrashing is performed by bullocks, two or more of which are yoked together, and driven over a quantity of sheaves spread on the ground; and thus the grain is trodden out very quickly. The rice or corn is then cleared from the husks by large fans, and the straw is formed into stacks for the cattle, as hay is not known in India.

RECENT EVENTS.

THE Afghan war has been followed by other events of much greater relative importance to the power of the British Empire, which is now more firmly established and more widely extended over India than that of the Moguls ever was, even under their most potent princes. The principal historical facts to be recorded, are the conquest of Scinde, the revolution in the Punjab, and the victories of Gwalior, which have brought that state completely under the controul of the British government.

Immediately after the restoration of Dost Mahommed to the throne of

Cabul, fresh disputes arose between the English government and the Ameers of Scinde, relative to the free navigation of the Indus, and the cession, according to treaty, of certain forts with their territories on the banks of that river. A detachment of British troops was therefore sent into the country, under the command of Sir Charles Napier, with a view of forcing the Ameers to fulfil their engagements. This small force, which did not amount to three thousand men, was attacked near Hyderabad, by the whole Sindian army, composed of several warlike tribes, numbering, in all, above twenty thousand soldiers, commanded by the Ameers in person, who, after a long and well-fought battle, gave up the contest, and surrendered themselves prisoners on the field. The victors then took possession of the capital, Hyderabad, a mean town, consisting chiefly of mud hovels, at the base of an eminence, on the summit of which stands the fort, in which treasures were found, to the amount of above a million of money.

Although the principal Ameers had given themselves up to the English, great efforts were made by the other chiefs to maintain their independence, and another battle took place on the 24th of March, 1843, the result of which has added the province of Scinde to the British dominions. The Ameers were sent as state prisoners to Bombay, and Sir Charles Napier, the successful General, was appointed Governor of the country he had conquered. Slavery was immediately abolished throughout the whole territory of Scinde, and the River Indus was declared open to ships of all nations.

In the mean time, the kingdom of Lahore had been in a state of the utmost confusion, in consequence of the civil wars that followed the death of Kurruck Singh. The British government took no part in these dissensions, but maintained a friendly intercourse with Shere Singh, in order to secure for the troops in Afghanistan, a free passage through the Punjab, from Cabul to British India.

The condition of the country was, at this time, extremely wretched. The great Seik army, which had been organised by Runjeet Singh, on the European system, and which in his time had been a powerful force, commanded by European officers, was now disbanded; the roads were infested with banditti, who plundered the villages with impunity, and, in many instances, set them on fire; so that the miserable peasants were wandering about every where, without the means of procuring food or shelter, while the government was too weak to afford them protection, and the king was regarded in the light of a usurper by many of the greatest nobles of the kingdom.

Shere Singh, however, maintained his seat on the throne, until the month of September, 1843, when he was assassinated by some of the chiefs, in his gardens, during the celebration of a public festival; and his son shared the same fate. The citadel of Lahore was then seized by the conspirators; Dhyan Singh, the minister, was shot, and the wives and children of the murdered princes were barbarously massacred. But the success of the insurgents was of short duration, for they were defeated before the close of the same day, by the opposite faction, who captured their leader, and placed on the throne Dhulleep Singh, a boy only seven years of age, said to be a son of the great Runjeet. At present, the government is conducted by the minister Heera Singh, but the country is still in a very unsettled and miserable condition, and may probably, ere long, follow the fortunes of the rest of India, and submit to the authority of British rulers.

It now only remains to speak of the affairs of Gwalior, and to trace the circumstances that have at length destroyed the independence of that state, so long preserved under the government of the family of Sindia. The last of those powerful princes died in 1827, leaving no son to succeed him. In such cases it is customary in many parts of India for the widow of the deceased sovereign, to select from amongst his relatives, some youth to be his successor, and she acts as Regent until the adopted heir becomes of age, or she chooses to resign her authority.

This was the course pursued by Baiza Bye, the widow of Sindia, who ruled over the extensive dominions of her late husband, till the year 1831, when Jhundkoo Rao, the chosen prince, became impatient to possess the sovereign power, which she was not disposed so soon to relinquish. A violent contest ensued, which was terminated through the mediation of the British government, in favour of Jhundkoo Rao, who was acknowledged as Maharaja, while the queen consented to retire on a pension of ten lacs of rupees, or £100,000 a year, to be paid out of the revenues of the state. Jhundkoo Rao Sindia died in December, 1843, under the same circumstances, with regard to the succession as his predecessor; and as there was no direct heir, the British government interfered so far as to direct, or rather to sanction, the choice of the widowed Maharanee, or Queen, who adopted her deceased husband's nearest relative, Jyngee Rao Sindia, the boy who now bears the title of Maharaja.

The Mama Sahib, a chief known to be friendly to the British interests, was appointed Regent, during the minority; and for some time acted in that capacity; but he was no favourite with the Maharanee, who was, in fact, at the head of a faction hostile to the English, and desirous of deposing the Regent appointed by their authority. He was at length expelled, and a rival chief, the Dada Khasgee Walla, placed at the head of the government. This assumption of independence on the part of the Queen and her partizans, together with the conduct of the new minister, whose undisguised animosity towards the English, seemed likely to occasion some trouble, caused the Governor General of India to adopt prompt and decisive measures for future security, by reducing the dominions of Sindia to a more complete state of subjection. With this view, a British army, accompanied by the Governor General, entered the territories of Gwalior, towards the close of the year 1843, and proceeded direct towards the capital, where the Mahratta forces were in readiness to oppose them.

On the 29th of December, two great victories were gained in the neighbourhood of Gwalior, the one at Maharajpore, by Sir Hugh Gough; the other at Punniar, by General Grey. These two engagements cost the lives of many of our brave countrymen, but they have effectually put an end to the factions that threatened to disturb the peace of the Indo-British empire, and will most probably be the means of annexing a large and opulent state to our eastern dominions.

Fort of Gwalior.

The fort of Gwalior, so long celebrated for its commanding situation, and apparent impregnability, was surrendered immediately after these battles, when the queen and the leading chiefs, with the young Maharaja, presented themselves in the English camp, to make submission, and give up the obnoxious minister; a concession that had previously been demanded and refused.

The tranquillity of the state being thus restored, the young Maharaja was placed on the throne, and the government will, in future, be conducted under the superintendence of British authorities.

In closing the present volume, it may be proper to mention the recall of Lord Ellenborough from the Government of India, under an order of the Court of Directors of the East India Company, a subject which for some time engrossed much public attention.

The exercise of this authority on the part of that body, was made without any previous misunderstanding with the British Government, by which, however, it was subsequently sanctioned, and Sir Henry Hardinge, a clever and experienced officer, was, with the full concurrence of the ministers of the crown, nominated to succeed the late Governor.

This privilege of recalling a Governor General has never been exercised by the Court of Directors, except in this instance, though the late Sir William Bentinck was recalled by that body from his government of Madras.

It may here be added, that till the year 1773 the East India Company had been allowed the free exercise of its authority over all its servants, whom it appointed or recalled without control. This privilege was more clearly defined in 1784, during the ministry of Mr. Pitt; when by a bill, called the East India Bill, the right of recalling any officer, even a Governor General, was distinctly given both to the Crown and the Court of East India Directors, independently of each other; and the provisions of this bill have since been renewed upon more than one occasion.

THE WAR IN THE PUNJAB, AND GENERAL AFFAIRS OF INDIA SINCE 1843.

SINCE the publication of this work, at the commencement of the year 1844, events of the deepest interest have taken place in our Indian Empire, which may now be truly said to extend over the whole of that vast region.

Lord Ellenborough was, as already stated, superseded in the year abovementioned, by Sir Henry Hardinge, an experienced officer, who served with great distinction in the long peninsular war, and at the famous battle of Waterloo, where he had the misfortune to lose his left arm. He arrived at Calcutta in July, 1844, and began his government by such measures as were most likely to maintain peace, and advance the civilisation of the country; but these pacific intentions were speedily frustrated, and he was compelled by circumstances to engage in a war, the success of which has not only extended the British dominion in India, but has probably been the means of preserving it, also.

Ever since the death of Kurruck Singh, the kingdom of Lahore had been one continued scene of anarchy. The government was too weak to keep the army in subordination, and that powerful body, like the Turkish Janissaries, before they were put down by the late Sultan Mahmoud, had assumed the right of setting up and deposing the rulers at their pleasure. The Ranee, or Queen Mother, who acted as Regent for her son, disliked the minister Heera Saigh, who was murdered in a rebellion of the soldiers, of which she was believed to be the instigator, at the beginning of 1845, after which, her own brother Jewahir, who had headed the insurrection, was made prime minister, and remained in power till the end of the year, when another revolution took place, and he met with a fate similar to that of his predecessors. The confusion and misrule that prevailed at Lahore, and certain indications of a hostile disposition towards the British Government, induced the Governor General to send several regiments to the frontiers, to protect the British possessions, in case of invasion, but with a full determination not to go to war, unless the safety of the empire was endangered.

The troops were stationed on the banks of the Sutlej, which is the largest of the streams that flow into the Indus, and forms the eastern boundary of the Punjab, separating that country from the British territories.

While the Governor General was thus preparing for a war in the north of India, Sir Charles Napier was earning fresh laurels in Scinde, where the British authority was still resisted by some of the mountain tribes, whose depredations in the districts around the locality, prevented the establishment of good order; and acted as a check upon the industry of the peaceful inhabitants.

In the month of January, 1845, the gallant conqueror of Scinde undertook an expedition against this formidable banditti, with a force of 7000 men; and after a long search, and the endurance of many hardships in a rugged, barren country, he discovered the principal chief Beejar Khan, with his people, in a strongly-fortified position on the summit of a lofty ridge of hills. Our troops forced their way through a narrow defile, which was the only approach to the fort, into which, after some firing on both sides, they effected an entrance. Very little resistance was offered. Several chiefs surrendered themselves prisoners; while their followers, consisting of three different tribes, being thus left without leaders, made no farther opposition. Beejar Khan escaped; but he has since offered to submit, on condition that his life shall be spared, and some land granted him. It was resolved that the three predatory tribes should be settled on the banks of the Indus, where lands were to be given them to cultivate; while their mountain country was made over to the Murrees, a friendly nation already under the protection of the British Government.

In the meantime, the signs of a war with the Seiks were growing more manifest, 'till at length little doubt could be entertained that they were contemplating an attack on the British territories.

The Government of Lahore continued in a very unsettled state; and although the Ranee and her ministers pretended to the British authorities that the hostile movements of the troops were not sanctioned by them, it is well known they encouraged the invasion as a means of ridding themselves of a turbulent soldiery, of whom they were in perpetual fear. The Court astrologer was even consulted as to the best day for the march of the troops, and he narrowly escaped falling a sacrifice to their fury for naming one more distant than suited their inclinations. In short, the war was determined upon at Lahore, and the Seik army, consisting of not less than 50,000 warlike men, furnished with one-hundred and eight pieces of artillery, and well-trained in the European system of warfare, advanced towards the Sutlej, in hostile array. It certainly appears to have been a most unprovoked aggression on the part of the Seiks; and as they sought the war without even a pretext of quarrel or complaint, their fate is the less to be compassionated; and the greatest cause of regret is that so many of our gallant soldiers have fallen in the contest.

In consequence of the information he had received, the Governor General left Calcutta on the 22nd September, and proceeded, by way of Agra and Delhi, to join the army on the Sutlej, where he offered his services as second in command to Sir Hugh Gough, who was Commander in Chief.

The Seiks began to cross the river on the 11th December, and took up a position at Ferozeshah, a village about ten miles from the populous town of Ferozepore, and an equal distance from the village of Moodkee, the British head quarters. Orders had been sent to the troops at Umballa to join the army without delay; and by forced marches, they performed the journey, (one hundred and fifty miles,) along heavy roads of sand, in six days, suffering greatly from fatigue and thirst, as no water was to be procured on the way.

On their arrival at Moodkee, on the 18th December, they found the enemy was then advancing in order to battle, and though nearly worn out with toil, they had scarcely one hour to rest and refresh themselves, before the action commenced. It lasted from three o'clock in the morning, 'till some time after night fall, for the Seiks fought with the utmost bravery, and it was not without considerable loss on our part that they were at length driven from the field, leaving behind them seventeen of their guns, which had been captured during the engagement, and some thousands of their fallen comrades.

Among the distinguished officers who fell at the battle of Moodkee, was Sir Robert Sale, who with his lady, had lately returned to India, having been in England since his memorable campaign in Affghanistan.

After this defeat, the Seiks retreated to Ferozeshah, where, for three days, they occupied themselves in raising strong entrenchments around their camp, which, on the 21st December was attacked by Sir Hugh Gough, who had been reinforced by a detachment of troops from Ferozepore. This was a more severe conflict than that at Moodkee, for the Seiks had the advantage of firing from behind their batteries, which could not be destroyed without a frightful sacrifice of life. Ere the close of day, however, this was partially effected; but the event of the battle was still uncertain, for while it was yet raging, the night set in, and obliged the combatants to cease for awhile their deadly strife. It was very cold and dark. The weary soldiers, without food or extra covering, laid down among their dead and dying companions, exposed to the cannonading of the enemy, which was kept up during the whole night. Sir Henry Hardinge, and the rest of the generals, remained in the field with the men, doing all in their power to revive their spirits; and when daylight appeared, the attack was renewed, the enemy put to flight, and the camp taken.

Seventy-three pieces of cannon were captured in this engagement. But the numbers of the barbarians seemed inexhaustable, for the victors had scarcely congratulated each other on their success, when a fresh army was seen advancing, led by one of the chiefs who had just fled; and our brave troops had to begin a fresh battle under all the disadvantages of exhausted strength and spirits. By exertions almost superhuman, this second army was put to flight, some of the chiefs were killed, and the British remained masters of the camp, in which were found stores of grain and ammunition, both of which were greatly needed. The whole force of the Seiks who had taken the field, is estimated at about sixty-thousand; while that of the British, did not amount to more than one-third of that number.

Among the many distinguished officers who were present at the battles of Moodkee and Ferozeshah, was Prince Waldemar, of Prussia, first cousin to the present King of that country, from whom he obtained permission, in 1844, to visit the British dominions in India. He is a young man, a Colonel of Dragoons in the Prussian guards; and being desirous of gaining some military experience, he did not lose the opportunity, and fought most gallantly during the whole of these severe engagements. He was accompanied by two Prussian officers of rank, who also highly distinguished themselves; and by his physician, who unfortunately was killed in the action at Ferozeshah.

The government of India has granted a medal, inscribed with the word "Ferozeshah," to every individual engaged in the battle, to be worn with the general uniform.

The Seiks had retired to the other side of the Sutlej, and were assembling again in great force; so that it was evident that another battle would soon take place. They formed a solid bridge of boats across the river, over which they came in parties, on plundering expeditions; and about the middle of January, 1846, established a camp within the bounds of the British territory, where they soon mustered to the amount of about twenty thousand.

The position they occupied was opposite the wealthy and populous city of Loodiana, from which a part of the protective force had been withdrawn, so that some fears were entertained for its safety; and Major General Sir Harry Smith was, therefore, dispatched from the main army with a body of troops, to unite with those remaining there, for the purpose of repelling any attacks in that quarter. The enemy being so posted as to intercept his march, the gallant commander did not accomplish his object without some severe skirmishing; but, at length, by a successiön of skilful manœuvres, he formed a junction with the Loodiana forces, and having been strengthened by other detachments, advanced towards the Fort of Budhowal, the station of the Seik Chief, who drew off his army to a position on the Sutlej, a few miles off; while the British took possession of the abandoned fort. The General led on his army, which was now sufficiently strong to attack the Seiks in their new encampment; but as they had been re-inforced with more troops and cannon, they boldly advanced, and the two armies met at the villiage of Aliwal, which has given its name to one of the most memorable battles recorded in the history of British India.

The battle of Aliwal, which is termed by Sir Hugh Gough, the Waterloo of India, was fought on the 28th of January, 1846, and ended in a complete victory over the enemy, whose loss was terrific; for, in andition to the many hundreds slain in the combat, great numbers perished in their despairing efforts to make their way across the river. Rich shawls and gold bracelets in abundance fell into the hands of the victors.

The immediate consequence of this engagement was that the whole of the territory on the left bank of the Sutlej submitted to the British government, and the Lahore troops evacuated every fort that they had held on that side of the river.

But there was yet more to be done, for the main body of the Seik army was still encamped on the opposite side of their fortified bridge, at the village of Sobraon, and until that army was entirely broken up, it was obvious that any pacific measures would be useless. Notwithstanding their repeated losses, they yet numbered about 30,000 men, and had seventy pieces of cannon remaining; added to which, they occupied a port that was very strongly fortified; so that our troops had before them the prospect of another sanguinary engagement.

Sir Harry Smith, with his forces, rejoined the Commander-in-Chief, and on the 10th of February, the battle of Sobraon terminated this eventful campaign.

The entrenched camp was attacked and taken by storm, after a most desperate struggle, in which thirteen British officers were killed, and above one hundred wounded, the losses in the ranks being great in proportion. The victory, however, although so dearly purchased, was decisive; and has, as far as human foresight can judge, secured to Great Britain the full and peaceable possession of her Indian empire. The Seik army was almost totally destroyed, every gun captured, and scarcely a vestage left of that formidable power which, but for the ability of our commanders, and the bravery of our soldiers, might, at least, have shaken the power of the British government in India, and have occasioned far greater calamities than those which have attended this brief and most successful warfare.

Immediately after the battle of Sobraon, the victorious generals encamped in the Punjab, at Kussoor, about sixteen miles from the bank of the river, and thirty-two from the capital.

In the meantime, the utmost confusion prevailed at the court of Lahore, where a very remarkable person was acting in the capacity of prime minister. This was the Rajah Gholab Singh, the uncle of Heera, and brother of Dhyan Singh. He was a powerful chief, with plenty of men and money at his command; but since the death of his brother, Dhyan, he had resided at his fortress of Jamoo, among the mountains, watching the course of public events. On the breaking out of the war, he brought his army, with abundance of stores and money, to the capital, but avoided taking any decided part in the contest.

After the battle of Aliwal, the Ranee, though his personal enemy, was induced to appoint him prime minister, in the hope of obtaining his assistance, which he did not refuse, but still delayed his departure for the camp under various pretences, and was yet at Lahore when the news of the total defeat of the army at Sobraon changed the whole face of affairs.

The Ranee and her party were now anxious to make peace on the best terms they could, and Gholeb Singh was commissioned to proceed at once to the British camp, for that purpose. The Rajah wisely insisted that they should first sign an agreement to abide by such terms as he should make, and thus invested with full power to negociate, he arrived at Kussoor on the 15th of February, accompanied by several of the most influential of the Sirdars.

The Governor General received him without the usual ceremonies; and after alluding to the unjustifiable conduct of the Seik government in beginning a war without the slightest pretext, he referred the minister to his agent and secretary, who were in possession of the terms on which he would pardon the late aggression, and renew the friendly alliance between the Seik and British governments.

These conditions were, the cession of the whole territory between the Sutlej and Beas rivers; the payment of a million and a half sterling, as an indemnity for the expenses of the war; the surrender of all the rest of the cannon that had been pointed against the British; and the total disbanding of the army, to be newly constituted upon principles approved by the British government.

The Rajah signed the treaty, and the Governor General issued a proclamation to the effect that, as he had been forced into this war by an unprovoked attack on the part of the Seiks, he felt it necessary to adopt such measures as should secure the British dominions from such aggressions in future; and that, as it was not the wish of the British government to take advantage of the success of its arms to enlarge its territories, he should endeavour to re-establish the Seik government in the Punjab, on such a footing as should enable it to exercise authority over its soldiers, and protect its subjects.

It was then stipulated that the Maharaja and principal chiefs should repair to the British camp, to tender their submission. The summons was promptly obeyed, and the young Prince, mounted on an elephant, and attended by Gholab Singh, and about twelve of the Sirdars, had an interview with the Governor General, when his submission was tendered by the minister, and it was then declared that he would, in future, be treated as a friend and ally.

These arrangements being all completed, Dhulleep Singh, who is only ten years of age, was conducted back, in state, to his palace, in the citadel of Lahore, by a large escort of European and native troops, who formed, altogether, a grand and imposing spectacle; the youthful sovereign, surrounded by his chiefs, in all the pomp of barbaric splendour, riding amid the victorious troops, who might be regarded both as his conquerors and protectors.

The treaty of peace had, however, still to be ratified; and as the Lahore government was not able to pay the sum that had been stated, it became necessary to alter the conditions. It was, therefore, settled that half a million, in money, should be paid, instead of one million and a half; and that as an equivalent for the deficient million, all the country should be ceded that lies between the Beas and the Indus, including the beautiful vale of Cashmere. The greater part of this territory is bestowed in full sovereignty on Gholab Singh, in consideration of the neutrality he preserved during the war; and who, in return for so valuable an acquisition of territory, is to pay seventy-five lacs of rupees, equal to three quarters of a million sterling.

A treaty containing sixteen articles was drawn up and signed at Lahore, on the 10th of March, 1846, by the representatives of the late contending powers, and was afterwards confirmed by the seals of the Governor General and the Maharajah. A separate treaty was then concluded with Gholab Singh, who has thus become a sovereign prince under the supremacy of the British government, which he is to acknowledge by an annual present, or tribute, of a horse, twelve shawl goats, and three pairs of Cashmere shawls; besides which, like the crown vassals of the feudal times, he is bound to assist the superior power, with all his military force, in any wars in the states adjoining his territories.

The Queen mother remains at the head of the government, and a body of British troops is stationed at Lahore, for the protection of the Maharajah, who, when these arrangements were finally completed, received a visit of congratulation from the Governor General, who was accompanied by the Commander-in-Chief, with the rest of the most distinguished British officers, and Sir Charles Napier, who had just arrived from the province of Moultan, where he had lately achieved another conquest.

Thus has terminated the war in the Punjab, the importance of which may be in some degree estimated by the magnitude of the rewards bestowed on those who conducted it.

To the Governor General of India the Queen has granted the dignity of Viscount; and to the Commander-in-Chief, that of Baron; in addition to which, large pensions will be granted to them, both by Parliament and the East India Company. Sir Harry Smith has also received a Baronetcy, as a reward for his services at Aliwal. It is stated that the newly-acquired territory is extremely fertile, and will yield an enormous revenue; that the climate is healthy; and that the change of its rulers is hailed with joy by the Mohammedan part of the population.

And now it is to be hoped that the measures for the general improvement of the contry and people, which were interrupted by the war, will be resumed; and that the illustrious Governor of India will be able to carry out the beneficial plans with which he began his administration. One of the most important of these, related to the education of the natives of Bengal, and the employment of them in the public service.

Soon after his arrival at Calcutta, Sir Henry Hardinge published a document, stating, that in all appointments to public offices throughout Bengal, preference would be given to those among the candidates who had been educated in the government schools, especially to such as had distinguished themselves by their attainments; and this regulation was to apply to the subordinate as well as to the higher situations; so that in appointing a public officer, even of the lowest grade, a man who can read and write is preferred to one who cannot. With such encouragement, it can scarcely be doubted that education will make rapid progress among the lower orders, as it has already among the higher classes of the Hindoo population.

Among the projected improvements, is the formation of railroads in India, for which purpose a company was established at Bombay, last year, to co-operate with the company in London. If this great work should be accomplished, the benefits will, no doubt, be very great, especially if they can be made available in transporting the produce of the interior to the ports, and of conveying troops from station to station. It is certain, in so vast a country, where the means of travelling are slow, difficult, and insecure, that such a mode of transit would prove one of the best boons ever conferred by science on mankind.

Steam navigation was making great progress. Last year, steam-boats had begun to ply from Bombay to the Indus, and a company had been formed, with a view of establishing a regular communication between Guzerat, Scinde, and Bombay, and also between Bombay and Ceylon.

THE END.